A TEXT BOOK OF

ENGINEERING PHYSICS

For
SEMESTER – I & II
FIRST YEAR DEGREE COURSE IN B.Tech
(COMMON FOR ALL BRANCHES)

Strictly According to New Revised Syllabus of
Bharati Vidyapeeth Deemed University, Pune

(EFFECTIVE FROM ACADEMIC YEAR 2014)

Dr. Mrs. GLADY PAUL
M. Sc., M. Phil., M. Ed., Ph. D
Assistant Professor
Imperial College of Engineering & Research
Formerly Lecturer in Physics Dept.,
BVDU's College of Engineering
Katraj, Dhankawadi, Pune.

Dr. S. P. JAGTAP
M. Sc. (Physics), Ph. D, B. Ed.
Assistant Professor, Applied Science Dept.,
RMD Sinhgad School of Engineering,
Warje, Pune.
Formerly - BVDU's College of Engineering,
Katraj, Dhankawadi, Pune.

N 1056

Engineering Physics (F.Y. B. Tech Sem. I & II BVDU) ISBN 978-93-5164-103-2

Third Edition : July 2015
© : Authors

The text of this publication, or any part thereof, should not be reproduced or transmitted in any form or stored in any computer storage system or device for distribution including photocopy, recording, taping or information retrieval system or reproduced on any disc, tape, perforated media or other information storage device etc., without the written permission of Authors with whom the rights are reserved. Breach of this condition is liable for legal action.

Every effort has been made to avoid errors or omissions in this publication. In spite of this, errors may have crept in. Any mistake, error or discrepancy so noted and shall be brought to our notice shall be taken care of in the next edition. It is notified that neither the publisher nor the authors or seller shall be responsible for any damage or loss of action to any one, of any kind, in any manner, therefrom.

Published By :	POLYPLATE	Printed By :
NIRALI PRAKASHAN Abhyudaya Pragati, 1312, Shivaji Nagar, Off J.M. Road, PUNE – 411005 Tel - (020) 25512336/37/39, Fax - (020) 25511379 Email : niralipune@pragationline.com		**Repro Knowledgecast Limited** Thane

☞ DISTRIBUTION CENTRES

PUNE
Nirali Prakashan : 119, Budhwar Peth, Jogeshwari Mandir Lane,Pune 411002, Maharashtra
 Tel : (020) 2445 2044, 66022708, Fax : (020) 2445 1538
 Email : bookorder@pragationline.com, niralilocal@pragationline.com
Nirali Prakashan : S. No. 28/27, Dhyari,Near Pari Company, Pune 411041
 Tel : (020) 24690204 Fax : (020) 24690316
 Email : dhyari@pragationline.com, bookorder@pragationline.com

MUMBAI
Nirali Prakashan : 385, S.V.P. Road, Rasdhara Co-op. Hsg. Society Ltd.,
 Girgaum, Mumbai 400004, Maharashtra
 Tel : (022) 2385 6339 / 2386 9976, Fax : (022) 2386 9976
 Email : niralimumbai@pragationline.com

☞ DISTRIBUTION BRANCHES

JALGAON
Nirali Prakashan : 34, V. V. Golani Market, Navi Peth, Jalgaon 425001,
 Maharashtra, Tel : (0257) 222 0395, Mob : 94234 91860

KOLHAPUR
Nirali Prakashan : New Mahadvar Road,KedarPlaza, 1st Floor Opp. IDBI Bank
 Kolhapur 416 012, Maharashtra. Mob : 9850046155

NAGPUR
Pratibha Book Distributors : Above Maratha Mandir, Shop No. 3, First Floor,
 Rani Jhanshi Square, Sitabuldi, Nagpur 440012, Maharashtra
 Tel : (0712) 254 7129

DELHI
Nirali Prakashan : 4593/21, Basement, Aggarwal Lane 15, Ansari Road, Daryaganj
 Near Times of IndiaBuilding, New Delhi 110002
 Mob : 08505972553

BENGALURU
Pragati Book House : House No. 1, Sanjeevappa Lane, Avenue Road Cross,
 Opp. Rice Church, Bengaluru – 560002.
 Tel : (080) 64513344, 64513355,Mob : 9880582331, 9845021552
 Email:bharatsavla@yahoo.com

CHENNAI
Pragati Books : 9/1, Montieth Road, Behind Taas Mahal, Egmore,
 Chennai 600008 Tamil Nadu, Tel : (044) 6518 3535,
 Mob : 94440 01782 / 98450 21552 / 98805 82331,
 Email : bharatsavla@yahoo.com

niralipune@pragationline.com | www.pragationline.com
Also find us on www.facebook.com/niralibooks

PREFACE TO THE THIRD EDITION

We are glad and excited to announce that the Second Edition of this book received an overwhelming response from the engineering student community, compelling us to release its Third Edition within a very short period of time.

This thoroughly revised Third Edition has been updated with additional matter, many Solved Problems, including Solution to all University Examination Solved Paper and Numerous Exercises for Practice.

Special care has been taken to maintain high degree of accuracy in the theory and numericals throughout the book.

We take this opportunity to express our sincere thanks to Shri. Dinesh Furia of Nirali Prakashan, a reputed pioneer in the publication filed. Our special thanks to Jignesh Furia for their effective cooperation and great care in bringing out this revised edition. We also appreciate the efforts of M P Munde, Mrs. Deepali Lachake (Co-ordinator) and the entire staff of Nirali Prakashan, namely Mrs. Ulka Chavan, Mrs. Pratibha Bele and Miss. Megha Khedkar for bringing this book to the students in a timely manner.

We sincerely hope that this "Third Edition" will also be warmly received by all concerned as in the past.

Valuable suggestions from our esteemed readers to improve the book are most welcome and highly appreciated.

July 2015
Pune   **Authors**

PREFACE TO FIRST EDITION

It gives us great pleasure to present the book of "**Engineering Physics**" for First Year B.Tech Students. This text book has been prepared in accordance with the Revised syllabus prescribed by the Bharati Vidyapeeth's Deemed University, Pune.

Each chapter has been dealt in detail. Sufficient number of problems have been given and exercises have been set. Emphasis has been given to University Solved Numericals and Questions.

We take this opportunity to thank a number of colleagues and our teachers who have helped us in clearing a concept.

We are specially thankful to Prof. Israr Shaikh (Physics) for his kind help.

We gratefully acknowledge the co-operation from Shri Dineshbhai Furia, Shri Jignesh Furia and Shri M.P. Munde and team namely Mrs. Pallavi Deshpande, Mrs. Ulka Chavan and Mrs. Pratibha.

Last but not the least we thank our families and friends who have also contributed in no small measure to the publishing of this book.

Constructive suggestions, criticisms and comments are always welcome from our well wishers, patrons, colleagues and students for the further improvement of this book.

August 2014
Pune   **Authors**

SYLLABUS

Unit – I (08 hours)

Modern Physics : Motion of a charged particle in electric and magnetic fields, Electrostatic and Magnetostatic focussing, Wavelength and resolution, Specimen limitation, Depth of field and focus, Electron microscope, Positive rays, Separation of isotopes by Bainbridge mass spectrograph.

Nuclear Physics : Nuclear fission, Liquid drop model of nucleus, Nuclear fission in natural uranium, Fission energy, Critical mass and size, Reproduction factor, Chain reaction and four factor formula, Nuclear fuel and power reactor, Nuclear fusion and thermonuclear reactions, Merits and demerits of nuclear energy, Particle accelerators, Cyclotron, Betatron,

Unit – II (08 hours)

Solid State Physics : Band theory of solids, Free electron theory, Fermi-Dirac probability function and position of Fermi level in intrinsic semi-conductors (with derivation) and in extrinsic semi-conductors, Band structure of p-n junction diode under forward and reverse biasing, Conductivity in conductor and semi-conductor, Hall effect and Hall coefficient, Photovoltaic effect, Solar cell and its characteristics.

Superconductivity : Introduction, Properties of a super conductor, Meissner's effect, Critical field, Types of superconductors, BCS theory, High temperature superconductors, Application of superconductors.

Unit – III (08 hours)

Thermodynamics : Zeroth law of thermodynamics, first law of thermodynamics, determination of j by Joule's method, Applications of first law, heat engines, Carnot's cycle and Carnot's engine, second law of thermodynamics, entropy, change in entropy in reversible and irreversible processes, third law of thermodynamics.

Nanoscience : Introductions of nanoparticals, properties of nanoparticals (Optical, electrical, Magnetic, structural, mechanical), synthesis of nanoparticals(Physicaland chemical), synthesis of clloids, growth of nanoparticals, synthesis of nanoparticals by colloidal rout, applications.

Unit - IV : Optics - I (08 hours)

Interference : Interference of waves, Visibility of fringes, interference due to thin film of uniform and non-uniform thickness, Newton's rings, Engineering applications of interference (optical flatness, interference filter, non-reflecting coatings, multi-layer ARC.

Diffraction : Classes of diffraction, Diffraction at a single slit (Geometrical method), Conditions for maximum and minimum, Diffraction at a circular aperture (Result only), Plane diffraction grating, Conditions for principal maxima and minima, Rayleigh's criterion for resolution, Resolving power of grating and telescope.

Unit - V : Optics - II (08 Hours)

Polarisation : Introduction, Double refraction and Huygen's theory, Positive and negative crystals, Nicol prism, Dichroism, Polaroids, Elliptical and circular polarisation, Quarter and half wave plates, Production of polarised light, Analysis of polarised light, half shade polarimeter, LCD.

Lasers : Spontaneous and stimulated emission, Population inversion, Ruby laser, Helium-Neon laser, Semiconductor laser, Properties of lasers, Applications of lasers (Engineering/industry, medicine, communication, Computers), Holography.

Unit - VI

Architectural Acoustics : Elementary acoustics, Limits of audibility, Reverberation and reverberation time, Sabine's formula, Intensity level, Sound intensity level, Sound absorption, Sound absorption coefficient, different types of noise and their remedies, Sound absorption materials, basic requirement for acoustically good hall, factors affecting the architectural acoustics and their remedies.

Quantum Mechanics : Electron diffraction, Davisson and Germer's experiment, Wave nature of matter, De-Broglie waves, Wavelength of matter waves, Physical significance of wave function, Schrodinger's time dependant and time independent wave equation, Application of Schrodinger's time independent wave equation to the problems of Particle in a rigid box and non rigid box.

CONTENTS

Unit - I

Chapter 1 : Modern Physics	1.1.-1.28
Chapter 2 : Nuclear Physics	2.1-2.40

Unit - II

Chapter 3 : Solid State Physics	3.1-3.40
Chapter 4 : Superconductivity	4.1-4.22

Unit - III

Chapter 5 : Thermodynamics	5.1-5.20
Chapter 6 : Nanoscience	6.1-6.16

Unit - IV

Chapter 7 : Interference	7.1-7.44
Chapter 8 : Diffraction	8.1-8.36

Unit - V

Chapter 9 : OPTICS - II - Polarization	9.1-9.36
Chapter 10 : Laser	10.1-10.22

Unit - VI

Chapter 11 : Architectural Acoustics	11.1-11.22
Chapter 12 : Quantum Mechanics	12.1-12.46

- **Solved University Question Paper (December 2014)** P.1 – P.4
- **University Question Paper (May 2015)** P.5 – P.6

✠ ✠ ✠

Unit - I

CHAPTER 1
MODERN PHYSICS

1.1 INTRODUCTION

It is a known fact that cathode rays consist of electrons moving with a high speed. Electrons enter into the constitution of any kind of matter. Therefore, before commencing the study of any electronic device, it is imperative to understand the behaviour or motion of the electron under the action of electric and magnetic fields. The first part of the chapter is devoted to this.

The properties of the electrons of being deflected by electric and magnetic fields and of producing scintillations on a fluorescent screen are made use of in the construction and action of a CRO and an electron microscope. The electron microscope has gained a place as an invaluable device to professionals dealing with the ultra small in a number of spheres. The second part of the chapter deals with these instruments and the principles of focussing of electrons required for the functioning of an electron microscope.

Microscopy is now an invaluable tool for the study of the finer and smaller details of matter. A preliminary discussion of scanning electron microscopy and scanning tunneling microscopy is given here.

The last part of the chapter concentrates on positive rays and their analysis, which led to the discovery of isotopes with the help of mass spectroscopy. Details of the most elegant of the mass spectrographs, the Bainbridge mass spectrograph are given in this section.

1.2 MOTION OF AN ELECTRON IN AN ELECTRIC FIELD

1.2.1 Motion of an Electron in a Parallel Electric Field

A and B are two large plane parallel plates separated by a distance 'd'. V is the potential difference between them. $E = \dfrac{V}{d}$ is a uniform electric field (uniform, if the size of plates is large as compared to the separation d) which would exert an attractive force on a free moving electron placed on plate A. Under the effect of this force, the electron would move towards the plate B. The equations of motion for an electron can be written knowing the force acting on it.

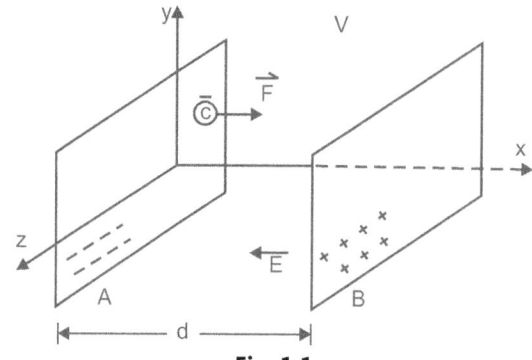

Fig. 1.1

(a) From the definition of the electric field, we have,

$$F = eE \quad \ldots (1.1)$$

where, e is the charge of the electron.

By second law of motion, we have,

$$F = ma \quad \ldots (1.2)$$

where 'm' is the mass of the electron and 'a' its acceleration along the X-axis. F is directed from A to B while E is directed from B to A.

From (1.1) and (1.2), we have,

$$ma = eE = \frac{eV}{d} \quad \left(\text{as } E = \frac{V}{d}\right)$$

$$\therefore \quad a = \frac{e}{m} \cdot \frac{V}{d} \quad \ldots (1.3)$$

i.e., acceleration of an electron is proportional to the potential applied between the plates.

(b) Velocity of the electron at an instant 't' can be found using the relation,

$$v = u + at$$

As the electron starts from the plate A, where it is at rest, initial velocity u = 0.

$$\therefore \quad v = at$$

Substituting the value for 'a' from equation (1.3),

$$v = \frac{e}{m} \cdot \frac{V}{d} \cdot t \quad \ldots (1.4)$$

(c) Displacement of the electron along the X-axis, during time 't' is obtained by using the relation,

$$s = ut + \frac{1}{2}at^2$$

If the displacement in time 't' along X-axis is x, then, we can write,

$$x = \frac{1}{2}at^2 \quad (\text{as } u = 0)$$

Substituting the value for 'a' from equation (1.3), we have,

$$x = \frac{1}{2} \cdot \frac{e}{m} \cdot \frac{V}{d} \cdot t^2 \quad \ldots (1.5)$$

(d) From equation (1.5), we get,

$$t^2 = \frac{2 \cdot m \, d}{eV} \cdot x$$

$$t = \sqrt{\frac{2 \cdot md}{eV} \cdot x} \qquad \ldots (1.6)$$

Substituting in equation (1.4), we get,

$$v = \frac{e}{m} \cdot \frac{V}{d} \sqrt{\frac{2 \, md}{eV} \cdot x}$$

$$= \sqrt{\frac{2 \, eV}{md} \cdot x} \qquad \ldots (1.7)$$

i.e., velocity of the electron is proportional to the square root of the displacement along X-axis at any given instant of time.

(e) From equation (1.7), the impact velocity can be found by putting $x = d$.

$$v_i = \sqrt{2 \frac{e}{m} \frac{V}{d} \cdot d}$$

$$\therefore \quad v_i = \sqrt{\frac{2 \, eV}{m}} \qquad \ldots (1.8)$$

i.e., velocity of impact is proportional to the square root of the potential difference.

(f) Time taken by the electron to travel from A to B is found from expression (6),

$$T = \sqrt{\frac{2 \, md^2}{eV}} \qquad (\therefore x = d)$$

T is the time of transit which is constant for a given p.d. V.

1.2.2 Motion of an Electron in a Perpendicular Electric Field

A and B are two parallel plates separated by a distance 'd'. If plate A is positively charged and plate B is negatively charged, then electric field E is directed from A to B.

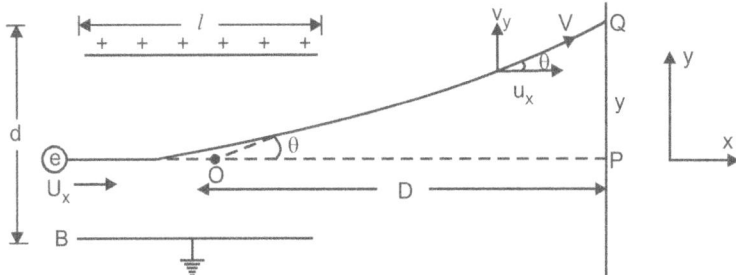

Fig. 1.2

Consider an electron of charge 'e' and mass 'm' moving with an initial velocity u_x along the X-axis. As it enters the plates A and B perpendicular to E, it is acted upon by a force. Along with the axial velocity u_x, a vertical component of the velocity v_y is introduced. While passing through the plates, the electron gets accelerated along the Y-axis. Axial velocity u_x remains unchanged, as there is no force along the X-axis. After emerging from the plates, the electron finally strikes the screen at point Q. If V is the p.d. between the plates separated by a distance 'd' then vertical force F is given by

$$F = ma_y = eE = \frac{eV}{d}$$

$$\therefore \quad a_y = \frac{e}{m} \cdot \frac{V}{d} \quad \ldots (1.9)$$

a_y is directed along the Y-axis towards the plate A.

Along the X-axis :

$F_x = 0 \quad a_x = 0$ and u_x = constant.

The electron remains in the region of the plates of length l for a time t given by

$$t \approx \frac{l}{u_x} \quad \ldots (1.10)$$

The final vertical velocity v_y of the electron as it leaves the electric field is given by

$$v_y = u_y + a_y t$$

As initial vertical velocity u_y is zero,

$$v_y = a_y t \quad \ldots (1.11)$$

Substituting from (1.9) and (1.10) in (1.11),

$$v_y = \frac{e}{m} \cdot \frac{V}{d} \cdot \frac{l}{u_x} \quad \ldots (1.12)$$

The electron leaves the region of the plates with a resultant velocity v.

$$v = \sqrt{v_x^2 + v_y^2}$$

where $v_x = u_x$ and v_y is given by relation (1.12). Velocity v is a constant, as there is no field outside the plates.

Inside the plates, it can be shown, by using Newton's law, that the path of the electron is a parabola. However, it can be assumed that the electron beam travels straight until centre O of the plates. Here the beam suddenly deflects by an angle $\theta = \tan^{-1}\left(\frac{v_y}{u_x}\right)$ with the X-axis.

If y is the vertical deflection on the screen then,

$$y = D \tan\theta \quad \ldots (1.13)$$

where D is the distance from the centre of the plates to the screen.

From Fig. 1.2,

$$\tan\theta = \frac{v_y}{u_x} \quad \ldots (1.14)$$

From (1.13) and (1.14),

$$y = D \cdot \frac{v_y}{u_x} \quad \ldots (1.15)$$

Substituting the value for v_y from relation (1.12) in relation (1.15), we have

$$y = D \cdot \frac{e}{m} \cdot \frac{V}{d} \cdot \frac{l}{2 u_x^2} \qquad \ldots (1.16)$$

Hence, vertical displacement is inversely proportional to the square of the axial velocity. Before entering the field, if the electron is accelerated through a p.d. V_A then,

$$\frac{1}{2} m u_x^2 = e V_A$$

$$\therefore \quad u_x^2 = 2 \cdot \frac{e V_A}{m}$$

Substituting the value for u_x^2 in relation (1.16), we have,

$$y = D \cdot \frac{e}{m} \cdot \frac{V}{d} \cdot \frac{l \cdot m}{2 \, e V_A}$$

$$\therefore \quad y = \frac{1}{2} \cdot \frac{D \cdot l}{d} \cdot \frac{V}{V_A} \qquad \ldots (1.17)$$

1.3 MOTION OF AN ELECTRON IN A TRANSVERSE MAGNETIC FIELD

1.3.1 Extensive Magnetic Field

Consider an extensive magnetic field of strength B, acting on an electron of charge e, mass m and velocity v perpendicular to the field. A radial magnetic force equal to Bev, acts on the (direction of F is given by Fleming's left hand rule) electron. Under the action of a continuous, transverse magnetic force directed towards the centre, the electron takes up a circular orbit.

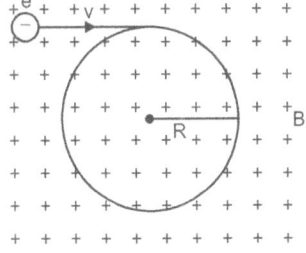

Fig. 1.3

The circular motion of the electron is governed by,

$$\text{Centripetal force} = \text{Magnetic force}$$

$$\frac{mv^2}{R} = Bev \text{ (where R is the radius of the orbit)}$$

$$\therefore \quad R = \frac{mv}{Be} \qquad \ldots (1.18)$$

Time period of circular motion is

$$T = \frac{2\pi R}{v}$$

Substituting the value for R from (1.18),

$$T = \frac{2\pi m}{Be} \qquad \ldots (1.19)$$

1.3.2 Limited Field

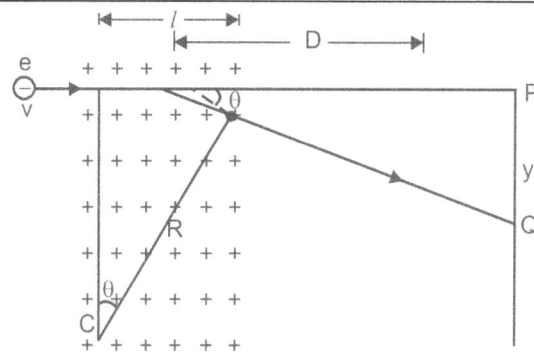

Fig. 1.4

Let a magnetic field of strength 'B' be confined to a region of length 'l'. Consider an electron of charge 'e', mass 'm' and moving with a velocity 'v' perpendicular to the magnetic field. The electron describes a circular arc AB of radius R and centre C. It emerges from the field tangentially at B, the point of exit, along a straight line to finally strike the screen at point Q.

From Fig. 1.4,

Vertical deflection $\qquad y = D \tan\theta \qquad \ldots (1.20)$

(where, D is a separation of screen from the centre of the field)

For extremely small deflections,

$$\tan\theta = \frac{AB}{R} \approx \frac{l}{R} \qquad \ldots (1.21)$$

From (1.20) and (1.21), we have

$$y = \frac{Dl}{R}$$

Substituting for R from relation (1.18),

$$y = D \cdot \frac{e}{m} \cdot l \cdot \frac{B}{v} \qquad \ldots (1.22)$$

i.e., vertical displacement in a magnetic field is inversely proportional to the axial velocity of the electron.

1.4 MOTION OF AN ELECTRON IN CROSSED ELECTRIC AND MAGNETIC FIELDS

Consider the motion of an electron in a perpendicular electric field E applied between two plane, parallel plates. Let a magnetic field B be applied simultaneously, transverse to both electric field and motion of electron. The magnetic field, as shown in Fig. 1.5 (pointing inwards) would produce a downward deflection. However, it would be attracted upwards by the electric field between the two plates.

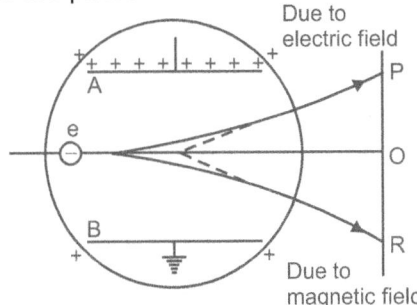

Fig. 1.5 : Crossed field

Electric force (directed upwards) = eE
Magnetic force (directed downwards) = Bev
If both the forces are equal, the electron would travel undeflected to strike the screen at O.

Then, $\quad eE = Bev$

$\therefore \quad v = \dfrac{E}{B}$ ... (1.23)

Such an arrangement of crossed fields is also called as a velocity selector. If a beam of electrons (or any other charged particle) with a range of velocities is passed through the selector then only those electrons will pass through whose velocity is given by relation (1.23). Other electrons would experience uneven forces and would be deflected so as to hit the plates. They would then be absorbed.

SOLVED EXAMPLES

Example 1.1 : A charged particle possessing 1000 times the mass of an electron and charge equal to that of an electron is accelerated through a potential difference of 1000 volts. Find the velocity attained by it and also its kinetic energy in joules and in eV.

Data : m = 1000 × 9.1 × 10^{-31} kg, V = 1000 volts, e = 1.6 × 10^{-19} C

Formulae : (i) $v = \sqrt{\dfrac{2 eV}{m}}$, (ii) K.E. = eV

Solution : (i) $\quad v = \sqrt{\dfrac{2 \times 1.6 \times 10^{-19} \times 1000}{1000 \times 9.1 \times 10^{-31}}}$

$= \sqrt{0.3516 \times 10^{12}} = 0.593 \times 10^{6}$ m/sec

(ii) $\quad E = eV$
$\quad = 1.6 \times 10^{-19} \times 1000$ J
$\quad = 1.6 \times 10^{-16}$ J
$\quad = 1000$ eV

Example 1.2 : An electron starts at rest at the negative plate of a plane parallel capacitor across which is applied a direct voltage of 1000 volts. The distance between the plates is 1 cm. How long will it take the electron to reach the positive plate ? Find its velocity at that instant.

Data : V = 1000 volts, d = 1 cm = 10^{-2} m

Formulae : (i) $t = \sqrt{\dfrac{2\,md^2}{eV}}$, **(ii)** $v = u + \dfrac{e}{m} \cdot \dfrac{V}{d}\, t$

Solution : (i)
$$t = \sqrt{\dfrac{2 \times 9.1 \times 10^{-31} \times (10^{-2})^2}{1.6 \times 10^{-19} \times 1000}}$$
$\quad = \sqrt{11.375 \times 10^{-19}}$
$\quad = \sqrt{1.1375 \times 10^{-18}} = 1.067 \times 10^{-9}$ sec.

(ii) $\quad v = u + \dfrac{e}{m} \cdot \dfrac{V}{d} \cdot t$
$\quad u = 0$
$$v = \dfrac{1.6 \times 10^{-19} \times 1000 \times 1.067 \times 10^{-9}}{9.1 \times 10^{-31} \times 10^{-2}}$$
$\quad = 0.1876 \times 10^8$ m/sec.

Example 1.3 : A charged particle with mass equal to 7344 times that of an electron and charge equal to twice that of the electron is accelerated from rest through a p.d. of 3×10^6 volts. Find the magnetic field required to bend the path of the particle into a circle of radius 2 metres if the particle enters the magnetic field (i) normally, (ii) inclined at an angle of 30° to the field.

Data : m = $7344 \times 9.1 \times 10^{-31}$, V = 3×10^6 volts, R = 2 m

Formulae : $v = \sqrt{\dfrac{2\,eV}{m}}$, $\quad B = \dfrac{mv}{eR}$

Solution :
$$v = \sqrt{\dfrac{2 \times 1.6 \times 10^{-19} \times 3 \times 10^6}{7344 \times 9.1 \times 10^{-31}}}$$
$\quad = \sqrt{0.0001436 \times 10^{18}}$
$\quad = \sqrt{1.436 \times 10^{14}} = 1.198 \times 10^7$ m/sec.
$$B = \dfrac{9.1 \times 7344 \times 10^{-31} \times 1.198 \times 10^7}{1.6 \times 10^{-19} \times 2}$$
$\quad = 25019.63 \times 10^{-5}$
$\quad = 0.25$ wb/m^2

Example 1.4 : A beam of electrons accelerated by a potential difference of 2000 volts passes between two co-axial coils, producing a magnetic field perpendicular to the electron beam. Find the radius of curvature of the beam in a region of 100×10^{-4} wb/sqm.

Data : V = 2000 volts, B = 100×10^{-4} wb/sqm

Formulae : $v = \sqrt{\dfrac{2\,eV}{m}}$; $R = \dfrac{mv}{Be}$

Solution :

$$v = \sqrt{\dfrac{2 \times 1.6 \times 10^{-19} \times 2000}{9.1 \times 10^{-31}}}$$

$$= \sqrt{0.7032 \times 10^{15}} = 2.652 \times 10^{7} \text{ m/sec}$$

$$R = \dfrac{9.1 \times 10^{-31} \times 2.652 \times 10^{7}}{100 \times 10^{-4} \times 1.6 \times 10^{-19}}$$

$$= 15.08 \times 10^{-3} \text{ mts} = 15.08 \text{ mm.}$$

Example 1.5 : Calculate the value of the electric field intensity which will give a proton an acceleration equal to the acceleration due to gravity.

Data : m = 1.67×10^{-27} kg, g = 9.8 m/sec^2

Formula : F = mg = e E

Solution :

$$E = \dfrac{mg}{e}$$

$$= \dfrac{1.67 \times 10^{-27} \times 9.8}{1.6 \times 10^{-19}}$$

$$= 10.23 \times 10^{-8} \text{ V/m}$$

Example 1.6 : An electron of 50 eV enters a perpendicular magnetic field of 0.04 wb/m^2. Find the r.p.m. of the electron and the radius of its path in the fields.

Data : K.E. = 50 eV, B = 0.04 wb/m^2

Formulae : $v = \sqrt{\dfrac{2\,eV}{m}}$; $R = \dfrac{mv}{Be}$; Rev./sec. = $\dfrac{v}{2\pi R}$

Solution :

$$v = \sqrt{\dfrac{2 \times 50 \times 1.6 \times 10^{-19}}{9.1 \times 10^{-31}}}$$

$$= 0.419 \times 10^{7} \text{ m/sec}$$

$$R = \dfrac{9.1 \times 10^{-31} \times 0.419 \times 10^{7}}{0.04 \times 1.6 \times 10^{-19}}$$

$$= 59.58 \times 10^{-5} \text{ m}$$

$$\text{Rev./sec.} = \dfrac{0.419 \times 10^{7} \times 7}{2 \times 22 \times 59.58 \times 10^{-5}}$$

$$= 1118 \times 10^{6} \text{ /sec.}$$

$$\text{r.p.m.} = 60 \times 1118 \times 10^{6} = 6.708 \times 10^{10} \text{ m}$$

Example 1.7 : An electron is accelerated through a certain potential difference and then enters a uniform magnetic field of 2×10^{-2} wb/m^2. The deflection of the magnetic field is perpendicular to the direction of motion of the electron. If the radius of the path of the electron is 1.18×10^{-2} m, calculate the p.d. through which the electron is accelerated.

Data : $B = 2 \times 10^{-2}$ weber/m^2, $R = 1.18 \times 10^{-2}$ m.

Formulae : $v = \dfrac{BeR}{m}$, $eV = \dfrac{1}{2} mv^2$

Solution :

$$v = \dfrac{2 \times 10^{-2} \times 1.6 \times 10^{-19} \times 1.18 \times 10^{-2}}{9.1 \times 10^{-31}}$$

$$= 0.415 \times 10^8 \text{ m/sec.}$$

$$V = \dfrac{mv^2}{2e}$$

$$= \dfrac{9.1 \times 10^{-31} \times (0.415 \times 10^8)^2}{2 \times 1.6 \times 10^{-19}}$$

$$= 0.4898 \times 10^4 \text{ volts} = 4.898 \text{ kV.}$$

Example 1.8 : An electron of energy 40 eV is circulating in a plane at right angles to a uniform magnetic field of strength 10^{-4} weber/m^2. Calculate the radius of its orbit and its period of revolution.

Data : K.E. = 40 eV, $B = 10^{-4}$ weber/m^2

Formulae : $v = \sqrt{\dfrac{2E}{m}}$; $R = \dfrac{mv}{Be}$; $T = \dfrac{2\pi m}{Be}$

Solution :

$$v = \sqrt{\dfrac{2 \times 40 \times 1.6 \times 10^{-19}}{9.1 \times 10^{-31}}}$$

$$= 3.75 \times 10^6 \text{ m/sec}$$

$$R = \dfrac{9.1 \times 10^{-31} \times 3.75 \times 10^6}{10^{-4} \times 1.6 \times 10^{-19}}$$

$$= 0.213 \text{ m}$$

$$T = \dfrac{2 \times 22 \times 9.1 \times 10^{-31}}{7 \times 10^{-4} \times 1.6 \times 10^{-19}}$$

$$= 35.75 \times 10^{-8} \text{ sec.}$$

$$= 0.3575 \text{ μ sec.}$$

Example 1.9 : An electron starts from rest and moves freely in an electric field $E = 24$ kV/m. Determine (a) the force on the electron, (b) it's acceleration.

Data : $E = 24$ kV/m $= 24 \times 10^3$ V/m

Formulae : $F = eE$; $a = \dfrac{F}{m}$

Solution : (a) $F = 1.6 \times 10^{-19} \times 24 \times 10^3$

$$= 38.4 \times 10^{-16} \text{ N}$$

(b) $a = \dfrac{38.4 \times 10^{-16}}{9.1 \times 10^{-31}}$

$= 4.22 \times 10^{15}$ m/sec^2

Example 1.10 : An electron is projected horizontally with an initial velocity v into a uniform vertical electric field acting upwards. Show that the trajectory of the electron inside the electric field is a parabola.

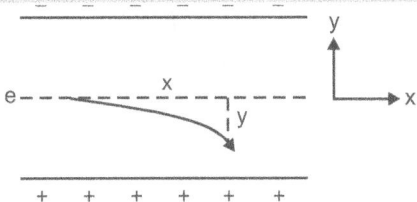

Fig. 1.6

Solution : Force acting on the electron due to the electric field E in the downward direction is,

$$F = eE$$

Also, $\quad F = ma$

$\therefore \quad a = \dfrac{eE}{m}$ ... (1)

After a time, t the electron traverses a distance say x in the horizontal direction. Let y be the vertical direction.

Then, $\quad x = vt$ ... (2)

$$y = ut + \dfrac{1}{2} at^2$$

as $\quad u = 0$

$$y = \dfrac{1}{2} at^2 = \dfrac{1}{2} a \cdot \dfrac{x^2}{v^2} \quad \text{[substituting for t from (2)]}$$

Substituting for a from (1),

$$y = \dfrac{1}{2} \cdot \left(\dfrac{e}{m} E\right) \cdot \dfrac{x^2}{v^2}$$

This is the equation of a parabola. It is similar to the motion of a projectile in the earth's gravitational field.

Example 1.11 : If a stream of electrons each of mass m, charge e and velocity 1.6×10^7 m/sec. is deflected by 0.3 m in traversing a distance of 0.5 m through an electric field of 3500 volts/m perpendicular to their path, find e/m in coulombs/kg.

Data : $u_x = 1.6 \times 10^7$ m/sec., y = 0.3 m^3, l = 0.5 m, E = 3500 V/m

Formula : $y = \dfrac{1}{2} \cdot \left(\dfrac{eE}{m}\right) \dfrac{l^2}{u_x^2}$

Solution :

$$\frac{e}{m} = \frac{2 \cdot y \cdot u_x^2}{E \cdot l^2}$$

$$= \frac{2 \times 0.3 \times (1.6 \times 10^7)^2}{3500 \times (0.5)^2} = 1.76 \times 10^{11} \text{ C/kg.}$$

Example 1.12 : An electron moving in a horizontal direction with a speed of 6×10^7 m/sec. enters a region where there is a uniform electric field of 30 volts/cm directed upwards in the plane of its motion. Find the electron's co-ordinates referred to the point of entry and the direction of its motion 2×10^{-8} seconds later.

Data : $u_x = 1.6 \times 10^7$ m/sec., E = 30 V/cm, t = 2×10^{-8} sec.

Formulae : $y = \frac{1}{2}\left(\frac{e}{m}E\right)t^2$; $x = u_x t$; $\tan \theta = \frac{y}{x}$

Solution :

$$y = \frac{1}{2} \times \frac{1.6 \times 10^{-19}}{9.1 \times 10^{-31}} \times 3000 \times (2 \times 10^{-8})^2$$

$$= 1.05 \times 10^{-1} = 0.105 \text{ m}$$

$$x = 6 \times 10^7 \times 2 \times 10^{-8} = 1.2 \text{ m}$$

∴ Electron's co-ordinates are (1.2 m, 0.105 m)

$$\tan \theta = \frac{0.105}{1.2} = 0.0875$$

$$\theta = \tan^{-1}(0.0875) = 5° 04'$$

The electron path is inclined at an angle of 5° 04' with the X-axis.

1.5 ELECTROSTATIC

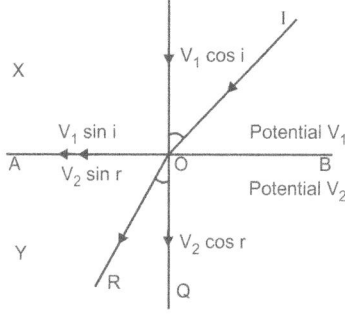

Fig. 1.7

Let AB be an interface between two regions X and Y. The electrostatic fields in the two regions are generated by voltages V_1 and V_2. The electrons moving through these regions will acquire velocities V_1 and V_2. If $V_2 > V_1$ then velocity V_2 will be larger than V_1.

Let an electron beam be incident along IO on the interface AB, from region X, at an angle of incidence i. Let it get refracted along OR, in region Y, making a refracting angle r. If the electron of charge 'e' and mass 'm' is accelerated through a p.d. V in region X then the energy acquired is given by,

$$\frac{1}{2} m v_1^2 = e V_1 \qquad \ldots (1.24)$$

Similarly, in region Y, the electrons acquire an energy

$$\frac{1}{2} m v_2^2 = e V_2 \qquad \ldots (1.25)$$

From (1.24) and (1.25),

$$\frac{v_1^2}{v_2^2} = \frac{V_1}{V_2} \text{ or } \frac{v_1}{v_2} = \sqrt{\frac{V_1}{V_2}} \qquad \ldots (1.26)$$

As AB is an equipotential surface, the component of velocities parallel to AB do not change.

Hence $\qquad v_1 \sin i = v_2 \sin r$

$$\therefore \qquad \frac{\sin i}{\sin r} = \frac{v_2}{v_1} \qquad \ldots (1.27)$$

From (1.26) and (1.27), $\qquad \dfrac{\sin i}{\sin r} = \dfrac{v_2}{v_1} = \sqrt{\dfrac{V_2}{V_1}}$

Therefore, if $V_2 > V_1$ then the electron gets accelerated in the medium and is deflected towards the normal while if $V_1 > V_2$ then it gets decelerated and is deflected away from the normal.

Electrostatic Lens :

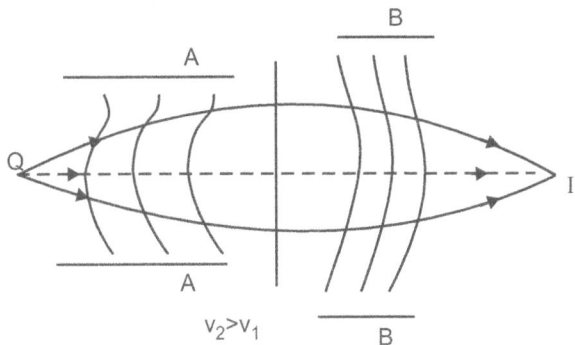

Fig. 1.8

The electrostatic lens consist of two pairs of electrodes AA and BB which are kept at different potentials and are separated by a gap. Potential V_2 on electrodes BB is greater than the potential V_1 on electrodes AA. The equipotential surfaces are such that in first region (AA), the field lines converge the beam whereas in the second region (BB), the field lines diverge the beam.

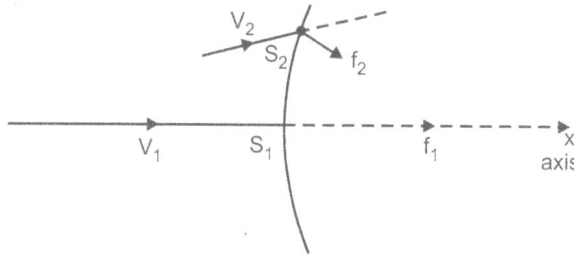

Fig. 1.9

Let an electron strike the equipotential surface at S with velocity v_1. Force $f_1 = eE$ acts on the electron, acting normal to the surface at S_1. The motion of the electron remains along the X-axis. Let an electron now strike the surface at S_2. A force $f_2 = eE$, acting normal to S_2 changes the direction of motion of the electron as well as its velocity. The electron takes up a resultant path which is directed towards the axis. In Fig. 1.9, the electron beam from source O travels from a region at low potential to the region of high potential. In this region, it gets deflected towards the normal. By adjusting the potentials, the beam can be focussed to any point J. To increase the focussing effect, a third electrode pair CC is inserted between AA and BB which is at a lower positive or negative potential with respect to the other two. Electrostatic lens of this type is commonly used in CRO and in some electron microscopes.

1.6 MAGNETOSTATIC FOCUSSING

This type of focussing can be achieved either by a permanent magnet or by passing current through a coil of wire, whose axis coincides with the beam axis. The focussing coil surrounds the tube. Magnetic lines of force are parallel to the direction of electron motion. If the lines of force and the electron motion are in the same direction, then the electron is urged to move only by the attractive force of the anode.

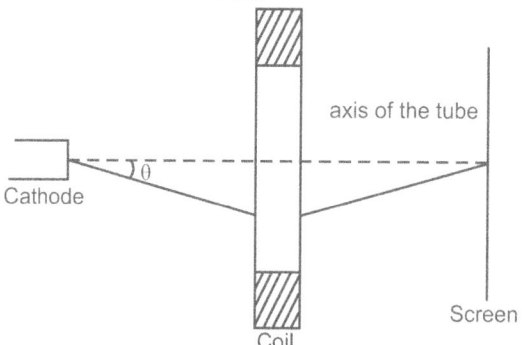

Fig. 1.10

Consider an electron at O (See Fig. 1.11) inside a magnetic field of intensity B moving with a velocity v in a direction at an angle θ with that of the field. Resolving the velocity into two components v cos θ along OR (the direction of the field) and v sin θ along OQ (at right angles to the field).

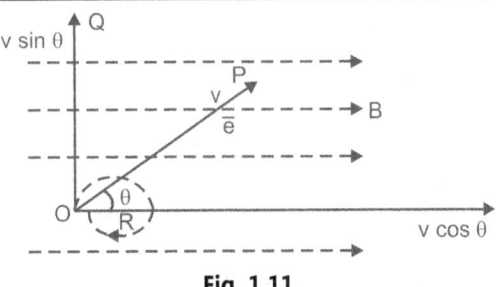

Fig. 1.11

The electron leaving the cathode at an angle to the axis of the system experiences a magnetic force at right angles to the direction of motion of the electron and to the magnetic line of force. The forces cause the electron to move in a spiral path (or a helix). It is urged forward by the anode and sideways by the magnetic force. When this electron path is projected on a screen, it is a circle. If the electron completes the circle by the time it reaches the screen then, it must lie on the axis of the tube just opposite to the point where it was emitted. All other electrons emerging from a point are brought to focus at a corresponding point on the screen.

The circular motion is governed by the relation

$$B e v \sin \theta = \frac{m (v \sin \theta)^2}{r}$$

or

$$v \sin \theta = \frac{B e r}{m} \qquad \ldots (1.28)$$

The time taken to complete one circle or one turn of the helix is,

$$T = \frac{2 \pi r}{v \sin \theta}$$

$$T = \frac{2 \pi r}{B e r / m}$$

$$= \frac{2 \pi}{B (e/m)} \quad \text{[from (1.28)]}$$

From this expression for 'T', it is evident that the time does not depend on the inclination 'θ' with the axis of the tube and the velocity of the electron. So the electron starting from O and moving away from its direction OR will be forced by the uniform field to arrive at R which is at a distance l along the direction of the field.

'l' is the distance covered by the electron during time 't' along OR (direction of the field) and is called the pitch of the helix.

∴

$$l = v \cos \theta \cdot T$$

$$= v \cos \theta \cdot \frac{2 \pi}{B \cdot e/m}$$

By varying the magnetic field strength (determined by the amount of current flowing through the focussing coil and the number of turns in the coil), electrons can be focussed on the screen.

Magnetic Lens :

One form of the magnetic lens is shown in Fig. 1.12. PQ is the section of the coil of the electromagnet. The electromagnet coil is surrounded with an iron shield except in the regions of gaps. 'a' and 'b' are the small gaps in opposite positions. The field lines are symmetric about the axis $O_1 O_2$ of the coil. The electrons entering the lens at O_1 get focussed at O_2. The focal length of the lens is very small and can be altered by suitably changing the strength of the magnetic field.

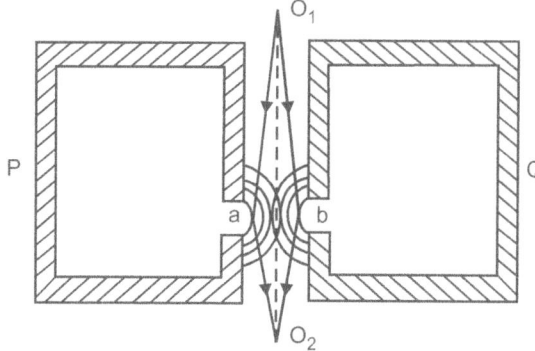

Fig. 1.12

1.7 WAVELENGTH AND RESOLUTION

Microscope is a device which magnifies small-sized objects which cannot be seen by an unaided eye. Unlike an optical microscope which uses light rays and optical lenses, the electron microscope uses a beam of electrons which can be focussed by either electrostatic or magnetostatic fields. An electron microscope normally uses magnetic fields.

With a naked eye one can observe particles of smallest size of dimension ~0.02 cm. To observe particles of size smaller than this dimension, an optical microscope is used. The smallest size that can be observed with an optical microscope has a limit of 2×10^5 cm. This depends on the resolving power of the microscope given by,

$$\text{R.P.} = 1/d$$

where, $$d = \frac{\lambda}{2 \times (\text{N.A.})}$$

(where λ is the wavelength of light used, N.A. is the numerical aperture of the lens)

The smallest value of λ is $\sim 6 \times 10^{-5}$ cm.

Principle :

The discovery of two principles led to the construction of the electron microscope.

(1) The wave nature associated with microscopic particles like electrons.
(2) The focussing of electrons using electric and magnetic fields.

According to DeBroglie every moving particle of mass 'm' and velocity 'v' has an associated matter wave whose wavelength is given by $\lambda = \dfrac{h}{mv} = \dfrac{h}{\sqrt{2meV}}$ where V is the p.d. through which the electrons have been accelerated. By changing p.d. V, wavelength λ can be varied through a wide range of values.

For high magnification, two important conditions need to be satisfied : (i) high resolution, (ii) good clarity. With an optical microscope, it was seen that the limit for magnification is due to the wavelength of light used for magnifying the object and not due to any kind of imperfections in the instrument.

The expression for R.P. shows that it varies inversely with wavelength λ and directly with the N.A. of the lens. For electrons accelerated through a p.d. of 60 kV, the De Broglie wavelength will be 5×10^{-10} cm. This value is 10^5 times smaller than the λ of visible light. Therefore, the R.P. of an electron microscope is 10^5 times larger than an optical microscope. Unlike an optical microscope, here clarity can be achieved by focussing the electron beam on the object to reveal a large amount of detail.

1.8 SPECIMEN LIMITATIONS

All the specimens have to be in high vacuum. Because of this they will have to undergo changes caused by drying and evacuation. The intense electron beam acting for a long time on the specimen may distroy the specimen. As the electron beam cannot penetrate through a metallic surface, study of metals will have to be carried out by an indirect method called "replica method". In this method a very thin replica of the surface is made and it is analysed with the instrument.

1.9 ELECTRON MICROSCOPE

Construction :

The electron microscope is of two types :

(a) Emission type, (b) Transmission type.

The standard microscope is of transmission type which uses magnetic lenses. This microscope has similarity in stages of magnification with an optical microscope. As shown in Fig. 1.13, in optical microscope, 'L' is the source. Light rays incident from the source are collected by the condenser lens L. The parallel light scattered by the object is passed through the objective lens O. This gives the first magnified image. The final image is obtained by the projector lens P.

Electron Microscopes are of Two Types :

(a) Transmission Type (Transmission Electron Microscope or TEM) : This is the first type of electron microscope to be developed and is similar to the light microscope except that a focussed beam of electrons is used instead of light to see through the specimen.

(b) Emission Type (Scanning Electron Microscope or SEM) : In this the image is formed by a detector synchronized with a focused beam of electrons scanning the object.

Electron Source : It produces a fine beam of electrons by thermionic emission, by heating the filament F in the electron gun G.

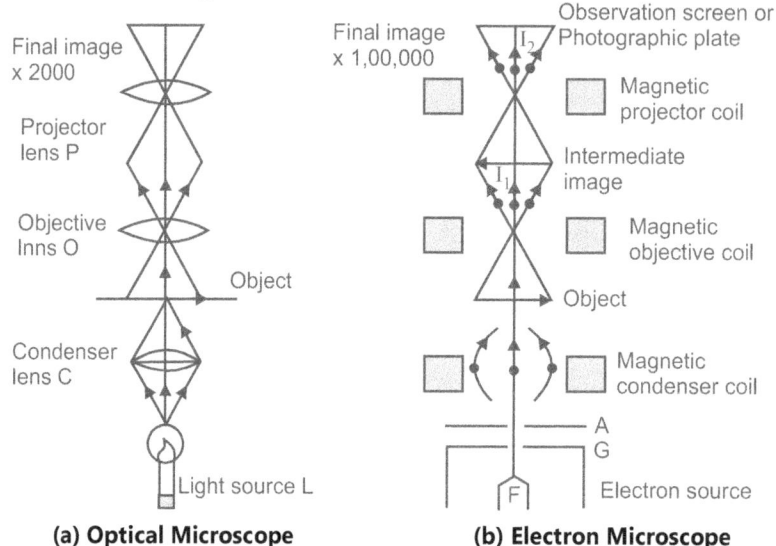

(a) Optical Microscope   (b) Electron Microscope

Fig. 1.13

Condenser Lenses : Electrons leaving the gun are directed on to the object by a pair of magnetic condenser lenses. The lenses reduce the region of cross over and focus the beam on the object. The system contains an aperture which restricts the size of the beam.

Specimen (Object) : It is mounted on a grid which rests above a circular hole in a specimen holder. Pressure in the interior of the microscope is kept very low with the help of vacuum pumps. To protect the specimen from contamination, a device known as 'cold finger' is incorporated in the specimen holder which captures any stray molecules before they can reach the object. Specimens include biological tissues, amorphous solids, ferromagnetic materials etc.

Objective Lens : This lens is the most important component in the microscope as it determines the resolving power of the instrument.

Projector Lens : It magnifies the intermediate image that the objective lens has produced.

The lenses in the electron microscope are not moved up or down as in an optical microscope but the focal length can be changed by varying the strength of the current flowing through the magnetic coils.

Recording System : Final image is examined on a fluorescent screen through a glass window.

Auxiliary Equipment :

- Vacuum pumps – For maintaining vacuum in the interior of the microscope.
- High voltage supply – For operating the microscope. It is generally of the orders of 20 to 100 kV.
- Lens current supply – For operation of magnetic lenses.

Working :

Electrons liberated from the cathode are accelerated through a p.d. of 60 kV. When current is passed through the coils surrounded by soft iron cylinders, a magnetic field is produced around them. When the beam of electrons is passed through the magnetic field, it is deflected and is focussed in the same way as an optical lens focusses light rays. The beam of electrons is subjected to a magnetic field by first magnetic lens acting as a condenser. It concentrates the beam of electrons on the object to be magnified. The second lens acts as an objective. The third lens is the projector lens which focusses the enlarged electron pattern. When the beam falls on a fluorescent screen, an image is formed which can be observed through a window.

Uses of an Electron Microscope :

- Due to its high resolution and high magnification, electron microscope is used in medicine and biological research to study viruses, disease causing bacteria, etc.
- It is also used in industries to investigate structure of textiles, fibres, paints, etc.
- Crystal structures can be studied in great detail by using an electron microscope.

1.10 POSITIVE RAYS

In 1886, a German Physicist E. Goldstein set up a discharge tube with a perforated cathode which was exhausted to a pressure of 1 N/m^2 (10^{-5} atmosphere pressure). A large p.d. applied across the electrodes caused luminous streamers to appear in the space behind the cathode. They seemed to originate from the anode and to travel towards the cathode, and were hence called as positive rays. The rays caused fluorescence, affected photographic plates and showed deflection in magnetic and electric fields. These positive rays were, later on, found to consist of positive ions formed by ionisation in the gas. They are then drawn to the cathode by the electric field. The positive ions are massive (they are neutral gas atoms having lost one or more electrons) and therefore move with a velocity which is very small as compared to the velocity of cathode rays.

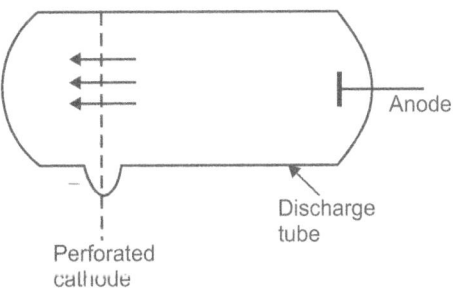

Fig. 1.14

1.11 MASS SPECTROGRAPH

Isotopes are elements having the same atomic number but different atomic weights.

For Example : $_1H^1$ and $_1D^2$; $_{92}U^{233}$, $_{92}U^{235}$ and $_{92}U^{238}$; $_{10}Ne^{20}$ and $_{10}Ne^{22}$

As the atomic number of isotopes is the same, they have the same electronic configuration and hence the same chemical properties. They can therefore be separated by physical methods and not by chemical methods.

To detect the presence of isotopes, to find an accurate value of isotopic masses and their abundance, F.W. Aston, an English Physicist, devised a mass spectrograph. This spectrograph brought about a separation between the isotopes on the basis of their masses. This was followed by Dempster's which has recently been superceded by Bainbridge's magnetic deflection mass spectrograph.

1.12 BAINBRIDGE MASS SPECTROGRAPH

Bainbridge used a power electromagnet and a velocity selector in his spectrograph and was able to obtain, a high resolving power, precise symmetric images and a linear mass scale which could not be obtained in Aston's or Dempster's spectrographs.

Principle :

Whatever be the velocities of the ions in the process of their generation, they are made perfectly homogeneous in velocity by the use of a special device called the velocity selector. They are then subjected to an extensive, transverse magnetic field and are brought to focus on a photographic plate.

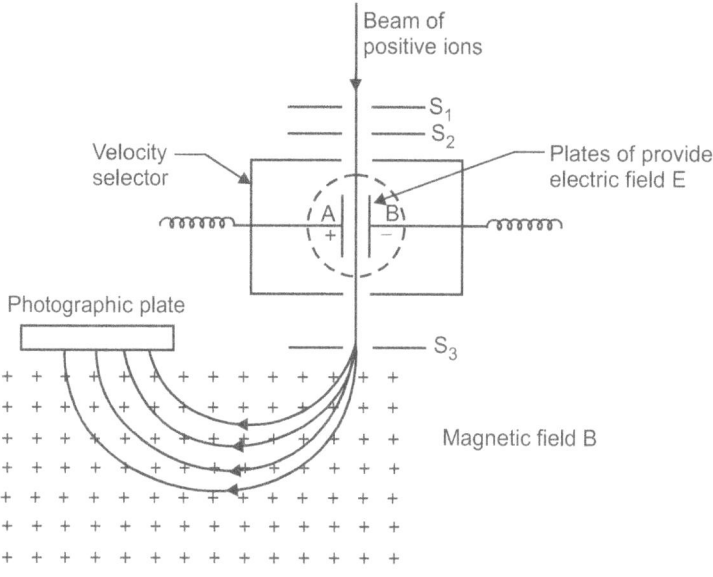

Fig. 1.15 : Bainbridge spectrograph

Apparatus :

The given beam of ions is collimated by two narrow parallel slits S_1 and S_2. It is then passed through a velocity selector, which consists of a transverse electric field E which is produced by maintaining plates A and B at a suitable p.d. Simultaneously a magnetic field B is applied perpendicular to both E and the motion of the ions. The magnetic field is obtained by an electromagnet represented by the dotted circle. The velocity selector allows only those ions to pass undeviated which possess the same velocity 'v' given by the following relation.

Inside the selector,

$$\text{Electric force} = \text{Magnetic force}$$
$$E q = B q v$$

(q is the charge of the ion moving with a velocity v).

$$\therefore \quad v = \frac{E}{B} \quad \ldots (1.29)$$

All other ions bend away the straight path due to the unbalanced effect of one of the two opposing fields. The ions emerging from slit S_3, at the exit of the selector, are introduced into a uniform magnetic field of intensity B' acting at right angles to the plane of the paper. Under the influence of this field they travel along circular paths which are governed by the following relation.

$$\text{Magnetic force} = \text{Centripetal force}$$

i.e.,
$$B' q v = \frac{m v^2}{r} \quad \ldots (1.30)$$

m is the mass of the ion whose circular path has a radius r.

From (1.29) and (1.30), we get

$$B' q = \frac{m}{r} \frac{E}{B}$$

$$\frac{q}{m} = \frac{E}{B \cdot B'} \cdot \frac{1}{r} \quad \ldots (1.31)$$

As E, B, B' are constants, q/m (specific charge ratio) is directly proportional to 1/r or $m \propto r$ and the mass scale is linear. Hence, after describing semi-circles, if the ions are made to fall on a photographic plate, they will strike it at different points depending on the value of mass. Lighter particles will trace small semi-circles while heavier ones will trace larger semi-circles. Traces are obtained on the photographic plate with the mass scale being linear.

Presence of isotopes is therefore detected by the production of spots on the photographic plate. Mass numbers of the isotopes can be found by comparing the plate with a standard calibrated plate. Relative abundance of the isotopes in a given beam of ions can be found by studying the relative intensity of the spots on the photographic plate.

Hence a Bainbridge mass spectrograph is used :
- to detect the presence of isotopes in a given beam of positive ions,
- to determine the mass number of the isotopes,
- to find out the relative abundance of the isotopes in the given beam of positive ions.

SOLVED EXAMPLES

Example 1.13 : In a Bainbridge mass spectrometer, if the magnetic field in the velocity selector is 1 wb/m^2 and ions having a velocity of 0.4×10^7 m/sec pass undeflected, find the electric field in the velocity selector.

Data : $v = 0.4 \times 10^7$ m/sec., $B = 1$ wb/m^2

Formula : $\qquad E = v \cdot B$

Solution : $\qquad E = 0.4 \times 10^7 \times 1 = 4 \times 10^6$ V/m

Example 1.14 : Singly ionised magnesium atoms enter a Bainbridge mass spectrograph with a velocity of 3×10^5 m/sec. Calculate the radii of the paths followed by the three most abundant isotopes of masses 24, 25, 26 when the magnetic flux density is 0.5 wb/m^2.

Data : $v = 3 \times 10^5$ m/sec., $B = 0.5$ wb/m^2, $q = 1.6 \times 10^{-19}$

Formula : $\qquad R = \dfrac{mv}{Bq}$

Solution : Mass of single ionised atom of Mg i.e.

$$m_{24} = \dfrac{24}{6.02 \times 10^{26}} \text{ kg} = 3.987 \times 10^{-26} \text{ kg}$$

$$R_{24} = \dfrac{M_{24} \cdot v}{B \cdot q} = \dfrac{3.987 \times 10^{-26} \times 3 \times 10^5}{0.5 \times 1.6 \times 10^{-19}}$$

$$= 14.95 \times 10^{-2} = 0.1495 \text{ m}$$

As $\qquad R \propto m$

$\therefore \qquad \dfrac{R_{24}}{R_{25}} = \dfrac{m_{24}}{m_{25}}$

i.e., $\qquad R_{25} = \dfrac{m_{25}}{m_{24}} \cdot R_{24}$

$$= \dfrac{25}{24} \times 0.1495 = 0.1557 \text{ m}$$

Similarly, $\qquad R_{26} = \dfrac{26}{24} \times 0.1495 = 0.1619$ m

Example 1.15 : A mixture of neon isotopes (Ne^{20} and Ne^{21}) is analysed using a Bainbridge mass spectrometer. Calculate the linear separation of isotopes when the field acting on the velocity selector is 80 kV/meter and the magnetic flux density is 0.55 weber/m^2.

Data : $E = 80$ kV/meter; $B = 0.55$ weber/m^2

Formulae : $v = \dfrac{E}{B}$, $R = \dfrac{mv}{Bq}$

Solution : $\qquad R = \dfrac{m(E/B)}{Bq} = \dfrac{mE}{qB^2}$

$$m_{20} = \dfrac{20}{6.025 \times 10^{26}} \text{ kg}$$

$$= 3.3195 \times 10^{-26} \text{ kg}$$

$$R_{20} = \frac{3.3195 \times 10^{-26}}{1.6 \times 10^{-19}} \times \frac{80 \times 10^3}{(0.55)^2}$$

$$= 548.678 \times 10^{-4}$$

$$= 0.0549 \text{ m}$$

As $\quad R \propto m$

$$\frac{R_{21}}{R_{20}} = \frac{m_{21}}{m_{20}}$$

∴ $\quad R_{21} = \frac{m_{21}}{m_{20}} \cdot R_{20}$

∴ $\quad R_{21} - R_{20} = \frac{m_{21}}{m_{20}} \cdot R_{20} - R_{20}$

$$= \left(\frac{m_{21}}{m_{20}} - 1\right) R_{20}$$

$$= \left(\frac{21}{20} - 1\right) \times 0.0549 = \frac{0.0549}{20}$$

$$= 0.00275 \text{ m}$$

The separation on the photographic plate is double that of the radii difference.

∴ Linear separation of isotopes on the photographic plate = $2 \times 0.00275 = 0.0055$ m.

SUMMARY

1. Motion of an electron in an electric field :
   (A) Parallel :
   (i) Displacement along X-axis in time 't' is
   $$x = \frac{1}{2} \cdot \left(\frac{e}{m}\frac{v}{d}\right) \cdot t^2$$
   (ii) Impact velocity,
   $$v_i = \sqrt{\frac{2eV}{m}}$$
   (iii) Time of transit,
   $$T = \sqrt{\frac{2md^2}{eV}}$$
   (B) Perpendicular :
   Vertical displacement,
   $$y = \frac{1}{2} \cdot \frac{lD}{d} \cdot \frac{V}{V_a} = D \cdot \frac{e}{m} \cdot \frac{V}{d} \cdot \frac{l}{u_x^2}$$

2. Motion of an electron in a transverse magnetic field :
   (A) Extensive magnetic field :
   (i) Radius of circular orbit, $R = \dfrac{mv}{Be}$.

   (ii) Time period of circular motion, $T = \dfrac{2\pi m}{Be}$

   (B) Limited magnetic field :
   Vertical displacement,
   $$y = D \cdot \dfrac{e}{m} \cdot l \cdot \dfrac{B}{v}$$

3. Motion of an electron in crossed electric and magnetic fields :
   $$\text{Velocity, } v = \dfrac{E}{B}$$
   This arrangement of crossed fields is called as velocity selector.

4. Ratio of charge to mass of an electron by Thomson's method :
   $$\dfrac{e}{m} = \dfrac{E}{B^2} \cdot \dfrac{d}{(ED \times OS)}$$

5. Electrostatic focussing :
   $$\dfrac{\sin i}{\sin r} = \dfrac{v_2}{v_1} = \sqrt{\dfrac{V_2}{V_1}}$$

6. Magnetostatic focussing :
   (i) Time period, $T = \dfrac{2\pi}{B(e/m)}$

   (ii) Pitch of the helix, $l = v \cos\theta \cdot T$.

7. Electron microscope is a device which magnifies small-sized objects that cannot be seen by the unaided eye. It is of two types :
   (i) Transmission type – TEM.
   (ii) Scanning type – SEM.

8. Scanning tunneling microscope is based on tunneling of electrons across a barrier.

9. Transmission electron microscope (TEM) uses a focussed beam of electrons to see through the specimen.

10. Scanning electron microscope (SEM) uses a focussed beam of electrons for scanning the object.

11. Bainbridge mass spectrograph is a device used to (i) detect the presence of isotopes, (ii) find an accurate value of isotopic masses, (iii) find their abundance. It uses the principle of a velocity selector.
    $$\dfrac{q}{m} = \dfrac{E}{B \cdot B'} \cdot \dfrac{1}{r}$$

IMPORTANT FORMULAE

- $a = \dfrac{e}{m} \dfrac{V}{d}$

- $v = \sqrt{\dfrac{2eV}{md}} \cdot x$

- $v_i = \sqrt{\dfrac{2eV}{m}}$

- $T = \sqrt{\dfrac{2md^2}{eV}}$

- $y = D \cdot \dfrac{e}{m} \cdot \dfrac{V}{d} \cdot \underset{\underset{x}{u}}{\dfrac{l}{2}} = \dfrac{1}{2} \cdot \dfrac{lD}{d} \cdot \dfrac{V}{V_a}$

- $R = \dfrac{mv}{Be}$

- $T = \dfrac{2\pi m}{Be}$

- $y = D \cdot \dfrac{e}{m} \cdot l \cdot \dfrac{B}{v}$

- $e/m = \dfrac{E}{B^2} \cdot \dfrac{d}{(ED \times OP)}$

  ED – extent of field.

  OP – distance from centre of field to screen.

- $l = v \cos\theta \cdot T$

  $T = \dfrac{2\pi}{B \cdot (e/m)}$

- Resolving (R.P.) $= \dfrac{1}{d}$

  $$d = \dfrac{\lambda}{2 \cdot (N.A.)}$$

  N.A. = Numerical aperture.

- $\dfrac{q}{m} = \dfrac{E}{B \cdot B'} \cdot \dfrac{1}{r}$

EXERCISE

1. Explain the motion of an electron in a parallel electric field.
2. Derive an expression for the displacement produced when an electric field acts perpendicular to the electron motion.
3. Derive an expression for the displacement produced when a magnetic field acts perpendicular to the electric motion.
4. What is a velocity selector ? Where is this principle utilized ?
5. Write the construction of an electron microscope and discuss the magnetic focussing in it.
6. Why is the resolving power of an electron microscope about 10^5 times larger than the resolving power of an optical microscope ?
7. Explain the construction and working of electrical focussing of electron microscope.
8. Explain with a neat diagram the principle and working of a Bainbridge Mass Spectrograph.
9. Explain use of Bainbridge Mass Spectrograph for detection of isotopes.
10. Explain electrostatic focussing using an electron lens.
11. Explain principle, construction and working of an electron microscope.
12. Show that a charged particle spirals around the field direction when allowed to enter at an angle with respect to field direction. What is magnetic focussing ?

PROBLEMS

1. Calculate the force acting on an electron of charge 4.8×10^{-10} e.s.u. moving in an electric field of strength 3000 volts/cm.

    Hint : 1 volt = $\frac{1}{300}$ e.s.u.   (**Ans.** 4.8×10^{-9} dynes)

2. For a proton initially travelling with a velocity 5×10^8 cm/sec., calculate the following :
    (i) Force experienced in a magnetic field B = 2000 j + 400 K gauss
    (ii) Acceleration experienced in the electric field E = 200 i + 100 j volts/cm
    (iii) Transverse deflection in travelling a length 10 cm in an electric field of 200 volts/cm.
    (**Ans.** (i) F = 1.6×10^{-8} (k − 2 j) dynes; (ii) a = 10^{14} (2 i + j) cm/sec^2; (iii) y = 0.04 cm)

3. A hydrogen atom is ionised in an electric field of 1 volt/cm. Calculate the velocity acquired and the distance travelled by the proton in 1 pico second having zero initial velocity.

   Given : e = 4.8 × 10^{-10} e.s.u.; m = 1.67 × 10^{-24} gm.

   (**Ans.** v = 1 cm/sec.; y = 5 × 10^{-13} cm)

4. Calculate the value of the electric field intensity which will give a proton an acceleration equal to the acceleration due to gravity.

   (**Ans.** E = 1.02 × 10^{-9} volt/cm)

5. Calculate energy in electron volts and velocity in cm/sec. of an alpha particle starting from rest and being accelerated by a potential of 1000 volts.

   Given : q = 2 × 4.8 × 10^{-10} e.s.u.; m = 2 × 1.6 × 10^{-24} gm.

   (**Ans.** E = 2000 eV; v = 3 × 10^7 cm/sec.)

6. Two parallel plates are situated 5 mm apart in vacuum and the p.d. between them is 250 volts. An electron is emitted from the negative plate with zero velocity. Calculate (i) K.E. of the electron in joules on reaching the positive plate, (ii) the velocity of the electron on reaching the positive plate.

   (**Ans.** (i) E = 4 × 10^{-17} joule; (ii) v = 9.48 × 10^6 m/sec.)

7. A proton moving with a velocity of 10^9 cm/sec enters a uniform magnetic field of strength 10^4 gauss at an angle of 30° with it. Find (i) Lorentz force, (ii) radius of the path.

   (**Ans.** (i) F = 8 × 10^{-8} dynes; (ii) r = 5 cm)

8. Find the mean velocity of protons selected by a velocity selector using crossed electric and magnetic fields when electric field is 60 kV and magnetic field is 2000 × 10^{-4} weber/sqm.

   (**Ans.** v = 3 × 10^5 m/sec.)

9. In a C.R.T. length of the deflecting plates is 2 cm, separation between the plates is 0.5 cm and distance of the fluorescent screen from the centre of the plates is 18 cm. Calculate deflection sensitivity in mm/volt if final anode voltage is (a) 500 volts, (b) 1500 volts.

   (**Ans.** (a) s = 0.72 mm/volt; (b) s = 0.24 mm/volt)

10. The spot of a C.R.T. is displaced vertically by a magnetic flux density 10^{-4} weber/sqm. Calculate the voltage which should be applied to the y-deflection plates placed 0.6 cm apart to return the spot to the centre of the screen. The final anode voltage is 450 volts and the length of the magnetic field is the same as that of the deflection plates.

    (**Ans.** V = 7.76 volts)

11. Two beams of U^{235} and U^{238} are separated by a 180° magnetic focussing (as in a mass spectrograph). Find the separation of the beams at the focus, if their velocities are equal and the U^{238} beam has a radius of 1 m in a field of 1 weber/sqm.

(Ans. Beam separation = 0.0255 m**)**

12. The electric field between the plates of a velocity selector in a Bainbridge mass spectrograph is 100 kV/m and the magnetic induction in both magnetic fields is 0.6 wb/m^2. A stream of singly charged neons moves in a circular path of radius 6 cm in the magnetic field. Find the mass number of the neon isotope.

(Ans. m = 21**)**

CHAPTER 2
NUCLEAR PHYSICS

2.1 INTRODUCTION

Rutherford, from his experiment on scattering of α-particles, suggested that an atom consists of a central nucleus surrounded by extra-nuclear electrons. The nucleus is positively charged and this charge is due to the protons present in the nucleus. The number of protons in the nucleus of an atom gives the atomic number 'Z' of the element to which the atom belongs. The nucleus also contains neutrons, which are electrically neutral. The number of neutrons in the nucleus is given by A – Z, where, 'A' is the mass number of the element. Nuclear size is about 10^{-15} m and the atomic size is about 10^{-11} m. An atom is electrically neutral, so the number of extra-nuclear electrons in an atom is always equal to the number of protons in the nucleus. A nucleus of an element is characterized by the mass number 'A' and the atomic number 'Z' of the element.

Nuclei of mass number upto 25 are called light nuclei. Nuclei of mass number between 25 and 85 are called intermediate nuclei and those of mass number above 85 are called as heavy nuclei. For elements of low mass number, the number of protons is nearly equal to the number of neutrons in the nucleus. e.g. for sodium, Z = 11, A = 23. So number of protons in sodium nucleus is 11 and number of neutrons is 12. Hence the neutron-proton ratio (n : p) for sodium is nearly equal to unity. Such nuclei, for which n : p ratio is nearly unity, are called stable nuclei. Light nuclei are stable. But with increase of mass number, the number of neutrons exceeds that of protons and n : p ratio exceeds unity. Such nuclei, for which n : p ratio exceeds 1.5, are called unstable nuclei. Heavy nuclei are unstable. e.g. for $_{92}U^{238}$, A = 238, Z = 92. Hence, n : p ratio is more than 1.5. So uranium is unstable. It exhibits radioactivity and disintegrates till stable end products are formed.

Henry Becquerel discovered that uranium gave out some type of radiations that could affect a photographic plate wrapped in a thick black paper. It was found that these radiations are highly penetrating, they ionize gases and cause scintillations on a fluorescent screen. The substances which emit these radiations are said to be radioactive. e.g. uranium, radium, polonium, radon, etc. The phenomenon of spontaneous emission of radiation from a substance is called as radioactivity. All naturally occurring elements with atomic numbers greater than 82 are found to be radioactive because their $\frac{n}{p}$ ratio exceeds 1.5.

The nuclear mass is the weight of the nucleus and it is equal to the sum of the masses of the neutrons and protons present in the nucleus. As the size of the nucleus is extremely small and its mass is very large, the nuclear density is enormously high, about 10^{17} kg/m^3. As mass of electron is negligible, the whole mass of an atom can be taken to be concentrated in its nucleus.

The ordinary chemical and physical properties of elements are to be attributed to peripheral electrons in their atoms. An atom can be singly ionized by removing one electron and it will then have one excess positive charge. When all the electrons of an atom are removed, the bare nucleus will be left behind with only the positive charge, and even then the atom still retains its individuality and intrinsic nature. When the nucleus itself is tampered with and its constituent particles are altered in kind and manner, the original atom ceases to exist giving birth to a new one. This phenomenon of conversion of one element into another is known as disintegration or transmutation of elements.

When transmutation is provoked by artificial means, it is called as artificial transmutation. It seemed possible that if atoms were bombarded with energetic particles, one of the latter might penetrate into a nucleus and cause transmutation. Alpha particles from natural radio nuclides were found to be effective for causing transmutation because of their relatively large energy and momentum. To reduce the probability of scattering of bombarding alpha particles and to increase the probability of disintegration, lighter elements were used as targets. The first artificial transmutation reaction observed by Rutherford was, when nitrogen was bombarded with α-particles. This transmutation can be represented as,

$$_7N^{14} + {_2}He^4 \rightarrow [{_9}F^{18}] \rightarrow {_8}O^{17} + {_1}H^1$$

Some of the artificially transmuted elements were found to be radioactive.

e.g. $_{13}Al^{27} + {_2}He^4 \rightarrow [{_{15}}P^{31}] \rightarrow {_{15}}P^{30*} + {_0}n^1$

$_{15}P^{30*}$ is radioactive and it disintegrates as

$_{15}P^{30*} \rightarrow {_{14}}Si^{30} + {_1}e^0 + \upsilon$ (neutrino)

(positron)

Such reactions led to the discovery of artificial radioactivity.

2.2 NUCLEAR FISSION

Transuranic elements are elements with atomic number greater than 92. e.g. $_{93}Np^{239}$, $_{94}Pl^{239}$ etc.

Nuclear fission was discovered as a result of attempts to make transuranic elements by means of (n, γ) reaction followed by β decay of the product nucleus.

The splitting up of a heavy nucleus into two or more medium sized nuclei with the release of a large amount of energy is called as fission.

Fission can occur spontaneously or it can be induced. Spontaneous fission was discovered by Flerov in 1940 in uranium. Many of the heavier isotopes of the elements with Z > 92 show spontaneous fission. In such cases, the number of protons in the nuclei are very large so that the electrostatic repulsion between them exceeds the nuclear binding force. Induced fission occurs whenever energy is supplied to a heavy nucleus by an impinging particle, making it unstable. Positively charged projectiles require sufficient energy to overcome the nuclear potential barrier of the target. Electron induced disintegrations are observed very rarely. Fission induced by γ-rays, called as photo-fission, was observed by Haxley in 1941.

Neutrons are the most effective fission producing agents. It was observed that heavy nuclei with even atomic number Z, and odd neutron number (A − Z), can be fissioned using thermal or slow neutrons. Such nuclei are less tightly held than those with even (A − Z). Thus, neutron binding energy alone is sufficient to cause fission in $_{92}U^{233}$, $_{92}U^{235}$ and $_{94}Pl^{239}$. Nuclei with even neutron number (A − Z) can be split only by fast neutrons. $_{90}Th^{232}$ is fissionable with neutrons of energy greater than 1.4 MeV. $_{92}U^{238}$ and $_{91}Pa^{231}$ require neutrons of energy greater than 1 MeV for their fission.

In 1938, Otto Hahn and his associates found that when $_{92}U^{235}$ is bombarded with thermal neutrons (energy = 0.025 eV), there is a splitting of uranium nuclei according to the following mode :

$$_{92}U^{235} + {_0}n^1 \rightarrow \left(_{92}U^{236} \right)^* \rightarrow {_{56}}Ba^{144} + {_{36}}Kr^{89} + 3\ {_0}n^1 + \text{energy}$$

These two fragments fly apart with a great velocity and tremendous energy is released during this process.

The fission fragments are not uniquely determined as several other combinations have since been observed.

2.2.1 Fission Process

It has been observed that fission fragments are not unique. There are over thirty different ways in which $_{92}U^{235}$ undergoes fission with thermal neutrons such as,

(i) $\ _{92}U^{235} + {_0}n^1 \rightarrow \left(_{92}U^{236} \right)^* \rightarrow {_{56}}Ba^{144} + {_{36}}Kr^{89} + 3\ ({_0}n^1) + E$

(ii) $\ _{92}U^{235} + {_0}n^1 \rightarrow \left(_{92}U^{236} \right)^* \rightarrow {_{40}}Zr^{98} + {_{52}}Te^{135} + 3\ ({_0}n^1) + E$

(iii) $\ _{92}U^{235} + {_0}n^1 \rightarrow \left(_{92}U^{236} \right)^* \rightarrow {_{42}}Mo^{95} + {_{57}}La^{139} + 2\ ({_0}n)^1 + E$

Whatever be the mode of fission, the fission process takes place in the following three stages.

(1) First Stage : The fissioning compound nucleus (excited, shown by star) splits into two primary fragments which lie in the middle of the periodic table. These fragments have mass numbers much greater than their stable isotopes. So they are unstable because of their excess neutrons. e.g. $_{56}Ba^{144}$ produced in the fission reaction of $_{92}U^{235}$ has 88 neutrons but its stable isotope $_{56}Ba^{138}$ has 82 neutrons.

(2) Second Stage : The neutrons alongwith the primary fragments are emitted with γ-rays. These neutrons are ejected immediately within a time interval of 10^{-14} sec and are called as prompt neutrons. Prompt neutrons constitute 99 % of the total neutrons ejected during fission of uranium.

(3) Third Stage : The unstable fission fragments decay by successive emission of β-particles till stable fission products are formed. This β - emission involves the emission of neutrons which get converted into protons and electrons. The process of emission of remaining 1 % neutrons during disintegration of primary fission products continues for several minutes after the actual fission process. So, these neutrons are called as delayed neutrons. The fraction of delayed neutrons is quite small but they play a vital role in the control of nuclear fission reactors.

Uranium was the first element to be fissioned. Later on it was found that there are other elements with higher mass number which can also be fissioned.

The relative abundance of isotopes of natural uranium is as follows,

$$_{92}U^{238} - 99.28 \%$$
$$_{92}U^{235} - 0.714 \%$$
$$_{92}U^{234} - 0.006 \%$$

Fission can also be induced by bombardment with particles other than neutrons. e.g. high speed protons of energy 6.9 MeV can induce fission in uranium and thorium, deuterons of energy greater than 8 MeV, α-particles of energy greater than 32 MeV and high energy γ-rays have also been found effective in producing fission.

2.2.2 Fission Products

The fission process occurs in many different modes. For U^{235} alone more than 60 different fission products are known. These vary from $_{30}Zn^{72}$ to $_{65}Tb^{161}$ and are known as primary fragments. They burst apart in opposite directions under their own electrostatic repulsion. The two fragments carry nearly equal momentum.

The fission products are radioactive. This creates serious problems not only in handling of materials but also in establishing a continuous fission reaction.

The fission product spectrum is shown in Fig. 2.1.

It can be seen from the figure that the most probable mass numbers that occur in about 6 % fissions are about 95 and 135. The symmetrical splitting with products of mass 118 occurs only about once in 20,000 fission events.

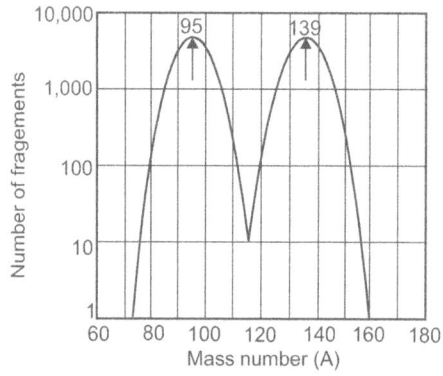

Fig. 2.1 : Fission fragment spectrum

2.2.3 Fission Neutrons

The fission process is carried forward from one fission nucleus to another with the help of neutrons produced in this reaction. This leads to the setting up of a chain reaction which spreads to the entire mass of fissionable material in a very short time. The number of neutrons emitted varies for different pairs of product nuclei and also depends upon the energy of the incident neutrons inducing fission. Thermal neutrons generally give a lower yield of neutrons. The number of neutrons resulting from fission of a single nucleus varies from zero to five. About 99 % of the fission neutrons are prompt neutrons, while the remaining 1 % are delayed neutrons.

2.3 LIQUID DROP MODEL OR BOHR AND WHEELER THEORY

2.3.1 Mechanism of Fission

The splitting up of a heavy nucleus into two moderately sized nuclei, with release of a large amount of energy is called as fission.

Heavy nuclei are unstable because n : p ratio is greater than 1.5. By releasing few neutrons, heavy nuclei gain equal no. of protons and neutrons. In this process, large amount of energy is released.

The theory of nuclear fission was explained by Bohr and Wheeler on the basis of liquid drop model for the nucleus. The similarities of the liquid drop model and nucleus may be discussed along the following lines :

- Constant density in both the cases which is independent of size.
- Spherical shape in both the cases, since a sphere has the smallest surface for a given volume and hence is most stable.
- Evaporation of a liquid drop corresponding to radioactive properties of nuclei i.e. disintegration of nucleus e.g. fission.
- Condensation of drops corresponding to the formation of compound nucleus in nuclear reaction e.g. fusion.
- The short range attractive forces of the atomic nuclei, play the role of surface tension in a liquid drop.

Bohr's liquid drop model can be explained with reference to Fig. 2.2.

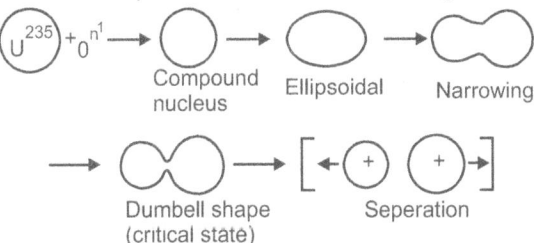

Fig. 2.2

Bohr and Wheeler explained fission by using the liquid drop model in which the nucleus is regarded similar to a drop of liquid. The surface energy of a nucleus, which is similar to the ordinary. Surface tension of a liquid drop, tends to make a nucleus acquire a spherical shape.

On absorption of incident neutrons by the target, a compound nucleus is formed. This spherical compound nucleus is in the excited state and it starts oscillating and changes its shape to become ellipsoidal. The restoring forces of the nucleus, which arise from short range nuclear forces, tend to make the nucleus to return to its original shape, while the extra energy tends to distort the shape still further. If the excitation energy is sufficient, the ellipsoid narrows to attain a dumb bell shape. With such a large distortion, the restoring forces cannot restore the nucleus to the spherical shape. The oscillations become violent and the coulombic repulsive forces increase the separation between the two nuclear lobes of the dumb-bell to finally split into two fragments. The two fragments are separated at a very high speed and are accompanied by the emission of neutrons and the release of a large amount of energy.

Fission reaction is as shown

$$_{92}U^{235} + {}_0n^1 \xrightarrow{Fission} {}_{56}Ba^{141} + {}_{36}Kr^{92} + 3\,({}_0n^1) + 200\text{ MeV}$$

For the compound nucleus U^{236} formed by the absorption of a slow neutron in U^{235}, the minimum energy required for producing enough distortion for fission is 5.3 MeV. The surface energy of U^{235} is 5.2 MeV. Obviously, U^{235} needs no further excitation after the capture of a slow neutron. U^{238} needs a neutron of atleast 1 MeV of initial kinetic energy for inducing fission.

2.3.2 Fission Energy

From the binding energy curve, we see that the heavy fissionable nuclides, whose mass numbers are about 240, have binding energies about 7.6 MeV/nucleon. Fission fragments, whose mass numbers are about 120, have binding energies of 8.5 MeV/nucleon. Hence 0.9 MeV/nucleon of energy (8.5 – 7.6) is released during each fission. i.e. nearly 0.9 × 235 = 212 MeV energy is released per fission of U^{235} nucleus. The fission is accompanied by the release of more neutrons which cause further fission. Thus, the firing of a single neutron under suitable conditions will set off a divergent chain reaction.

The energy released per fission can also be calculated by the consideration of masses of U^{235} and the fission products. For a maximum yield, the corresponding mass numbers of the fission products are nearly 95 and 139.

To calculate the mass defect of the reaction, consider the fission of U^{235} as

$$_{92}U^{235} + {}_0n^1 \rightarrow \left({}_{92}U^{236}\right)^* \rightarrow {}_{42}Mo^{95} + {}_{57}La^{139} + 2\,{}_0n^1 + Q.$$

At first sight, the above reaction might appear unbalanced as regards the charge. But it is so because β-emissions during the fission process have not been considered. (Each β-emission reduces atomic number by one unit).

Now, mass of U^{235} = 235.124 a.m.u.
mass of $_0n^1$ = 1.009 a.m.u.
mass of Mo^{95} = 94.946 a.m.u.
mass of La^{139} = 138.955 a.m.u.

∴ Mass defect of the reaction = (Total mass of reactants − Total mass of products)
= (236.133 − 235.919) a.m.u. = 0.214 a.m.u.

∴ Energy released per fission of U^{235} nucleus
= 0.214 × 931 MeV
= 200 MeV

2.4 CRITICAL MASS AND SIZE

The two chief sources of wastage of neutrons which lead to the collapse of the chain reaction are : (i) leakage of neutrons from the system and (ii) presence of non-fissionable material in the system, which absorb the neutrons.

The leakage of neutrons from the system may be reduced by a suitable choice of the size and shape of the fissionable material. If we consider a spherical shape of the material, then the ratio of rate of leakage of neutrons to the rate of their production in inversely proportional to the size of the material. This is so because rate of escape or leakage of neutrons is a surface effect dependent on the surface area $4\pi r^2$ of the fissionable material.

Rate of neutron production is proportional to the volume $\frac{4}{3}\pi r^3$ of the fissionable material.

The size of the material must be chosen large enough to keep the neutrons within the system. This decreases the probability of their escape before they hit the nucleus. The concept of critical size results from the fact that fission occurs throughout the volume of the reacting material whereas neutron escape or leakage takes place from its surface. As the ratio of the rate of escape of neutrons from the system to the rate of their production varies inversely as the radius, this ratio decreases with increase in size. A the radius is increased from a small value, a critical size is reached beyond which more neutrons are produced than are lost and the chain reaction can progress rapidly. This size of the material is called super critical. If the size of the material is less than the critical size, it is subcritical and loss of neutrons is greater than their production. Consequently, for subcritical size, chain reaction is not possible.

For a controlled self-sustaining chain reaction to occur, the size of the material must be critical.

The second source of loss of neutrons is their absorption by non-fissionable material present in the system. This loss may be reduced by (a) carefully purifying the fissionable material to reduce non-fissionable impurities that absorb neutrons and (b) by neutralizing the disturbing action of the non-fissionable material without actually removing it.

Critical size of the fissionable material is that size for which production of neutrons by fission is equal to their loss so that the reproduction factor is 1 and the chain reaction is just possible.

(a) Thus at critical size, K = 1 and the neutron population is constant. The mass corresponding to this size is called the critical mass and the chain reaction is possible.

(b) For subcritical size, K > 1 and the neutron population increases exponentially with time. This leads to an uncontrolled chain reaction.

(c) For subcritical size, K < 1 and the neutron population decreases exponentially with time which leads to the collapse of the chain reaction.
   1. Fission of uranium nuclei, with the emission of more neutrons than captured.
   2. Non-fission capture of neutrons by uranium.
   3. Non-fission capture of neutrons by the materials.
   4. Escape of neutrons without being captured.

If the loss of neutrons by the last three processes is less than or equal to the surplus produced by the first, the chain reaction occurs, otherwise it does not.

For getting neutron balance certain conditions on any system in which chain reaction is sought, one condition is on the size. There is a certain size called the critical size, for which the production of neutrons by fission is just equal to their loss by non-fission capture and escape, and a chain reaction is possible. If the size of the system is smaller than the critical size, a chain reaction cannot be sustained.

If the uranium is distributed in a regular way throughout the assembly, the neutron production depends on the volume of the system, while the probability of escape depends on the surface area. If the system is very small and the surface to volume ratio is large, most of the neutrons can escape, and it is impossible to achieve a chain reaction. The greater is the size of the assembly, it is less likely that a neutron escapes but loss by absorption will be more, hence chain reaction is difficult to achieve.

2.5 REPRODUCTOIN FACTOR

The number of second generation fissions in U^{235} per fission of U^{235} by a first generation neutron is called the reproduction factor or multiplication factor and is denoted by k

i.e. $\quad k = \eta \in pf$

2.6 NUCLEAR CHAIN REACTION AND FOUR FACTOR FORMULA

2.6.1 Chain Reaction in Uranium

Let us consider the chain reaction in $_{92}U^{235}$. When U^{235} nucleus is bombarded by slow neutrons, the nucleus is broken into two parts, Barium and Krypton. The process is accompanied by the emission of three neutrons. Nearly 200 MeV of energy is produced as a result of fission of one U^{235} nucleus. The neutrons produced in this process further attack other Uranium nuclei and produce fission. More neutrons are produced and an enormous amount of energy is released. This process continues and the series of fission reactions is called a chain reaction. If this process is allowed to continue uncontrolled, the whole U^{235} mass would disintegrate in almost no time and tremendous energy would be released.

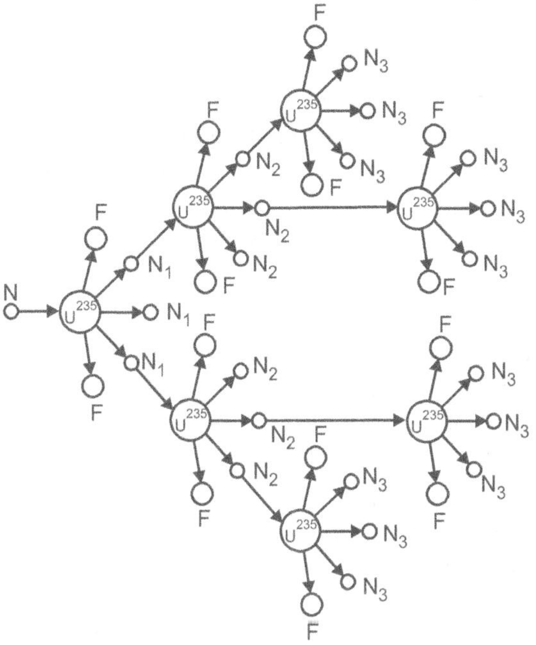

Fig. 2.3 : Chain reaction in U^{235}

The chain reaction process is not so simple as it appears because many causes work against the progressive neutron breeding essential for sustaining the chain reaction.

2.6.2 Chain Reaction in Natural Uranium

Natural uranium is a mixture of $_{92}U^{235}$ (0.714 %), $_{92}U^{238}$ (99.28 %) and $_{92}U^{234}$ (0.006 %).

Chain Reaction in Natural Uranium is Not Possible.

Consider a mass of natural uranium which is so large that leakage of neutrons from its surface is practically nil. If a thermal neutron is introduced in this mass to cause fission of a U^{235} atom, the neutrons released during fission reaction are fast neutrons. These neutrons can suffer (i) radiative capture, (ii) elastic or inelastic scattering, or (iii) can cause fission. Repeated collisions of these fast neutrons with U^{238} nuclei will reduce their energy slowly. The energy lost in a single collision is very small because of the large mass difference between U^{238} atom and the neutron. Therefore, the neutrons will linger for a long time in any given energy interval. The probability of resonance capture of these slowed down neutrons by U^{238} thus increases. On their capture, they would be lost forever and would not be available for inducing fission. Assuming that these fast neutrons can be thermalized, they can then induce fission in U^{235} but U^{235} isotope is present in very small amount in natural uranium. Hence, the probability of these thermalized neutrons colliding with U^{235} is negligible. In natural uranium, U^{238} is 140 times more abundant than U^{235}, hence collision of neutrons is more probable with U^{238} rather than U^{235}. As such, chain reaction cannot occur in natural uranium. Even if we use pure U^{235}, the chain reaction may not occur because the neutrons produced in earlier fission are fast neutrons and they have less affinity to induce fission. Secondly with small size of U^{235}, the neutrons produced in earlier fission events would escape from it before they had a chance to encounter other atoms.

Chain reaction can be made possible in natural uranium in two ways :

(i) By using a mixture of U^{238} and U^{235} having more percentage of U^{235}. This mixture is called as enriched uranium. When enriched uranium is used, neutrons from earlier fission are slowed down by U^{238} atoms to thermal energies and these thermal neutrons can then induce fission in U^{235} atoms to produce more fission neutrons which are further thermalized and the process continues.

(ii) Production of enriched uranium is very costly and it involves the isotopic separation of U^{238} and U^{235}. So we use a method of forcing a chain reaction in natural uranium itself. This is achieved by the use of certain artificial devices known as moderators. These reduce effectively the adverse absorption effect of U^{238} and thereby permit U^{235} to pursue its natural chain reaction. The essential function of a moderator is to slow down the fast fission neutrons very rapidly by elastic collisions to thermal energies, so that the chance of non-fission resonance capture by U^{238} becomes small. And consequently, the probability of fission of U^{235} increases. The moderator itself must have the property of not absorbing neutrons. Elements of low atomic weight are used as moderators. The commonly used moderators are heavy water, graphite, beryllium etc.

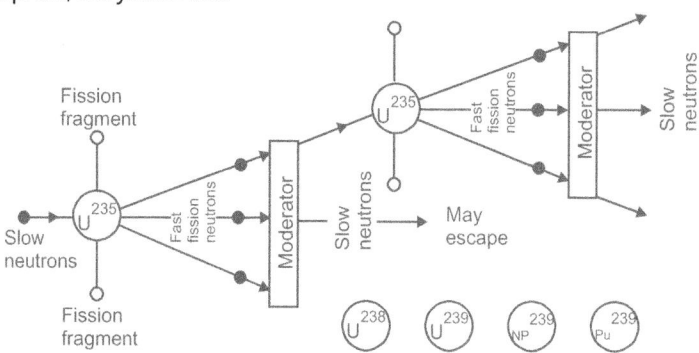

Fig. 2.4 : Chain reaction in natural uranium

2.6.3 Four Factor Formula of a Chain Reaction

For a chain reaction to sustain in a fissionable material, it is necessary that its size must be critical and reproduction factor be equal to unity.

The expression for the reproduction factor or multiplication factor (Four factor formula) of a chain reaction can be derived with the assumption that the size of the fissionable material is such that there is no leakage of neutrons from the system.

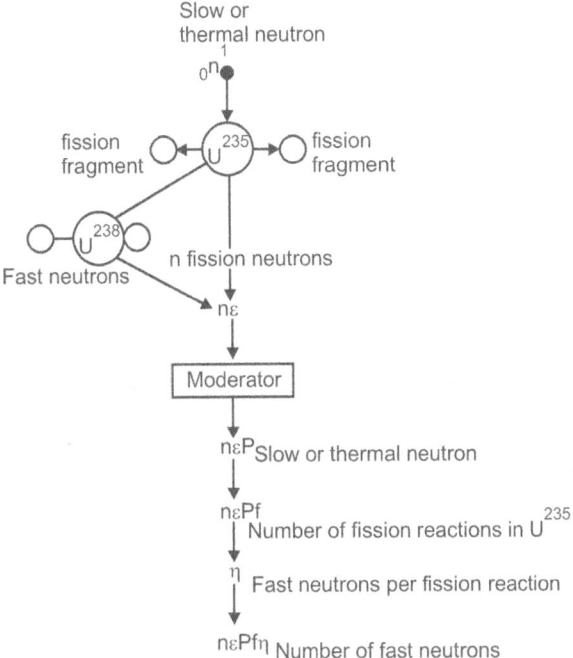

Fig. 2.5 : Chart showing neutron balance in a reactor

Consider a reactor assembly consisting of enriched uranium and a moderator. Let a single thermal neutron induce fission in U^{235} to produce 'n' fast neutrons. Of these, some neutrons will cause fission in U^{238} and therefore additional fast neutrons will be emitted. Let this small increase in fast neutrons be taken into account by introducing a factor ε called as the fast fission factor. The number of fast neutrons now available will be $n\varepsilon$ and their fission cross-section for enriched uranium is low. To obtain a large fission cross-section, the fast neutrons must be slowed down by elastic collisions with a moderator. During the time the fast neutrons are slowing down and passing through intermediate energies, some of them may be captured (by non-radiative process) by U^{238}. This is known as resonance absorption.

The resonance escape probability 'p' of neutrons gives the probability of neutrons being slowed down to thermal energies without being captured by U^{238} atoms at intermediate energies.

The number of neutrons surviving this capture and reaching thermal energies is $n\varepsilon p$. Only a fraction 'f' of these $n\varepsilon p$ thermal neutrons can induce fission in U^{235}. 'f' is called as the thermal utilization factor. The remaining thermal neutrons are absorbed by non-fission capture in the moderator, coolant and other materials in the reactor. Hence, the number of fission reactions of U^{235} is equal to $n\varepsilon pf$.

Let each fission reaction produce η fast neutrons. Therefore, number of fast neutrons is $n\varepsilon pf\eta$.

Reproduction factor, $K = \dfrac{\text{Number of neutrons present in any generation}}{\text{Number of neutrons present in immediately preceding generation}}$

$$K = \dfrac{n\,\varepsilon\,p\,f\,\eta}{n} = \varepsilon\,p\,f\,\eta$$

This is called as the four factor formula. For controlled chain reaction, K is slightly greater than one.

In designing a reactor, the fundamental problem is to maintain K at one to achieve a self-sustaining chain reaction. Of the four factors, η and ε are fixed for a given fuel. The other two factors p and f can be made to have suitable desired values by properly designing the reactor geometry, arranging a fuel and by proper choice of the moderator.

2.7 NUCLEAR FUELS

Nuclear fuels are fissionable materials used in reactors. The various nuclear fuels are :

- Natural uranium (99.28 % of $_{92}U^{238}$, 0.714 of $_{92}U^{235}$)
- Enriched uranium (containing a higher percentage of $_{92}U^{235}$)
- $_{92}U^{233}$ obtained from $_{90}Th^{232}$
- $_{94}Pu^{239}$ obtained from $_{92}U^{238}$

These fuels can be classified as fertile fuels and fissile fuels. A fuel like U^{238} which can be transformed into a fissionable substance is called a fertile fuel. Th^{232} is also a fertile fuel. Fissile fuels are those which undergo fission when bombarded by projectiles like neutrons. U^{235}, U^{233}, Pu^{239} are fissile fuels. Natural uranium may be considered as a fissile as well as a fertile fuel as it contains 0.714 % of U^{235} and 99.28 % of U^{238}. The fuel rods in a reactor may be of pure uranium, uranium oxide or an alloy of uranium and aluminium. These rods are either cylindrical or rectangular in shape and are covered with stainless steel or aluminium or zirconium to prevent contamination with air or coolant and also to preserve the fission products. Due to constant emission of X-rays, γ-rays etc. the fuel rods undergo a change in dimension and mechanical properties. In course of time, the fission products increase, while the fissile nuclei decrease. So, the fuel has to be extracted periodically and fresh fuel is to be charged in the reactor.

For achieving fusion, the two nuclei should have sufficient K.E. to overcome the mutual coulomb repulsion. Fusion reactions can, therefore, be achieved by heating the fuel to extremely high temperature. Due to the requirement of such high temperatures, the fusion reactions are called thermonuclear reactions. When a gas is heated to such a very high temperature, the electrons are stripped off the atoms, and the bare positive nuclei and the negative electrons move about freely. This mixture is known as plasma, which is regarded as the fourth state of matter. The plasma as a whole is electrically neutral. In the state of plasma and at temperature of the order of 10^8 K, the nuclei will have energies of the order of a few keV and the bare nuclei have a probability to overcome Coulomb repulsion and produce fusion reactions.

2.8 POWER REACTOR

2.8.1 Nuclear Reactor

One of the most important practical applications of nuclear fission is a nuclear power plant. The constant power production required for industrial purposes is achieved by a slow neutron reacting system called the reactor or pile.

A nuclear reactor is a device or an apparatus in which nuclear fission is produced under a self sustaining, controlled chain reaction. It is an arrangement of nuclear fuels alongwith moderators, circulating coolant and controlling devices such that self sustaining chain reaction can be maintained under controlled conditions. A reactor may be looked on as a nuclear furnace which burns fuels like U^{235} or Pu^{239} and provides in turn energy, useful products like neutrons, heat, radio isotopes etc. The large amount of energy released in fission together with the emission of more than one neutron has made it possible to use the fission process as a source of energy. The emission of an average of 2.5 neutrons in the fission of U^{235} nucleus permits a chain reaction in which these neutrons produce more fission, more neutrons and so on. Thus a self sustaining, controlled, chain reaction is a source of nuclear energy. A chain reaction is controlled in a reactor by choosing a critical size of the material (size for which reproduction factor K = 1) and a critical mass of the fuel. The achievement of a chain reaction in uranium depends on a favourable balance among four competing processes.

- fission of uranium nuclei with emission of more neutrons than are captured.
- non-fission capture of neutrons by uranium.
- non-fission capture of neutrons by other materials.
- escape of neutrons without being captured.

If the loss of neutrons by the last three processes is less than or equal to the surplus produced by the first, chain reaction occurs otherwise it does not.

The need for a favourable neutron balance sets certain conditions on any system in which chain reaction is sought, one condition is on the size. Chain reaction is possible only when the critical size is used for which the production of neutrons by fission is just equal to their loss by non-fission capture and escape. If the size of the system is less than the critical size, chain reaction cannot be sustained.

2.8.2 Classification of Nuclear Reactors

Nuclear reactors can be classified into different categories depending on the purpose for which the reactor is made, the fuel composition, coolant, neutron energies and the moderators used.

(1) The Purpose
  (a) Research tool
  (b) Production of fissile material
  (c) Power generation

(2) The Fuel
  (a) Natural uranium
  (b) Enriched uranium
  (c) Pu^{239}
  (d) U^{238}

(3) The Composition
  (a) Heterogeneous
  (b) Homogeneous

(4) Coolant
  (a) Air, CO_2 or He
  (b) Water or other liquids
  (c) Liquid metal

(5) Neutron Energies
  (a) High energy
  (b) Intermediate energy
  (c) Low energy (Thermal)

(6) Moderators
  (a) Graphite
  (b) Water
  (c) Heavy water
  (d) Beryllium or beryllium oxide.

In homogeneous reactors the nuclear fuel and moderator are mixed to form a homogeneous mixture. For e.g. enriched uranium salts dissolved in ordinary water as a moderator. In heterogeneous reactors the fuel and the moderator are isolated.

2.8.3 Power Reactor

Power reactors are those which are primarily intended for the production of usable power. They transform the heat produced from the energy released in fission into electricity. The heat is transferred to a fluid passing through the core of the reactor. The hot fluid is then passed through a heat exchanger where energy is transferred and utilized to produce steam. The steam so generated drives a turbine which is coupled to an electric generator. The electric power produced can be used for, running factories, lighting cities, driving ships, submarines or planes.

A thermal, natural uranium, graphite moderated heterogeneous, liquid sodium cooled, power reactor is shown diagrammatically in Fig. 2.6.

2.8.4 Essentials of a Nuclear Power Reactor

(1) Reactor Core : This is the main part of the reactor. Nuclear fission chain reaction takes place here with the liberation of fission energy. The energy liberated is in the form of heat which is used for operating power conversion equipments.

The core normally has the shape of a right circular cylinder of diameters from 0.5 m to 15 m. It consists of an assembly of fuel elements, control rods, coolant and moderator. The pressure vessel where the core is placed is also considered as the core. The fuel element uranium is either in the shape of a rod or a plate. It has a stainless steel, aluminium or zirconium coating to avoid rusting.

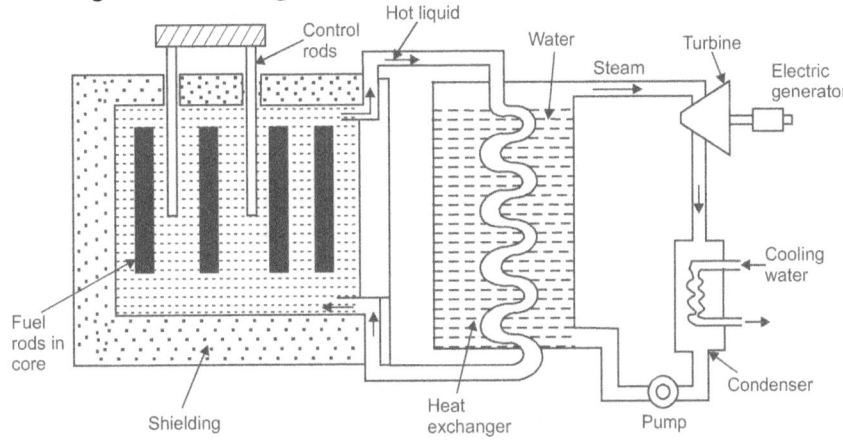

Fig. 2.6 : Power reactor

(2) Reflector : The region surrounding the core is called the reflector. It is a thick layer of a material which is the same as that of the moderator. This is done to reflect back into the core as many neutrons as possible.

(3) Control Mechanism : The control rods or arrestors are cadmium or boron rods which can be inserted in or withdrawn from slots passing through the core. When the reactor is not in operation, several arrestors are inserted in a number of slots which bring down the multiplication constant below one. To start the operation the arrestors are slowly pulled out and adjusted so that the intensity of the neutrons emitted begins to increase. By careful adjustment of the arrestors the reactor can be made to work at a constant power level. The adjustments of the arrestors can be done manually or automatically. The materials used as arrestors are normally very good absorbers of slow neutrons and they also have the advantage of not becoming radioactive due to neutron capture. Thus the control mechanism helps in starting the reactor, maintaining a steady power output and for shutting down.

(4) Moderator : The function of a moderator is to slow down the fission neutrons to thermal energies so that they are available for producing further fission. The moderators should have a small neutron absorption cross-section, high boiling point and high neutron scattering cross-section. Elements of low atomic weight are particularly suited to serve as moderators, because they reduce the energy of the neutrons considerably at each collision. The commonly used moderators are heavy water (D_2O), graphite, beryllium or beryllium oxide.

(5) Coolants : The fission process generates an intense amount of heat. The function of the coolants is to remove this heat energy and bring it out for useful purposes. Cooling can be done either by blowing gas such as air, hydrogen or helium, or by circulating liquid coolants like water, organic liquids, liquid metals, heavy water etc. throughout the reactor.

(6) Reactor Shielding : There is a radiation shield around the entire assembly. This is to weaken the γ - rays and neutrons coming out of the reactor, so that they are no longer hazardous to persons working in the immediate vicinity. (The thick walls of cement and concrete built around the reactor serve as the shield). In high power reactors there are two shields

- **(a) Thermal Shield :** It is very close to the reactor core and consists of a thick iron or steel covering. It absorbs most of the rays and protects the biological shield from overheating.
- **(b) Biological Shield :** It is a layer of concrete, a few decimetres thick and it surrounds the thermal shield and the reactor core. Its function is to absorb the γ - rays and neutrons coming out from the inner shield.

2.8.4.1 Working

The actual operation of a reactor begins when a sufficiently large number of fuel rods are brought together in the presence of a moderator. A single stray neutron (either from spontaneous fission or cosmic radiation) strikes a U^{235} nucleus and causes it to disintegrate to release product nuclei and some more neutrons. These neutrons are slowed down from energies of several MeV to thermal energies by collisions with moderator nuclei. They, then, proceed to induce further fission. In order to control the rate of the chain reaction rods made of Cadmium or Boron are used. These rods readily absorb neutrons. As the rods are inserted further and further into the reactor, the reaction rate is reduced.

2.8.5 Applications of Reactors

- The great advantage of nuclear power plants is that the production of energy involves only a small consumption of fuel.
- The combustion of fuel does not require any additional material like oxygen. Hence the proper controlling of nuclear energy will enable powerful engines to be built. They will be capable of working for long periods without refueling.
- Reactors are used to produce fissile fuel like plutonium and U^{233}.
- They are used to produce other radioactive materials required for research purposes.
- Reactors are used to produce radio active isotopes and energetic neutrons.
- They are used for digging canals and for driving ships.
- Compact and portable reactors can be designed for use in planes and ships.

2.9 NUCLEAR FUSION

Nuclear fusion is a process in which two lighter nuclei combine together to form a heavier and stable nucleus. As the mass of the product nucleus formed is less than the sum of the mass of the nuclei fused, there is a mass defect in nuclear fusion reaction. The energy equivalent of this mass defect is released during fusion process and this amount is very large. The fusion energy can be calculated by using Einstein's mass-energy relation.

For example, consider the fusion of two deuterons to form an alpha particle.

$$_1H^2 + {_1H^2} \rightarrow {_2He^4}$$

The deuteron nuclei, being positively charged, repel each other when they are brought close to each other. For fusion reaction to take place, the internuclear distance must be 10^{-14} m. If deuteron fusion has to take place, high energy must be imparted to deuteron nuclei so that they may overcome the repulsive force. This is achieved by raising the temperature to an excessively high value. Reactions produced at such high temperatures are called as thermonuclear reactions. It is believed that the energy liberated in the sun and other stars is due to the nuclear fusion reactions occurring at very high stellar temperature of about $3 \times 10^7\,°C$.

From the binding energy curve (Fig. 2.1), it is clear that the binding energy per nucleon is greater for helium than for hydrogen. The binding energy per nucleon goes on increasing for heavier nuclei upto $_{26}Fe^{56}$ and then decreases upto elements of mass number of about 240. Thus for the lighter elements, it is advantageous for the nuclei to combine to form heavier nuclei. e.g. it is advantageous for hydrogen atoms to fuse together to form helium which is very stable. This fusion process can be written as,

$$4\,_1H^1 \rightarrow {_2He^4} + 2\,_{+1}e^0 + 24.7 \text{ MeV}$$

The annihilation of positrons supplies an additional energy of 2 MeV so that total energy released in this fusion is 26.7 MeV.

The fusion energy released may also be calculated from the loss of mass during the fusion reaction.

For e.g. in the above reaction

$$4\,_1H^1 = 4 \times 1.008144 \text{ a.m.u.} = 4.032576 \text{ a.m.u.}$$
$$_2He^4 = 4.003873 \text{ a.m.u.}$$
$$2\,_{+1}e^0 = 2 \times 0.000558 \text{ a.m.u.} = 0.001115 \text{ a.m.u.}$$

∴ Loss of mass or mass defect of the reaction, Δm

$$= 4.032576 - (4.003873 + 0.001115) \text{ a.m.u.}$$
$$= 0.028857 \text{ a.m.u.}$$

∴ Energy released $= 0.028857 \times 931$ MeV
$$= 26.7 \text{ MeV}$$

2.10 THERMONUCLEAR REACTIONS

The basic exothermic reaction in stars and hence the source of energy is due to fusion of hydrogen nuclei into helium nuclei. It is the source of almost all of the energy in the universe. This fusion reaction can take place under stellar conditions in two different series of processes.

(1) Proton – Proton Cycle

The primary energy source in the sun is fusing of hydrogen into helium and it occurs as follows :

Step I :

Two protons fuse to give a deuteron nucleus, position and a neutrino.

$$_1H^1 + {}_1H^1 = {}_1H^2 + {}_1e^0 + v$$

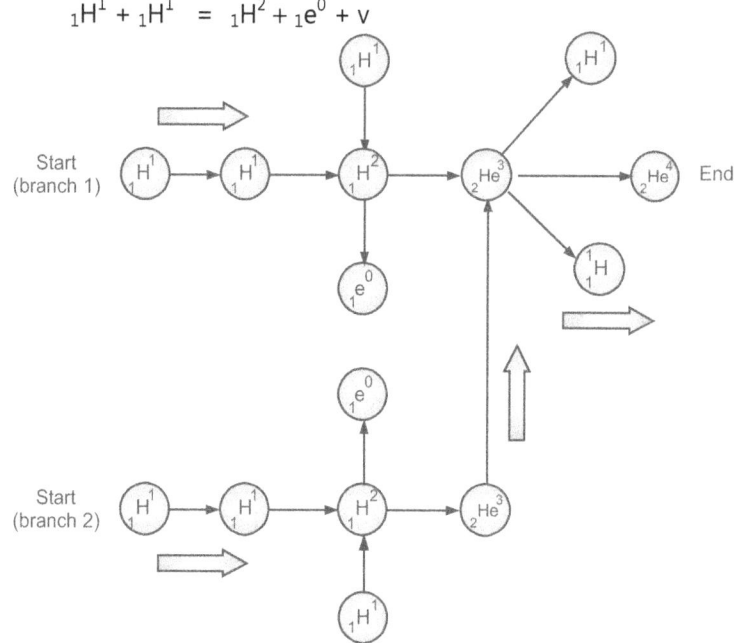

Fig. 2.7 : Proton – proton cycle

Step II :

Deuteron nucleus captures another proton to give $_2He^3$ and emits a gamma ray,

$$_1H^2 + {}_1H^1 \rightarrow {}_2He^3 + \gamma$$

Step III :

Above reaction takes place simultaneously in two separate branches and two $_2He^3$ nuclei are formed. These two $_2He^3$ nuclei fuse to form a helium nuclei with the release of two protons.

$$_2He^3 + {}_2He^3 \rightarrow {}_2He^4 + 2{}_1H^1 + Q$$

The net reaction can be written as

$$4{}_1H^1 \rightarrow {}_2He^4 + 2{}_{+1}e^0 + Q$$

Where Q = 24.7 MeV. The two positions annihilate to give 2 MeV of energy. Therefore total energy released in p-p cycle is 26.7 MeV.

(2) Carbon – Nitrogen Cycle (CN)

In 1939, Be the proposed the second set of reactions by which hydrogen might be converted into helium in the sun. It is called the **carbon cycle, CN cycle** or **CNO cycle** since carbon, nitrogen and oxygen serve as nuclear catalysts.

The reaction occurs in the following steps :

Step I : A proton fuses with $_6C^{12}$ to form a $_7N^{13}$, γ-ray photon and some energy.
$$_6C^{12} + {_1H^1} \rightarrow {_7H^{13}} + \gamma$$

Step II : The nitrogen-13 is unstable and decays to $_6C^{13}$ and emits a positron.
$$_7N^{13} \rightarrow {_6C^{13}} + {_{+1}e^0} + \gamma$$

Step III : The $_6C^{13}$ captures a portion and becomes $_7N^{14}$
$$_6C^{13} + {_1H^1} \rightarrow {_7N^{14}} + \gamma$$

Step IV : $_7N^{14}$ captures another proton to form 8O15 with the emission of gamma ray
$$_7N^{14} + {_1H^1} \rightarrow {_8O^{15}} + \gamma$$

Step V : The $_8O^{15}$ decays to $_7O^{15}$ and positron
$$_8O^{15} \rightarrow {_7N^{15}} + {_{+1}e^0} + \gamma$$

Step VI : Finally, $_7N^{15}$ captures another proton go give $_6C^{12}$ and $_2He^4$.
$$_7N^{15} + {_1H^1} \rightarrow {_6C^{12}} + {_2He^4}$$

On adding all the equations, we have,
$$4\ {_1H^1} \rightarrow {_2He^4} + 2\ {_{+1}e^0} + 24.7\ \text{MeV}$$

The annihilation of the positrons supplies an additional 2 MeV of energy so that the total energy released is 26.7 MeV.

All the above reactions are given in the cyclic form as shown in Fig. 2.8.

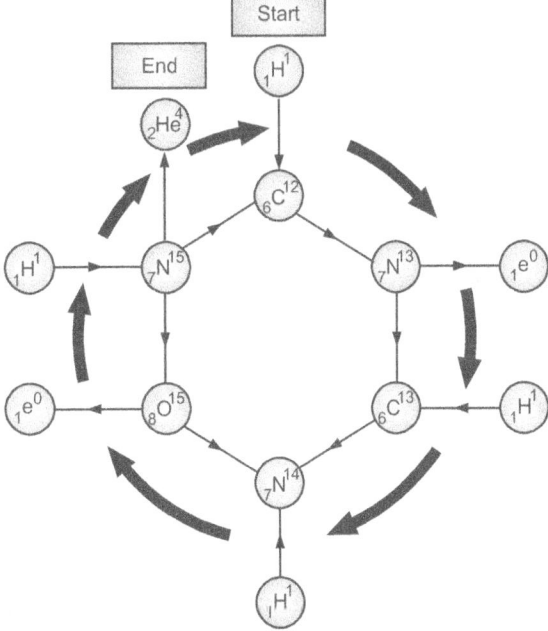

Fig. 2.8 : Carbon – nitrogen cycle

2.11 MERITS AND DEMERITS OF NUCLEAR ENERGY
2.11.1 Merits

- As the energy generated during the fission reaction is 200 MeV, sustained chain reaction is capable of generating large amounts of energy in a very short time. Power production through nuclear energy is more economical and easier to manage than production of hydroelectricity or thermo-electricity. Most of the power requirement of many countries is fulfilled through power generated by nuclear reactors. 75 % of power in France comes from nuclear plants as does 70 % of power in Belgium. However, in India nearly about 1500 MW of the total required power comes from nuclear plants.
- Another area of nuclear application is the use of radioisotopes in the field of medicine. Radioisotopes are introduced into the body to study the problem at hand. Thus, it is used as a non-invasive, non-surgical, diagnostic tool. It has also proved to be useful for diagnosis and treatment of thyroid cancer.
- India is an agricultural country but problems of short shelf life, insect infestation and the increased use of chemicals in agriculture has made it difficult to make optimal use of the harvest potential. Food irradiation is a technique which is used to preserve foods. In this treatment, food is subjected to γ-rays, X-rays and fast electrons of very low energy levels. The food then remains nutritionally, microbiologically and toxicologically active. It also inhibits sprouting of food like onions. It enables storage between six months and an year. It does away with the use of chemicals and helps delay the ripening of fruits if so required.
- Nuclear science also helps in conservation of the environment. Sciences like spectroscopy help to pinpoint environmental problems like ozone depletion. This is done by recording the frequencies and amplitudes of the sample air. According to patterns thus read, gases present and their magnitudes can be determined. In a reactor, spectroscopy is used to monitor the heavy water.
- Nuclear reactors apart from being sources of energy, can serve as sources of fuel, e.g. Pu^{239} which can be derived from U^{238} as in a breeder reactor. This is particularly useful as nuclear fuel is in short supply.
- Nuclear energies released being very high, can also serve as a tool of research leading to an understanding of microscopic particles in the nucleus.
- A research reactor provides a series of research possibilities. One can study the characteristics of the reactor, the nuclear effects produced by excess neutrons, and the properties and behaviour of materials made by the reactor.
- Beta or electron irradiation produces promise structural changes in molecules, particularly in high polymers. By this means, rubber can be vulcanized and the melting temperature of polyethylene can be raised.

2.11.2 Demerits

- Fuel required for nuclear reactors is very expensive. Moreover, U^{235} is not available in India in large quantities.
- As very large amount of energy is released in a very short time, chances of the reaction turning unmanageable is high. This could be destructive.
- There is always the danger of a nuclear accident. This could lead to radioactive contamination resulting in mutation of genes, burning of skin and the infliction of deadly diseases.
- Radioactive waste that emanates from a power plant could prove harmful to human life. Though the radioactive wastes are buried much below the water table, as there are some radioactive materials having half lives for more than thousand years, the danger seems great.
- Nations in possession of deadly nuclear weapons can be a constant threat to humanity.

SOLVED EXAMPLES

Example 2.1 : When a slow neutron is captured by U^{235} nucleus, fission results in the release of 200 MeV energy. If the output power of a nuclear reactor is 1.6 MW, calculate the number of nuclei undergoing fission per sec.

Solution :
Energy released in the fission of one $_{92}U^{235}$ nucleus = 200 MeV
$$= 200 \times 10^6 \times 1.6 \times 10^{-19} \text{ J}$$
$$= 3.2 \times 10^{-11} \text{ J}.$$
Power of the nuclear reactor = 1.6 MW
$$= 1.6 \times 10^6 \text{ J/sec}$$
∴ Number of nuclei undergoing fission per sec.
$$= \frac{1.6 \times 10^6}{3.2 \times 10^{-11}} = 5 \times 10^{16}$$

Example 2.2 : Express the energy released by 1 gm atom of U^{235} during fission in MeV.

Solution :
Energy released in the fission of one U^{235} atom ≈ 200 MeV
$$= 200 \times 10^6 \times 1.6 \times 10^{-19} \text{ J}$$
$$= 3.2 \times 10^{-11} \text{ J}$$
Number of atoms in 1 gm - atom of U^{235} = 6.05×10^{23}
Energy released in the fission of 1 gm-atom
$$= 6.025 \times 10^{23} \times 3.2 \times 10^{-11} \text{ J}$$
$$= 19.28 \times 10^{12} \text{ J} = 120.5 \text{ MeV}$$

Example 2.3 : A nuclear reactor needs to supply 45000 MWh of electrical energy per day. The reactor has an efficiency of 30 %. Find the mass of U^{235} needed for a single days operation.

Solution :

$$\text{Efficiency} = \frac{\text{electrical energy (output)}}{\text{nuclear energy (input)}}$$

$\therefore$ Nuclear energy input $= \dfrac{45000 \text{ MWh}}{0.30} = 1,50,000$ MWh

1 MWh $= 10^3 \times$ kWh $= 10^3 \times 36 \times 10^5$ J

$\therefore$ Nuclear energy input required per day

$= 1,50,000 \times 36 \times 10^8$ J
$= 54,00,000 \times 10^8$ J

Energy released per fission of U^{235} nucleus

$= 200$ MeV $= 3.2 \times 10^{-11}$ J.

$\therefore$ Number of nuclei required per day

$= \dfrac{\text{nuclear energy input per day}}{\text{energy released per fission of } U^{235}}$

$= \dfrac{54,00,000 \times 10^8}{3.2 \times 10^{-11}} = 168.75 \times 10^{23}$

235 gm of U^{235} contain 6.02×10^{23} atoms.

$\therefore$ 168.75×10^{23} atoms correspond to a mass

$= \dfrac{168.75 \times 10^{23}}{6.02 \times 10^{23}} \times 235 = 6587$ gm $= 6.587$ kg.

2.12 PARTICLE ACCELERATORS

The development of machines for the acceleration of charged particles is closely related to the advance of nuclear physics, and is an example of the interplay between the invention of new instruments and the progress of physical science.

An atom of an element defines the individual nature and properties of that element. The kernel of the atom is the positively charged nucleus and it gives the essential individuality to the atom. The negatively charged, light, electrons gyrating around the nucleus are responsible for most of the physical and chemical properties of the element. For transmutation to take place, the nucleus has to be altered. The nuclear dimension is about 10^{-15} m. Therefore, a small projectile capable of penetrating the electron groups surrounding the nucleus and overcoming the positively charged potential barrier is required. The projectiles that have been successfully used for transmutation are cosmic rays, α-particles, γ-rays, protons, neutrons, deuterons and electrons. Of these, cosmic rays, γ-rays and α-particles are considered to be natural projectiles while the rest are artificial projectiles. The drawback of the natural projectiles is that they are beyond the control of man. The desire to control the conditions of the experiment led the physicist to go for artificial projectiles. The physicist wanted to be able to choose the kind of projectile and to regulate the speed and intensity with which the projectile strikes the target. Hence, special techniques have been designed for the acceleration of artificial projectiles. The apparatus so devised are called as particle accelerators.

Here we shall discuss briefly the subject of particle accelerators, with the object of presenting some of the basic ideas underlying the design of accelerators. Several types of particle accelerators are now available, each with its own distinctive feature, but most of them may be grouped into two broad classes.

(i) They are direct voltage accelerators in which the projectiles move in straight paths through a long vacuum tube, impelled by the maximum voltage of the discharge. e.g. Van de Graff machine, Cockcroft and Walton machine.

(ii) Resonance accelerators in which particles are started at relatively low speeds and are brought to the high energies required for the bombardment of the target by the repeated push of periodic pulses of voltage. e.g. the cyclotron, betatron.

2.12.1 Classification of Accelerators

Accelerators can also be classified on the basis of the energies that the projectiles attain.

(1) Static Accelerators : This accelerator accelerates charged particles like electrons, protons, deuterons and α-particles upto 12 MeV.

(2) Linear Accelerator : Energies upto 40 GeV can be achieved for electrons and 50 MeV for protons.

(3) Lawrence Cyclotron : Particles accelerated by the accelerator are protons, deuterons and α-particles. They reach an energy upto 40 MeV.

(4) Synchro Cyclotron : This is a modification of Lawrence cyclotron which can accelerate particles to still higher energies.

(5) Betatron : It is used for accelerating electrons and gives energies upto 300 MeV.

(6) Electron Cyclotron : Modification of a betatron which gives electron energies upto 6 GeV.

(7) Proton Cyclotron : It is similar to electron cyclotron and accelerates protons to an energy of 10 GeV.

The accelerators which will be studied in detail here are Cyclotron and Betatron.

Particles are accelerated to very high energies using electric and magnetic fields. A charged particles of charge of acquires energy qV when it is accelerated through a potential difference V. Choosing V very large, it should be possible to achieve any desired energy. In practice, the maximum voltage that one can produce, limits the maximum energy which can be imparted in a single step to the particles. The production of maximum voltage depends on the ability of providing adequate insulation. The problems of insulation can be bypassed if we use modest voltages and accelerate the particles through successive small steps. By making the number of steps large, we can produce energetic charged particle beam.

2.13 LAWRENCE CYCLOTRON

Lawrence cyclotron is also known as a fixed frequency cyclotron.

2.13.1 Construction

The cyclotron consists essentially of a flat, cylindrical evacuated chamber C inside which two semicircular metal boxes D_1 and D_2 called the dees (on account of their shape like the letter D), are arranged with a small parallel air gap between them. [Fig. 2.9 (a)].

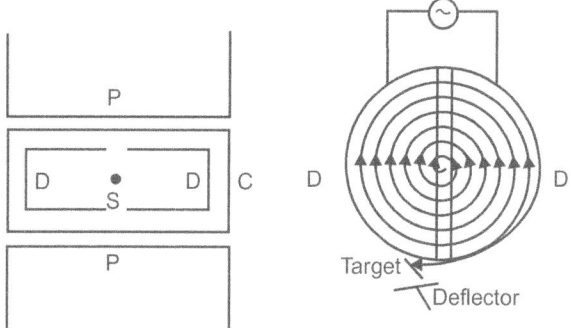

Fig. 2.9 : The Cyclotron (a) Sketch, (b) Principle of Action

An alternating potential of the order of 10,000 volts and of high frequency (10^7 cycles) is applied between the dees. The chamber containing the dees is situated between the pole pieces PP of a huge electromagnet. The magnet is capable of producing fields of flux density of a few weber per m^2 so that a strong magnetic field can be established perpendicular to the flat faces of the dees. A source S, arranged at the centre of the dees supplies the positive ions to be accelerated.

2.13.2 Principle and Working

The principle of action of a cyclotron is illustrated in Fig. 2.9 (b). The positive ion produced at S will be drawn into that dee which happens to be negative at that moment. When once inside the dee, the ion, being in a field free space, will move with a constant speed. Due to the magnetic field acting in a perpendicular direction, the ion will describe a semicircular path before arriving at the gap between the dees. Now, if the frequency of the alternating potential and the magnetic field strength be so chosen, that the time required to describe this semicircle corresponds to one half cycle, then the ion will reach the gap just at the proper time to be further accelerated by the new reversed electric field across the gap into the opposite dee. Since the particle is now moving with greater velocity, it will describe a semicircle of greater radius in the second dee. But it is easily seen that the time taken to describe a semicircle is independent of both the radius of the path and the velocity of the ion. Hence, the ion describes all semicircles, whatever be their radii in exactly the same time, the larger velocity of the ion compensating for the longer path to be traversed.

Thus, it is clear that the ion will arrive each time at the gap between the dees exactly at the moment when the alternating potential can accelerate it further. By this means, several hundred separate accelerating impulses can be given to each ion. In consequence, the ion will describe a series of semicircles of ever increasing radii in the two dees. It will gradually spiral outwards and finally emerge at the outer rim of the dees. For each complete turn of the spiral, the ion gains an energy equal to twice the potential applied between the dees. It will emerge therefore with an energy corresponding to a potential very much higher than that used in the accelerating process (given by 2nV, where n is the number of revolutions executed by the ion and V is the applied potential). At the periphery of the dees, an auxiliary negative electrode deflects the accelerated ions to the target to be bombarded.

2.13.3 Theory

When a particle of mass m and charge 'q' moves with a velocity 'v' in a perpendicular magnetic field of induction 'B', it experiences a force equal to Bqv, and it moves along a circular path of radius r. The centripetal force of circular motion is provided by the magnetic force.

$$\therefore \quad Bqv = \frac{mv^2}{r}$$

or
$$v = \frac{Bqr}{m} \quad \ldots (2.4)$$

Equation (2.4) shows that for a constant magnetic field B and for a constant value of q for a given particle, the velocity of the particle is directly proportional to the radius. It means that the time of travel of a particle is the same whether it moves along a circle of larger or smaller radius.

Let 'V' be the equivalent voltage through which the particle has been accelerated.

Then,
$$\frac{1}{2} mv^2 = qV \quad \ldots (2.5)$$

From equations (2.4) and (2.5),

$$V = \frac{q}{2m} B^2 r^2 \quad \ldots (2.6)$$

For resonance between the applied a.c. voltage and the moving particle, the time taken by the particle to travel a semicircular path within any of the dees must be equal to half the time period of the applied a.c. field.

$$\therefore \quad \frac{T}{2} = \frac{\pi r}{v}$$

or
$$T = \frac{2\pi r}{v} \quad \ldots (2.7)$$

From equations (2.4) and (2.7),

$$T = \frac{2\pi m}{Bq} \quad \ldots (2.8)$$

It is seen that the time taken to describe a semicircle is independent of r and v, and it is the same for ions of same q/m i.e., the ions describe all semicircles of different radii in exactly the same time.

The cyclotron resonant frequency is given by,

$$f = \frac{1}{T} = \frac{Bq}{2\pi m} \qquad \text{... (2.9)}$$

The kinetic energy of the particle in the cyclotron is

$$E = \frac{1}{2}mv^2$$
$$= \frac{1}{2}m\left(\frac{Bqr}{m}\right)^2$$
$$= \frac{q^2 B^2 r^2}{2m} = qV \text{ (from equation (2.5))} \qquad \text{... (2.10)}$$

If R is the radius of the outermost orbit, then the energy of the particle emerging out of the cyclotron is

$$E_{max} = \frac{1}{2}\frac{q^2 B^2 R^2}{m} \qquad \text{... (2.11)}$$

2.14 BETATRON

It is used for speeding up electrons to extremely high energies with the help of an expanding magnetic field and was invented by Kerst. Betatron differs from a cyclotron mainly in two fundamental aspects :

(1) In betatron, the electrons are accelerated by an expanding magnetic field.
(2) The circular orbit of the electrons has a constant radius.

2.14.1 Construction

It consists of a highly evacuated annular tube known as a doughnut chamber placed between the poles of an electromagnet excited by an alternating current usually of frequency 60 to 180 Hz. The doughnut lies in that part of the air gap of the electromagnet where the flux density is one half of the main flux density. The field traversing the doughnut is called the guide or control field and its function is to stabilize the electrons in an orbit of constant radius. (Fig. 2.10)

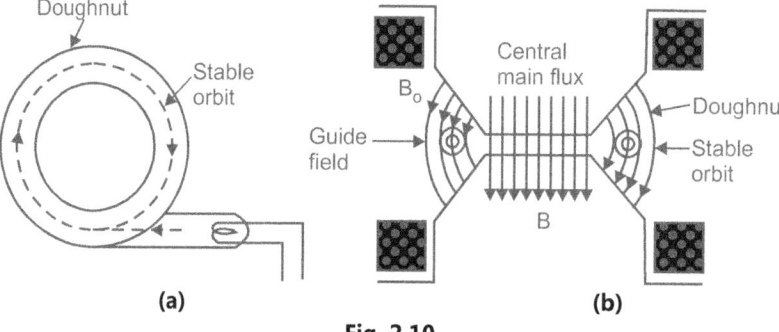

Fig. 2.10

The high velocity electrons from an electron gun are injected into the doughnut when the main flux is rising in one direction i.e. at the beginning of each cycle of this flux. (Fig. 2.11).

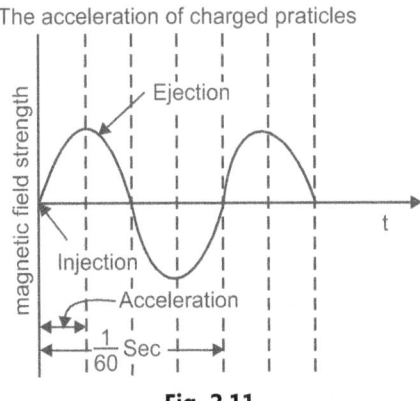

Fig. 2.11

This increasing magnetic field gives rise to a voltage gradient (i.e., electric field) around the doughnut which accelerates the orbiting electrons and so increases their energy.

2.14.2 Principle

The action of the betatron depends on the same principle as that of the transformer in which an alternating current applied to the primary coils induces a similar current in the secondary windings. The primary current produces an oscillating magnetic field which, in turn, induces an oscillating potential in the secondary coil. The betatron is a transformer in which a cloud of electrons, located inside an annular, doughnut shaped vacuum chamber, takes the place of secondary windings. When an electron is injected in the doughnut, then the alternating magnetic field has two effects.

(i) an e.m.f. is produced in the electron orbit by the changing magnetic flux and it gives an additional energy to the electron.

(ii) a radial force is produced, by the action of the magnetic field, which is perpendicular to the electron velocity and it keeps the electron moving in a circular path.

Operation :

Electrons from the electron gun are injected into the doughnut shaped vacuum chamber when the magnetic field is just rising from its zero value in the first quarter cycle (as shown in Fig. 2.11).

The electrons now make several thousand revolutions and gain energy. When the magnetic field has reached its maximum value i.e. at the end of the quarter cycle, the electrons are pulled out from their orbit. They either strike a target and produce X-rays or emerge from the apparatus through a window.

2.14.3 Theory

Consider an electron moving in a circular orbit of radius 'r' in the magnetic field. Let at any instant, B be the magnetic field at this orbit and ϕ_B the total magnetic flux through the orbit.

The flux ϕ_B increases at the rate of $\dfrac{d\phi_B}{dt}$ and the induced e.m.f. in the orbit is given by Faraday's laws of electromagnetic induction.

Induced e.m.f. $= -\dfrac{d\phi_B}{dt}$

Work done on the electron in one revolution = Induced e.m.f. × charge

$$W = -\dfrac{d\phi_B}{dt} \times e \qquad \ldots (2.12)$$

This work done must be equal to the tangential force F acting on the electron multiplied by the length of the orbit path.

Work done = Force × Distance traversed

i.e. $\qquad W = F \times 2\pi r$

or $\qquad F = \dfrac{W}{2\pi r} = -\dfrac{e}{2\pi r}\dfrac{d\phi_B}{dt}$ (by using 2.12) $\qquad \ldots (2.13)$

This force F increases the electron energy which in turn would tend to increase the radius of the orbit. In order to maintain the radius of the orbit a constant, the force experienced by the electron must be counteracted. When the electron of mass 'm' moves in an orbit of radius 'r' with velocity 'v' under the action of a perpendicular magnetic field B, we have,

$$Bev = \dfrac{mv^2}{r}$$

or $\qquad mv = Ber$

Now, force is the rate of change of momentum

$\therefore \qquad F = \dfrac{d}{dt}(mv) = \dfrac{d}{dt}(Ber)$

$$= er\dfrac{dB}{dt} \qquad \ldots (2.14)$$

To maintain the radius constant, the value of F given by equations (2.13) and (2.14) should be numerically equal.

$\therefore \qquad \dfrac{e}{2\pi r}\dfrac{d\phi_B}{dt} = er\dfrac{dB}{dt}$

$\qquad \dfrac{d\phi_B}{dt} = 2\pi r^2 \dfrac{dB}{dt}$

On integrating, we get,

$$\phi_B = 2\pi r^2 B$$

This is the betatron condition.

2.14.4 Energy Gained in the Betatron

Energy gained by the electron during one revolution = Force × Displacement

Using equation (2.13),

$$\text{energy / rev.} = \dfrac{e}{2\pi r}\dfrac{d\phi_B}{dt} \times 2\pi r$$

$$= \frac{e\, d\, \phi_B}{dt} \quad \ldots (2.15)$$

Let the main alternating flux be given by $\phi = \phi_m \sin \omega t$.

Work done during one revolution or energy gained per revolution

$$= e \frac{d\phi_B}{dt} = e \frac{d}{dt}(\phi_m \sin \omega t)$$

$$= e\, \omega\, \phi_m \cos \omega t$$

∴ Average increase in energy per revolution, $E_{av} = \dfrac{\text{Maximum value of energy}}{\pi/2}$

$$= \frac{e\omega\, \phi_m}{\pi/2} = \frac{2\, e\omega}{\pi}\, \phi_m$$

i.e. $\qquad E_{av.} = \dfrac{2}{\pi} e\, \omega\, \phi_m \quad \ldots (2.16)$

As the acceleration takes place during a quarter cycle,

i.e. in time $\qquad t = \dfrac{T}{4} = \dfrac{1}{4}\left(\dfrac{2\pi}{\omega}\right)$ (T being period of the cycle)

∴ $\qquad t = \dfrac{\pi}{2\omega}$

If v_{av} is the average velocity of the electron during this time,
then distance travelled by electron $= v_{av} \times t$

$$= v_{av}\, \frac{\pi}{2\omega}$$

∴ Number of revolutions completed by the electron during a quarter cycle

$$= \frac{\text{Total distance traversed}}{\text{Distance traversed in one revolution}}$$

$$= \frac{v_{av}\, \pi/2\omega}{2\pi r} = \frac{v_{av}}{4\omega r} \approx \frac{c}{4\omega r} \quad \ldots (2.17)$$

because the electron has a velocity almost equal to the speed of light.

Hence, total energy gained by the electron during a quarter cycle

$$= \begin{bmatrix}\text{Average energy} \\ \text{gained per revolution}\end{bmatrix} \times \text{Number of revolutions}$$

∴ From equations (2.16) and (2.17),

$$E = \frac{2}{\pi} e\omega\, \phi_m \times \frac{v_{av}}{4\omega r}$$

$$= \frac{e\, v_{av}\, \phi_m}{2\pi r} \approx \frac{ec\, \phi_m}{2\pi r} \quad \ldots (2.18)$$

Hence, the maximum value of main flux is

$$\phi_m = \frac{2\pi r E}{ec}$$

∴ The value of maximum flux density of main field is

$$B = \frac{\phi_m}{\pi r^2} = \frac{2\pi r E}{ec\pi r^2} = \frac{2E}{ecr}$$

The flux density of guide field is 1/2 the main flux density.

Maximum flux density of the guide field is,

$$B_0 = \frac{B}{2} = \frac{E}{ecr}$$

SOLVED EXAMPLES

Example 2.4 : A cyclotron, in which the flux density is 0.7 wb/m^2, is employed to accelerate deuterons. What should be the frequency of the alternating potential to be applied between the dees for the cyclotron resonance condition ? Mass of deuteron = 3.34 × 10^{-27} kg and charge q = 1.6 × 10^{-19} C.

Data : B = 0.7 wb/m^2, m = 3.34 × 10^{-27} kg, q = 1.6 × 10^{-19} C.

Formula : $\quad f = \dfrac{Bq}{2\pi m}$

Solution :

$$f = \frac{0.7 \times 1.6 \times 10^{-19}}{2 \times 3.14 \times 3.34 \times 10^{-27}}$$

$$= 0.053 \times 10^8 \text{ Hz} = 5.3 \text{ MHz}$$

Example 2.5 : Protons are accelerated in a cyclotron with dees of radius slightly greater than 32 cm and magnetic field of flux density 0.65 wb/m^2. Calculate (i) the velocity of the protons, (ii) the energy in MeV, (iii) frequency of the applied alternating potential between the dees.

Data : r = 32 cm, B = 0.65 wb/m^2, m = 1.67 × 10^{-27} kg, q = 1.6 × 10^{-19} C.

Formulae : (i) $v = \dfrac{Bqr}{m}$, (ii) $E = \dfrac{B^2 q^2 r^2}{2m}$, (iii) $f = \dfrac{Bq}{2\pi m}$

Solution :

(i) $\quad v = \dfrac{0.65 \times 1.6 \times 10^{-19} \times 0.32}{1.67 \times 10^{-27}}$

$\quad = 0.199 \times 10^8$ m/sec.

(ii) $\quad E = \dfrac{(0.65 \times 1.6 \times 10^{-19} \times 0.32)^2}{2 \times 1.67 \times 10^{-27}}$

$\quad = 0.03316 \times 10^{-11}$ J = 2.07 MeV

(iii) $$f = \frac{0.65 \times 1.6 \times 10^{-19}}{2 \times 3.14 \times 1.67 \times 10^{-27}}$$
$$= 9.92 \text{ MHz.}$$

Example 2.6 : A cyclotron with a dee radius of 50 cm is used to accelerate deuterons. The frequency of the oscillator is 2 MHz. Calculate their energy as they emerge.

Data : $r = 50$ cm, $f = 2$ MHz, $m = 2 \times 1.67 \times 10^{-27}$ kg, $q = 1.6 \times 10^{-19}$ C.

Formula : $E = 2 m f^2 \pi^2 r^2$

Solution :
$$E = 2 \times 3.32 \times 10^{-27} \times [2 \times 10^6 \times 3.14 \times 0.5]^2$$
$$= 65.467 \times 10^{-15} \text{ J}$$
$$= 40.97 \times 10^4 \text{ eV}$$

Example 2.7 : In a betatron, the maximum magnetic field at the electron orbit is 0.5 wb/m². The diameter of the stable orbit is 1.5 m. If the frequency of the alternating current through the electromagnet coils is 50 Hz, calculate for the electrons

(i) Final energy
(ii) Average energy gained per revolution.

Data : $B = 0.5$ wb/m², $r = 1.5$ m, $f = 50$ Hz

Solution :

Number of revolutions in a quarter cycle
$$= \frac{c}{4\,wr} = \frac{c}{4\,(2\pi f)\,r} = \frac{c}{8\,\pi f r}$$
$$= \frac{3 \times 10^8}{8 \times 3.14 \times 50 \times 0.75}$$
$$= 3.18 \times 10^5 \text{ revolutions}$$

Final energy gained by the electron
$$E = \frac{ec\,\phi_m}{2\,\pi r}$$
$$= \frac{ec\,2\pi r^2 B}{2\,\pi r} \quad (\text{as } \phi_m = 2\pi r^2 B)$$
$$E = ecrB$$
$$= 1.6 \times 10^{-19} \times 3 \times 10^8 \times 0.75 \times 0.5 \text{ J}$$
$$= \frac{1.8 \times 10^{-11}}{1.6 \times 10^{-19}} \text{ eV} = 1.125 \times 10^8 \text{ eV}$$

$\therefore$ Average energy gained per revolution
$$= \frac{1.125 \times 10^8}{3.18 \times 10^5}$$
$$= 0.35 \times 10^3 \text{ eV}$$

Example 2.8 : Find the maximum energy and the corresponding wavelength of γ rays produced by suddenly stopping in matter electrons, which have been accelerated in a betatron under the following conditions,

period of acceleration = 4×10^{-4} sec, orbit radius = 10 cm

The flux within the orbit increases from zero at a constant rate of 15 wb/sec.

Solution :

Number of revolutions made in one second

$$= \frac{c}{2\pi r} = \frac{3 \times 10^8}{2 \times 3.14 \times 0.1}$$

$$= 4.77 \times 10^8 \text{ rev/sec.}$$

∴ Number of revolutions made in 4×10^{-4} sec.

$$= 4.77 \times 10^8 \times 4 \times 10^{-4} \text{ sec}$$

$$= 19.1 \times 10^4 \text{ revs.}$$

Energy increase per revolution

$$= e \frac{d\phi}{dt} \text{ J}$$

$$= \frac{d\phi}{dt} \text{ eV} = 15 \text{ eV}$$

∴ Maximum energy gained for 19.1×10^4 revolutions

$$= 15 \times 19.1 \times 10^4 \text{ eV}$$

$$= 286.5 \times 10^4 \text{ eV}$$

Wavelength of γ rays, λ :

$$E = h\nu = \frac{hc}{\lambda}$$

$$= \frac{6.625 \times 10^{-34} \times 3 \times 10^8}{286.5 \times 10^4 \times 1.6 \times 10^{-19}}$$

$$= 0.0043 \times 10^{-10} \text{ m}$$

$$= 0.0043 \text{ A}°$$

Example 2.9 : The protons in a cyclotron describe a circle of radius 0.4 m just before emerging from the dees. If the magnet intensity is 1.5 wb/m², what is

(i) the maximum K.E. of the protons ?

(ii) the frequency of the alternating voltage applied ?

($m_p = 1.67 \times 10^{-27}$ kg)

Data : $B = 1.5$ wb/m² ; $m_p = 1.67 \times 10^{-27}$ kg; $R = 0.4$ m, $q = 1.6 \times 10^{-19}$ C

Formulae : (i) $E = \frac{B^2 q^2 R^2}{2m}$, (ii) $f = \frac{Bq}{2\pi m}$

Solution :

(i) $$E = \frac{(1.6 \times 10^{-19} \times 1.5 \times 0.4)^2}{2 \times 1.67 \times 10^{-27}}$$
$$= 0.276 \times 10^{-11} \text{ J}$$
$$= 0.17 \times 10^8 \text{ eV} = 17 \text{ MeV}$$

(ii) $$f = \frac{1.5 \times 1.6 \times 10^{-19}}{2 \times 3.14 \times 1.67 \times 10^{-27}}$$
$$= 0.23 \times 10^8 \text{ Hz} = 23 \text{ MHz}.$$

Example 2.10 : In a betatron, the maximum magnetic field transversing the electron orbit is 0.8 wb/m². Operating frequency of it is 50 Hz and the stable orbit diameter is 0.8 m. Calculate average energy gained per revolution and the final energy of electron assuming maximum possible time for acceleration.

Data : $B = 0.8$ wb/m², $f = 50$ Hz, $R = \frac{0.8}{2} = 0.4$ m

Formulae : $mv = BeR$; revolution $= \frac{c}{4\omega R}$

Solution :

In a betatron, $v \approx c$
$$E = mc^2 = mc \cdot c = BeRc$$
$$= 0.8 \times 1.6 \times 10^{-19} \times 0.4 \times 3 \times 10^8 \text{ J}$$
$$= 1.536 \times 10^{-11} \text{ J} = 0.96 \times 10^8 \text{ eV}$$

Number of revolutions $= \frac{c}{4\omega R} = \frac{c}{4(2\pi f)R}$
$$= \frac{3 \times 10^8}{8 \times 3.14 \times 50 \times 0.4}$$
$$= 5.97 \times 10^5 \text{ cycles}$$

Energy per revolution $= \frac{\text{Total energy}}{\text{Number of revolutions}}$
$$= \frac{1.536 \times 10^{-11}}{5.97 \times 10^5}$$
$$= 0.26 \times 10^{-16} \text{ J/rev}^n$$
$$= 0.16 \times 10^3 \text{ eV/rev}^n$$
$$= 160 \text{ eV/rev}^n$$

Example 2.11 : Calculate the energy in kWh obtained when 3.6 gm of uranium is completely converted into energy.

Data : $m = 3.6$ gm $= 3.6 \times 10^{-3}$ kg

Formula : $E = mc^2$

Solution :

$$E = (3.6 \times 10^{-3})(3 \times 10^8)^2$$
$$= 32.4 \times 10^{13} \text{ J} = 32.4 \times 10^{13} \text{ W-sec.}$$
$$= \frac{32.4 \times 10^{-3}}{36 \times 10^5} \text{ kWh}$$
$$= 9 \times 10^7 \text{ kWh}$$

Example 2.12 : Calculate the energy in kWh released by fission of 10 gm of U^{235}. Given that the energy released per fission of U^{235} is 200 MeV and Avogadro number is 6.025×10^{26}/kg.

Data : m = 10 gm, N = 6.025×10^{26} / kg, E/fission = 200 MeV

Solution :

Energy released per fission of U^{235}
$$= 200 \text{ MeV}$$
$$= 200 \times 10^6 \times 1.6 \times 10^{-19} \text{ J}$$
$$= 3.2 \times 10^{-11} \text{ J}$$

Number of atoms in 10 gm of $U^{235} = \dfrac{10 \times 6.025 \times 10^{23}}{235}$
$$= 0.256 \times 10^{23}$$

∴ Energy released in the fission of 10 gm of U^{235}
$$= 0.256 \times 10^{23} \times 3.2 \times 10^{-11} \text{ J}$$
$$= \frac{0.256 \times 10^{23} \times 3.2 \times 10^{-11}}{36 \times 10^5} \text{ kWh}$$
$$= 22.76 \times 10^4 \text{ kWh.}$$

Example 2.13 : A cyclotron with dees of radius 2m has a magnetic field of 0.75 wb/m². Calculate the maximum energies to which it can accelerate (i) protons, (ii) α - particles.

Data : mass of proton = 1.67×10^{-27} kg
mass of α-particle = 6.643×10^{-27} kg

Formula : $E_{max} = \dfrac{B^2 q^2 R^2}{2m}$

Solution :

(i) For proton,
$$E_{max} = \frac{(0.75 \times 1.6 \times 10^{-19} \times 2)^2}{2 \times 1.67 \times 10^{-27}} \text{ J}$$
$$= \frac{1.72 \times 10^{-11}}{1.6 \times 10^{-13}} \text{ MeV} = 107.78 \text{ MeV}$$

(ii) For α - particle, q = $2 \times 1.6 \times 10^{-19}$ C
$$E_{max} = \frac{(0.75 \times 3.2 \times 10^{-19} \times 2)^2}{2 \times 6.643 \times 10^{-27}} \text{ J}$$

$$= \frac{1.734 \times 10^{-11}}{1.6 \times 10^{-13}} \text{ MeV} = 108 \text{ MeV}$$

Example 2.14 : The magnetic flux within a stable orbit in a betatron changes from 1.384×10^3 wb to 8.44×10^2 wb in half a minute. What would be the energy of an electron which undergoes 2×10^6 revolutions ?

Data : $t = 1/2$ min $= 30$ sec. $\phi_1 = 1.384 \times 10^3$ wb, $\phi_2 = 8.44 \times 10^2$ wb,
No. of revolutions, $N = 2 \times 10^6$

Formula : $E = Ne \dfrac{d\phi}{dt}$

Solution :

Increase in energy per revolution $= e \dfrac{d\phi}{dt}$

$$= e\left(\frac{\phi_1 - \phi_2}{t}\right) J = \frac{(\phi_1 - \phi_2)}{t} \text{ eV}$$

Final energy after N revolutions $= N \dfrac{(\phi_1 - \phi_2)}{t}$

$$= 2 \times 10^6 \left(\frac{1.384 \times 10^3 - 0.844 \times 10^3}{30}\right) \text{eV}$$

$$= 0.036 \times 10^9 \text{ eV} = 36 \text{ MeV}$$

Example 2.15 : In a thermonuclear reaction, 1.00×10^{-3} kg of hydrogen is converted into 0.993×10^{-3} kg helium. Calculate energy released.

Data : $m_1 = 1.00 \times 10^{-3}$ kg, $m_2 = 0.993 \times 10^{-3}$ kg

Formula : $\Delta E = \Delta mc^2$

Solution :

$$\Delta E = (m_1 - m_2) c^2 = (1.00 - 0.993) \times 10^{-3} \times (3 \times 10^8)^2 \text{ J}$$

$$= 0.063 \times 10^{13} \text{ J}$$

Example 2.16 : A reactor produces 200 MW of electric power. The thermal efficiency is 30 %. The energy per fission of U^{235} is 200 MeV. Calculate the mass of uranium used.

Data : Power P = 200 MW, E/fission = 200 MeV

Solution :

Power of nuclear reactor
$$= 200 \times 10^6 \text{ W} = 200 \times 10^6 \text{ J/sec.}$$

Nuclear energy output of the reactor
$$= \frac{30}{100} \times 200 \times 10^6 = 60 \times 10^6 \text{ J/sec.}$$

Energy released per fission of U^{235} = 200 MeV = 3.2×10^{-11} J.

∴ Number of U^{235} nuclei required per sec. to give an output of 6×10^6 J

$$= \frac{60 \times 10^6}{3.2 \times 10^{-11}} = 18.75 \times 10^{17}$$

18.75×10^{17} nuclei correspond to a mass of

$$= \frac{18.75 \times 10^{17}}{6.025 \times 10^{23}} \times 235$$

$$= 731.32 \times 10^6 \text{ gms}$$

In a day the mass of U^{235} required is

$$= 6.3 \times 10^{13} \text{ gms} = 6.3 \times 10^{10} \text{ kgs}$$

Example 2.17 : Calculate the power output of a nuclear reactor which consumes 10 kg of U^{235} per day. Assume that the energy released per fission of U^{235} is 200 MeV.

Solution :

Number of atoms in 10 kg of U^{235} is

$$= \frac{6.025 \times 10^{26}}{235} \times 10 = 2.56 \times 10^{25} \text{ atom}$$

Energy released per fission of U^{235} = 200 MeV = 3.2×10^{-11} J.

∴ Energy released in the fission of 10 kg

$$= 2.56 \times 10^{25} \times 3.2 \times 10^{-11} \text{ J} = 8.912 \times 10^{14} \text{ J}$$

$$\text{Power} = \frac{\text{Energy}}{\text{Time}} = \frac{8.912 \times 10^{14} \text{ J}}{1 \text{ day}}$$

$$= \frac{8.912 \times 10^{14}}{3600 \times 24} = 9.48 \times 10^9 \text{ W} = 9480 \text{ MW}$$

SUMMARY

1. Atomic nucleus occupies a very small volume with a diameter of 10^{-14} m. It consists of Z protons and A-Z neutrons. Proton and neutrons are collectively called as nucleons.
2. Nucleons are held in the nucleus through short range nuclear forces.
3. Masses of nucleons and nuclei are expressed in atomic mass units (amu)

$$1 \text{ amu} = 1.67 \times 10^{-27} \text{ kg}$$

4. Mass defect of a nucleus is the difference between its theoretical mass and its actual mass.
5. The B.E. of a nucleus is the amount of energy which has to be supplied to a nucleus to split it up into its constituent particles. It is given by

$$\Delta E_B = [Z m_p + (A - Z) m_n - M_n] \times 931 \text{ MeV}$$

6. Binding energy curve is a plot of binding energy per nucleon as a function of mass number.
7. An encounter between a nucleus and a nuclear particle that results in a rearrangement of their constituent parts is called a nuclear reaction.

8. In Bohr's liquid drop model of a nucleus a nucleus is considered similar to a liquid drop because the properties of a liquid drop are similar to that of a nucleus.
9. The energy released or absorbed in a nuclear reaction is called the nuclear reaction energy or the energy balance of the reaction. It is called the Q-value of the nuclear reaction.
10. Q-value is positive for exothermic reactions. Energy is released during the reaction.
11. Q-value is negative for endothermic reactions. Energy is absorbed during the reaction.
12. Nuclear cross-section (σ) is a measure of the probability of occurrence of the nuclear reaction.
13. Slow thermal neutrons which are in thermal equilibrium with the medium through which they pass are called as thermal neutrons.
14. The splitting of a heavy nucleus into two or more medium sized nuclei with the release of a large amount of energy is called as fission.
15. Neutrons are the most effective fission inducing agent. Heavy nuclei with even atomic number Z and odd neutron number (A–Z) can be fissioned using thermal or slow neutrons. Ex. $_{92}U^{235}$.
16. Nuclei with even neutron number (A-Z) can be split only by first neutrons. Ex. $_{92}U^{238}$.
17. Bohr and Wheeler explained the process of nuclear fission by using the liquid drop model.
18. A nuclear fission reaction can develop into sustained chain reaction provided there is a minimum mass of fissionable material and if reproduction factor K $\cong$ 1.
19. Reproduction factor or multiplication factor 'K' is defined as the ratio of number of neutrons in any generation to the number of neutrons in the preceding generation.
20. Four factor formula, K = $\in$ pfη.
21. Nuclear fuels are fissionable materials used in nuclear reactors. They can be classified as fertile fuels and fissible fuels.
22. Nuclear fusion is the process in which two higher nuclei combine together to form a heavy nucleus. This is accompanied by release of energy.
23. Fusion reactions take place only at very high temperatures. There are known as thermonuclear reactions.
24. Particles accelerators are devices used to accelerate charged particles so that they may be used as projectiles for effecting artificial transmutation.
25. Lawrence cyclotron is a fixed frequency cyclotron. $\left(f = \dfrac{Bq}{2\pi m}\right)$ used to accelerate positively charged particles.
26. Betatron is used for accelerating electrons to high energies with the help of an expanding magnetic field.

27. $\phi_B = 2\pi r^2 B$ is the betatron condition.

28. Number of revolutions made by the electron in the betatron is given by $\frac{c}{4wr}$.

29. Total energy gained by the electron in the betatron is, $E = \frac{ec\phi_m}{2\pi n}$.

IMPORTANT FORMULAE

- $\Delta E_B = [Zm_p + (A - Z) m_n - M_n] \times 931$ MeV
- $Q = (M_0 + M_1) - (M_2 + M_3) = E_2 + E_3 - E_1$
- $K = \dfrac{\text{Rate of production of neutrons}}{\text{Rate of loss of neutrons}} = \dfrac{P}{A + L} = \dfrac{NF/A}{1 + L/A}$
- $K = \epsilon p f \eta$
- $T = \dfrac{2\pi m}{Bq}$
- $f = \dfrac{Bq}{2\pi m}$
- $E_{max} = \dfrac{q^2 B^2 R^2}{2m} = qV$
- $\phi_B = 2\pi r^2 B$
- $E = \dfrac{ec\phi_m}{2\pi r}$
- $\dfrac{E}{rev^n} = e \dfrac{d\phi_B}{dt}$

EXERCISE

1. What is nuclear fission ? Explain it on the basis of Bohr & Wheelers liquid drop model.
2. Write a note on energy released in the fission of one uranium atom.
3. Explain chain reaction in nuclear fission.
4. How is a chain reaction produced in natural uranium ? Why is it not possible in natural uranium ?
5. Write a note on nuclear fuels.
6. Derive the four factor formula.
7. What are thermal neutrons ?
8. What is nuclear fusion ?
9. Enumerate on thermonuclear reactions.

10. What is stellar energy ?
    Explain : (i) Proton - Proton cycle
             (ii) Carbon - Nitrogen cycle.
11. Distinguish between fission and fusion.
12. Discuss the merits and demerits of nuclear energy.
13. Describe working of cyclotron. Derive resonance frequency.
14. Explain working of a betatron. Obtain betatron condition.
15. What are thermal neutrons ? How are they produced ?
16. Give construction and working of a betatron. Show that in a betatron, the total magnetic flux ϕ is twice the value of magnetic flux through the electron orbit if the flux density B were uniform throughout the orbit.
17. Describe the theory of cyclotron and hence discuss its limitations.
18. Write a note on liquid drop model of an atom.
19. Distinguish between nuclear fission and fusion. Define multiplication factor and nuclear cross-section.
20. Write a note on chain reaction in natural uranium.
21. Explain what is meant by nuclear fusion. Give an account of proton-proton and carbon-nitrogen cycle in fusion reaction.
22. Distinguish between a cyclotron and a betatron.
23. Write a note on nuclear fusion and stellar energy.
24. Explain the working of betatron. Obtain betatron condition.
25. Derive four factor formula.
26. Explain principle, construction, operation of betatron and derive betatron condition.
27. What is nuclear fission ? Explain it on the basis of Bohr and Wheeler liquid drop model.
28. Write a note on cyclotron.
29. What are advantages of microtron over cyclotron ?
30. Explain working of microtron. Derive formula for resonance condition.

PROBLEMS

1. Calculate the equivalent energy of one gram in kWh. (**Ans.** 2.5×10^7 kWh.
2. A reactor is developing nuclear energy at the rate of 50,000 kW. (i) How many atoms of U^{235} undergo fission per second ? (ii) What mass of U^{235} (in kg) would be used in 3000 hours of operation, assuming that 200 MeV of energy is released per fission ?
   (**Ans.** (i) 1.56×10^{18} (ii) 6.58 kg)
3. A nuclear reactor converts nuclear energy into electrical energy with an efficiency of 25 %. If the reactor supplies 1000 MWh per day using the nuclear fuel U^{235}, find the mass of U^{235} needed for a days operation. (**Ans.** 1.76 kg)

4. A cyclotron, in which flux density is 1.4 wb/m², is employed to accelerate protons. What should be the frequency of the alternating field applied to the dees ? Given : mass of proton
   = 1.67×10^{-27} kg and charge = 1.6×10^{-19} C. **(Ans. 21.3 MHz)**

5. Deuterons in a cyclotron describe a circle of 32 cm just before emerging from the dees, the frequency of the applied a. c. voltage being 10 MHz.
   Find (i) flux density of the magnetic field.
   (ii) the velocity of deuterons emerging out of the cyclotron.
   Mass of deuteron = 3.32×10^{-27} kg, charge = 1.6×10^{-19} C.
   (Ans. 1.3 wb/m², 2×10^7 m/sec.)

6. In a 70 MeV betatron, the radius of the stable orbit is 28 cm. Calculate,
   (i) the angular velocity of the electrons
   (ii) the frequency of the applied electric field.
   (iii) the maximum value of the magnetic flux density at the orbit for this energy (assume velocity of electron = velocity of light in vacuum)
   (Ans. (i) 1.07×10^7 rad/sec. (ii) 1.7×10^8 Hz, (iii) 0.833 wb/m²)

7. Determine the frequency of a generator feeding a cyclotron that accelerates deuterons upto 4 MeV when the maximum radius of the particular orbit is 75 cm, mass of deuteron = 3.34×10^{-27} kg. **(Ans. 4.15×10^6 Hz)**

8. The magnetic flux within a stable orbit of a betatron changes at a constant rate of 15 Wb/sec. What would be the energy of an electron which undergoes 10^6 revolutions ?
   (Ans. 15 MeV)

9. A cyclotron with dees of radius 2m has a magnetic field of 0.65 Wb/m². Calculate the maximum energies to which (a) protons (b) deuterons can be accelerated. For proton, m = 1.67×10^{-27} kg, q = 1.6×10^{-19} C; for deuteron, m = 3.34×10^{-27} kg, q = 1.6×10^{-19} C.

10. If the frequency of the oscillator potential applied to the dees of a cyclotron is 9 MHz, what must be the magnetic flux density B to accelerate α- particles ? Mass of α-particles = 6.643×10^{-27} kg. **(Ans. 1.17 Wb/m²)**

11. Calculate the frequency of the alternating potential that must be applied to the cyclotron dees in which deuterons are accelerated, given that maximum flux density is 3 Wb/m².
    (Ans. 23 MHz)

✠ ✠ ✠

Unit - II

CHAPTER 3
SOLID STATE PHYSICS

3.1 INTRODUCTION

From the engineering point of view, knowledge of electric, magnetic and dielectric properties of materials is very essential. Basically, solids can be classified into different categories such as conductors, insulators and semiconductors. The classification of materials from electrical point of view into conductors, semiconductors and insulators is based according to their resistivity range. For conductors the resistivity ranges from 1.6×10^{-8} to 1.4×10^{-6} ohm-m. The resistivity range of semiconductors and insulators is respectively from 10^{-4} to 10^{6} ohm-m and from 10^{7} to 10^{16} ohm-m. Considering the rapid development of semiconductor electronics, stress has been given to discuss the semiconductor devices in this chapter. Semiconductor devices are highly compact, low power consuming and efficient. They have replaced vacuum tubes to a great extent. For a better knowledge of semiconductors, one should understand the properties of semiconductors on the basis of band theory of solids. For this, elementary knowledge of electronic configuration of atoms and quantum numbers is quite essential.

3.1.1 Electron Configuration of Atoms

Different physical and chemical properties of various elements are attributed to different configuration of electrons in their atoms. The four quantum numbers that specify the electron state in an atom are n, l, m_l and m_s.

As per **'Pauli's Exclusion Principle'**, no two electrons in an atom can have the same set of quantum numbers n, l, m_l and m_s. This principle gives the arrangement of electrons in different orbits.

The various subshells are filled in the following manner :

- As we go from one atom to the next in the order of increasing atomic numbers, the electrons are added one by one to various shells.
- Electrons enter different subshells in the order of increasing energy. The subshell of lower energy is filled up first while the higher energy subshell is filled up later.

The sequence of filling different subshells can be remembered from Fig. 3.1.

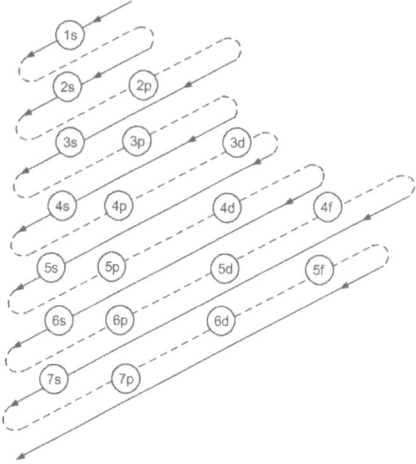

Fig. 3.1

- As per Pauli's principle, an orbital cannot have more than two electrons.
- According to Hund's rule, electron pairing does not take place in p, d, f orbitals until all the orbitals of the given subshell contain one electron each with parallel spin.

For example, the filling of various orbitals of nitrogen (Z = 7) can be

$$1s^2\, 2s^2\, 2p_x^1\, 2p_y^1\, 2p_z^1$$

↑ ↓	↑ ↓	↑ ↑ ↑
1s	2s	2p

3.1.2 Electron Energy States of an Isolated Atom

An isolated atom of an element with atomic number Z and mass number A consists of a positively charged nucleus, with Z protons and (A − Z) neutrons around which Z electrons revolve in different orbitals. The orbits are characterized by a set of four quantum numbers n, l, m_l, and m_s. The distribution of electrons in an atom i.e., energy states decide the properties of the element to which the atom belongs. The energy of an electron in an atom depends on n as well as l i.e. energy of the electron is a function of n, l, or $E = E(n, l)$. As n and l can have only discrete values, the energy E will have discrete values. The energy states characterized by n, l numbers are generally degenerate i.e. electrons with different set of quantum numbers will have the same energy, due to different m_l values for a given l. The state with same n and l will be $(2l + 1)$ degenerate. The number of electrons that can have the same energy $E(n, l)$ with given n and l is $2(2l + 1)$, the factor 2 is due to two possible values of m_s for each m_l. The state s is non-degenerate and has two electrons. But p, d, f states are respectively 3-fold, 5-fold, 7-fold degenerate and the number of electrons in those states are 6, 10, 14 respectively.

As such the energy states of an isolated atom will be quite discrete. The energy states of an isolated lithium atom are shown in Fig. 3.2.

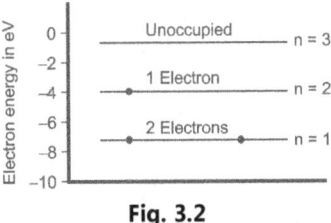

Fig. 3.2

3.2 BAND THEORY OF SOLIDS

A solid is an aggregate of atoms in very close proximity. For example, a crystal is a periodic arrangement of atoms in which the structure is built up by a regular repetition of a small unit called a **'Unit Cell'**.

The energy states of an isolated atom consist of discrete energy levels. But when the atoms are brought into close proximity as in a crystal, the outermost or valence electrons of adjacent atoms interact with each other. The inner or non-valence electrons do not interact significantly at any realizable interatomic distance because they are too closely associated with the nuclei. As per Pauli's exclusion principle, since not more than two interacting electrons may have the same energy level, new levels must be established which are discrete but only infinitesimally different. The separation between split energy sublevel is of the order of 10^{-20} eV. This group of related levels in a polyatomic material is called an **'Energy Band'**. In short, in crystals or solids, the allowed energy levels of an atom are modified by the proximity of other atoms in such a way that the discrete energy levels of the individual atoms become bands in solids. Each band contains as many discrete levels as there are atoms in the material. In a solid containing N atoms, there are N possible energy levels in each band such that, only two electrons of opposite spin may occupy the same energy level. Thus, the N levels will accommodate a maximum of 2N electrons. In other words, a band formed from N atoms contains 2N energy states.

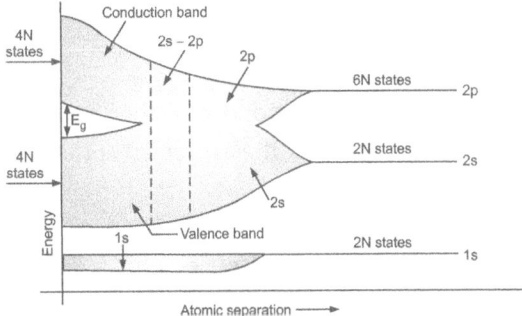

Fig. 3.3 : Formation of energy bands in a diamond crystal

The imaginary formation of a diamond crystal from isolated carbon atoms is shown in Fig. 3.3. Each isolated carbon atom has an electron structure $1s^2\ 2s^2\ 2p^2$. Each atom has available two 1s states, two 2s states and six 2p states and higher states. If we consider N atoms, there will be 2N states of 1s type, 2N states of 2s type and 6N states of 2p type. As the interatomic spacing decreases, these energy levels split into bands beginning with the outer (n = 2) shell. As the 2s and 2p bands grow, they merge into a single band composed of a mixture of energy levels. This band of '2s–2p' levels contains 8N available states. As the distance between atoms approaches the equilibrium interatomic spacing of diamond, this band splits into two bands separated by an energy gap or band gap E_g. The upper band is known as the **'Conduction Band'** while the lower one is known as the **'Valence Band'**. Thus, the conduction band contains 4N states and the valence band also contains 4N states. So, apart from the low lying and tightly bound 1s levels, the diamond crystal has two bands of available energy levels separated by energy gap E_g. The energy gap E_g does not contain allowed energy levels for electrons to occupy. This gap is also called as **'Forbidden Band'**.

The lower 1s band is filled with 2N electrons which originally resided in the collective 1s states of the isolated atoms. However, there were 4N electrons in the original isolated n = 2 shell. (2N in 2s states and 2N in 2p states). These 4N electrons must occupy states in the valence band or the conduction band in the crystal. At 0 K, the electrons will occupy the lowest energy states available to them. In the case of the diamond crystal, there are exactly 4N states in the valence band available to the 4N electrons. So at 0 K every state in the valence band will be filled while the conduction band will be completely empty of electrons. This arrangement of completely filled and empty energy bands has an important effect on the electrical conductivity of the material. As conduction band is completely empty, the diamond will serve as an insulator.

3.2.1 Valence Band, Conduction Band and Forbidden Energy Gap

Energy Band :

In solids or crystals, allowed energy levels are modified by the proximity of other atoms in such a way that discrete energy levels of individual atoms are converted into series of energy levels. The difference in the energy sublevels is of the order of 10^{-28} eV. This series of energy levels is called **'Energy Band'**.

Valence Band :

The electrons in the inner shells are strongly bonded to their nuclei while the electrons in the outermost shells are not strongly bonded to their nuclei. It is these electrons which are most affected, when a number of atoms are brought very close together during the formation of a solid. The electrons in the outermost shell are called **'Valence Electrons'**. The band formed by a series of energy levels containing the valence electrons is known as **'Valence Band'**. The valence band may be defined as a band which is occupied by valence electrons or highest occupied energy band. The valence band is completely filled with electrons at 0 K.

Conduction Band :

The next higher permitted energy band is called the **'Conduction Band'**. This band may be either empty or partially filled with electrons. Conduction band may be defined as the lowest unfilled permitted energy band. It lies just above the valence band. The electrons occupying conduction band are known as **'Conduction Electrons'** and these electrons move freely in the conduction band.

Forbidden Gap :

The conduction band and valence band are separated by a region or a gap known as **'Forbidden Band'** or **'Forbidden Gap'**. This band is collectively formed by a series of nonpermitted energy levels above the top of the valence band to the bottom of the conduction band and is a measure of E_g. Thus, E_g is the amount of energy that should be imparted to the electron in the valence band for its migration to the conduction band. These bands are shown in Fig. 3.4.

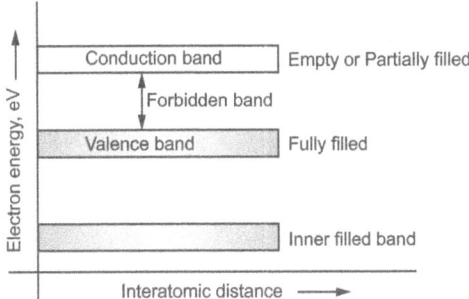

Fig. 3.4 : Valence band, conduction band and forbidden gap at T = 0 K

If a valence electron happens to absorb enough energy, it jumps across the forbidden energy gap and enters the conduction band. Also, if a conduction electron happens to radiate too much energy, it will suddenly reappear in the valence band once again.

3.3 CONCEPT OF ELECTRICAL CONDUCTIVITY

The electrons in a partially filled conduction band are relatively free to move in the specimen as they are not bound to any atom but are in a band which is shared by the entire crystal. These electrons are called as **'Free Electrons'**.

The electrons well inside the specimen are surrounded by positive ion cores from all the sides, hence net force exerted by the iron cores (or lattice points) on electrons is zero. Due to the thermal energy, the electrons are in constant motion with average velocity of 10^5 m/s at room temperature. But the direction of motion of electron is totally random and take a very complex path. This results in net zero current. On the way electrons collide with the lattice points which are in vibration motion due to thermal energy. This reduces the velocity of electrons and comes to almost rest. This results in small amount of resistivity and the loss of energy is converted into thermal energy.

The average time between collisions is called the **'Mean Free Time'** and the length of the path during this free time is called the **'Mean Free Path'**. The mean free paths have different lengths. Fig. 3.5 (a) shows motion of electrons under equilibrium conditions.

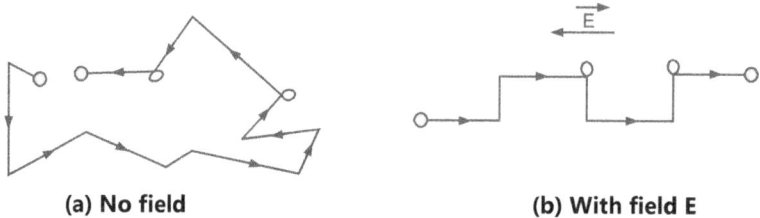

(a) No field   (b) With field E

Fig. 3.5 : Motion of free electrons

In presence of field $\vec{E}$, the direction of motion will be directed along the electric field. This results into net current flowing in a particular direction. As the electron tries to move in the field, the number of collisions increases. In fact, the external field simply bends the path of the electron between two collisions. In general, the conductivity depends on number of charge carriers and their freedom to move.

3.3.1 Free Electron Theory of Metals

The free electron theory of metals was first proposed by Drude and later improved by Lorentz and hence the theory is called the Drude-Lorentz theory. Following are the basic assumptions made in the theory.

- All metals contain a fixed number of valence electrons forming an **Electron Gas**, which are free to move throughout the volume of the metal like molecules of a gas.
- The electron velocities in metals obey the classical **Maxwell-Boltzmann Distribution** of velocities.
- The positive ions which can vibrate about their mean position, cannot move from one lattice site to another. The repulsive force between the negatively **Charged Electron** is ignored and the electric field due to the positive ions is assumed to be uniform.
- The electrons move from one point to another randomly with **Random Velocity** which is temperature dependent. At room temperature, this velocity is about 4×10^5 m/s.
- The **Kinetic Energy** of the electron is given by $3kT/2$, where k is Boltzmann's constant and T is absolute temperature.
- In absence of external electric field, the electrons move in **Random Directions**, making collisions from time to time with positive ions, which are fixed in lattice. This makes net current zero.
- When an electric field is applied, free electrons move towards positive terminal of the supply. Thus, the electrons will experience two motions – random motion due to temperature and drift motion due to applied voltage. As a result the electron will move in **Opposite Direction to the Electric Field** while maintaining their random motion.

- While drifting towards positive of the supply, the electrons colloid with positive ions. During each collision the electron loses all its drift velocity and starts from rest once again. The average distance covered by an electron between collisions is known as **Mean Free Path** 'λ' and time taken to cover this distance is termed as relaxation time 'τ'.
- As the temperature increases, the vibration of the ion core increases, this increases the probability of electron-core collision. As a result, **Resistivity Increases with Increase in Temperature**.

3.3.2 Free Electron Theory - Quantum Mechanical Treatment

Quantum mechanical behaviour of electron gas was first investigated by Sommerfeld. The main failure of the classical theory was that it was developed on the basis of Boltzmann statistics. The quantum theory was developed on the basis of Fermi-Dirac statistics and is successful in explaining the behaviour of electron cloud.

In Sommerfeld's model, it is assumed that the free electrons are the valence electrons of the atoms of the metals. The alkali metals contribute one electron per atom. These electrons are free to move within the metal but cannot come out of the metal surface due to presence of high potential barrier at the surface. The potential inside the conductor is zero. Thus, the metal acts as a potential well for the free electrons.

3.3.3 Drawbacks of Classical Free Electron Theory

The free electron theory, successfully established Ohm's law, showed that the resistivity is directly proportional to the temperature and the Wiedemann-Franz relation was proved. However, the theory has many drawbacks.

The main drawbacks are:

- The specific heat capacity value based on classical theory shows that it is independent of temperature. But as per quantum theory, it directly depends on temperature i.e. it increases with the increase in temperature.
- As per classical theory, the paramagnetic susceptibility is inversely proportional to the temperature. But experimental results show that it is almost independent of temperature.
- The classical theory failed to explain occurrence of long mean free paths (10^8 or 10^9 times interatomic spacing).
- Classification of solids on band theory i.e. metals, semimetals, semiconductors and insulators cannot be done by classical theory.
- The positive values of Hall coefficient of metals could not be explained by classical theory.
- Classical theory also failed to explain photoelectric effect, Compton effect and black body radiation.

3.4 FERMI ENERGY

3.4.1 Fermi Level in Conductors or Metals

The statement that a solid is composed of N atoms implies that each atomic level splits into N-energy levels and bands of energy are formed. The filling of the bands follows a simple rule. States of lowest energy are filled first, then the next lowest and so on, till all the electrons are accommodated. The highest filled state is called the **Fermi Level** and its corresponding energy is called the '**Fermi Energy**' E_F. The magnitude of E_F depends on the number of electrons per unit volume in the solid because the electron density determines how many electrons must go into the bands. At 0 K, all states upto E_F are full and all states above E_F are empty. At higher temperatures, the random thermal energy will empty a few states below E_F by elevating a few electrons to yet higher energy states. No transitions to states below E_F occur as they are full. Thus, an electron cannot change its state unless enough energy is provided to take it above E_F.

The highest filled state in the highest energy band which contains electrons in a metal, at 0 K, is called the Fermi level and its corresponding energy is called the Fermi energy E_F.

3.4.2 Fermi Level in Semiconductors

In semiconductors, the Fermi level is a reference level that gives the probability of occupancy of states in conduction band as well as in valence band.

In case of intrinsic semiconductors, the band picture consists of a band of completely filled states called as the '**Valence Band**' separated from a band of unoccupied states called as the '**Conduction Band**', by an energy gap E_g. For an intrinsic semiconductor, the Fermi level lies at the centre of the forbidden band, indicating that the states occupied in conduction band are equal to the states unoccupied in valence band. In other words, for every electron in the conduction band, there is a hole in the valence band.

So Fermi level in the semiconductors may be defined as the energy which corresponds to the centre of gravity of conduction electrons and holes when 'weighted' according to their energies.

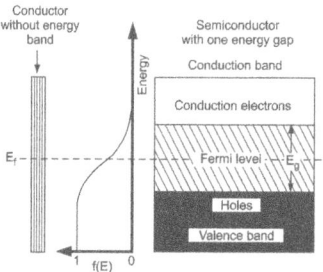

Fig. 3.6

However, it is to be noted that Fermi level is only an abstraction. A hollow body can have a centre of gravity at the centre where there is no matter. Similarly, a material can have a Fermi level at an energy which is forbidden to all electrons. For example, in an intrinsic semiconductor, the Fermi level is at the centre of the forbidden band.

3.5 FERMI-DIRAC PROBABILITY DISTRIBUTION FUNCTION

Electrons in solids obey Fermi-Dirac statistics. In the development of this type of statistics, the wave nature of electrons and the Pauli's exclusion principle will have to be taken into consideration. The result of the statistical arrangement gives the distribution of electrons over a range of allowed energy levels at thermal equilibrium.

i.e. $$P(E) = \frac{1}{1 + e^{(E - E_F)/kT}} \quad \ldots(1)$$

where k is Boltzmann's constant.

The Fermi-Dirac distribution function P(E) gives the probability that an energy state of energy E will be occupied by an electron at absolute temperature T. The quantity E_F is the Fermi energy.

(i) For an energy E equal to the Fermi level E_F, the probability of occupation is given by

$$P(E_F) = [1 + e^{(E - E_F)/kT}]^{-1} \quad \ldots(2)$$

$$P(E_F) = \frac{1}{2}$$

Thus, an energy state at the Fermi level has a probability $\frac{1}{2}$ of being occupied by an electron for a temperature T > 0 K.

(ii) At T = 0 K for E < E_F, the term $e^{(E - E_F)/kT} = 0$ so that P(E) = 1; i.e. the probability of finding an electron with energy less than Fermi energy is unity. Or it can be said that at T = 0 K all energy states below E_F, have a probability of occupancy of unity i.e. they are certainly occupied.

(iii) At T = 0 K for E > E_F, the term $e^{(E - E_F)/kT} = \infty$ so that P(E) = 0; i.e. the energy states above E_F have zero probability of occupancy and they are therefore empty. The probability function plotted for different temperatures is shown in Fig. 3.7.

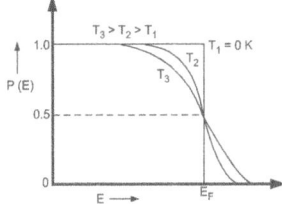

Fig. 3.7 : The Fermi-Dirac distribution function

The rectangular distribution implies that at 0 K every available energy state upto E_F is filled with electrons and all the states above E_F are empty. At temperatures higher than 0 K, some probability exists for states above Fermi level to be filled. When the temperature is raised, there is a greater possibility of electrons being found above the Fermi level with an equal probability of finding a hole below the Fermi level.

3.6 POSITION OF FERMI LEVEL IN INTRINSIC SEMICONDUCTORS

The Fermi-Dirac probability function is

$$P(E) = \frac{1}{1 + e^{(E - E_F)/kT}} \quad \ldots (1)$$

and it gives the probability of an electron occupying a state of energy E.

The derivation of the position of Fermi level in intrinsic semiconductors is based on the following assumptions :

- The widths of the valence band and conduction band are small when compared to the forbidden gap E_g.
- As band widths are small, all levels in the band have the same energy. The levels in the conduction band have energy E_c while levels in valence band have energy E_v.
- At 0 K, the solid is like an insulator i.e. no conduction is possible as valence band is completely filled and conduction band is completely empty.

    At any other temperature say T,

    Let n_c = number of electrons in the conduction band.

    n_v = number of electrons in the valence band.

    $N = n_c + n_v$ = number of electrons in both the bands

From the probability theory, we have

$$P(E_c) = \frac{n_c}{N}$$

i.e. $\quad n_c = N\,P(E_c) \quad \ldots (2)$

where $P(E_c)$ is the probability of an electron having an energy E_c in the conduction band.

So, according to Fermi-Dirac probability distribution function defined in equation (1), we have,

$$P(E_c) = \frac{1}{1 + e^{(E_c - E_F)/kT}} \quad \ldots (3)$$

From equations (2) and (3), $\quad n_c = \dfrac{N}{1 + e^{(E_c - E_F)/kT}} \quad \ldots (4)$

Similarly, $\quad n_v = \dfrac{N}{1 + e^{(E_v - E_F)/kT}} \quad \ldots (5)$

Substituting (4) and (5) in $N = n_c + n_v$,

$$\therefore N = \frac{N}{1 + e^{(E_c - E_F)/kT}} + \frac{N}{1 + e^{(E_v - E_F)/kT}}$$

Or $[1 + e^{(E_c - E_F)/kT}][1 + e^{(E_v - E_F)/kT}] = 1 + e^{(E_c - E_F)/kT} + 1 + e^{(E_c - E_F)/kT}$

This gives $e^{(E_c + E_v - 2E_F)/kT} = 1$

i.e. $\dfrac{E_c + E_v - 2E_F}{kT} = 0$

or $E_c + E_v - 2E_F = 0$

$$\therefore E_F = \frac{E_c + E_v}{2}$$

Thus, Fermi level in intrinsic semiconductors is exactly in the middle of the forbidden gap as shown in Fig. 3.8.

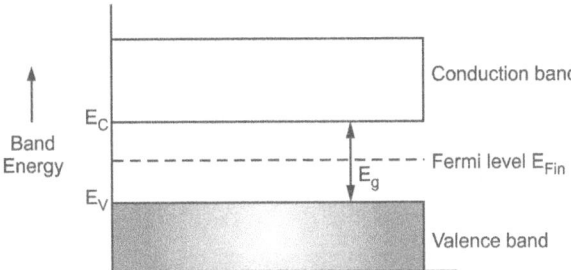

Fig. 3.8 : Position of Fermi level in intrinsic semiconductor

3.7 POSITION OF FERMI LEVEL IN EXTRINSIC SEMICONDUCTORS

(a) Position of Fermi Level in N-Type Semiconductor :

The N-type or pentavalent impurity semiconductor has more conduction electrons than holes. This moves the 'centre of gravity' up so that the Fermi level is above the middle of the forbidden band. Donors represent isolated energy levels located very close to the bottom of the unfilled conduction band. (Normally for Ge, 0.01 eV below the lower edge of conduction band). Hence, very little energy is required to raise an electron from the donor level into the conduction band where it is free for conduction of electricity.

In Fig. 3.9, the energy levels of the impurity atom (donor) are shown as isolated circles not as a band because here atoms are isolated from each other. E_{Fin} represents the position of Fermi level in the case of intrinsic semiconductors.

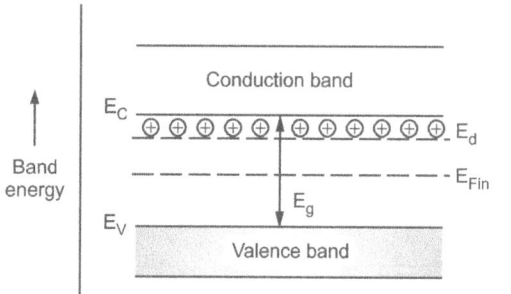

Fig. 3.9 : Indicates donor level

The position of Fermi level in the case of extrinsic semiconductor depends both on the doping and on the temperature. At 0 K all the donor levels are occupied and there are no electrons in the conduction band. Since P(E) = 1 upto the donor levels and P(E) = 0 at the conduction band, Fermi level E_F must be somewhere in the range $E_d \leq E_F \leq E_c$. (See Fig. 3.10).

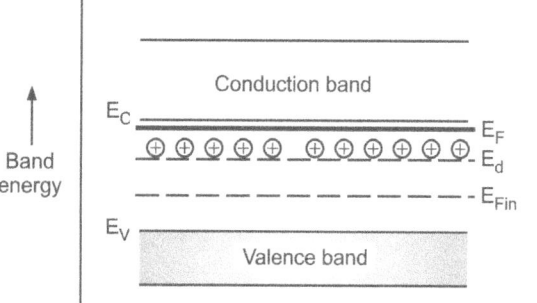

Fig. 3.10 : Position of E_F at T = 0 K

(b) Position of Fermi Level in P-Type Semiconductor :

In P-type semiconductor, the concentration of holes is greater than that of electrons.

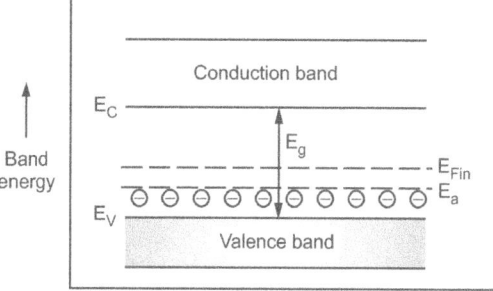

Fig. 3.11 : Indicates acceptor level

This makes the **'Centre of Gravity'** move down, so that Fermi level is below the middle of the forbidden band. Acceptors represent isolated energy levels, and lie close to the top of filled valence band. In Ge, this discrete energy level is only 0.01 eV above the valence band. Hence, a very small amount of energy is required for an electron to leave the valence band and occupy the acceptor energy level. Thus, holes are created in the valence band. Fig. 3.11 indicates the acceptor level in a P-type semiconductor.

At T = 0 K the Fermi level lies somewhere in the range between $E_v \leq E_F \leq E_a$ (See Fig. 3.12). At this temperature, the conduction band is empty.

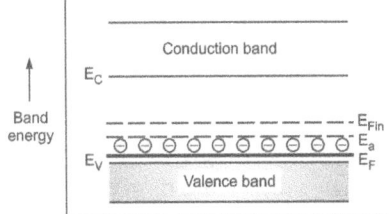

Fig. 3.12 : Indicates position of E_F at T = 0 K

3.8 P-N JUNCTION DIODE

When the crystal of a pure semiconductor is doped so that one half of it is P-type and the other half is N-type, then the border between P-type and N-type is called **'P-N Junction'**. The P-N junction have non-linear resistance which is the basis for all solid state electronic devices.

The junction diode is a two terminal device having one P-N junction. The junction diode passes a large current in one direction and almost no current in the other direction. Therefore, such a diode can be used as a rectifier. The Fermi level in P-type material is located close to the top of the valence band, whereas in N-type material Fermi level lies close to the bottom of the conduction band.

The P-type material has more holes than free electrons and the N-type material has more free electrons than holes. When the junction is made between these materials, the holes would tend to move from P-type material into the N-type material and electrons would tend to move from the N-type material into the P-type material, due to the difference in the concentration of holes and electrons on either side of a P-N junction. This process is called as **'Diffusion'**. The two materials then equalise their Fermi levels. The diffused charge carriers combine at the junction to neutralize each other. Due to this neutralisation, a charge free space called **'Depletion Layer'**, of width of the order of a few microns, is formed near the junction.

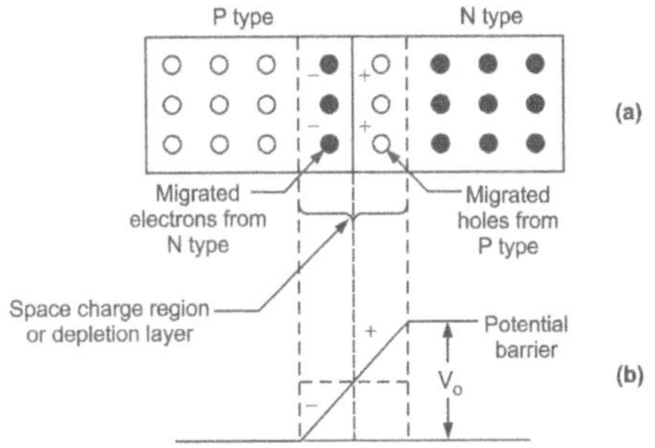

Fig. 3.13 : (a) P-N junction (after joining), (b) Potential barrier

Due to the diffusion of holes from P to N region, negative ions are produced in P region Similarly, due to the diffusion of electrons from N into P region, positive ions are produced in

N-region. Both these negative and positive ions are immobile and form parallel rows of opposite charges facing each other across the depletion layer. Because of this charge separation, an electric potential V_O develops across the junction under an equilibrium condition, i.e. with the junction externally isolated. This potential is called as the **'Junction Potential'**, or **'Barrier Potential'** and it can be represented by a battery called as the **'Space Charge Equivalent Battery'**. Once the potential barrier is established, further diffusion of majority charge carriers across the junction is prevented. On applying external voltage to P-N junction, diode conduction can occur only in one direction, so it is used as a rectifier.

3.9 ENERGY BAND PICTURE OF A P-N JUNCTION DIODE

3.9.1 Zero Bias

Consider a P-N junction formed by fusing a P-type and an N-type semiconductor under unbiased condition. Under this condition, the Fermi level will have to realign such that it exists as a single energy level for the entire specimen. This Fermi level in P-type is located close to the top of the valence band whereas in N-type it is close to the bottom of the conduction band. Because the Fermi level is lower on the P-side relative to the N-side, electrons move across the boundary to the P-side and thereby equalize the Fermi levels. The band edges in the two specimen shift themselves to make the alignment of Fermi levels possible and the energy band diagram remains no more the same (See Fig. 3.14) but assumes a shape as shown in Fig. 3.15.

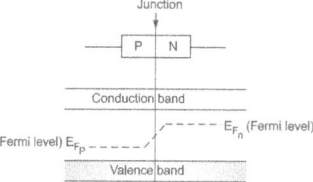

Fig. 3.14 : Non-equilibrium energy band picture of a p-n junction

The conduction band of P-type is shifted upwards by eV_B over the conduction band of N-type where V_B is the **'Potential Barrier'** across the junction. The minority electrons in the conduction band of P-type are at a higher energy than the majority electrons in the conduction band of N-type. Hence, the electrons crossing the junction from P-region will not encounter the potential barrier while the electrons crossing the junction from N-region side will face the potential barrier. The band picture for a zero bias diode at equilibrium is shown in Fig. 3.15.

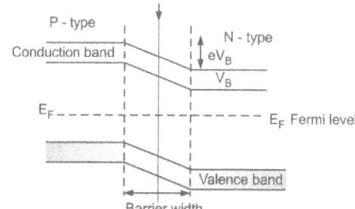

Fig. 3.15 : Shifting of the band in P and N-type semiconductors

3.9.2 Forward Bias

Under forward biasing the P-side is connected to the positive terminal and N-side to the negative terminal of the battery. Due to the forward bias, equilibrium conditions are disturbed and therefore energy bands and the Fermi levels are altered. Since in forward bias, negative terminal of the battery is connected to N-type side, the energy of the electrons in the N-side increases by an amount eV, where V is the externally applied voltage. Consequently, Fermi level raises by eV and the energy bands adjust their positions so as to suit the elevation of Fermi level. Due to the increase in energy in N-type side, the potential barrier is reduced to $e(V_B - V)$ and the barrier width is reduced. Hence the electrons crossing the junction from N-side will now face a low potential barrier and they can easily cross the junction.

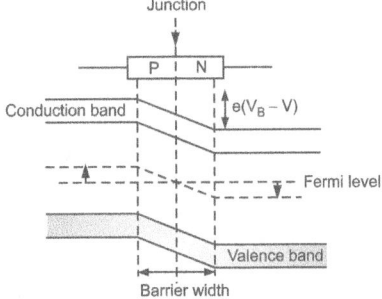

Fig. 3.16 : Forward bias

For conduction to take place in a P-N diode, the forward bias potential should be greater than the barrier potential. Band picture of P-N junction diode in forward bias condition is shown in Fig. 3.16.

3.9.3 Reverse Bias

In this case, N-side is connected to the positive terminal and P-side to the negative terminal of the battery. This lowers the Fermi level on N-side by an amount eV raising the barrier height to $e(V_B + V)$ and thereby increasing the width of the depletion layer. See Fig. 3.17.

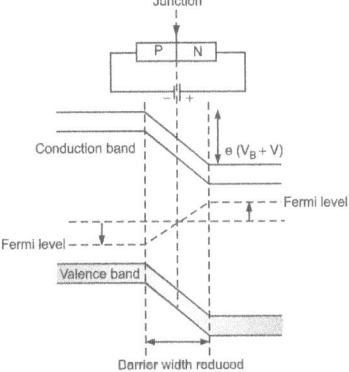

Fig. 3.17 : Reverse bias

The electrons which are the majority carriers in the N-side will now face a greater potential barrier in crossing the junction. Therefore the number of electrons crossing from N-side to P-side decreases and hence the current is very much reduced.

3.10 ELECTRICAL CONDUCTIVITY OF CONDUCTORS AND SEMICONDUCTORS

3.10.1 Conductivity of Conductors

According to the free electron model of an atom, the valence electrons are not attached to individual atoms. They move about freely along all directions among the atoms. These free electrons are called as conduction electrons and they form the **'Free Electron Cloud'** or **'Free Electron Gas'** or **'Fermi Gas'**.

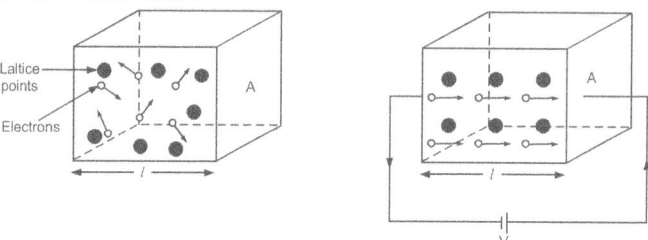

(a) Random motion   (b) Directed motion

Fig. 3.18 : Current flow in conductors

In the absence of an external electrical field, the electrons move randomly in all directions [See Fig. 3.18 (a)]. When an electric field is applied to the metal, the random motion becomes directed [See Fig. 3.18 (b)]. This type of directed motion is known as **'Drift'**. The drift velocity v of the electrons depends upon the electron mobility μ_e and the applied electric field E.

The drift velocity v is given by

$$v = \mu_e E \qquad \ldots (3.1)$$

Let A = conductor cross-section area

n = electron density (i.e. number of free electrons per unit volume of the conductor)

l = length of the conductor

V = voltage applied across the two ends of the conductor

E = electric field applied.

Then the charge crossing the cross-section 'A' of the conductor in unit time is equal to $n \times (v \times A)$ e. This rate of flow of charge constitutes the current.

i.e. $$I = nvAe \qquad \ldots (3.2)$$

Substituting for v from equation (3.1), we get

$$I = n \mu_e E A e \qquad \ldots (3.3)$$

Now, substituting for $E = \dfrac{V}{l}$ in equation (3.3), we get

$$I = n\mu_e \dfrac{V}{l} A e \qquad \ldots (3.4)$$

$$\therefore \quad \dfrac{V}{I} = \dfrac{l}{A} \cdot \dfrac{1}{nm_e e} \qquad \ldots (3.5)$$

By Ohm's law, we have,
$$R = \dfrac{V}{I} \qquad \ldots (3.6)$$

$$\therefore \quad R = \dfrac{l}{A} \cdot \dfrac{1}{n m_e e} \qquad \ldots (3.7)$$

But
$$R = \rho \dfrac{l}{A} \qquad \ldots (3.8)$$

where ρ is the resistivity of the conductor. Comparing equations (3.7) and (3.8), we get,

$$\rho = \dfrac{1}{n m_e e} \qquad \ldots (3.9)$$

The unit of ρ is ohm-m.

Conductivity 'σ' is defined as the reciprocal of resistivity.

$$\therefore \quad \text{Conductivity, } \sigma = \dfrac{1}{r} = n e \mu \text{ mho/m} \qquad \ldots (3.10)$$

Now, current density J is defined as the current flowing across the unit cross section.

From (3.3), we have,
$$J = \dfrac{I}{A} = n e \mu_e E \qquad \ldots (3.11)$$

From (3.10) and (3.11), we have $J = \sigma E \quad$ or $\quad \sigma = \dfrac{J}{E}$

3.10.2 Conductivity in a Semiconductor

Fig. 3.19 current flow in a semiconductor. This current is a sum of current flow due to electron flow and hole flow.

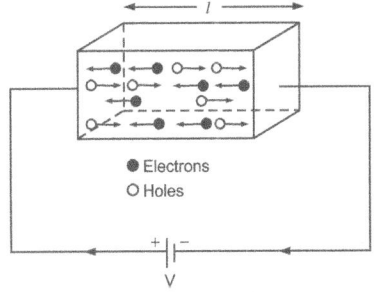

Fig. 3.19 : Current flow in a semiconductor

In a semiconductor, let

n_e = electron density in the conduction band
n_p = hole density in valence band
μ_e = electron mobility
μ_p = hole mobility
v_e = drift velocity of electrons
v_p = drift velocity of holes
A = cross section of the semiconductor
V = voltage applied across the semiconductor of length l

The current due to electrons is given by

$$I_e = n_e v_e A e \qquad \ldots (3.12)$$

and the current due to holes is given by

$$I_p = n_p v_p A e \qquad \ldots (3.13)$$

Therefore, total current flowing through the semiconductor will be,

Total current, $I = I_e + I_p$

$$I = n_e v_e A e + n_p v_p A e$$

$$\therefore I = A e (n_e v_e + n_p v_p) \qquad \ldots (3.14)$$

The drift velocity of a charged particle in electric field E is,

$$v = \mu E$$

∴ For electrons, $\quad v_e = \mu_e E$

and for holes, $\quad v_p = \mu_p E$

But $\quad E = \dfrac{V}{l}$

∴ $\quad v_e = \mu_e \dfrac{V}{l} \qquad \ldots (3.15)$

$\quad v_p = \mu_p \dfrac{V}{l} \qquad \ldots (3.16)$

Substituting equations (3.15) and (3.16) in equation (3.14), we get

$$I = A e \left(n_e \mu_e \dfrac{V}{l} + n_p \mu_p \dfrac{V}{l} \right)$$

$$I = \dfrac{A e V}{l} (n_e \mu_e + n_p \mu_p) \qquad \ldots (3.17)$$

∴ $\quad R = \dfrac{V}{I} = \dfrac{l}{A e (n_e \mu_e + n_p \mu_p)} \qquad \ldots (3.18)$

But $\quad R = r \dfrac{l}{A} \qquad \ldots (3.19)$

∴ Resistivity of the given semiconductor is given by [comparing equations (3.18) and (3.19)],

$$\rho = \frac{1}{e(n_e \mu_e + n_p \mu_p)} \text{ ohm-m} \qquad \ldots (3.20)$$

The conductivity is reciprocal of resistivity.

∴ Conductivity $\quad \sigma = \frac{1}{r} = e(n_e \mu_e + n_p \mu_p)$ mho/m $\qquad \ldots (3.21)$

Hence, conductivity in a semiconductor is a sum of conductivity due to both electrons and holes.

Or $\qquad \sigma_{sc} = \sigma_e + \sigma_p$

From equation (3.14), $\quad \frac{I}{A} = e(n_e \mu_e + n_p \mu_p) E$

∴ The current density $\quad J = \frac{I}{A} = e(n_e \mu_e + n_p \mu_p) E \qquad \ldots (3.22)$

From (3.21) and (3.22), $\quad J = \sigma E$

Case (i) : Intrinsic Semiconductor :

$$n_e = n_p = n_i$$

∴ Conductivity of an intrinsic semiconductor is

$$\sigma_i = e n_i (\mu_e + \mu_p)$$

Case (ii) : N-Type Extrinsic Semiconductor :

For N-type semiconductors, electron concentration is much greater than the hole concentration.

∴ $\quad n_e \gg n_p \quad$ or $\quad n_e \mu_e \gg n_p \mu_p$

Hence $\quad \sigma^N \approx e n_e \mu_e$

If n_d is electron concentration or concentration of donor atoms,

then, $\quad \sigma^N \approx e n_d \mu_e \quad$ (as $n_e \approx n_d$)

Case (iii) : P-Type Extrinsic Semiconductor :

In P-type semiconductor, electron concentration is negligibly small in comparison to hole concentration.

Then $\quad n_p \gg n_e \quad$ or $\quad n_p \mu_p \gg n_e \mu_e$

∴ $\quad \sigma_p \approx e n_p \mu_p$

If n_a is acceptor atom concentration then $\sigma_p \approx e n_a \mu_p$ (as $n_p \approx n_a$)

SOLVED EXAMPLES

Example 3.1 : Calculate the current produced in a small Germanium plate of area 1 cm² and of thickness 0.3 mm when a P.D. of 2 V is applied across the faces.

Given : $\qquad n_i = 2 \times 10^{19} / m^3$

$$e = 1.6 \times 10^{-19} C$$

$$\mu_e = 0.36 \, m^2/\text{volt-sec}$$

Data :
$\mu_h = 0.17$ m²/volt-sec
$A = 1 \times 10^{-4}$ m³
$V = 2$ volts
$l = 0.3$ mm $= 0.3 \times 10^{-3}$ m

Formula : $I = n^i e (\mu_e + \mu_h) \dfrac{V}{l} \cdot A$

Solution :

$$I = 2 \times 10^{19} \times 1.6 \times 10^{-19} (0.36 + 0.17) \dfrac{2 \times 10^{-4}}{0.3 \times 10^{-3}}$$

$$= \boxed{1.13 \text{ amp.}}$$

Example 3.2 : Calculate the conductivity of pure silicon at room temperature when the concentration of carriers is 1.5×10^{16} /m³ and the mobilities of electrons and holes are 0.12 and 0.05 m²/V - sec respectively at room temperature.

Data : $n_i = 1.5 \times 10^{16}$ /m³, $\mu_e = 0.12$ m²/V-sec, $\mu_h = 0.05$ m²/V-sec.

Formula :
$\sigma_{in} = \sigma_n + \sigma_p$
$\sigma_{in} = n^i e (\mu_e + \mu_h)$

Solution :

$$\sigma_{in} = 1.5 \times 10^{16} \times 1.6 \times 10^{-19} (0.12 + 0.05)$$

$$= \boxed{4.1 \times 10^{-4} \text{ mho/m}}$$

Example 3.3 : Calculate the conductivity of the Germanium specimen if a donor impurity is added to the extent of one part in 10^8 Germanium atoms in room temperature.

Given :
Avogadro number $= 6.02 \times 10^{23}$ atoms/moles
At. wt. of Ge $= 72.6$
Density of Ge $= 5.32$ g/cm³
Mobility $\mu_e = 3800$ cm²/ V-sec

Formula : $\sigma \approx e\, n_d\, \mu_e$

Solution :

Concentration of Ge atoms

$$= \dfrac{6.02 \times 10^{23}}{72.6} \times 5.32$$

$$= 4.41 \times 10^{22} \text{ /cm}^3$$

Since there is one donor atom per 10^8 Germanium atoms then

$$n_d = \dfrac{4.41 \times 10^{22}}{10^8} = 4.41 \times 10^{14} \text{ / cm}^3$$

In N-type semiconductor, n > p

$$\text{then } \sigma = e \, n_d \, \mu_e$$
$$= 1.6 \times 10^{-19} \times 4.41 \times 10^{14} \times 3800$$
$$= \boxed{0.268 \text{ mho/cm.}}$$

Example 3.4: The resistivity of an n-type semiconductor is 10^{-6} Ω cm. Calculate the number of donor atoms which must be added to obtain the resistivity.

Given: $\mu_e = 1000$ cm²/V-sec.

Data:
$$\rho = 10^{-6} \text{ Ω cm}$$
$$\mu_e = 1000 \text{ cm}^2\text{/V-sec}$$

Formula: Resistivity $\rho \approx \dfrac{1}{n_d \, e \, m_e}$

Solution:
$$n_d = \dfrac{1}{r \, e \, m_e}$$

$$\therefore \quad n_d = \dfrac{1}{10^{-6} \times 1.6 \times 10^{-19} \times 1000}$$
$$= \boxed{6.25 \times 10^{21} \text{ atoms.}}$$

Example 3.5: Calculate the conductivity of extrinsic silicon at room temperature if the donor impurity added is 1 in 10^8 silicon atoms.

Given:
At room temperature,
$$n_i = 1.5 \times 10^{10} \text{ per cm}^3$$
$$\mu_e = 1300 \text{ cm}^2 / \text{volt-sec}$$
and number of silicon atoms per unit volume $= 5 \times 10^{22}$.

Formula: $\sigma_n \approx n e \mu_e$

Solution:
If there is 1 donor atom per 10 silicon atoms, then the number of donor atoms per cm³

$$n_d = \dfrac{\text{number of silicon atoms/unit volume}}{10^8}$$

$$= \dfrac{5 \times 10^{22}}{10^8} = 5 \times 10^{14}$$

Assuming all the donors are ionised and n >> p, hole conduction can be neglected.

$$\therefore \quad \sigma_n = n \, e \, \mu_e$$
$$\sigma_n = n_d \, e \, \mu_e$$
$$= 5 \times 10^{14} \times 1.6 \times 10^{-19} \times 1300$$
$$= \boxed{0.104 \text{ mho/cm.}}$$

Example 3.6 : In Germanium, the energy gap is 0.75 eV. What is the wavelength at which Germanium starts to absorb light ?

Data : $E_g = 0.75$ eV

Formula : $E_g = h\upsilon = \dfrac{hc}{\lambda}$

Solution :

Energy gap in a semiconductor is the minimum energy required to shift an electron from the top of valence band to the bottom of the conduction band. If photons of minimum energy $h\upsilon$ are absorbed by a material to enable electrons to cross the energy gap, then

$$h\upsilon = E_g$$

$$\therefore\quad E_g = h\upsilon = h\dfrac{c}{\lambda} = \dfrac{6.625 \times 10^{-34} \times 3 \times 10^8}{\lambda}\ \text{J}$$

$$= \dfrac{6.625 \times 10^{-34} \times 3 \times 10^8}{1.6 \times 10^{-19} \times \lambda}\ \text{eV}$$

i.e. $\quad E_g = \dfrac{12400}{\lambda}\ \text{eV, if } \lambda \text{ is in A.}$

$$\therefore\quad \lambda \cong \dfrac{12400}{E_g} = \dfrac{12400}{0.75}$$

$$\therefore\quad \boxed{\lambda = 1653\ \text{A}^\circ}$$

Example 3.7 : Calculate the average thermal velocity, the drift velocity and the mobility of electrons in copper in an electric field of 100 V/cm. Calculate also the density of the electric currents. The resistivity of copper is 1.72×10^{-8} ohm-m at 25°C. Boltzmann constant is 1.38×10^{-23} J/K, density of copper is 8.9×10^3 kg/m³ and At. wt. is 63.54.

Data : $E = 100$ V/cm, $\rho = 1.72 \times 10^{-8}\ \Omega$-m,
$k = 1.38 \times 10^{-23}$ J/K, density $= 8.9 \times 10^3$ kg/m³, At. wt. $= 63.54$.

Formulae : (i) $v = \sqrt{\dfrac{3kT}{m}}$, (ii) $v_d = \mu E$, (iii) $\sigma = ne\mu = \dfrac{1}{r}$.

Solution :

At equilibrium, the electrons follow the Maxwell-Boltzmann distribution. So their average K.E. for each degree of freedom is $\dfrac{1}{2}kT$. For particles moving in three dimensions, we can write,

$$\dfrac{1}{2}mv^2 = \dfrac{3}{2}kT$$

$$\therefore\quad v = \left(\dfrac{3kT}{m}\right)^{1/2} = \left(\dfrac{3 \times 1.38 \times 10^{-23} \times 298}{9.1 \times 10^{-31}}\right)^{1/2}$$

$$v = 1.16 \times 10^5\ \text{m/sec.}$$

Since each copper atom contributes one valence electron to the conduction band, the number of electrons/m³ will be equal to the number of copper atoms/m³.

$$\therefore \text{No. of electrons/m}^3 = n = \frac{6.02 \times 10^{26} \times 8.9 \times 10^3}{63.54}$$

$$= 0.84 \times 10^{29} \text{ atoms/m}^3$$

$$\text{Mobility } \mu = \frac{1}{r \cdot n \cdot e}$$

$$\mu = \frac{1}{1.72 \times 10^{-8} \times 0.84 \times 10^{29} \times 1.6 \times 10^{-19}}$$

$$= 4.33 \times 10^{-3} \text{ m}^2/\text{volt-sec}$$

$$\text{Drift velocity } v_d = \mu \cdot E$$

$$= 4.33 \times 10^{-3} \times 100$$

$$\therefore \boxed{v_d = 0.433 \text{ m/sec.}}$$

Example 3.8 : Calculate the conductivity of pure silicon at room temperature when the concentration of carriers is $1.6 \times 10^{10}/\text{cm}^3$.

Data :
μ_e = 1500 cm²/volt-sec
μ_h = 500 cm²/volt-sec at room temperature
n_i = 1.6 × 10¹⁰/cm³
μ_e = 1500 cm³/V-sec
μ_n = 500 cm³/V-sec

Formula : $\sigma_{in} = \sigma_n + \sigma_p$

Solution :

$$\sigma_{in} = n_i e (\mu_e + \mu_n)$$
$$= 1.6 \times 10^{10} \times 1.6 \times 10^{-19} (1500 + 500)$$
$$= \boxed{5.12 \times 10^{-6} \text{ mho/cm}}$$

3.11 HALL EFFECT AND HALL COEFFICIENT

3.11.1 Hall Effect

It often becomes necessary to determine whether a material is an N-type or a P-type semiconductor. Measurement of conductivity alone does not give this information as no distinction can be made between hole and electron conduction. Hall effect is used to differentiate between the two types of carriers. It provides a means of determining the density and mobility of charge carriers and gives information about the sign of the predominant charge carrier.

If a piece of conductor (metal or semiconductor) carrying a current is placed in a transverse magnetic field, an electric field is produced inside the conductor in a direction normal to both the current and the magnetic field. This phenomenon is known as **'Hall Effect'** and the voltage so generated is called as **'Hall Voltage'**.

Explanation of the Effect :

Assume that the sample material is an N-type semiconductor. The current flow consists, almost entirely, of electrons moving from right to left. This movement corresponds to the direction of conventional current from left to right as shown in Fig. 3.20 (a). If v is the drift velocity of the electrons moving perpendicular to the magnetic field B, there is a downward force Bev acting on each electron. This causes the electrons to be deflected in the downward direction. This makes negative charges to accumulate on the bottom face of the slab [See Fig. 3.20 (b)] leaving positive ions on the top surface. This gives rise to a potential difference along the top and bottom faces of the specimen across points M and N with the bottom face being negative. This potential difference causes a field E_H in the negative y-direction and so a force eE_H acts on the electrons in the upward direction. Under equilibrium, the upward force due to the electric field just balances the downward force due to the magnetic field.

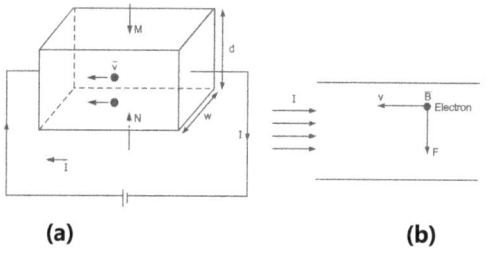

(a)   (b)

Fig. 3.20 : Hall Effect

Thus, $\quad e E_H = e B v$

$\therefore \quad E_H = v B \quad \ldots (1)$

If I is the current in the x-direction then,

$$I = n v A e$$

or $\quad v = \dfrac{I}{neA} \quad \ldots (2)$

where n is the concentration of charge carriers.

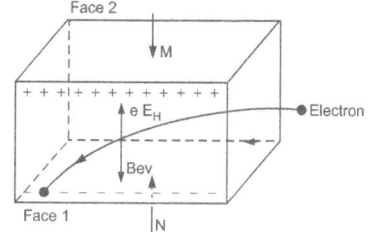

Fig. 3.21 : Motion of electrons in an N-type semiconductor

$\therefore \quad E_H = \dfrac{B I}{neA} \quad \ldots (3)$

Also $\quad E_H = \dfrac{V_H}{d}$

where V_H is the Hall voltage named after the scientist Hall who first predicted and measured the Hall voltage.

$\therefore \quad V_H = E_H d \quad \ldots (4)$

Substituting this in expression (3),

$$V_H = \frac{1}{ne} \cdot \frac{BId}{A} \qquad \ldots (5)$$

or
$$V_H = R_H \frac{BId}{A} \qquad \ldots (6)$$

where $R_H = \frac{1}{ne}$ is the Hall coefficient for any charge e. ... (7)

If J_x is the current density of charge carriers in x-direction then,

$$V_H = \frac{1}{ne} \cdot BJd \quad \left(\text{as } J = \frac{I}{A}\right) \qquad \ldots (8)$$

In this specimen, as the dominant charge carriers are electrons,

$$\therefore \quad V_H = -\frac{1}{ne} BJd \qquad \ldots (9)$$

In expression (8), all three quantities V_H, B and J can be measured. Hence, Hall coefficient and current density can be found.

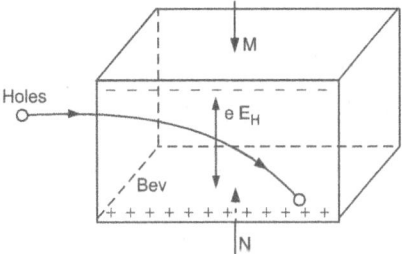

Fig. 3.22 : Motion of holes in P-type semiconductor

Similarly, formulae can be derived for P-type semiconductors. All the formulae are same except that the Hall coefficient will be positive.

The sign of the Hall voltage gives the sign of the charge carrier and this provides one of the few methods by which the sign of the charge carrier can be ascertained.

$$\therefore \quad \text{Hall voltage, } V_H = R_H \cdot \frac{BId}{A} = R_H BJd \qquad \ldots (10)$$

3.11.2 Hall Coefficient (R_H)

The Hall coefficient R_H is determined by measuring the Hall voltage that generates the Hall field. If V_H is the Hall voltage across the sample of thickness d then

$$V_H = E_H d \qquad \ldots (1)$$

Also, the Hall voltage is given by,

$$V_H = R_H \frac{BId}{A} \qquad \ldots (2)$$

If w is the width of the sample, then its cross-section will be d × w.

$$\therefore \quad V_H = R_H \frac{BId}{dw} = R_H \frac{BI}{w} \quad \ldots (3)$$

or
$$R_H = \frac{w}{BI} V_H = \frac{1}{nq} \quad \ldots (4)$$

As all quantities in relation (4) are measurable except for n, this relation is used to find the number of charge carriers per unit volume. For metals such as Na, Cu, Ag and Au, the value of n given by this equation is close to the number of valence electrons per unit volume. In the case of semiconductors, the interpretation becomes more complex. However, it should be noted that the Hall voltage varies inversely as n, so one would expect it to be larger for semiconductors than for metals.

3.11.3 Applications of Hall Effect

- **Determination of Type of Semiconductor :**

For an N-type semiconductor, the Hall coefficient is negative whereas for a P-type semiconductor, it is positive. Thus, the sign of Hall coefficient is used to determine whether a given semiconductor is N or P-type.

- **Calculation of Charge Carrier Concentration :**

The Hall voltage V_H is measured by placing two probes at the centre of the top and bottom faces of the sample. If $\vec{B}$ is the magnetic flux density, then

$$n = \frac{1}{e} \cdot \frac{BId}{A} \cdot \frac{1}{V_H}$$

Current I is measured using a current measuring device. Therefore, R_H and hence n can be calculated.

- **Determination of Mobility :**

If conduction is due to one type of charge carriers, for example electrons, then

$$\sigma = ne\,\mu_e$$

$$\mu_e = \frac{s}{ne} = \sigma R_H$$

$$\mu_e = \sigma \cdot \left(\frac{V_H A}{B I d}\right)$$

Knowing σ, and measuring other parameters as in the above applications, the mobility of electrons μ_e can be determined.

Example 3.9 : Find the drift velocity for the electron in silver wire of radius 1.00 mm and carrying a current of 2 amperes. Density of silver is 10.5 g/cm$_3$.

Data : r = 1.00 mm, I = 2 amp, density = 10.5 g/cc.

Formula :
$$v = \frac{I}{q \cdot n \cdot A}$$

Solution :

$$I = qnvA$$

Silver is monovalent. So each atom may be assumed to contribute one electron. One gram atomic weight of silver, 108 g, has 6×10^{23} atoms (Avogadro's number).

The density of silver is 10.5 g/cm^3. So 108 g will occupy $108/10.5 \approx 10.3$ cm^3.

∴ Number of electrons per unit volume, $n = \dfrac{6 \times 10^{23}}{10.3} \approx 6 \times 10^{22}$

or $n = 6 \times 10^{28}$ per m^3

The cross-sectional area of wire, $A = \pi r^2 = \pi (10^{-3})^2 \approx 3 \times 10^{-6}$ m^2

Now, $v = \dfrac{I}{q \times n \times A}$

$= \dfrac{2}{(1.6 \times 10^{-19}) \times (6 \times 10^{28}) \times (3 \times 10^{-6})}$

$\boxed{v = 7 \times 10^{-5} \text{ m/sec.}}$

Example 3.10 : Find the current density in the wire of the preceding example.

Solution :

Current density $J = \dfrac{I}{A} = \dfrac{2.0 \text{ amperes}}{3.0 \times 10^{-6} \text{ m}^2}$

∴ $\boxed{J = 6.7 \times 10^5 \text{ A/m}^2}$

Example 3.11 : A silver wire is in the form of a ribbon 0.50 cm wide and 0.10 mm thick. When a current of 2A passes through the ribbon perpendicular to a 0.80 T magnetic field, how large a hall voltage is produced along the width ? The density of silver is 10.5 g/cm^3.

Data : d = 0.50 cm, t = 0.10 mm, I = 2 amp, B = 0.80 T, density = 10.5 g/cc.

Formula : $V_H = \dfrac{1}{nq} \cdot \dfrac{BId}{A}$

Solution :

The atomic weight of silver is 108, so the number of atoms in 1 cm^3 is

$$n = (6 \times 10^{23}) \left(\dfrac{10.5}{108}\right) \approx 6 \times 10^{22} \text{ per cm}^3$$

Silver is monovalent and we can assume that each atom contributes one electron.

∴ Number of electrons per m^3 = 6×10^{28}

$A = 0.05 \times 0.001 = 5 \times 10^{-5}$ m^2

Hall voltage, $V_H = \dfrac{1}{nq} \cdot \dfrac{BI \cdot d}{A}$

$= \dfrac{1}{6 \times 10^{28} \times 1.6 \times 10^{-19}} \times \dfrac{0.80 \times 2.0 \times 0.05}{5 \times 10^{-5}}$

$\approx \boxed{1.67 \times 10^{-7} \text{ volt.}}$

Example 3.12 : A copper specimen having length 1 metre, width 1 cm and thickness 1 mm is conducting 1 amp current along its length and is applied with a magnetic field of 1 Tesla along its thickness. It experiences a Hall effect and a Hall voltage of 0.074 microvolts appears along its width. Calculate the Hall coefficient and the mobility of electrons in copper. Conductivity of copper is $\sigma = 5.8 \times 10^7 \, (\Omega m)^{-1}$.

Data : $l = 1$ m, $d = 1$ cm $= 10^{-2}$ m, $t = 1$ mm $= 10^{-3}$ m, $B = 1$ Tesla, $I = $ amp.
$V_H = 0.074 \times 10^{-6}$ volts, $\sigma = 5.8 \times 10^7 \, (\Omega m)^{-1}$

Formulae : (i) $V_H = R_H \cdot \dfrac{BId}{A}$, (ii) $\sigma = \dfrac{m}{R^H}$.

Solution :

(i) $R_H = \dfrac{V^H \cdot A}{BId} = \dfrac{0.074 \times 10^{-6} \times 10^{-2}}{1 \times 1 \times 10^{-2}} = \boxed{0.074 \times 10^{-6} \text{ m}^3/\text{coulomb}}$

(ii) $\mu = \sigma R_H = 5.8 \times 10^7 \times 0.074 \times 10^{-6} = \boxed{4.292 \text{ m}^2/\text{volt-sec.}}$

3.12 SOLAR CELLS

Solar cell is a type of photo-voltaic cell. Photo-electric cells are of three types :

1. Photo-emissive cell.
2. Photo-voltaic cell.
3. Photo-conductive cell

All these are based on the principle of photo-electric effect i.e. photon energy is being converted into electrical energy.

The photo-voltaic cells are based on the photo-voltaic effect which is the conversion of light into an electric current without the aid of an external battery. In this case, voltage is developed in the cell. Solar cells are the best example of this type.

3.12.1 Action of a Solar Cell

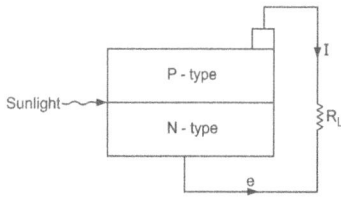

Fig. 3.23 : Solar cell p-n junction with load resistance R_L

(1) When a P-N junction is exposed to sunlight, photons of energy hv are absorbed, if hv is greater than the band gap E_g. Electron-hole pairs are then generated in both the P-side and N-side of the junction. The electrons and holes that are produced within a small distance of the junction reach the space charge region by diffusion.

(2)

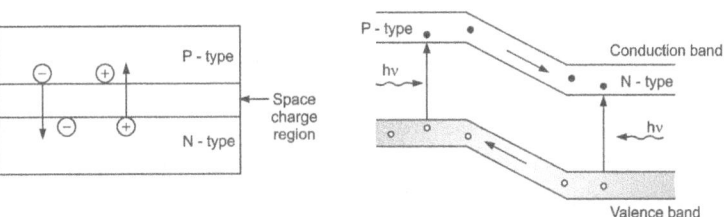

(a) Diffusion of electrons and holes

(b) Energy band diagram corresponding to diffusion of electrons and holes

Fig. 3.24

The electron-hole pairs are separated by the strong barrier field existing across the space charge region. Electrons in the P-side slide down the barrier potential to move to the N-side while holes in N-side move towards the P-side. [See Fig. 3.24 (b)]

(3) When the P-N junction is open circuited, the accumulation of electrons and holes on the two sides of the junction gives rise to an **'Open-Circuited Voltage'** V_{oc}. When a load resistance is connected across the diode, current flows in the circuit. This effect is known as **'Photovoltaic Effect'**.

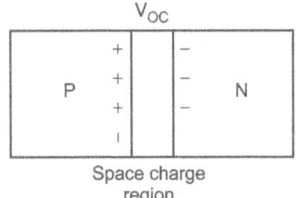

Fig. 3.25

(4) When the diode terminals are short circuited, the maximum current obtained is called the short **'Circuit Current'** I_{sc}.

The current flows as long as the diode is illuminated by sunlight. The magnitude of current flowing is proportional to the light intensity.

The electrical energy generated in the solar cell is in the form of dc voltage of approximately 0.5 V. The current varies with the surface area of photo-voltaic cell and with the intensity of the incident light falling on it. The efficiency of the solar cell is given by,

$$h = \frac{\text{Power output}}{\text{Incident solar power}}$$

3.12.2 I-V Characteristics of a Solar Cell

Fig. 3.26 shows I-V characteristics of a solar cell. The I-V characteristics of solar cell is studied by changing the load resistance R_L and measuring current flowing through and voltage appearing across it. When load R_L is zero maximum current flows through it but voltage will be zero, this current is called the **'Short-Circuit Current I_{SC}'**. As voltage is zero it will come on current axis. As load increase at a particular stage when R_L becomes infinity, the current will be zero and voltage will reach the maximum value. This maximum voltage is called **Open-Circuit Voltage V_{oc}** and is plotted on voltage axis. For maximum voltage V_{OC}, current is zero or vice-versa. So the product $V_{OC} I_{SC}$ will not give the maximum power drawn from the solar cell. For getting maximum power from the solar cell, draw a line at 45° passing from origin, the point (V_m, I_m) where the line will cut the curve will give maximum usable power. The ratio of maximum usable power to ideal power is called as **Fill Factor**.

$$\text{Fill factor 'f'} = \frac{\text{Usable power}}{\text{Ideal power}}$$

i.e. $\quad$ fill factor 'f' $= \dfrac{V_m \cdot I_m}{V_{oc} \cdot I_{sc}}$

where,

I_m and V_m are the maximum usable current and voltage obtained experimentally.

I_{sc} = short-circuit current

V_{oc} = open-circuit voltage

$V_{oc} \cdot I_{sc}$ = theoretically obtained maximum power of the solar cell.

$V_m \cdot I_m$ = experimentally obtained maximum power of the cell.

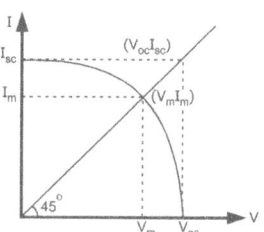

Fig. 3.26

As the potential difference increases, the recombination of electrons and holes also increases and hence potential difference cannot be increased beyond certain limits. To reduce the recombination, the upper region is of smaller width so that carriers can reach the junction before they recombine.

When photovoltaic cells are connected in series or parallel, they form a solar battery.

3.12.3 Advantages

- It is an environmentally clean source of energy.
- It is free and available in adequate quantities.
- It is used in satellite communication.
- It is used as power source in artificial satellites.
- It can be used to supply power to places in remote areas and in fuel starved areas.

3.12.4 Disadvantages

- **Dilute Source :** Even in the hottest region on earth, radiation flux rarely exceeds 1 kW/m² which is the value for technological utilization. It requires large collecting areas in moving application, which results in excessive cost. Thus, use is restricted because of its high price.
- Solar energy varies with time because of day-night cycle.

3.13 SOLAR CELL APPLICATIONS

Solar cells are used extensively in satellites and space vehicles for long duration power supply. Their first application was in 1958 to power Vangaurd I, a space satellite. Since then solar cells have remained as an important source of power in space applications due to their low weight, reliability and durability. Success of solar cells in space led to their terrestrial applications. For terrestrial use, there are three broad categories, namely : industrial, social and consumer applications.

3.13.1 Industrial Applications

- **Navigational Aids :** Marine beacons, remote light beacons near the airport and navigational lights around the world were earlier powered by kerosene/batteries having several maintenance problems. Now-a-days, they are powered by simple solar cells which are reliable and cost effective.
- **Alarm Systems :** Railway signals, alarm systems for fire, flood warnings, traffic lights, highway telephones, etc. are all being powered by solar cells.
- **Defence Equipments :** Many defence equipments for example, mobiles, telephones, remote radar, large instruments used in remote areas, etc. are now being effectively powered by solar cell.
- **Telecommunications :** Telecommunication equipments are often located in remote and inaccessible areas, for example, islands, deserts, etc. They now consume reduced power due to the use of solid-state devices. This has facilitated the use of solar cell as an economical and reliable power source.
- **Emergency Equipment :** Charging of batteries on rafts, boats and for providing essential services after natural disasters like earthquakes, floods, etc. can be done efficiently by a solar cell.
- **Automatic Meteorological Stations :** A meteorological station collects meteorological data at fixed time intervals at several locations and analyses them to predict weather forecasting accurately. A solar powered meteorological weather station is reliable, economical and is relatively free of maintenance problems.

3.13.2 Social Applications

- Providing electric power to remote villages and islands, specially in developing countries, by solar cell. These villages are unconnected to the main grid. A small stand-alone type solar cell can provide a rural house enough power for lighting tubes, TV and a small refrigerator.
- Solar cell powered pumps are being installed to provide potable water and for irrigation purposes.
- Special solar cell powered portable refrigerators are being used for the transportation and storage of vaccines. These vaccines are used for mass immunisation programmes for improving rural standards and reducing infant mortality rate.
- Providing electricity to TV, for schools, for educational and recreational purposes.

3.13.3 Consumer Applications

A large number of consumer items which are low powered are now being powered by solar cells. Some of these products are pocket calculators, clocks, torches, watches, radios, lights, electric fans, toys, battery chargers, etc.

Example 3.13 : Calculate the conductivity of a Germanium sample if a donor impurity is added to the extent of one part in 10^7 Ge atoms at room temperature.

Given : Avogadro number $N_a = 6.02 \times 10^{23}$ atoms/gm-mole
Atomic weight of Ge = 72.6
Density of Ge = 5.32 gm/cc
Mobility $\mu_e = 3800$ cm^2/V-sec

Formula : $\sigma = e\, n_d\, \mu_e$

Solution :
Concentration of Ge atoms

$$= \frac{6.02 \times 10^{23}}{72.6} \times 5.32$$

$$= 4.41 \times 10^{22} / \text{cm}^3$$

Since there is one donor atom per 10^7 Ge atoms then

$$n_d = \frac{4.41 \times 10^{22}}{10^7} = 4.41 \times 10^{15} /\text{cm}^3$$

$\therefore \quad \sigma = 1.6 \times 10^{-19} \times 4.41 \times 10^{15} \times 3800$

$$\boxed{\sigma = 2.68 \text{ mho/cm}}$$

Example 3.14 : Calculate the energy gap of silicon, given that it is transparent to radiation of wavelength greater than 11000 A°.

Given : $\lambda = 11000$ A°

Formula : $E_g = h\upsilon = \dfrac{hc}{\lambda}$

Solution :

$$E_g = \frac{hc}{\lambda}$$

$$E_g = \frac{6.63 \times 10^{-34} \times 3 \times 10^8}{11000 \times 10^{-10}}$$

$$E_g = 1.808 \times 10^{-19} \text{ J}$$

$$\boxed{E_g = 1.13 \text{ eV}}$$

Example 3.15 : Calculate the number of donor atoms which must be added to an intrinsic semiconductor to obtain resistivity as 10^{-6} Ωm.

Given : $\mu_e = 1000$ cm^2/V-sec

Solution :
See example 3.4.

Example 3.16 : Calculate the number of acceptors to be added to a Germanium sample to obtain the resistivity of 10 Ω-cm.

Given : $\mu = 1700$ cm^2/volt-sec
Data : $\rho = 10$ cm
   $\mu = 1700$ cm^2

Formula : $\rho = \dfrac{1}{n_a m_a e}$

Solution :

$$n_a = \dfrac{1}{r\, m_a\, e}$$

$$n_a = \dfrac{1}{10 \times 1700 \times 1.6 \times 10^{-19}}$$

$$\boxed{n_a = 3.6 \times 10^{14} / \text{cm}^3}$$

Example 3.17 : Calculate the mobility of charge carriers in a doped silicon whose conductivity is 100 per Ω-m and the Hall coefficient is 3.6×10^{-4} m^3/Coulomb.

Data : $\sigma = 100$ per Ω-m
   $R_H = 3.6 \times 10^{-4}$ m^3/Coulomb

Formula : $\mu = 6\, R_H$

Solution :

$$\mu = 6\, R_H$$
$$\mu = 100 \times 3.6 \times 10^{-4}$$
$$\boxed{\mu = 0.036 \text{ m}^2/\text{V-sec}}$$

Example 3.18 : In an N-type semiconductor the Fermi level lies 0.3 eV below the conduction band at room temperature. If the temperature is raised to 330 K, find the position of Fermi level.

Data : $E_C - E_F = 0.3$ eV at room temperature $T = 27°C$

Formula : $E_F = E_C - kT \ln\left(\dfrac{N_d}{N_c}\right)$

Solution :

At $T = 300$ K

$$E_C - E_F = kT \ln\left(\dfrac{N_d}{N_c}\right)$$

$$0.3 = k \times 300 \ln\left(\dfrac{N_d}{N_c}\right)$$

∴ $k \ln\left(\dfrac{N_d}{N_c}\right) = \dfrac{0.3}{300}$

At $T = 330$ K

$$E_C - E_F = 330 \times \frac{0.3}{300}$$

∴ $\boxed{E_C - E_F = 0.33 \text{ eV}}$

Fermi level lies 0.33 eV below the conduction band.

Example 3.19 : Calculate the band gap energy in Germanium. Given that it is transparent to radiation of wavelength greater than 17760 A°.

Data : $\lambda = 17760$ A°

Formula : $E_g = h\upsilon = \dfrac{hc}{l}$

Solution :

$$E_g = \frac{6.63 \times 10^{-34} \times 3 \times 10^8}{17760 \times 10^{-10}}$$

$$E_g = 1.12 \times 10^{-19} \text{ J}$$

$$E_g = \frac{1.12 \times 10^{-19}}{1.6 \times 10^{-19}}$$

$\boxed{E_g = 0.7 \text{ eV}}$

Example 3.20 : Intrinsic silicon is doped with phosphorus, with the atomic ratio of 10^8 (Si) : 1 (P). Calculate the conductivity of N type of silicon thus formed. Given mobility of electrons in silicon $\mu_e = 1400$ cm^2 Vs^{-1}. Atomic weight of intrinsic silicon = 28.085, Avogadro's number = 6.022×10^{23} atoms per mole, Density of silicon = 2.33 gm/cm^3.

Data :   Avogadro number = 6.022×10^{23} atoms/moles

At. wt. of Si = 28.085

Density of Si = 5.32 gm/cm^3

Mobility μ_e = 1400 cm^2 Vs^{-1}

Formula : $\sigma \approx e\, n_d\, \mu_e$

Solution :

Concentration of Si atoms

$$= \frac{6.022 \times 10^{23}}{28.085} \times 2.33 = 4.996 \times 10^{22} / \text{cm}^3$$

Since there is one donor atom per 10^8 Si atoms,

then, $n_d = \dfrac{4.996 \times 10^{22}}{10^8} = 4.996 \times 10^{14} / \text{cm}^3$

The conductivity is, $\sigma = e\, n_d\, \mu_e$

$$= 1.6 \times 10^{-19} \times 4.996 \times 10^{14} \times 1400$$

$$= 1.119 \times 10^{-1} \text{ mho/cm} = 0.1119 \text{ mho/cm}$$

Example 3.21 : A specimen having length 1.00 cm, width 1.00 mm and thickness 0.1 mm is made to conduct with 1.00 mA current and is placed in a magnetic field of 1.0 Wb/m², acting along the thickness. Calculate the Hall voltage in case of (i) N type semiconductor with Hall coefficient of -3.44×10^{-8} m³/C and (ii) Aluminium with Hall coefficient of -0.3×10^{-10} m³/C. Which of these materials is more sensitive to Hall effect ? Why ?

Data : l = 1.00 cm, d = 1.00 mm, t = 0.1 mm, I = 1.00 mA, B = 1.0 Wb/m².
For semiconductor, $R_H = -3.44 \times 10^{-8}$ m³/C.
For aluminium, $R_H = -0.3 \times 10^{-10}$ m³/C

Formula : $$V_H = R_H \cdot \frac{BId}{A}$$

Solution :

(1) For N-type semiconductor,

$$V_H = -3.44 \times 10^{-8} \times \frac{1 \times 1 \times 10^{-3} \times 1 \times 10^{-3}}{0.1 \times 10^{-3} \times 1 \times 10^{-3}}$$

∴ $\boxed{V_H = -3.44 \times 10^{-7} \text{ V}}$

(2) For aluminium, $$V_H = -0.3 \times 10^{-10} \times \frac{1 \times 1 \times 10^{-3} \times 1 \times 10^{-3}}{0.1 \times 10^{-3} \times 1 \times 10^{-3}}$$

$\boxed{V_H = -0.3 \times 10^{-9} \text{ V}}$

N-type semiconductor is more sensitive to Hall effect than aluminium. Because for same experimental setup, it gives more Hall voltage.

SUMMARY

- The energy levels of an isolated atom are discrete.
- In crystals or solids, the allowed energy levels of an atom are modified by the proximity of other atoms in such a way that the discrete energy levels of the individual atoms become bands. Each band contains as many discrete levels as there are atoms in the material.
- Elements are classified as (i) conductors, (ii) semiconductors and (iii) insulators.
- The band formed by a series of energy levels containing the valence electrons is known as valence band.
- The lowest unfilled permitted energy band is called the conduction band.
- The energy required for an electron to jump from the valence band to the conduction band is called the 'band gap' or forbidden gap of the semiconductor.
- Materials having properties intermediate between those of conductors and insulators are known as semiconductors.
- Semiconductors are of two types : (i) intrinsic and (ii) extrinsic.

- Intrinsic semiconductors are those which are pure (free from electroactive and crystalline defects).
- Doping is the process of adding an impurity to intrinsic semiconductors to increase its conductivity.
- Extrinsic semiconductors are obtained by doping an intrinsic semiconductor. They are of two types : (i) p-type extrinsic semiconductor, (ii) n-type extrinsic semiconductor.
- An extrinsic semiconductor formed by doping a trivalent impurity is called a p-type semiconductor. In this type, holes are the majority charge carriers and electrons are the minority charge carriers.
- An extrinsic semiconductor formed by doping a pentavalent impurity is called as n-type semiconductor. In this type, electrons are the majority charge carriers and holes are the minority charge carriers.
- For a metal, electrical conductivity,
$$\sigma = n_e e \mu_e$$
- For a semiconductor,
$$\sigma_{sc} = e(n_e \mu_e + n_p \mu_p)$$
- For an intrinsic semiconductor,
$$\sigma_{in} = e n_i (\mu_e + \mu_p)$$
- For a p-type extrinsic semiconductor,
$$\sigma_p \approx e n_p \mu_p \approx e n_a \mu_p$$
- For an n-type extrinsic semiconductor,
$$\sigma_n \approx e n_e \mu_e \approx e n_d \mu_e$$
- When a current carrying specimen (I) is placed in a transverse magnetic field (B), an electric field 'E' is induced in the specimen perpendicular to both I and B. This phenomenon is called as Hall effect and the voltage hence developed is called as Hall voltage.

Hall voltage, $V_H = R_H \cdot \dfrac{BId}{A}$

Hall coefficient, $R_H = \dfrac{1}{nq}$.

- The highest filled state in the highest occupied energy band at 0 K is called the Fermi level for a metal. The corresponding energy is called the Fermi energy (E_F).
- Fermi level in semiconductors is defined as the energy which corresponds to the centre of gravity of conduction electrons and holes when weighted according to their energies. It is a reference level that gives the probability of occupancy of states in conduction band as well as in valence band.
- The Fermi-Dirac probability distribution function P(E) gives the probability that an energy state of energy E is occupied by an electron at T K.

$$P(E) = \dfrac{1}{1 + e^{(E - E_F)/kT}}$$

- The Fermi level in intrinsic semiconductors is exactly in the middle of the forbidden gap.

$$E_F = \frac{E_c + E_v}{2}$$

- The position of the Fermi level in a p-type extrinsic semiconductor is close to the valence band as holes are the majority charge carriers.
- The Fermi level in an n-type extrinsic semiconductor is close to the conduction band as electrons are the majority charge carriers.
- When a pn junction is illuminated with light, it has the property of producing an e.m.f. This effect is called as photovoltaic effect.
- Solar cell is a semiconducting device that converts sunlight into electricity. It works on the principle of photovoltaic effect.
- Due to their low weight, reliability and durability, solar cells are used widely in industrial, social and consumer applications.

IMPORTANT FORMULAE

- $v = \mu_e E$
- $I = n\,\mu_e\,\dfrac{V}{l}\cdot A \cdot l$ (for metals)
- $\rho = \dfrac{1}{n\,e\,m_e}$
- $\sigma = \dfrac{1}{r} = n \cdot e\,\mu_e$ (for conductors/metals)
- $I = l \cdot A \cdot \dfrac{V}{r}\,(n\,\mu_e + p\,\mu_p)$ (for semiconductors)
- $\rho = \dfrac{1}{e\,(n\,\mu_e + p\,\mu_p)}$ (for semiconductors)
- $\sigma = \dfrac{1}{r} = e\,(n\,\mu_e + p \cdot \mu_p)$ (for semiconductors)
- $\sigma_i = e\,n_i\,(\mu_e + \mu_p)$ (for intrinsic semiconductors)
- $\sigma_n = n_e\,e\,\mu_e \approx n_d\,e\,\mu_e$ (for n-type semiconductors)
- $\sigma_p = n_h e \mu_p \approx n_a e \mu_p$ (for p-type semiconductors)
- $V_H = R_H \cdot \dfrac{BId}{A}$
- $R_H = \dfrac{1}{nq}$
- $\mu = \sigma\,R_H$.

EXERCISE

1. Describe in brief the formation of energy bands in solids.
2. Explain the terms valence band, conduction band and forbidden energy gap.
3. Classify the elements into conductors, insulators and semiconductors on the basis of band theory of solids.
4. Give the energy band picture of lithium, beryllium, sodium, diamond and silicon.
5. Derive an expression for conductivity in a metal.
6. Derive an expression for conductivity in an intrinsic and extrinsic semiconductor.
7. Discuss dependence of conductivity on temperature.
8. Explain Hall effect and Hall coefficient.
9. What is Fermi energy ? Show the location of Fermi energy levels in intrinsic and extrinsic semiconductors.
10. What is Fermi function ? Show that the Fermi level lies at the centre of the energy gap in an intrinsic semiconductor.
11. Explain why a potential difference develops across an open circuited P-N junction.
12. Give the energy band picture of a P-N junction diode and explain the effect of biasing on the band picture.
13. "P-N junction is a unidirectional device". Explain.
14. Explain the working of a P - N junction diode under forward and reverse bias.
15. Explain the process that takes place in and around the depletion layer.
16. What are transistors ? Explain the working of PNP / NPN transistor.
17. Discuss the working of an NPN transistor with respect to the energy band diagram.
18. Write a note on construction and characteristics of a solar cell.
19. Explain the working of a solar cell. Give the significance of the cell parameters I_{SC}, V_{OC} and fill factor.
20. Discuss applications of a solar cell.
21. Explain effect of temperature and impurity atoms on the position of Fermi level.
22. Write a short note on drift current and diffusion current.
23. Explain free electron theory in short. Give its short comings.
24. Derive an expression for conductivity of
    (i) Intrinsic semiconductor and (ii) Extrinsic semiconductor.
25. Obtain an expression for the conductivity of an
    (i) intrinsic semiconductor, (ii) extrinsic semiconductor.
26. Derive an expression for the conductivity in intrinsic and extrinsic semiconductors.
27. Derive an expression for the conductivity in an intrinsic and extrinsic semiconductor.
28. Derive an expression for conductivity of semiconductors.
29. Derive an expression for conductivity in an intrinsic and extrinsic semiconductor.
30. Obtain an expression for conductivity of semiconductors.
31. Draw energy band picture of P-N junction when it is
    (i) Forward biased and (ii) Reverse biased.

32. Define :
    (i) Valence band. (ii) Conduction band and
    (iii) Forbidden energy gap and draw energy band diagram of P-N junction when it is
        (i) forward biased and (ii) reverse biased.
33. Discuss with the help of energy diagrams, the working of a P-N junction diode in
    (i) forward bias and (ii) reverse bias.
34. Give energy band picture of a P-N junction diode and explain the effect of biasing on the band picture.
35. Draw energy band diagram of P-N junction diode under forward bias and reverse bias condition.
36. What is Fermi energy level ? Explain the working of P-N junction diode on the basis of Fermi energy level in forward biased mode.
37. Comparing with zero biasing explain the working of PN junction diode in forward bias and reverse bias on the basis of energy level diagram.
38. Draw energy band diagram for PN junction diode in forward and reverse biased conditions.
39. Draw energy band diagrams for PN junction diode in forward biased and reverse biased conditions.
40. If the base of the transistor is made thick, explain the changes in their properties. Draw the energy level diagram for P-N-P transistor.
41. What is Hall effect ? Obtain an expression for the Hall voltage and for the Hall coefficient.
42. What is Hall effect ? Obtain an expression for Hall voltage. State applications of Hall effect.
43. What is Hall effect ? Obtain an expression for the Hall voltage and Hall coefficient.
44. Explain Hall effect in semiconductors. Derive the equations for Hall voltage and Hall coefficient.
45. What is Hall effect ? Obtain an expression for Hall voltage and Hall coefficient. State applications of Hall effect.
46. What is Hall effect ? Derive relation for Hall voltage and Hall coefficient.
47. Explain I-V characteristics of a solar cell. State any one merit and demerit of solar cell.
48. Explain photo-voltaic effect. How is the fill factor obtained for a solar cell from its IV characteristics ?
49. (1) State merits and demerits of solar cell.
    (2) State any two applications of solar cell.
50. Explain the construction and working of solar cell. Explain its characteristic curve.
51. Define Fermi level for a semiconductor. Show the position of Fermi level for extrinsic semiconductors.
52. With the help of neat diagram, show the position of Fermi level for extrinsic semiconductor (n-type and p-type) at 0 K and higher temperature.
53. Using Fermi-Dirac probability distribution function, derive the position of Fermi level in the intrinsic semiconductor.

54. Define Fermi level in semiconductors. Show that the Fermi level in intrinsic semiconductor lies exactly at the centre of the forbidden gap.
55. Using Fermi-Dirac probability distribution function, derive the position of Fermi level in the intrinsic semiconductor.
56. Using Fermi-Dirac probability distribution function, derive an expression for the position of Fermi energy level in the intrinsic semiconductor.
57. Write down an expression for the probability of occupancy of a particular energy state of an electron in an intrinsic semiconductor. Represent it graphically at 0°K and at room temperature.
58. Write the formula for the Fermi-Dirac Probability Distribution Function. Draw in the same figure the Fermi-Dirac Probability versus Electron energy at T = 0 K, T_1 and T_2 (where $T_2 > T_1 > 0$ K). Explain the significance of the figure.

UNSOLVED PROBLEMS

1. The mobilities of carriers in intrinsic germanium sample at room temperature are μ_e = 3600 cm^2/volt-sec and μ_p = 1700 cm^2/volt-sec. If the density of electrons is same as holes and is equal to 2.5×10^{13} per cm^3, calculate the conductivity. **(Ans.** 2.12 mho/m)
2. Calculate the number of acceptors to be added to a Germanium sample to obtain the resistivity ρ = 10 ohm. cm. Given μ = 1700 cm^2/volt-sec. **(Ans.** 3.676×10^{14} per cm^3)
3. At room temperature the conductivity of a silicon crystal is 5×10^{-4} mho/cm. If the electron and hole mobilities are 0.14 m^2/volt-sec and 0.05 m^2/volt-sec, determine the density of carriers. **(Ans.** 1.64×10^{16} / m^3)
4. The specific density of tungsten is 18.8 g/cm^3 and its atomic wt. is 184.0. Assume that there are two free electrons per atom. Calculate the concentration of free electrons. Av. No. = 6.025×10^{23} / gmole. **(Ans.** 2.5×10^{23}/cm^3)
5. Compute the conductivity of copper for which μ_e = 34.8 cm^2/volt-sec and d = 8.9 gm/cm^3. Assume that there is one free electron per atom.
   Av. No. = 6.025×10^{23} / g mole, at. wt. of Cu = 63.5.
   If an electric field is applied across such a copper bar with an intensity of 10 V/cm, find the average velocity of free electrons. **(Ans.** 47.02×10^{-4} mho/cm, 348 cm/sec.)
6. The resistivity of copper wire of diameter 1.03 mm is 6.51 ohm per 300 m. The concentration of free electrons in copper is 8.4×10^{28} / m^3. If the current is 2 A, find (a) mobility, (b) drift velocity, (c) conductivity.
   (Ans. 0.413 m^2/volt-sec, 0.286×10^{-20} m/sec, 55.5×10^8 mho/m)
7. Calculate the energy gap in silicon if it is given that it is transparent to radiation of wavelength greater than 11000 A°. **(Ans.** 1.13 eV)
8. An N-type semiconductor is to have a resistivity of 10 ohm-cm. Calculate the number of donor atoms which must be added to achieve this. **(Ans.** 12.5×10^{23})
   Assume μ_e = 500 cm^2/volt-sec.

✠ ✠ ✠

CHAPTER 4
SUPERCONDUCTIVITY

4.1 INTRODUCTION

Superconductivity is one of the most exciting phenomena because of its special feature when compared to conductors and has wide range of applications in industry. Experimentally, superconductivity was discovered by Dutch physicist, Heike Kamerlingh Onnes in 1911. While studying the temperature dependence of resistance of metals, he discovered that the electrical resistance in certain metals such as lead and mercury suddenly disappears at around 4 K.

In 1933, W. Hans Meissner revealed that the superconductors repel the magnetic lines of force when it is placed in an external magnetic field. The theoretical explanation of superconductivity was given by John Bardeen, Leon N. Cooper and J. Robert Schreiffer in 1957. The theory is famous as **BCS Theory** which explained superconductivity based on pairing of electrons called **'Cooper Pair'**. Some important features of superconductivity are as follows :

- The electrical resistance drops to zero at critical temperature.
- The magnetic flux lines are excluded from the bulk of superconductor.

4.2 INTRODUCTION TO SUPERCONDUCTIVITY

It is a known fact that the resistivity of pure metals decreases with decreasing temperature. When the temperature falls below a certain value (the exact value depending on the substance), the resistivity vanishes entirely.

In metals, both the thermal vibrations of atoms and the presence of impurities or imperfections scatter the moving conduction electrons. This gives rise to electrical resistivity. The variation of resistivity for a pure metal and superconductor is shown in Fig. 4.1.

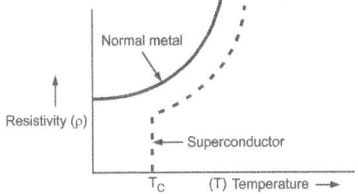

Fig. 4.1 : Variation of resistance with temperature

At the beginning of the twentieth century, in 1908, H. Kamerling Onnes, a Dutch Physicist, successfully liquified helium. As helium boils at 8.2 K, it therefore became possible to study the properties of materials at low temperature. In 1911, he observed that the electrical resistivity of pure mercury dropped suddenly to zero at about the boiling point of helium. He concluded that mercury had passed into a new state, which he called the **Superconducting**

State due to its remarkable electrical properties. The temperature at which the material changes its state from a state of normal resistivity to a superconducting state, is called the **Transition or Critical Temperature T_c**. A conductor having zero (or almost zero) electrical resistance is called a **Superconductor** and this phenomenon is called as **Superconductivity**.

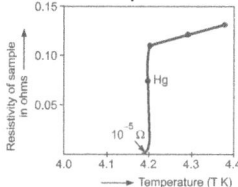

Fig. 4.2 : Resistance of mercury as a function of temperature showing a transition from normal state to superconducting state at a critical temperature of 4.2 K

The superconducting transition is found to be very sharp for a pure metal and it is broad for an impure metal. The zero magnetic induction in a superconductor is responsible for levitation effects. In a famous levitation experiment, a horizontal bar magnet was suspended from a chain. It was lowered over a sheet of lead, which had been cooled to the superconducting state. As the magnet came nearer to the superconducting state, the magnet remained floating horizontally over the lead sheet. The field of the approaching magnet induces a current on the surface of the superconductor. As the resistance is zero in the superconductor, the current persisted and the field due to the current repelled the bar magnet. This persistence of currents is found uniquely in superconductors. Certain experiments on the study of decay of these super currents in a solenoid found decay time to be greater than 10^5 years.

4.3 PROPERTIES OF SUPERCONDUCTORS

Following are the properties of superconductors :

4.3.1 Zero Electrical Resistance

A superconductor is characterized by zero electrical resistance. The temperature below which the resistance of the material vanishes is called as the **'Transition Temperature'** or **'Critical Temperature'**. It is referred as T_c. As it is not possible to test experimentally whether the resistance is zero, the specimen is connected in a circuit as shown in Fig. 4.3.

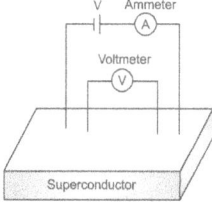

Fig. 4.3

When the material is in normal conducting state, a voltage drop is measured across its ends. As the material is cooled below its transition temperature T_c, the voltage drop disappears as its resistance drops to zero ($R = V/I$).

A more sensitive method devised by K. Onnes consists in measuring the decrease of current in a closed ring of superconducting wire.

Table 4.1 : A List of Some Superconductors alongwith their Critical Temperature

Sr. No.	Material	T_c in K
1.	Copper, silver, gold	Non-superconducting
2.	Rhodium	240×10^{-6}
3.	Aluminium	1.1
4.	Tin	3.72
5.	Mercury	4.15
6.	Lead	7.2
7.	Niobium	9.3
8.	Niobium-titanium alloys	9-11
9.	Lead molybdenum sulphide	14
10.	Niobium-tin	18.3
11.	Vanadium-gallium	15.4
12.	Niobium-germanium	23.3

It has been observed that traces of paramagnetic elements in the specimen can lower the transition temperature. Hence, it becomes necessary to remove these traces completely. Non-magnetic impurities have no marked effect on the transition temperature.

4.3.2 Meissner Effect

Meissner and Ochsenfeld discovered in 1933 that a superconductor completely expels any magnetic field lines that were initially penetrating it in its normal state. This property is independent of the path by which the superconducting state is reached.

Path 1 :

The sample is in superconducting state and is brought to the magnetic field. It is found that the magnetic flux is totally expelled from the sample.

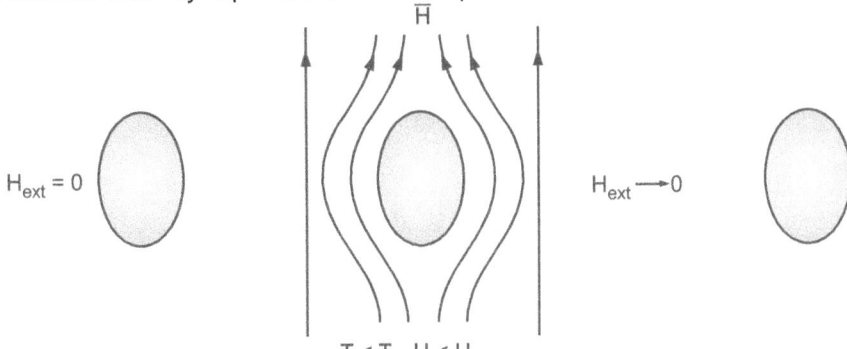

(a) Superconductor is initially outside the magnetic field

(b) When the superconductor is transported into the magnetic field, it pushes the field lines aside

$T < T_c, H < H_c$

(c) When the magnetic field is switched off

Fig. 4.4

Path 2 :

The magnetic field is applied first to the sample in the normal state. Then the material be cooled to below T_c in the presence of the magnetic field. Meissner and Ochsenfeld found that the magnetic flux is totally expelled from the sample as it becomes superconducting. This expulsion of magnetic flux during the transition from normal to superconducting state is called as **'Meissner Effect'**.

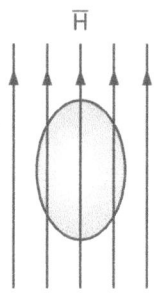
$T > T_c, H > H_c$

(a) Superconductor in a magnetic field at $T > T_c$, magnetic field penetrates the body in normal state

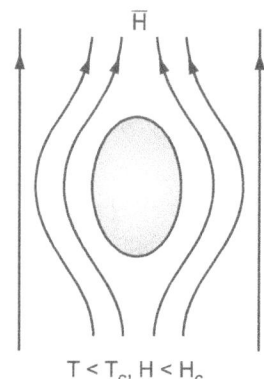
$T < T_c, H < H_c$

(b) On cooling the superconductor in the presence of magnetic field, it expels the flux lines within the specimen at $T = T_c$. This is Meissner effect

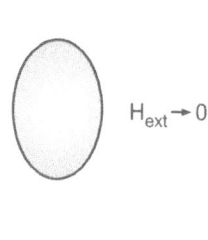
$H_{ext} \to 0$

(c) When the field is switched off, field is not trapped within the superconductor. Superconductivity is thus characterized by perfect diamagnetism

Fig. 4.5

Explanation of Meissner Effect :

When a superconducting sample is placed in a magnetic field, it induces currents which circulate on the surface of the specimen in a manner that it creates a magnetic field everywhere equal and opposite to the applied magnetic field.

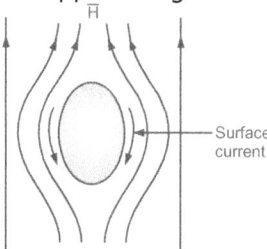

Fig. 4.6 : Meissner effect

Meissner effect cannot be explained by the assumption that a superconductor is a resistanceless conductor. A superconductor is not just a perfect conductor but has an additional property. A material in the superconducting state does not permit any magnetic flux to exist within the body of the material.

When a perfect conductor is cooled in a magnetic field until its resistance becomes zero, the magnetic field in the material is frozen or trapped in the material. It cannot change subsequently, irrespective of the applied field. Therefore, a conductor does not exhibit diamagnetic behaviour even slightly.

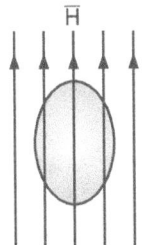
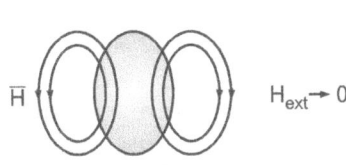

(a) Conductor held in magnetic field is cooled to the state of zero electrical resistance

(b) When magnetic field H_{ext} is switched off, magnetic field is trapped in the ideal conductor

Fig. 4.7

The magnetic induction inside the specimen is given by,

$$B = \mu_0(H + M) \quad \text{(Normal state } T > T_c)$$

where, H – external applied field

M – magnetisation produced within the specimen

For $T < T_c$, $B = 0$

$\therefore \quad \mu_0(H + M) = 0$

$\Rightarrow \quad H = -M$ (Superconducting state)

The susceptibility of the material,

$$\chi = \frac{M}{H} = -1 \quad \text{(Perfect diamagnetism)}$$

Thus, the superconducting state is characterized by perfect diamagnetism. Meissner effect conclusively proves whether a particular material has become a superconductor or not. Because of Meissner effect, superconducting materials strongly repel external magnets, it leads to both **'Levitation Effect'** and **'Suspension Effect'**.

4.3.3 Critical Field : Effect of External Magnetic Field

K. Onnes discovered in 1913 that, when a superconductor is placed in an increasing magnetic field, it loses superconductivity at a certain value H_c of the field. The magnetic field strength at which superconductivity gets destroyed is called the **'Critical Magnetic Field'** H_c. This value is a characteristic of the metal and depends on its orientation in the magnetic field and the temperature.

The relation between superconductivity and magnetic field plays an important role in the study of properties of superconductors. Obviously, the value of H_c varies with temperature. Fig. 4.8 shows the variation of H_c with temperature for a typical superconductor.

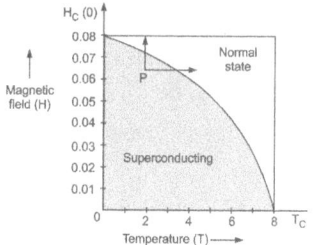

Fig. 4.8

From Fig. 4.8, consider point P, where the temperature and the magnetic field are within the shaded region, the metal is in the superconducting state. On increasing either the temperature or the field, it can be driven into the normal state. Hence, it can be seen that a superconductor has two possible states : (i) the superconducting one which is resistanceless and perfectly diamagnetic and (ii) a normal state which is the same as a normal metal.

At any temperature $T < T_c$, the material remains superconducting until a corresponding critical magnetic field is applied. When the magnetic field exceeds the critical value, the material goes into the normal state. The critical field required to destroy the superconducting state decreases progressively with increase in temperature.

For example, a magnetic field of 0.04 T will destroy the superconductivity of mercury at $T \approx 0$ K, whereas a field of 0.02 T is sufficient to destroy its superconductivity at $T \approx 3$ K.

The variation of critical field with temperature is given by the relation

$$H_c(T) = H_c(0)\left[1 - \left(\frac{T}{T_c}\right)^2\right]$$

where $H_c(0)$ is the critical magnetic field at 0 K.

4.3.4 Persistent Currents

Consider a superconducting ring placed in a magnetic field. When cooled to below the critical temperature, it becomes superconducting. The external field induces a current in the ring. When switched off, the current will continue to keep flowing, on its own accord, around the loop, as long as the loop is held below the critical temperature. Such a steady current flowing with undiminished strength is called **Persistent Current**. This current does not need external power to maintain it as there does not exist I^2R losses. If the superconducting ring has a finite resistance R, the current circulating in the ring would decrease according to the relation,

$$I(t) = I(0)\, e^{-Rt/L}$$

where L is the inductance of the ring.

Calculations show that once the current flow is initiated, it persists for more than 10^5 years. Persistent current is one of the most important properties of a superconductor. Superconductor coils with persistent currents produce magnetic fields. They can therefore be used as magnets which do not require a power supply to maintain its magnetic field.

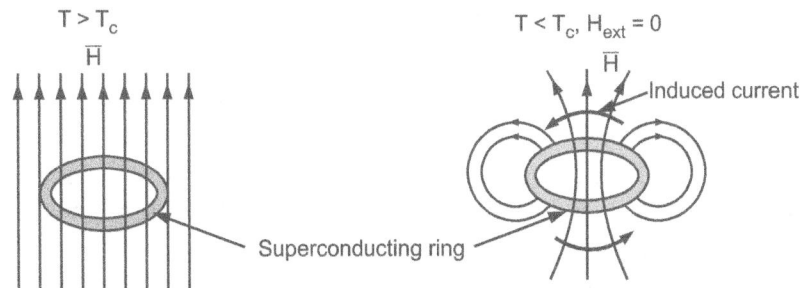

(a) **Superconducting ring is cooled in the presence of a magnetic field**

(b) **At T < T_c, the magnetic field is switched off. Persistent current is induced in the ring**

Fig. 4.9

4.3.5 Isotope Effect

Maxwell and Reynolds found independently that the critical temperature of superconductors varies with isotopic mass. It is found to decrease with increasing isotopic mass M.

Since a heavier isotopic mass lowers the lattice vibrations, this indicates that superconductivity is due to an interaction between electrons and lattice vibrations. To get an idea of the magnitude of the effect for mercury, T_c varies from 4.185 K to 4.146 K as the isotopic mass M varies from 199.5 to 203.4. The transition temperature changes smoothly when different isotopes of the same element are mixed. The experimental results within each series of isotopes can be given by the relation :

$$T_c \propto \frac{1}{\sqrt{M}}$$

i.e. $T_c \propto M^{-1/2}$

or $M^{1/2} \cdot T_c = $ constant.

4.3.6 Critical Current Density (Jc)

The magnetic field which destroys superconductivity, need not be due to an externally applied field, but it may be the field produced as a result of current flow in the superconductor ring itself. If the field produced by itself exceeds H_c, the superconductivity of the ring is destroyed.

Thus, if a superconducting material carries a current and if the magnetic field produced by it is equal to H_c, then superconductivity disappears. The maximum current density J at which superconductivity vanishes is called the **'Critical Current Density'** J_c. For $J < J_c$, the current can sustain itself while for $J > J_c$, the current cannot sustain itself. A superconducting ring of radius R loses its superconductivity when the current is,

$$I_c = 2\pi R H_c$$

∴ The critical current density,

$$J_c = \frac{\text{Critical current}}{\text{Area of the ring}}$$

$$J_c = \frac{2\pi R H_c}{\pi R^2} = \frac{2H_c}{R}$$

This sets a limit to the maximum current a superconductor can carry without disturbing its superconducting state.

As the temperature is raised, the maximum current that a superconductor can carry decreases as the temperature is raised and falls to zero at the transition temperature T_c. This maximum current leads to a maximum applied magnetic field. As critical current falls with the temperature, the critical magnetic field will also decrease as the transition temperature is approached. The variation of critical current density J_c and critical magnetic field H_c with temperature is shown in Fig. 4.10.

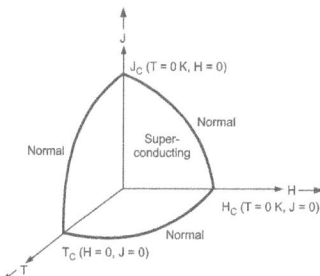

Fig. 4.10

Fig. 4.10 shows the combined effects of temperature, current density and magnetic field on a superconductor. The boundary separates superconducting and normal states. Within the boundary, the state is superconducting.

In the superconduction state,

$$T < T_c$$
$$H < H_c$$
and $$J < J_c$$

4.4 TYPES OF SUPERCONDUCTORS

There are two types of superconductors : type I and type II. There is no difference in the mechanism of superconductivity in both the types. Both have similar thermal properties at the transition temperature in zero magnetic field. The difference lies in their behaviour in a magnetic field, particularly in Meissner effect.

4.4.1 Type-I Superconductors

In a type-I superconductor, the transition from a superconducting state to normal state, in the presence of a magnetic field, occurs sharply at the critical value H_c. At this point, the field penetrates completely. Below H_c, type-I superconductors are perfectly diamagnetic. They completely expel the magnetic field from the interior of the specimen. Upto the critical field strength, magnetization of the material grows in proportion to the external field. At the transition temperature, it suddenly drops to zero to the normal conducting state. The magnetic field penetrates only the surface layer and current flows only in this layer. Aluminium and lead are examples of type-I superconductors. As superconductivity gets destroyed at low values of critical field, type-I superconductors cannot be used in solenoids for producing large magnetic fields. Such superconductors are also called as **'Soft Superconductors'**.

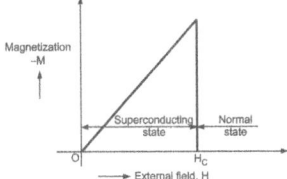

Fig. 4.11 : Magnetization curve for a type-I superconductor

4.4.2 Type-II Superconductors

Type-II superconductor, also known as **'Hard Superconductor'** is characterized by two critical fields H_{c1} and H_{c2}. ($H_{c1} < H_c < H_{c2}$). It exists in three states : superconducting, mixed and normal.

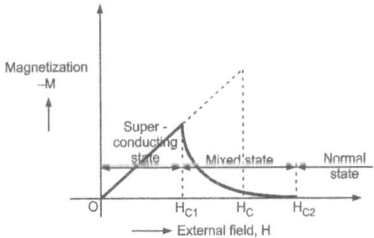

Fig. 4.12 : Magnetization curve in type-II superconductor

(i) Superconducting State :

This occurs upto a critical field H_{c1}. The magnetization increases with the applied magnetic field and the external magnetic flux is completely expelled from the interior of the material.

(ii) Mixed State :

This region extends from H_{c1} to H_{c2}. At H_{c1}, the magnetic flux penetrates the material. Between H_{c1} and H_{c2}, the material is in a mixed state magnetically but electrically it is a superconductor. Meissner effect is incomplete. In this region, the superconductor is threaded by flux lines and is said to be in a **'Vortex State'**. Value of H_{c2} may be 100 times higher than H_c (~20 to 50 Wb/m^2). As superconductivity is retained upto high values of magnetic fields, type-II superconductors are found useful in applications where high magnetic fields are created. Commercial solenoids wound with type-II superconductors produce high, steady magnetic fields above 10 T. Once the magnetic field is created by a superconductor solenoid, it does not require electrical power to maintain it. But the solenoid must be kept below critical transition temperature.

(iii) Normal State :

When the magnetic field exceeds critical field strength H_{c2}, magnetization vanishes completely. The sample is penetrated by the external field and superconductivity is destroyed. The specimen reverts from superconducting state to normal state.

Type-II superconductors have a distinguishing feature. The supercurrents arising in an external magnetic field can flow not only on the surface but also in its bulk. The magnitude of the currents carried is also large when the magnetic field is between H_{c1} and H_{c2}.

Table 4.2 : Types of Superconductor - Differences :

Sr.	Property	Type-I Superconductor	Type-II Superconductor
1.	Variation of magnetic field with temperature	Graph of Magnetic field (H) vs Temperature (T) showing H_c curve separating Superconductor region (below) from Normal state (above), meeting at T_C.	Graph of Magnetic field (H) vs Temperature (T) showing H_{c2} and H_{c1} curves, with SC region at bottom, Mixture of normal and superconducting state between, and Normal state above, meeting at T_C.
2.	Critical magnetic field	Has one critical magnetic field H_c.	Has two critical magnetic fields H_{c1} and H_{c2}.
3.	Transition from superconducting to normal state	Transition from superconducting state to normal state in the presence of a magnetic field occurs sharply at the critical value H_c.	If external magnetic field is less than H_{c1}, material remains superconductor. When external magnetic field increases above H_{c2}, their superconductivity is destroyed.
4.	Magnetization below and above critical magnetic field	They are perfectly diamagnetic below H_c and completely expel magnetic field from interior of the superconducting phase.	For $H_{c1} < H < H_{c2}$ they exist in magnetically mixed and electronically superconducting state.
5.	Change in magnetization with external magnetic	Upto H_c magnetization of the material grows in proportion to the external field and then abruptly drops to zero at the transition to the normally	The magnetization of Type-II superconductors grows in proportion to the external field upto H_{c1}. The external magnetic flux is expelled from the interior

	field	conducting state.	of the material till then. At H_{c1}, magnetic field lines begin penetrating the material. As magnetic field increases further, the magnetic flux through the material increases. At H_{c2}, magnetization vanishes completely. External magnetic field penetrates completely and superconductivity is destroyed.
6.	Current carrying capacity	They are poor carriers of electrical current.	They are good carriers of electrical current.
7.	Magnetic field generation capacity	About 0.01 to 0.2 Wb/m^2 (value of H_c).	About 20 to 50 Wb/m^2 (Value of H_{c2}).
8.	Applications as magnets	Not much useful due to low H_c.	Useful due to high H_{c2}.
9.	Examples	Aluminium, lead, indium	Transition metals and alloys consisting of niobium, silicon and vanadium, Nb-Ti alloys, Nb3Sn, etc.

4.5 BCS THEORY

Two theories were advanced to explain the phenomenon of superconductivity :
- The London theory,
- Gorter and Casimi theory.

However, none of them were experimentally proved. Then, in the year 1957, came the BCS (named after the American physicists, John Bardeen, Leon N. Cooper and John Robert Schrieffer) quantum theory of superconductivity, which was successful in giving an explanation.

The superconducting state is known to be an ordered state of the conducting electrons of the metal. The order lies below the transition temperature. Above it, they are disordered. The BCS theory explained the nature and origin of the electron ordering.

According to this theory, there is an electron - lattice - electron interaction resulting from the interactions of the electrons with the vibrations of the atoms in the lattice. This results in an overall attraction between two electrons. At low temperatures, this attraction overcomes the coulomb repulsion.

(a) Base of the Theory

This theory is based on the concept of electron-lattice-electron interaction.

(b) Approach of Electron and Lattice Distortion :

When an electron approaches an ion in the lattice, there is coulomb attraction between the electron and the lattice ion. This produces a distortion in the lattice. The distortion causes an increase in the density of ions in the region of distortion. The higher density of ions in the distorted region will attract, in turn, a nearby electron. The interaction between the lattice and the electron can be thought of as the constant emission and reabsorption of phonons by the lattice. Thus, a free electron exerts a small attractive force on another electron through phonons, which are quanta of lattice vibrations.

(c) Formation of Cooper Pair :

An electron of wave factor k as shown in Fig. 4.11 emits a phonon q which is absorbed by an electron of wave vector k'. This scatters k into k–q and k' into k' + q. This process is virtual and energy need not be conserved. Hence, the phonons are called as **'Virtual Phonons'**. The nature of the resulting interaction depends on the relative magnitudes of electronic energy change and phonon energy ($h\omega_q$). If this phonon energy exceeds the electronic energy, the interaction is attractive.

As a result of this interaction, electrons form together bound pairs. A pair of free electrons thus coupled through a phonon is called a **Cooper Pair**. The energy of pairing i.e., the net attraction is very weak. Only a tiny temperature is needed to throw apart the electrons by thermal agitation and convert them back to normal electrons.

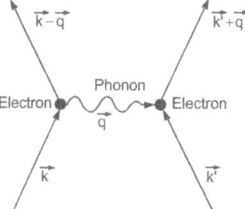

Fig. 4.13 : Electron-Phonon-Electron Interaction

(d) Almost Zero Resistance Below Critical Temperature :

When the temperature is sufficiently low, the electrons try to get into the lowest state by forming Cooper pairs. Several pairs occupy the same state at the same time. This state is the ground state. Thus, the superconducting state is an ordered state of the **'Conduction Electrons'**. The motion of all Cooper pairs is the same. Either they are at rest, or if the superconductor carries a current, they drift with the same velocity. As the density of Cooper pairs is very high, even large currents require a small velocity. The small velocity of Cooper pairs combined with their precise ordering minimizes collisions and it leads to vanishing resistivity. Once particles get into the ordered state, it would be very difficult to change the state of any one of them.

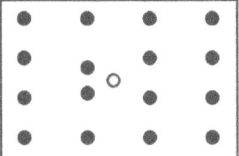 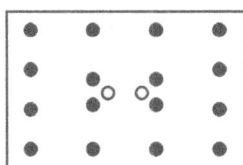 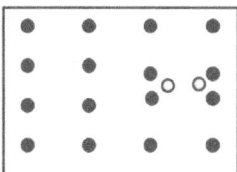

(a) Electron approaches lattice and lattice ions are attracted towards electrons resulting development of positive charge on the electron

(b) Another electron is attracted towards the positive regions surrounding to the first electron

(c) As first electron moves ahead, second electron follows it and both move together as "Cooper Pair"

Fig. 4.14

Conclusions from BCS Theory :
- The electron-lattice-electron interaction is attractive at low temperature and can overcome the coulomb repulsion between the electrons.
- The electrons of a Cooper pair have a lower energy than two unpaired electrons. Hence, the energy spectrum shows an energy gap. The Cooper pairs occupy the lower state. The energy gap prevents the pairs from breaking apart.
- The theory explains Isotope effect and Meissner effect in a natural manner. The London penetration depth, etc. are natural consequences of the BCS ground state.
- The BCS theory predicts a relation for T_c (critical temperature) which is also found to be satisfied qualitatively by experimental results.
- Magnetic flux through a superconducting ring is quantized and the effective unit of charge is 2e rather than e. This can be understood when one considers the BCS ground state involving pairs of electrons.

4.6 HIGH TEMPERATURE SUPERCONDUCTORS

Superconductors whose critical temperature (T_c) is greater than 77 K are called 'high temperature superconductors'. This temperature is much higher than critical temperature 4.2 K for mercury. Hence, they are termed as high temperature superconductors. This temperature can be achieved by liquid nitrogen which is less expensive and easy to handle. Also, liquid nitrogen has a larger heat capacity and is therefore, a better coolant than liquid helium.

In general, high T_c superconductors are ceramic materials. Several new oxide superconductors have T_c above 90 K. The superconductivity has not yet been achieved at room temperature, but experiments are going on to achieve it. The superconductivity at room temperature has not been ruled out theoretically.

High Tc superconductors are prepared from the oxides of barium, copper, yttrium, etc. The unit cells of these types of superconductors are complicated. The unit cells consists of one rare earth metal atom, two barium atoms and three copper atoms and seven oxygen atoms.

The number of atoms of each metal element give name 1-2-3 superconductors to this class. The 1-2-3 superconductors form layer of copper and oxygen atoms sandwiched between layers of other elements in the compound.

Fig. 4.15 shown $YBa_2Cu_3O_7$ (YBCO), a ceramic oxide superconductor.

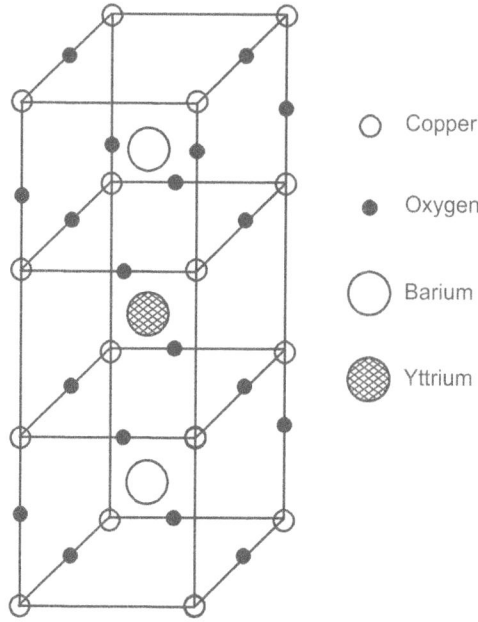

Fig. 4.15 : Unit cell of $YBa_2Cu_3O_7$ (YBCO)

The rare earth oxide systems La-Sr-Cu-O and Y-Ba-Cu-O has stable superconducting transition temperatures ranging from 80 K to 100 K.

4.7 APPLICATIONS OF SUPERCONDUCTIVITY

The phenomenon of superconductivity finds numerous applications which can be broadly classified into two types.

1. **Large-Scale Applications :**

These are applications requiring large currents, long lengths of superconductors in environments where the magnetic field may be several tesla (1 tesla = 10^4 Oersted). Examples include magnets and power transmission lines, transformers and generators, where current densities of atleast 10^5 amps/cm^2 are required. Superconductors are more advantageous than normal conductors because of their lower resistance and hence smaller power loss.

2. **Small-Scale Applications :**

These are applications involving minute amounts of current or fields. Examples are detection systems like SQUIDS.

4.7.1 Large-Scale Applications

The cost of energy consumption in the world and the electrical energy in particular are staggering. It is said that about one-fifth the power generated is lost due to I^2R losses. The elimination of even a small fraction of the resistive load will have a staggering impact. Another important area of application is the use of high temperature superconductors in the production of strong magnetic fields above the 2 Tesla level. This will eliminate the use of iron cores in motors, generators and transformers resulting in reduced size, weight and losses from iron cores.

1. **Wires and Superconducting Magnets :**

As R = 0 for a superconductor, there are no I^2R losses. There is no energy dissipation associated with the flow of a current through a superconductor. A current set up in a closed loop of a superconductor persists, almost forever, without decay. Superconducting wires could be used for very economical long distance power transmission, as energy dissipation is low and electrical power transmission can be done at a lower voltage level. Electric generators made with superconducting wire are more efficient than conventional generators wound with copper wire.

2. **Magnetic Levitation (Maglev) :**

The zero magnetic induction in a superconductor is responsible for levitation effects.

This phenomenon has led to one of the most spectacular applications, maglev or magnetically levitated train. Superconducting magnetic coils produce the magnetic repulsion required to levitate the train. Maglev trains will not slide over the rails but will float on an air cushion over a magnetised track. As there is no mechanical friction, speeds upto 500 km/hr can be achieved easily. As these trains are capable of very high speeds, they can compete with short hop plane flights in crowded air corridors.

There are several maglev train test strips and there is talk about a 13 mile commercial line in the Orlando-Florida area and a longer one between Los Angeles and Las Vegas. One proposal is to use an on-board electromagnet to levitate the train above the laminated iron rail in the guide with ~1 cm air gap. A second proposal is to use superconducting wire coils in the vehicle to produce a magnetic field of the same polarity as coils in the guides, the repulsive force lifts the vehicle above the track (about 10-15 cm). As iron is not required for the magnetic field, the vehicle could be much lighter.

3. **Electronics Industry :**

Superconductors will change the face of the electronics industry, particularly IC fabrication. Currently, due to large amounts of heat generated (I^2R losses) there is a limit to the number of components that can be placed on a single chip. With the use of superconductors, more densely packed chips may be used. With the use of superconducting chips in digital electronics, logic delays of 13 pico seconds and switching times of 9 pico seconds have been achieved. By using basic Josephson junctions (refer small-scale applications), sensitive microwave detectors, magnetometers and stable voltage sources have been manufactured.

4. Computer Industry :

Currently, logic elements operate at speeds of nanoseconds. By using Josephson junctions, information can be transmitted more rapidly and by several orders of magnitude. Research is being conducted on 'petaflop' computers. A petaflop is a thousand-trillion floating point operations per second. Today's fastest computer has only achieved 'teraflop' speeds - trillions of operations per second.

5. Superconducting Magnets :

The most important use of superconductivity has been in the production of high magnetic fields (> 10^5 Gauss or 10 Tesla) over large volumes without a large consumption of electrical power.

As superconductors are capable of carrying, without energy loss, about 100 times larger current densities as compared to normal conductors like copper, they can be used for building light weight, high intensity, compact magnets useful in various applications. Relatively small superconducting magnets have very economically replaced gigantic water-cooled copper conductor magnets which dissipate several megawatts of electrical power. Superconducting magnets (SCM) find application in many areas in technology, including energy storage devices for electrical power industry, electric motor windings, electromagnetic pumps, etc.

Superconducting magnets are also used in the field of medicine for NMR (Nuclear Magnetic Resonance) imaging particularly for producing NMR tomography. This is of particular importance for investigating pathological changes in the brain. By applying a strong magnetic field from a superconducting magnet across the body, hydrogen atoms inside the body are forced to take up energy from the magnetic field. This energy is then released at a frequency that can be detected and displayed on a computer. This method is called as Magnet Resonance Imaging (MRI) and is widely used in hospitals.

Superconducting magnets are also used in high energy physics experiments. Large particle accelerators employ magnets producing high fields for bending and guiding the accelerated particles. Controlled nuclear fusion requires confining high temperature plasma within a closed region. This is done by using superconducting magnets. Superconducting magnets have also been employed for magnetically separating refining ores, isotopes and chemicals.

6. Military Applications :

- Superconductors have found a wide variety of applications in the military. HTSC (high temperature superconductors) are being used to detect mines and submarines.
- Smaller motors are being built by Navy ships using superconducting wires.
- 'E-bombs' have been used by the US army in March 2003 when US forces attacked Iraq. These are devices that use strong superconducting magnets to create a fast, high intensity electromagnetic pulse to disable an enemy's electronic equipment.

4.7.2 Small-Scale Applications of Superconductivity

Brian D. Josephson, a graduate student at Cambridge University, in 1962, predicted that electrical current would flow between two superconducting materials even when they are separated by a non-superconductor or insulator. This tunneling phenomenon is called as the **'Josephson Effect'**. It has been applied to electronic devices such as the SQUID, an instrument capable of detecting and measuring extremely weak magnetic fields.

4.8 JOSEPHSON EFFECT

Josephson Junction :

Two superconductors connected by a thin layer of insulating material (~ 1-2 nm) is called a **'Josephson Junction'**. Under suitable conditions, Josephson found that remarkable effects were associated with the tunneling of superconducting electron pairs from a superconductor, through a layer of an insulator, into another superconductor. This junction is called a **Weak Link**. The effect found to be associated with the pair tunneling is called **Josephson Effect**.

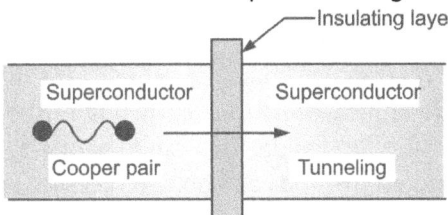

Fig. 4.16 : Josephson Junction

4.8.1 DC Josephson Effect

When two superconductors are separated by a thin insulating layer, Cooper pairs tunnel through the junction and current flows across the junction without any external applied voltage. If this current does not exceed critical current I_c, voltage across the junction is zero. This effect is known as **DC Josephson Effect**. The Cooper pairs on each side of the junction can be represented by a wave function. The dc current obtained due to the tunneling of Cooper pairs through the insulating layer is given by $I_J = I_C \sin \phi$, where ϕ is the phase difference between wave functions of Cooper pairs on either side.

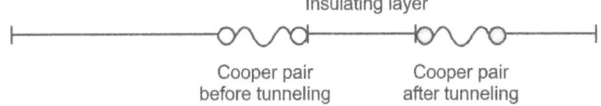

Fig. 4.17 : DC effect

4.8.2 AC Josephson Effect

When a dc voltage is applied to the Josephson junction and the current I_J through the junction exceeds a critical value I_c, a potential difference V appears across the Josephson junction and the junction current I_J varies sinusoidally with time. This effect is known as ac **Josephson Effect**. In such a case, the energies of the Cooper pair on both the sides of the barrier differ by 2 eV. The alternating supercurrents are accompanied by the emission or absorption of electromagnetic radiation.

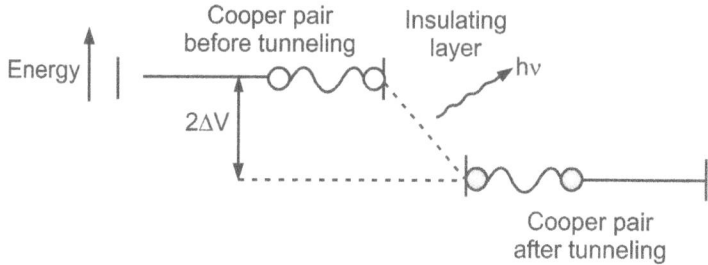

Fig. 4.18 : AC effect

If ΔV is the finite potential difference between the superconductors, the electron pairs on opposite sides of the barrier differ in energy by an amount $2\Delta V = 2$ eV. Hence, frequency υ of the associated photon will be given by,

$$h\upsilon = 2 \text{ eV} \quad \text{or} \quad \upsilon = 2\left(\frac{e}{h}\right)V.$$

Josephson suggested the determination of h/e from this relation after measuring applied voltage and frequency of emitted radiation. This experiment was carried out between 1967 and 1968. It is one of the simplest methods available to measure the fundamental constant.

SOLVED EXAMPLE

Example 4.1 : The critical temperature of a superconductor with isotopic mass 200 is 5 K. Calculate the critical temperature of the superconductor when isotopic mass is 196.

Data : $M = 200, \quad T_{200} = 5$ K

Formula : $T_C \propto M^{-1/2}$

Solution :

$$\frac{T_{200}}{T_{196}} = \frac{200^{-1/2}}{196^{-1/2}} \quad T_{196} = \frac{196^{-1/2}}{200^{-1/2}} \cdot 5$$

$$T_{196} = \sqrt{\frac{200}{196}} \cdot 5$$

$$\boxed{T_{196} = 5.05 \text{ K}}$$

The critical temperature for $M = 196$ is 5.05 K.

SUMMARY

- A conductor having zero electrical resistance is called a superconductor and this phenomenon is called as superconductivity.
- The temperature below which superconductivity is exhibited is called as critical transition temperature (T_c).
- Superconductivity vanishes if temperature, magnetic field and current density exceed the critical value. For superconducting state, $T < T_c$, $H < H_c$ and $J < J_c$.
- BCS theory states that the superconducting state is an ordered state of a pair of conduction electrons coupled through a phonon called a Cooper pair.
- The expulsion of magnetic field/flux from the interior of the specimen, when cooled below the critical temperature is called as Meissner effect.
- Critical temperature for different isotopes varies with the mass.

    $$M^{1/2} T_c = \text{constant}.$$

- Variation of critical magnetic field with temperature is given by

    $$H_c(T) = H_c(0) \left[1 - \frac{T}{T_c}\right]^2$$

    where $H_c(0)$ is the critical magnetic field at 0 K.

- Persistent currents : When a current is induced in a superconducting ring or loop held below the critical temperature, it persists undiminished as long as the temperature remains below the critical temperature T_c.
- Type-I superconductors are pure specimens which expel completely magnetic field lines. They exhibit perfect diamagnetism. They are also called as soft superconductors.
- Type-II superconductors are characterized by two critical fields. Between the two critical fields, the magnetic flux partially penetrates the material. Above the upper critical field flux, penetration is total. They are also called as hard superconductors.
- Tunneling of current between two superconductors separated by an insulator is known as Josephson effect.
- The flow of a dc current across the Josephson junction, in the absence of any electric or magnetic field is known as dc Josephson effect.
- When a dc voltage is applied across the Josephson junction, RF current oscillations are setup across the junction along with the emission or absorption of electromagnetic radiation. This is known as ac Josephson effect.

IMPORTANT FORMULAE

- Isotope effect, $M^{1/2} T_C$ = constant.
- $\lambda = \dfrac{\lambda_o}{\left[1-\left(\dfrac{T}{T_C}\right)^4\right]}$.
- $H_C = H_o \left[1-\left(\dfrac{T}{T_C}\right)^2\right]$.

EXERCISE

1. Explain BCS theory to explain superconductivity.
2. What is superconductivity ? What are the characteristics of superconductors ?
3. Explain Meissner effect, isotope effect, critical temperature and critical field.
4. What are the types of superconductors ? Where do they find application ?
5. Enumerate the different applications of superconductors. How are they advantageous as compared to normal conductors ?
6. Explain some properties of type-I and type-II superconductors.
7. What is superconductivity ? What are the characteristics of superconductors ?
8. Explain zero electrical resistance of the superconductors.
9. State and explain (i) Critical field and (ii) Meissner effect.
10. State and explain (i) Meissner effect and Critical field.
11. Explain the isotope effect and its significance.
12. Explain the Meissner effect. What important property of superconductors it explains ?
13. Explain :
    (i) Critical field
    (ii) Zero electrical resistance of superconductors.
14. State and explain
    (i) Meissner effect.
    (ii) Persistent currents.
    (iii) Isotope effect for superconductors.
15. Explain zero resistance and its significance in superconductors.

16. Explain :
    (i) Persistent of currents.
    (ii) Meissner effect.
    (iii) Critical magnetic field for superconductors.
17. What is superconductivity ? State and explain :
    (i) Critical magnetic field.
    (ii) Meissner effect.
    (iii) Persistent current.
18. State and explain :
    (1) Meissner effect.
    (2) Isotope effect.
19. Explain :
    (i) Meissner effect.
    (ii) Effect of external magnetic field on superconductors.
20. Explain the terms :
    (1) Meissner effect.
    (2) Critical magnetic field.
21. Explain the following properties of superconductors :
    (a) Meissner effect
    (b) Critical field.
22. Explain the term : Persistent current.
23. State and explain : (1) Meissner effect and (2) Isotope effect.
24. Explain what is the significance of critical temperature, critical magnetic field and critical current density for superconductors.
25. State and explain Meissner effect. Hence show that susceptibility is negative in superconducting state.
26. Explain the BCS theory of superconductors.
27. Explain BCS theory of superconductivity.
28. Explain how BCS theory explains superconductivity.
29. Explain BCS theory of superconductivity.

30. Following paragraph gives 6 statements regarding BCS theory. Rewrite the statements and underline if they are incorrect :

    (a) BCS theory indicates electron-lattice-electron interaction through a quantum of lattice vibration called phonon.

    (b) An electron, while passing through lattice distorts it, and another electron while passing across the distorted lattice gets attracted due to accumulated positive charge in the distorted lattice.

    (c) Two electrons cannot exist together despite the presence of phonons.

    (d) Cooper pairs are Bosons and thus any number of Cooper pairs can be accommodated in a single low energy state.

    (e) This leads to coherent propagation of the Cooper pairs with lowest possible speeds and thus hindrances are minimized. This leads to the superconducting state.

    (f) BCS theory explains why superconductivity is a high temperature, high magnetic field phenomenon.

31. Differentiate between type-I and type-II superconductors.

32. What is superconductivity? Differentiate between type-I and type-II super-conductors.

33. Explain the phenomenon of superconductivity. Explain type-I and type-II superconductors.

34. Explain type-I and type-II superconductors.

35. Differentiate between type-I and type-II superconductors, on the basis of their response to the magnetic field and exhibition of the Meissner effect. Support your explanation with the figures.

36. State the applications of superconductivity. Explain any one of them.

37. Explain any two applications of superconductivity.

38. State the applications of superconductivity. Explain any one of them.

39. Explain the phenomenon of superconductivity. State any two applications of superconductivity.

40. Elaborate on any two applications of superconductors.

41. Write a note on Josephson effect.

Unit - III

CHAPTER 5
THERMODYNAMICS

5.1 INTRODUCTION

The branch of physics which deals with the heat in motion is called **Thermodynamics**. Also, Thermodynamics can be defined as a subject that deals with exchange of mass, mechanical work and other form of energy between a system and its surroundings. The principles of thermodynamics are very general and give a relation between heat and various forms of energy like electrical chemical, optical etc.

A system can be defined as a portion of matter or region of space separated from other objects, to which the attention is focused and the physical parameters are discussed. A system may be (i) closed or (ii) open or (iii) isolated. In a closed system the matter is not exchanged but energy can be exchanged with surroundings. The best example of a closed system is a mass of gases enclosed in a cylinder by means of a piston. Here no mass can flow in or out but by pushing the piston in or out the mechanical work can be done.

On other hand when mass and energy both are exchanged with the surroundings the system is said to be open system. In an air compressor, air enters in with low pressure and exits with high pressure. Thus both, energy as well as mass is exchanged with surroundings.

When a system does not exchange energy and mass, both, with the surroundings the system is called isolated system.

5.2 ZEROTH LAW OF THERMODYNAMICS

When two bodies are in contact with each other and no exchange of heat takes place between them, they are said to be in thermal equilibrium.

The 'Zeroth Law of Thermodynamics' states that of two systems are in thermodynamic equilibrium with a third system, the two original systems are in thermal equilibrium with each other. Basically, if a system A is in thermal equilibrium with system C and system B is also in thermal equilibrium with system C, the system A and B are in thermal equilibrium with each other. The Fig. 5.1 illustrates the zeroth law of thermodynamics.

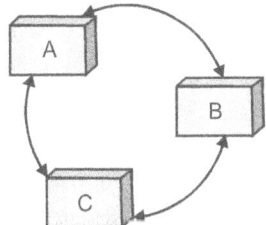

Fig. 5.1 : Zeroth law of Thermodynamics

The zeroth law logically provides the basis for first and second laws of thermodynamics and is assumed in these laws. Also it forms the basis of temperature.

5.3 FIRST LAW OF THERMODYNAMICS

The first law of thermodynamics is based on the principles of conservation of energy. Here, we are interested in the conservation of heat into work and establish equivalence between mechanical work and the thermal energy.

According to the '**First Law of Thermodynamics**', a finite amount of mechanical work is needed to produce definite amount of heat and vice versa, i.e. the ratio of the work done and the heat produced is always constant. It W is the work done in producing amount of heat H, according to the first law.

$$W \propto Q$$

or

$$\frac{W}{Q} = J \qquad \text{....(i)}$$

Where J is the proportionality constant and is known as Joule's constant. This is also called mechanical equivalent or heat and is equal to the amount of work done required to produce unit quantity of heat.

The value of J is 4.2×10^7 of erg/cal in C.G.S and 4.2 Joules/cal in M.K.S system.

When heat is supplied to a system, a part of the heat energy is used to increase the internal energy of the system, thereby raising the temperature and the rest is used for doing external work. If U_i and U_f are initial and final internal energy of the system respectively, then the work done is,

$$Q = U_f - U_i + W \qquad \text{...(ii)}$$

If the heat supplied is very small i.e. dQ the increate in the internal energy is dU and work done dW, then.

$$dQ = dU + dW \qquad \text{...(iii)}$$

This is differential form of the first law of thermodynamics.

5.4 DETERMINATION OF J BY JOULE'S METHOD

The aim of experiment was to determine the ratio between work done and heat produced. The Joule's experiment was performed to,
- establish that the heat is a form of energy and is not a material substance like caloric fluid.
- always same amount of heat is produced by a given amount of mechanical work.

Construction : The apparatus consists of a specially designed calorimeter placed in a wooden box C with felt to avoid heat losses to the surroundings. A number of vanes, VV projects from the walls of the calorimeter in its interior. A spindle carrying a number of boxes peddles PP act as a churner and it is so pivoted at the bottom that the peddle PP are capable of turning between the fixed vanes V. The spindle can be attached to a drums D by means of screw S' wherever desired. The drum D can be rotated by the handle H or by the falling weights WW which are attached to two pieces of string passing over the pulleys; P_1 and P_2 and wrapped round the drum. Two vertical scales are fixed to note the vertical distances through which the weights falls.

Working : The two weights WW are allowed to fall through a height 'h'. In doing so, they turn the spindle and thereby turn the paddles PP immersed in a known mass (m) of water contained in calorimeter. The water is thus churned but not allowed to rotate due to fixed vanes and the potential energy of the falling weight is converted into kinetic energy of paddles. Due to friction offered by paddles, kinetic energy is converted into heat. As a result of it, the temperature of the water in calorimeter rises. The rise, in the temperature is measured by an accurate thermometer T inserted in the calorimeter. The process is rapidly repeated several times such that there is an accurately measurable rise in the temperature of water.

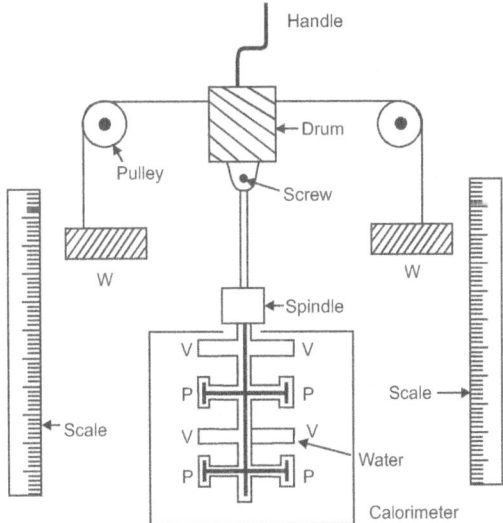

Fig. 5.2 : Determination of J

Observation and Calculation :

The water equivalent of calorimeter = W g

Mass of the water in the calorimeter = M g

Mass of each weight falling down = m g

Height through which weight falls = h m

Number of falls = n

Rise in temperature of water = t°C.

The work down by falling weights.
$$W = n \times (mgh + mgh)$$
$$W = 2nmgh \quad \ldots(i)$$

Heat produced product = Heat gained by water + Heat gained by calorimeter
$$Q = MSt + Wt$$
$$Q = (MS + W)t \quad \ldots(ii)$$

Where, S = Specific heat capacity of water

As,
$$J = \frac{W}{Q} \quad \ldots(iii)$$

Substituting (i) and (ii)
$$J = \frac{2nmgh}{(MS + W)t}$$

Here it is assumed that the whole of potential energy lost by the falling weight is given to the water.

But in practice some of the potential energy lost is converted into kinetic energy of the weights. If v is the velocity of each weight before reaching the ground, the kinetic energy aquired by each weight will be v. Thus the kinetic energy of both the weights will be mv^2 (i.e. $\frac{1}{2}mv^2 + \frac{1}{2}mv^2$) Hence the actual energy transmitted to the water will be $2mgh-mv^2$.

$$\therefore \quad J = \frac{(2mgh - mv^2)n}{(MS + W)t} \quad \ldots(iv)$$

5.5 APPLICATIONS OF FIRST LAW OF THERMODYNAMICS

(i) Adiabatic Relation : From the first law of thermodynamic
$$dQ = dU + PdV \quad \ldots(i)$$

But
$$dU = C_v \, dT$$

and for an adiabatic process $dQ = 0$

$$\therefore \quad C_v \, dT + pdV = 0$$

For one more of an ideal gas
$$P = \frac{RT}{V}$$

$$\therefore \quad C_v \, dT + \frac{RT}{V} d_1 V = 0$$

But $\quad C_p - C_v = R$

$$\therefore C_v dT + \frac{(C_p - C_v) T dV}{V} = 0$$

$$C_v V\, dT + (C_p - C_v) T\, dV = 0$$

or, $\quad V\, dT + \left(\dfrac{C_p}{C_v} - 1\right) T\, dV = 0$

$$(\gamma - 1)\frac{dV}{V} = -\frac{dT}{T} \qquad \text{where } \gamma = \frac{C_p}{C_v}$$

Integrating

$$(\gamma - 1) \ln V = -\ln T + \ln A$$

where A is a constant

$$\ln V^{\gamma-1} = -\ln T + \ln A$$
$$\ln TV^{\gamma-1} = \ln A$$

or $\quad TV^{\gamma-1} = A \qquad\qquad\qquad (ii)$

As $\quad T = \dfrac{PV}{R}$

$$\frac{PV}{R} V^{\gamma-1} = A$$

$$PV^{\gamma} = AR = B \qquad\qquad\qquad (iii)$$

Also, $\quad V = \dfrac{RT}{P}$

$$\therefore P\left(\frac{RT}{P}\right)^{\gamma} = B$$

$$T^{\gamma} P^{1-\gamma} = \frac{C}{R^{\gamma}} C$$

$$\frac{T^{\gamma}}{P^{\gamma-1}} = C \qquad\qquad\qquad (iv)$$

where A, B, and C are constants

The eq. (2), (3) & (4) are known as adiabatic relations of an ideal gas.

(ii) Modulus of Elasticity :

The bulk modulus of elasticity of a gas is defined as

$$K = \frac{-dP}{dV|v} = -V\frac{dP}{dV} \qquad\qquad\qquad (i)$$

Expressing P as a function of temperature T and volume V,

$$P = f(T, V) \qquad \text{(ii)}$$

Therefore,

$$dP = \left(\frac{\delta P}{\delta T}\right)_V dT + \left(\frac{\delta P}{\delta V}\right)_T dV$$

for an isothermal process, dT = 0

$$\therefore \quad dP = \left(\frac{\delta P}{\delta V}\right)_T dV$$

$$\therefore \quad \frac{dP}{dV} = \left(\frac{\delta P}{\delta V}\right)_T$$

But, $\qquad PV = RT \quad \text{or} \quad P = \frac{RT}{V}$

$$\therefore \quad \left(\frac{\delta P}{\delta V}\right)_T = RT \frac{d}{dv}\left(\frac{1}{V}\right)$$

$$\left(\frac{\delta P}{\delta V}\right)_T = \frac{-RT}{V^2} = -\frac{PV}{V^2}$$

$$\left(\frac{\delta P}{\delta V}\right)_T = \frac{P}{V} \qquad \text{(iii)}$$

Hence the isothermal bulk modulus is given by

$$K_{iso} = -V \left(\frac{\delta P}{\delta V}\right)_T$$

$$K_{iso} = -V \left(-\frac{P}{V}\right) = P \qquad \text{...(iv)}$$

For an adiabatic process

$$PV^\gamma = B \text{ (constant)}$$

$$\therefore \quad P = \frac{B}{V^\gamma}$$

$$\left(\frac{dP}{dV}\right)_{adia.} = \frac{B \, d}{dV}(V^{-\gamma})$$

$$= -\gamma P V^\gamma V^{-\gamma-1}$$

$$= -\gamma P v^{-1}$$

$$= -\frac{\gamma P}{V} \qquad \text{...(v)}$$

So the adiabatic bulk method is

$$K_{adia} = -V\left(\frac{dP}{dV}\right)_{adia.}$$

$$= -V\left(-\frac{\gamma P}{V}\right)$$

$$= \gamma P \qquad \ldots(vi)$$

From (5) and (6)

$$\frac{K_{adia}}{K_{iso}} = \frac{\gamma P}{P} = \gamma \qquad \ldots(vii)$$

5.6 CARNOT'S CYCLE AND CARNOTS ENGINE

For theoretical explanation Carnot assumed an ideal heat engine, free from all imperfection of an actual engine. As it is not possible to achieve this in practice, so he made some assumption about ideal engine. An ideal engine consists of

- A cylinder of perfectly non-conducting wall and perfectly conducting bottom.
- The moment of piston is in horizontal direction and is frictionless.
- The working substance is air which is supposed to behave like a perfect gas.
- A source of heat of constant temperature.
- A sink which receives the rejected heat at a constant temperature T_2.
- An insulating cap which can be connected to the bottom of the cylinder.

Carnot Cycle

The working substance receives some heat from the source, a major part of it is converted into mechanical work and the remaining heat is rejected to the sink. The Carnot's engine works in following four stage called **Carnot Cycle**.

The Fig. (a) shows Carnot's engine and Fig. (b) shows Carnot's cycle

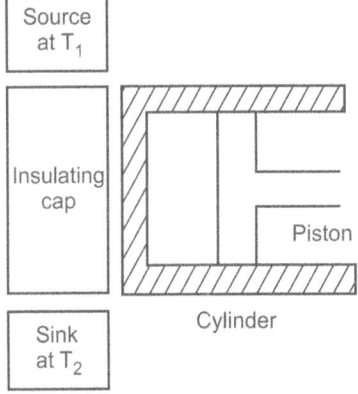

Fig. 5.3(1) : Carnot's Engine

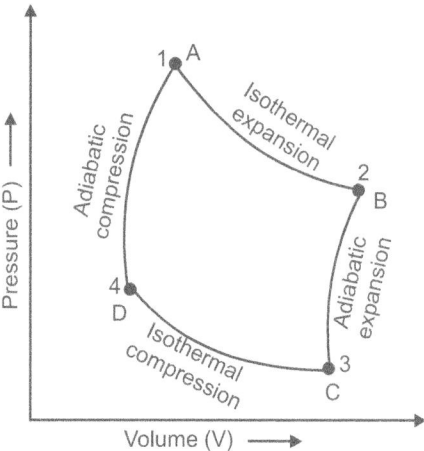

Fig. 5.3 (2) : Carnot's cycle

Let us assume that the mass of air enclosed in the cylinder is m. The starting point of the cycle is A, at which the volume, pressure and temperature of gas is V, P, and T_1 respectively.

(1) First Stage

The insulating cap is removed and the cylinder bottom is connected to the source. The piston is made to move slowly in outward direction. Due to this the expansion of the gas takes place and, therefore, the temperature of gas falls. The low temperature gas absorbs the heat from the source at constant temperature. This represents isothermal expansion (portion AB of the graph). If the heat absorbed by the gas is Q_1, The work done will be,

The work done by the air, W_1

$$= mRT_1 \log_e\left(\frac{V_2}{V_1}\right) \quad \ldots \text{(I)}$$

Where, V_1 and V_2 are volumes of gas before and after expansion

$$\therefore \quad Q_1 = \frac{MRT_1 \log_e\left(\frac{V_2}{V_1}\right)}{J} \quad \ldots \text{(II)}$$

Take $1/J$ = A (Constant)

$$\therefore \quad Q_1 = MRT_1 A \log_e\left(\frac{V_2}{V_1}\right) \quad \ldots \text{(III)}$$

(2) Second Stage

Now, the source is removes and the non-conducting cap is brought is contact with the bottom of the cylinder. The air is allowed to expand in further. This is a diabatic expansion as no heat is exchanged with surroundings. Therefore, the work done during this stage (portion BC of the graph) is,

$$W_2 = \frac{P_2 V_2 - P_3 V_3}{\gamma - 1} \quad \ldots (I)$$

$$W_2 = \frac{mR(T_1 - T_2)}{\gamma - 1} \quad \ldots (II)$$

(3) Third Stage

Now the insulating cap is removed and the sink is brought in contact with the bottom of the cylinder which is at temperature T_2. The air is now compressed isothermally to a volume V_4. As the compression takes place at constant temperature T_2, the heat is rejected to the sink. Hence work done on the air (portion CD of the graph),

$$W_3 = -mRT_2 \log_e\left(\frac{V_4}{V_3}\right) \quad \ldots (V)$$

or

$$W_3 = mRT_2 \log_e\left(\frac{V_3}{V_4}\right) \quad \ldots (VI)$$

$$\therefore \quad Q_2 = \frac{mRT_2}{J} \log_e\left(\frac{V_3}{V_4}\right)$$

If $\quad \dfrac{1}{J} = A$

then

$$Q_2 = mRT_2 \, A \log_e\left(\frac{V_3}{V_4}\right) \quad \ldots (VII)$$

4. Fourth Stage

The insulating cap is again brought in contact with the bottom of the cylinder by disconnecting sink. Now the air is compressed adiabatically as no heat is exchange with surroundings. The temperature of the air rises to T_1 and the initial condition of gas is restored completing the cycle. The work done during this cycle (Portion DA of the graph) is

$$W_4 = \frac{P_4 V_4 - P_1 V_1}{\gamma - 1}$$

or

$$W_4 = \frac{mR(T_2 - T_1)}{\gamma - 1} \quad \ldots (VIII)$$

5.7 SECOND LAW OF THERMODYNAMICS

The first law of thermodynamics says that mechanical work can be converted to heat or vice-versa. But it does not tells us any thing about the conditions under which conversion of heat into work or vice-versa can take place. Also it does not give any idea about the direction of flow of heat. The second law takes care of these two conditions and can be stated as,

Clausius Statement : It is impossible, for a self-acting machine working in a cylinder process unaided by any external agency to convey heat from a body at lower temperature to a body at higher temperature.

In simple woods, heat can not flow from a cold body to a hot body without the performance of work by some external agency.

Kelvin's Statement : It is impossible to derive continuous supply of a work by cooling a body to a temperature lower than that of the coldest of its surroundings.

The above statement can be interpreted that no heat engine can convert whole of the heat energy supplied to it into useful work. The ratio of heat converted into work and the heat taken in by the engine is always less than one and is called the **Thermal Efficiency**.

5.8 ENTROPY

A P-V diagram is a useful representation of displacement work in which work is represented by an arc on the diagram. An Arrangement similar to P-V diagram can be made for heat transfer in a process by using absolute temperature and a new property called **Entropy**. This forms a thermodynamic diagram in which heat transfer is represented by an area. The concept of entropy is very useful while dealing with thermodynamic conditions of gases in engines and refrigerators.

The literature meaning of entropy is transformation and is denoted by ϕ.

In an operation either heat is rejected or received, the quantity of heat rejected or received divided by absolute temperature at that time measures the change of entropy. If a working substance is given heat Q at constant temperature T, then the increase in entropy is given by

$$d\phi = \frac{Q}{T} \qquad \ldots \text{(I)}$$

or

$$\phi_1 - \phi_2 = \frac{Q}{T} \qquad \ldots \text{(II)}$$

where, ϕ_1 = Initial entropy

and ϕ_2 = Final entropy

If small quantity of heat dQ is supplied at T K, there will be no charge in temperature T as dQ is very small. The small charge of entropy is,

$$d\phi = \frac{dQ}{T} \qquad \ldots \text{(III)}$$

By integrating we can get the total charge in entropy.

$$\int_{\phi_1}^{\phi_2} d\phi = \int_{T_1}^{T_2} \frac{dQ}{T} \qquad \ldots \text{(IV)}$$

A graph between entropy and temperature is known as temperature entropy or T-ϕ or T-S diagram. The area had the T-ϕ diagram gives the total heat diagram gives the total heat rejected or received. The Fig. 3. shows T-ϕ diagram for heating process.

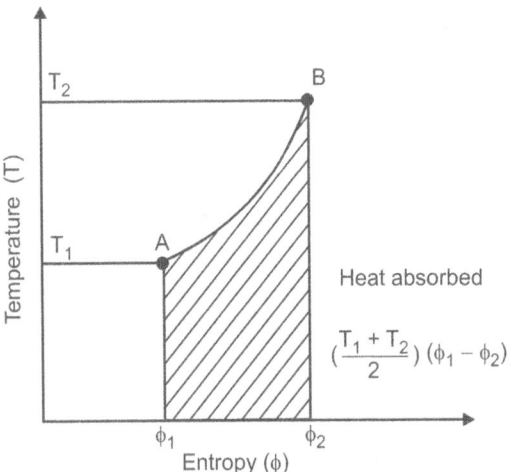

Fig. 5.4 : Entropy of a system

The change in entropy can be also defined as a measure of the rate of availability of heat for transformation into work.

The maximum work done dW obtainable from an amount of heat dQ is given by the Carnot cycle. The efficiency of Carnot cycle is given by $\left(1 - \dfrac{T_2}{T_1}\right)$.

Therefore, $\qquad dW = dQ\left(\dfrac{T_1 - T_2}{T}\right)$ ... (I)

or $\qquad dW = \dfrac{dQ}{T}$ ... (II)

The entropy is measured in heat units per degree temperature per unit mass. Generally we are not interested in absolute valve of entropy. Usually we are concerned only with change of entropy.

5.9 CHANGES IN ENTROPY IN A REVESSIBLE AND IRRVERSIBLE PROCESS

Consider a reversible process such as Carnot cycle ABCDA, shown in Fig. 2. The working substance absorbs heat energy Q_1 at temperature T_1 from A to B. As the amount of heat decreased by Q_1, at temperature T_1 from the source, the gain in the entropy of the working substance from A to B will be Q_1/T_1. As BC is an adiabatic expansion, there is no change from B to C. The working substance rejects heat Q_2 at temperature T_2 from C to D. Hence the loss of the entropy of substance is Q_2/T_2. Again, from D to A as it is adiabatic there will be no change in entropy.

Therefore the net gain in the entropy of the working substance in one compile cycle ABCDA is

$$= \dfrac{Q_1}{T_1} - \dfrac{Q_2}{T_2} \qquad \text{... (I)}$$

For reversible process we have

$$\frac{Q_1}{T_1} = \frac{Q_2}{T_2} \qquad \ldots (II)$$

Hence the charge in the entropy in a reversible process is zero i.e. in a reversible process the entropy remains same.

Consider an irreversible process such as conduction or radiation in which heat is lost by a body at higher temperature T_1 and gained by the body at lower temperature T_2 ($T_1 > T_2$).

If at temperature T_2 heat gained by the body is Q and at temperature T_1, the heat lost by the body is Q. Considering hot and cold bodies as one system.

Gain in entropy of the cold body $= \dfrac{Q}{T_1}$

Loss of entropy of the hot body $= \dfrac{Q}{T_2}$

Therefore, the net change in the entropy of the system,

$$= \frac{Q}{T_2} - \frac{Q}{T_1}$$

As $T_1 > T_2$, the change in the entropy is positive quantity. Thus we can say entropy increases in all irreversible process.

SOLVED EXAMPLES

Example 5.1 : A heat engine operates between two thermal reservoirs which are at 900 K and 300 K. The heat engine receives 500 kJ heat from the source and rejects 300 kJ to heat sink at 300 K. Determine if this heat engine violates the second law of thermodynamics on the basis of (a) Clausius inequality and (b) the Carnot principle.

Solution :

Refer Fig. 5.30.

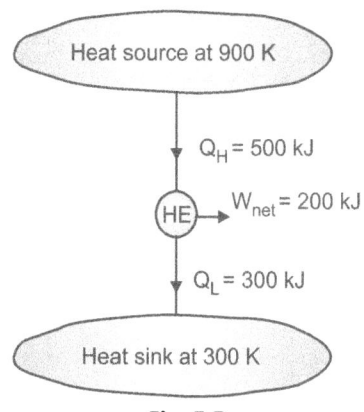

Fig. 5.5

(a) The cyclic integral of $\dfrac{\delta Q}{T}$ for the heat-engine cycle under consideration is,

$$\oint \dfrac{\delta Q}{T} = \dfrac{Q_H}{T_H} - \dfrac{Q_L}{T_L} = \dfrac{500 \text{ kJ}}{900 \text{ K}} - \dfrac{300 \text{ kJ}}{300 \text{ K}}$$

$$= -0.444 \text{ kJ/kg}$$

The value is negative, this satisfies the Clausius inequality and the second law of thermodynamics.

(b) To check Carnot principle,

$$\eta_{th} = 1 - \dfrac{Q_L}{Q_H} = 1 - \dfrac{300}{500} = 0.4$$

$$\eta_{th\,rev} = 1 - \dfrac{T_L}{T_H} = 1 - \dfrac{300}{900} = 0.66$$

The efficiency of reversible engine (0.66) is higher than the efficiency of actual heat engine (0.4) i.e. $\eta_{th} < \eta_{th\,rev}$. The cycle that violates the Clausius inequality will also violate the Carnot principle.

Example 5.2 : In a heat exchanger, water flows through a tube which is surrounded by air. Water at 80°C and 1 bar pressure rejects 600 kJ heat to the air at 300 K. Assume the heat exchanger is insulated (water rejects heat to air only). Air flows through shell-side of the heat exchanger. Determine (a) the entropy change of the water, (b) the entropy change of air during the process and (c) whether this process is reversible, irreversible or impossible.

Solution :

(a) The temperature of flowing water is 80°C. Therefore, the entropy change of water during internally reversible, isothermal process (since temperature of water at 80°C will not change) can be found.

$$\Delta s_{water} = \dfrac{Q_{water}}{T_{water}} = \dfrac{-600 \text{ kJ}}{(80 + 273) \text{ K}} = -1.69 \text{ kJ/K}$$

Q_{water} is negative, since heat is rejected.

(b) The entropy change of air

Q_{air} = +600 kJ as it receives.

$$\Delta s_{air} = \dfrac{Q_{air}}{T_{air}} = \dfrac{600 \text{ kJ}}{300 \text{ K}} = 2.0 \text{ kJ/K}$$

(c) The total change of entropy for this process

$$\Delta s_{Total} = \Delta s_{water} + \Delta s_{air}$$

$$= -1.69 + 2.0 = 0.31 \text{ kJ/K}$$

The total energy change of the whole process is positive. Hence, it is an irreversible process.

Example 5.3 : A 100 kg iron casting at 600 K is put into a well having a large quantity of water at 285 K. Eventually, the iron casting attains thermal equilibrium with well water. The specific heat of cast iron is 0.5 kJ/kg·K. Determine (a) Entropy change of the cast iron block, (b) Entropy change of well water, (c) Total entropy change for this process.

Solution :

(a) Cast iron block is treated as incompressible substance.

$$\Delta s_{iron} = m(s_2 - s_1) = m \cdot c_{av} \log\left(\frac{T_2}{T_1}\right)$$

$$= 100 \text{ kg} \times 0.5 \text{ kJ/kg·K} \ln\left(\frac{285}{600}\right)$$

$$= -37.2 \text{ kJ/K}$$

(b) The well water acts as a thermal reservoir which does not experience increase in temperature.

$$Q_{iron} = m \cdot c_{av} \cdot (T_2 - T_1)$$

$$= 100 \times 0.5 \times (285 - 600)$$

$$= -15750 \text{ kJ}$$

$$Q_{well} = -Q_{iron} = +15750 \text{ kJ}$$

$$\Delta s_{well} = \frac{Q_{well}}{T_{well}} = \frac{15750 \text{ kJ}}{285 \text{ K}} = \mathbf{55.2 \text{ kJ/K}}$$

(c) The total entropy change for the process is,

$$\Delta s_{total} = \Delta s_{iron} + \Delta s_{well}$$

$$= -37.2 + 55.0 = \mathbf{18 \text{ kJ/K}}$$

The total entropy change is positive, hence the process is irreversible.

Example 5.4 : An iron cube at a temperature of 400°C is dropped into an insulated bath containing 10 kg water at 25°C. The water finally reaches a temperature of 50°C at steady state. Given that the specific heat of water is equal to 4186 J/kg·K. Find the entropy changes for the iron cube and the water. Is the process reversible? If so why?

Solution :

Given : Temperature of iron cube = 400°C = 673 K

Temperature of water = 25°C = 298 K

Mass of water = 10 kg

Temperature of water and cube after equilibrium = 50°C = 323 K

Specific heat of water, c_{pw} = 4186 J/kg·K

Entropy Changes for the Iron Cube and the Water :

Now, Heat lost by iron cube = Heat gained by water

$$m_i \, c_{pi} \, (673 - 323) = m_w \, c_{pw} \, (323 - 298)$$
$$= 10 \times 4186 \, (323 - 298)$$

$$\therefore \quad m_i \, c_{pi} = \frac{10 \times 4186 \, (323 - 298)}{(623 - 323)} = 2990$$

where, m_i = Mass of iron, kg, and
c_{pi} = Specific heat of iron, J/kg·K

The iron cube rejects heat = Q_{iron}

The entropy of iron = $m_i c_{pi} \ln\left(\frac{T_2}{T_1}\right)$

(a) Entropy of iron at 673 K = $m_i \, c_{pi} \ln\left(\frac{T_2}{T_1}\right)$

$$= 2990 \ln\left(\frac{323}{673}\right)$$
$$= \mathbf{-2195 \, J/K}$$

Water receives heat (Q_w is positive).

(b) Entropy of water at 298 K = $m_w \cdot c_{pw} \ln\left(\frac{T_2}{T_1}\right)$

$$= 10 \times 4186 \ln\left(\frac{298}{273}\right) = 10 \times 4186 \ln\left(\frac{323}{298}\right)$$
$$= \mathbf{3372 \, J/K}$$

(c) The total entropy change for the process is,

$$\Delta s_{total} = \Delta s_{iron} + \Delta s_{water}$$
$$= -2195 + 3372$$
$$= 1177 \, J/K$$

Net change in entropy = 3372.24 − 2195

Net change in entropy = 3372.24 − 2195 = **1177.24 J/K**

Since Δs > 0, hence, the process is **Irreversible.**

Example 5.5 : An ideal gas is heated from temperature T_1 to T_2 by keeping its volume constant. The gas is expanded back to its initial temperature according to the law pv^n = constant. If the entropy changes in the two processes are equal, find the value of n in terms of the adiabatic index γ.

Solution :

Change in entropy during constant volume process

$$= m\, c_v \ln\left(\frac{T_2}{T_1}\right) \qquad \ldots (i)$$

Change in entropy during polytropic process (pv^n = constant)

$$= m\, c_v\left(\frac{\gamma - n}{n - 1}\right)\ln\left(\frac{T_2}{T_1}\right) \qquad \ldots (ii)$$

For the same entropy, equating (i) and (ii), we have

$$\frac{\gamma - n}{n - 1} = 1$$

or $(\gamma - n) = (n - 1)$ or $2n = \gamma + 1$

$$\therefore \quad n = \frac{\gamma + 1}{2}$$

Example 5.6 : 1 kg of air has a volume of 56 litres and a temperature of 190°C. The air then receives heat at constant pressure until its temperature becomes 500°C. From this state the air rejects heat at constant volume until its pressure is reduced to 700 kN/m². Determine the change of entropy during each process stating whether it is on increase or decrease.

Take c_p = 1.006 kJ/kg·K and c_v = 0.717 kJ/kg·K

Solution :

Given :

Mass of air = m = 1 kg.
Initial volume of air = V_1 = 56 litres
Initial temperature of air = T_1 = 190 + 273 = 463 K
Final temperature of air = T_2 = 500 + 273 = 773 K
Final pressure of air = p_3 = 700 kN/m²

Calculate : (i) Change of entropy during each process.

The given process is drawn in Fig. 5.6.

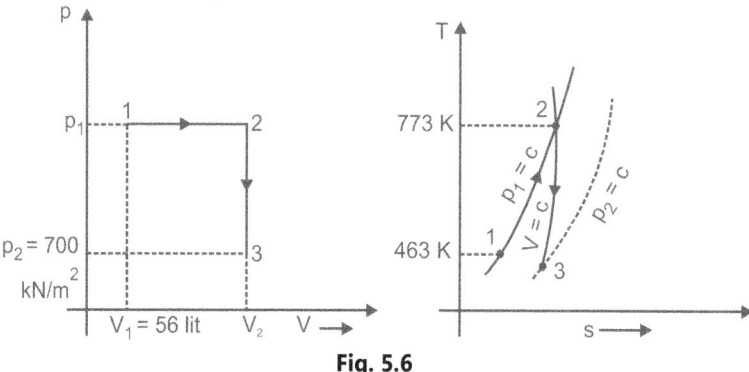

Fig. 5.6

For Process 1-2 (Constant Pressure Process) :

$$p_1 = p_2$$

By general gas equation,

$$\frac{p_1 V_1}{T_1} = \frac{p_2 V_2}{T_2}$$

$$\therefore \quad \frac{V_1}{T_1} = \frac{V_2}{T_1}$$

$$V_2 = \frac{V_1}{T_1} \times T_2 = \frac{56 \times 10^{-3}}{463} \times 773$$

$$\therefore \quad V_2 = 0.09353 \text{ m}^3$$

Using the equation of change of entropy,

$$s_2 - s_1 = mc_v \cdot \log_e \frac{T_2}{T_1} + mR \log \frac{V_2}{V_1}$$

$$= 1 \times 0.717 \log \frac{773}{463} + 1(1.006 - 0.717) \log \frac{0.09353}{0.056}$$

$$= 0.3675 + 0.48268$$

$$= \mathbf{0.85 \text{ kJ/kg·K (Increase)}}$$

Process 2-3 (Constant Volume) : $V_2 = V_3$

From general gas equation,

$$p_2 V_2 = mRT_2$$

$$\therefore \quad p_2 = \frac{mRT_2}{V_2} = \frac{1 \times 0.289 \times 773}{0.09353}$$

$$= \mathbf{2388.51 \text{ kN/m}^2}$$

and

$$\frac{p_2 V_2}{T_2} = \frac{p_3 V_3}{T_3}$$

$$\frac{p_2}{T_2} = \frac{p_3}{T_3} (\because V_2 = V_3)$$

$$\therefore \quad T_3 = \frac{p_3 T_2}{p_2} = \frac{700 \times 773}{2388.51}$$

$$T_3 = 226.54 \text{ K}$$

Using the equation of change of entropy,

$$s_3 - s_2 = mc_p \cdot \log_e \frac{T_3}{T_2} - mR \cdot \log_e \frac{p_3}{p_2}$$

$$= 1 \times 1.006 \log \frac{226.54}{773} - 1 \times 0.289 \log \frac{700}{2388.51}$$

$$= -1.23472 - (-0.3547)$$

$$= \mathbf{-0.88002 \text{ kJ/kg·K (Decrease)}}$$

Example 5.7 : A mass 'm' kg of a gas at temperature T_1 K is isobarically and adiabatically mixed with an equal mass of same gas at temperature T_2 K ($T_1 > T_2$). Show that the change in entropy of the universe during the process is given by :

$$(\Delta s)_{uni} = 2m \cdot c_p \ln\left[\frac{T_1 + T_2}{2\sqrt{T_1 \cdot T_2}}\right]$$

Solution :

Consider 'm' kg of gas at temperature T_1 in the compartment (A) and same mass i.e. 'm' kg of gas at temperature T_2 in another compartment (B). The gas from (A) and (B) is allowed to mix together as shown in Fig. 5.32.

The gases in compartment (A) and compartment (B) are allowed to mix together as shown in Fig. 5.32.

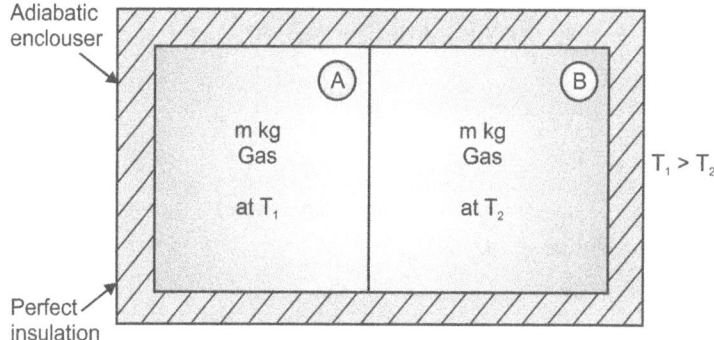

Fig. 5.7

Let the temperature of gas after mixing be T_3.

Heat given out by gas at T_1 = Heat lost by gas at T_2

∴ $mc_p(T_1 - T_3) = mc_p(T_3 - T_2)$

∴ $T_3 = \dfrac{T_1 + T_2}{2}$ ... (1)

(a) The change of entropy of gas in compartment (A) at constant pressure,

$$(\Delta s)_A = \int_{T_1}^{T_3} \frac{dQ}{T} = \int_{T_1}^{T_3} \frac{m \cdot c_p}{T} dT = mc_p \cdot \log_e \frac{T_3}{T_1} \quad ...(2)$$

(b) The change of entropy of gas in compartment (B),

$$(\Delta s)_B = \int_{T_2}^{T_3} \frac{m \cdot c_p}{T} dT = mc_p \cdot \log_e \frac{T_3}{T_2} \quad ...(3)$$

(c) The change of entropy of surroundings $(\Delta s)_{surr} = 0$ because it is an adiabatic process.

$$\therefore (\Delta s)_{universe} = (\Delta s)_A + (\Delta s)_B + (\Delta s)_{surr}$$

$$= m \cdot c_p \cdot \log_e \frac{T_3}{T_1} + m \cdot c_p \cdot \log_e \frac{T_3}{T_2} + 0 \quad \ldots (4)$$

Substituting value of T_3 from equation (1) in equation (4), we get,

$$(\Delta s)_{universe} = mc_p \left[\log_e \frac{T_1 + T_2}{2T_1} + \log_e \frac{T_1 + T_2}{2T_2} \right]$$

$$\therefore (\Delta s)_{universe} = mc_p \left[\log_e \left(\frac{T_1 + T_2}{2T_1} \right) + \log_e \left(\frac{T_1 + T_2}{2T_2} \right) \right]$$

$$= mc_p \cdot \log_e \left[\frac{(T_1 + T_2)^2}{(2\sqrt{T_1 T_2})^2} \right]$$

$$= mc_p \log_e \left[\frac{T_1 + T_2}{2\sqrt{T_1 T_2}} \right]^2$$

$$(\Delta s)_{universe} = 2 \cdot m \cdot c_p \log_e \left[\frac{T_1 + T_2}{2\sqrt{T_1 T_2}} \right] \quad \ldots (5)$$

Hence proved.

5.10 THIRD LAW OF THERMODYNAMICS

In all the heat engines there is always some heat loss due to radiation, condition or friction. Hence in a cycle, the change in entropy, is not zero but a positive quantity. As the engine cycle is repeated, the entropy of the system keeps on increasing and tends to a maximum value. Once the state of maximum entropy is reached, the engine no more can do any work and stage of stagnancy is reached.

With the increase in entropy, the disorder of the molecules of a substance increases. The heat is disordered energy. The measure of the disorder of the system in terms of mathematical concept is called **Entropy**. In short the energy becomes heat as soon as it is disordered.

The molecules of gases have more freedom as compared to liquid, therefore entropy of gas is more as compared to liquid. Same way entropy of liquid is more as compared to liquid.

As the temperature tends to absolute zero, the entropy tends to zero as the molecules are almost ordered. This is called **Third Law of Thermodynamics**.

SUMMARY

- The branch pf physics which deals with the heat in notice is called thermodynamics.
- If two systems are in thermodynamic equilibrium with a third system, the two systems are in thermal equilibrium with each other. – Zeroth Law of Thermodynamics.
- A finite amount of mechanical works is needed to produce definite amount of heat and vice-versa. – First Law of Thermodynamics.
- The heat can not flow from a cold body to hot body without the performance of work by some external agency.
- The measure of the disorder of the system is called entropy.
- The entropy in a reversible process is zero.
- The entropy in an irreversible process is positive.
- As temperature tends to absolute zero, the entropy tends to zero as the molecules are almost ordered. – Third Law of Thermodynamics

EXCERCIES

1. State and explain first law of thermodynamics.
2. What is zeroth law of thermodynamics.
3. Describe a method of determination the value of J.
4. State the second law of thermodynamics.
5. Explain any two application of first law of thermodynamics.
6. What do you understand by reversible and irreversible process.
7. Discuss entropy in reversible and irreversible process.
8. What are different stages of Carnot cycle ?
9. Discuss working of Carnot's engine.
10. What is entropy ? Discuss entropy is a reversible and irreversible process.
11. What is third law of thermodynamics ? Discuss it in detail.

✠ ✠ ✠

CHAPTER 6
NANOSCIENCE

6.1 INTRODUCTION

Nano, Greek for **'dwarf'**, means one billionth. The measurement at this level is in nanometer (abbreviated "nm") – billionth of a meter. To get a sense of nanoscale, a human hair measures roughly 75,000 nm, a bacterial cell measures a few hundred nanometers. On the other side, ten hydrogen atoms lined up end-to-end make up 1 nm. The smallest thing which can be seen with naked human eye is of the order of 10,000 nm.

'Nanoscience' is the study of the fundamental principles of molecules and structures with at least one dimension is in the size range of 1 to 100 nm. These structures are known as **'nanostructures'**. The research and application of the nanostructures into nanoscale devices is called **'nanotechnology'**.

6.2 NANOPARTICLES

An atom or small molecule in the form of vapour is smaller than a nanometer in size. But as they are in gaseous form and their molecules are not in arranged manner, hence do not fall in category of nanoscience. The nanostructures are the smallest solid things that is possible to make. At nanoscale, most of the physical properties like conductivity, hardness or melting point are totally different than when they are in gaseous or crystal form. At nanoscale these properties depend on not only on the material but also the size of the nanostructure.

At such a size, the classical Newtonian mechanics or thermodynamics is not able to explain the observed properties. So one has to apply quantum mechanics to explain the properties of nanoscale materials.

The basic nanoscience is not new, the chemist have been doing nanoscience for hundreds of years. The stained glass windows in medieval charges contain different size gold nano particles. The different size gold particles created different colours as orange, purple, red or greenish in the glass. The new about current nanoscience is aggressive focus on developing applied technology and the right tools for doing it.

Here, we will be studying different properties, methods of synthesis and applications of nanotechnology.

6.3 PROPERTIES OF NANOPARTICLES

The properties of nanoparticles are different from the properties when they are in bulk form (crystal) or in vapour form (gas). The nanoparticles are the smallest solid things possible to make. The properties of the materials are size dependent when it is below critical size (usually less than 100 nm). At such a small size, the shape of the nanostructure also decides the property of the material. By making nanomaterials of different size and shape, one can obtain desired property. These properties can be used in many applications in the fields of science, engineering, medicine and environment. Some of the major properties are as follows.

6.3.1 Optical

The stained glasses are made by mixing small amount of metal particles like gold, cobalt, nickel, etc. Basically, glass is transparent and the colour appearing on the glass is due to nanoparticles of metals of different sizes. The colour of nanoparticles are different from the colour of bulk material. When nanoparticles of gold are formed, they give bright red colour instead of yellow as it appears in bulk form.

In 1908, G. Mie explained the phenomenon by using classical electromagnetic theory. When a beam of light of intensity I_o and wavelength λ passes through a medium, the transmitted intensity is given by,

$$I = I_o e^{-\mu x} \quad \ldots (I)$$

where μ is the **'extinction coefficient'** and depends on number of particles in medium, volume of colloidal particles and extinction cross-section of a particle.

When the light is passed through a medium, a fraction is absorbed and a part is scattered, hence the extinction cross-section is the sum of **'absorption extinction'** and **'scattered extinction cross-section'**. The scattering coefficient of the light depends on wavelength λ and the absorption coefficient depends inversely on the volume of the colloidal particles i.e. $1/V$ or $1/R^3$ and dielectric constant.

Thus, the absorption is independent of particle size. This theory explained the observation of absorption of light for metal nanoparticle in visible range. But for particles of size less than ~10 nm failed to explain the size dependency of the optical properties. The Drude model explained the particle size dependency of optical properties. For explaining it he assumed that the dielectric constant not only depends on frequency but also on particle size. According to the Drude model, the electrons can be considered as plasma.

6.3.2 Electrical

The ease with which the material can conduct electricity is called **'conductivity'**. The conductivity of any material depends on the number of charge carriers, charge, mass of charge carrier and the relaxation time (time between two collisions with ion core). The inverse of conductivity is called **'resistivity'**.

When a voltage V is applied across the conductor, current flowing through it is given by Ohm's law and gives a linear graph as shown in Fig. 6.1 (a). But for nanoparticles, the variation of current with changing voltage is as shown in Fig. 6.1 (b).

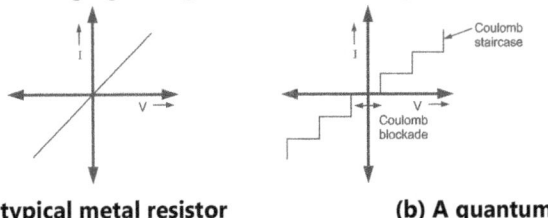

(a) A typical metal resistor (b) A quantum dot

Fig. 6.1 : Voltage versus current

If the dimensions of metal piece is reduced to 100 nm or less, there appears a region around zero voltage for which there is no current.

The electrons are transferred when the voltage is $\pm$ e/2C. A single electron is transferred by tunneling when the voltage is $\pm$ e/2C. Therefore, when the voltage is less than this, electrons cannot be transferred. This gives a region of zero current at low bias voltage and is known as **'Coulomb blockade region'**. The repeated tunneling of single electron produces **'Coulomb staircase'**.

In general, electrical resistivity of materials having nanosized grain is larger than the polycrystalline materials. When electrons are moving, they get scattered at grain boundaries. This results in higher resistivity. The materials having nanosized grains have larger number of grain boundaries than polycrystalline materials. This results in higher resistivity in materials having nanosized grains.

6.3.3 Magnetic

Basically, magnetism in bulk material is due to orbital and spin motion of the electrons around the nucleus. The magnetic materials have magnetic domains. Depending upon orientation of domains, magnetic materials are classified as paramagnetic or ferromagnetic materials. The magnetic materials have these domains to minimize the total magnetostatic energy of the system. Bulk of ferromagnetic materials have spontaneously magnetized domains. When the particle size is less than a critical size, domain formation is not favoured and material prefers to be single domain.

The single domain particles do not show coercivity or hysteresis. These type of particles are known as **'superparamagnetic particles'**. Fig. 6.2 shows magnetization of superpara-magnetic material on the application of external magnetic field.

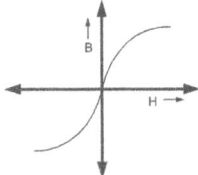

Fig. 6.2 : Magnetization of superparamagnetic particles

In superparamagnetic particles, spins are oriented in one direction and switches coherently in the opposite direction on the application of external magnetic field. Thus, we will get a curve as shown in Fig. 6.2 with no coercive field.

The nanoparticles have large surface to volume ratio. At the surfaces, the symmetry and lattice constant change. Due to this, some materials show ferromagnetic behaviour which are not ferromagnetic in the bulk form.

6.3.4 Structural

Starting with an individual atom, one can make bulk material by putting atoms in some particular manner. In nanostructures, small number of atoms are placed in the manner which is different from the arrangement of atoms in the bulk form. Thus, the nanoparticles are not just the fragments of bulk materials and have different structures. The structure formed is mainly affected by temperature and pressure. Starting from few atoms, nanoparticles undergo structural changes till they reach the bulk material. Fig. 6.3 (a) shows structural formation in silicon. The formation is not as the fragment of unit cell as shown in Fig. 6.3 (b) but is totally different as shown in Fig. 6.3 (c).

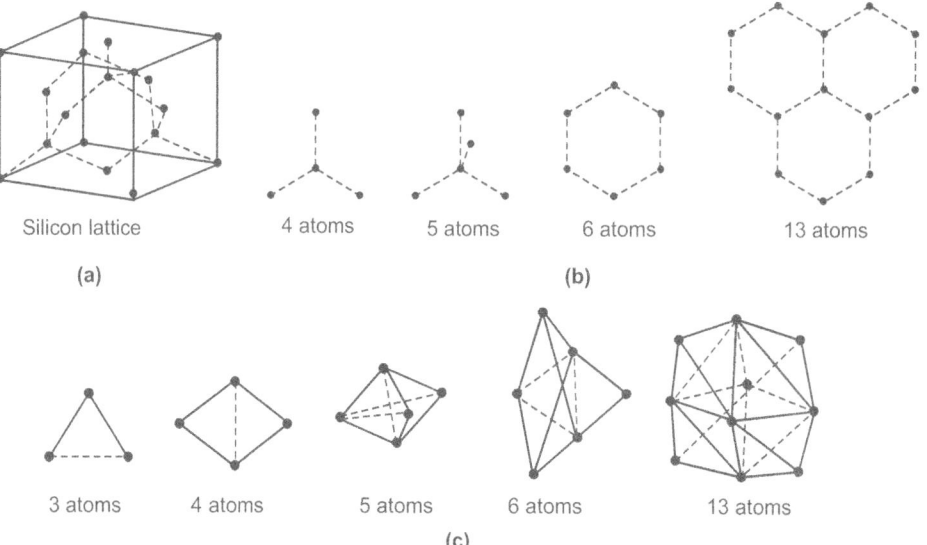

Fig. 6.3 : (a) Silicon atoms forming a unit cell, (b) Fragments of silicon unit cell and (c) Experimentally observed stable clusters of silicon

6.3.5 Mechanical

The mechanical properties of a material depend upon the composition and bonds between the atoms. The mechanical properties like elasticity, hardness, ductility, etc. are result of this. The presence of impurities and imperfections in crystalline forms change these properties.

For a nanoscale material, the material tends to form a single crystal. The nanocrystals are highly pure and free of imperfections.

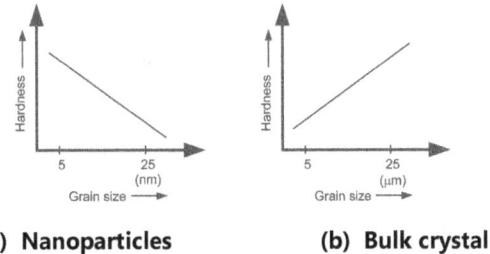

(a) Nanoparticles   (b) Bulk crystal

Fig. 6.4 : Hardness variation with grain size

It has been observed that in metallic nanocrystals, Young's modulus reduces drammatically. For example, magnesium nanocrystal has Young's modulus equal to 3900 N/mm^2 against 4100 N/mm^2 for polycrystalline form.

For bulk material, the hardness increases linearly with the grain size. But in nanomaterials, the hardness increases linearly with decrease of the particle size as shown in Fig. 6.4.

But the density of nanocrystalline pellet is often low as some pores are left when the powder is compressed to form pellets. When the deposition is done at high temperature, the densities approach the density of polycrystalline materials.

6.4 BRIEF INTRODUCTION TO DIFFERENT METHODS OF SYNTHESIS OF NANOPARTICLES

As it has been discussed earlier, the physical properties of material change drammatically when they are reduced to nanoscale. The process by which the nanoscale particles are obtained is termed as **'nano-fabrication'** or **'nanoscale manufacturing'** or **'synthesis'**. For getting nanoparticles one can start from a bulk material and can cut down to the nanoscale. This particular type of nanofabrication is called **'top-down nanofabrication'**, because it starts with a large structure and proceeded to make it smaller. Conversely, starting with individual atoms and building up a nanomaterial is called **'bottom-up nanofabrication'**.

Large number of techniques are available to manufacture (synthesis) different types of nanomaterials in different forms i.e. colloids, cluster, powder, thin films etc. There are various physical, chemical, biological and hybrid techniques to synthesize nanomaterials. The chart shows different commonly used techniques. The technique selected is decided by the material of interest, type of nanostructure, size, quality and quantity.

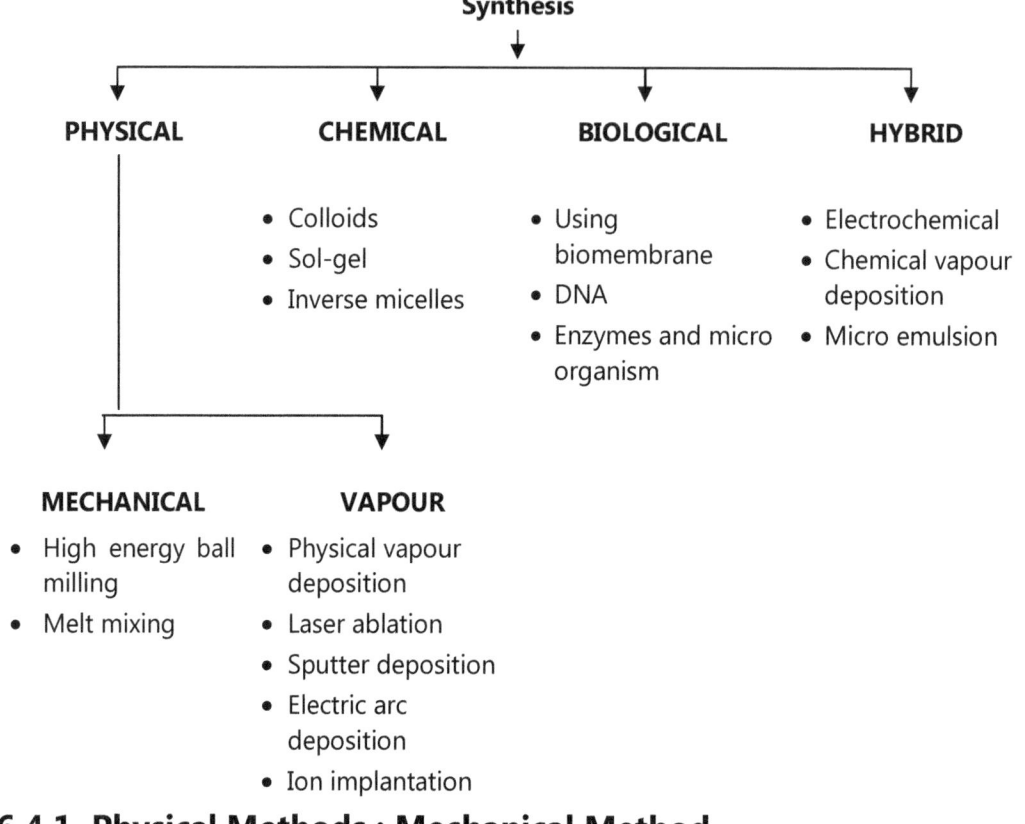

6.4.1 Physical Methods : Mechanical Method

High Energy Ball Milling :

This is one of the simplest methods of making nanoparticles of some metals and alloys. This gives nanoparticles in powder form. This is top-down nanofabrication where the material in powder or flakes of dimensions less than 50 μm are reduced to nanoparticles in powder form. The different types of mills used are planetary, vibratory, rod etc. Usually one or more containers are used and the container size depends on the quantity of nanoparticles to be fabricated.

Hardened steel or tungsten carbide balls are put in container along with powder or flakes of the bulk material. The initial material is in bulk form and is of arbitrary size and shape. The ratio of the balls and material is 2 : 1 and container should be less than half filled as shown in Fig. 6.5. If the container is more than half filled, the efficiency of milling reduces. Use of large balls increases the impact energy on collision and hence gives smaller grain size but produces larger defects in the particles. In the process, some impurities may be added from balls. The air present in the container may also contaminate the nanoparticles. The whole process is carried out in a tight lid container. The containers are rotated at high speed around own axis. In addition to this, they may be rotated around some central axis and are called as **'planetary ball mill'**. Due to collisions, the temperature may rise from 100 to 1100°C, but a lower temperature is favoured. Generally, liquid nitrogen is used to dissipate the heat generated.

When the containers are rotating around the central axis, the material is forced to the walls and is pressed against the walls due to centrifugal force. But due to the motion of containers around their own axis, the material is forced to other region of the container as shown in Fig. 6.6.

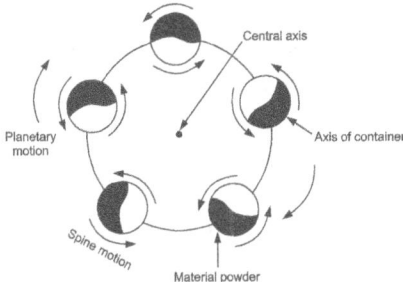

Fig. 6.5 : Planetary ball mill

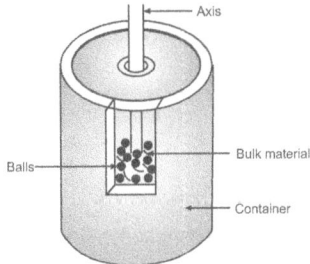

Fig. 6.6 : Ball mill container

Controlling the speed of rotation, planetary as well as axial, a fine powder of uniform size (few nm to few tens of nm) can be obtained. The nanoparticles of Co, Cr, Al-Fe, Ag-Fe etc. can be synthesized in short time. The amount obtained is few 'milligrams' to few 'kilograms'.

6.4.2 Chemical Method

In chemical method, the nanoparticles are obtained in colloidal form, which can be filtered or centrifuged and dried to obtain powder. A thin film can be obtained by electrodeposition, etching etc. The advantages of chemical synthesis are :

- Less expensive.
- Requires low temperature.
- Doping is possible during synthesis.
- Variety of shapes and sizes can be obtained.
- Large quantity can be obtained.
- Particles are in colloidal form and can be converted to powder easily.

In most of the cases, the nanoparticles obtained are in the colloidal form.

Colloids

Colloids are class of materials in which two or more phases (solid, liquid or gas) of same or different materials co-exist with at least one dimension less than a micrometer. The nanomaterials are a sub-class of colloids, in which one of the dimensions are in nano range (< 100 nm). More generally, it is defined as very small particles (within 1 nm to 1000 nm range) that remain dispersed in a liquid for a long time. Their small size prevents them from being filtered easily or settled rapidly. Some examples of colloids are fog (liquid in gas), tinted glass (solid in solid) and foam (gas in liquid).

The colloids can be used for self-assembly of nanoparticles on a neutral base. In colloidal self-assembly, colloids assemble themselves into useful alignments. Fig. 6.7 shows self-assembly of nanoparticles dissolved in ethanol. As the temperature rises and the ethanol evaporates, the surface of the liquid moves down the plate, making it easier for nanoparticle spheres floating nearby to stick to the plate. As ethanol level goes down, more and more particles deposit themselves on the plate, forming an orderly pattern. When all the ethanol is evaporated, the first layer is completed. The number of layers can be added by repeating the process. The process is called **colloidal self-assembly**. Fig. 6.7 illustrates the process.

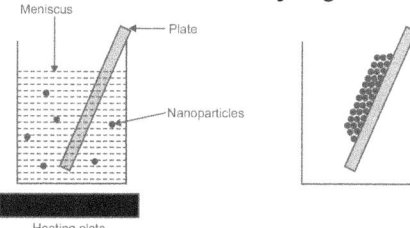

Fig. 6.7 : Self-assembly process

The synthesis of colloids will be discussed in later part of the chapter.

6.5 SYNTHESIS OF COLLOIDS

'**Colloids**' are phase separated nanoparticles suspended in some host matrix in various shapes such as spheres, rods, tubes, fibres, plates etc. Colloids of metals, semiconductors and insulators of various shapes can be synthesized in aqueous (water) or non-aqueous media. The particles acquire surface charge in the media. The coulomb force acting on them stabilizes and stops the further growth. In general, the colloids in liquid can have positive, negative charges or may be neutral. But in most of the cases, they are charged. The various sources by which colloids acquire charge through composition of colloidal material, properties of dispersing medium and concentration of colloids.

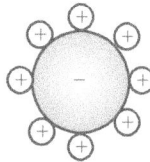

Fig. 6.8 : Charges on colloids

Soon charges develop on particles, ions of opposite charges accumulate around them. The oppositely charged ions are known as **'counter ions'**. Fig. 6.9 shows accumulation of counter ions on a particle. This accumulation of counter ions leads to formation of an electric double layer.

When two charged colloidal particles come closer, they start repelling each other. This stabilizes the colloids. Nanoparticles are special class of colloidals where colloids have one dimension in the range of nanoparticles.

Making nanoparticles using colloidal route goes back to 19th century when M. Faraday synthesized gold nanoparticle by chemistry method. The particles developed are still stable.

Fig. 6.10 illustrates a simple arrangement for synthesis of nanoparticles by colloidal method. The chemical reaction in which colloids are obtained is carried out at very slow rate by keeping concentration and temperature low. The whole reaction is carried out in a glass reactor of suitable size. The reactor has provision to introduce some precursors, gases and measure temperature, pH etc. Usually a trineck flask is used as a reactor. The reaction is carried out in an inert atmosphere (argon or nitrogen gas) to avoid unwanted oxidation of the nanoparticles. The reaction temperature can be controlled by a thermostatic heater. Magnetic stirrer is used during the reaction for proper mixing of the reactants.

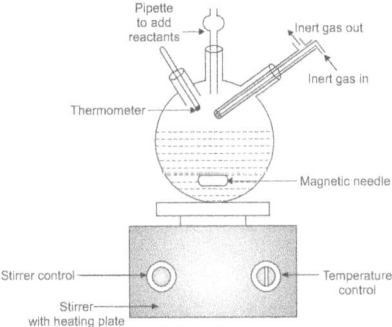

Fig. 6.9 : Chemical reactor to synthesize nanoparticles

6.6 GROWTH OF NANOPARTICLES

Chemical method is a **'bottom-up fabrication'**, where the particle size grows. Monodispersed nanoparticles i.e. particles of nearly same size can be obtained by controlling various steps involved. The **'nucleation'** and **'growth'** of particles can be understood by LaMer diagram as shown in Fig. 6.11.

As the concentration increases, at certain concentration C_O, the formation of nuclei begins. A further increase in the concentration increases the nuclei formation. The nucleation (formation of nucleus) increases upto a concentration C_N above which there is **'supersaturation'**. The concentration C_N denotes the maximum rate of nucleation. After saturation, no new nuclei can be formed and crystal growth reduces the concentration. Thus, again at C_O the minimum concentration of nucleation is reached. This gives an equilibrium at concentration C_S. If new nuclei are formed during the growth, the growth will be in different stages i.e. growth of nuclei formed earlier and growth of new nuclei formed. This results in various sized nanoparticles. Thus, the concentration is to be properly adjusted so that no fresh nuclei are formed once the concentration reaches C_N.

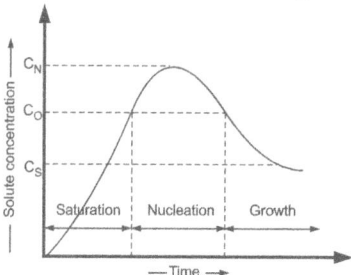

Fig. 6.10 : LaMer diagram

The larger particles have lower surface free energy, hence the larger particles are more stable and grow at the expense of smaller particles. This growth is known as **'Ostwald ripening'**.

Aggregation of particles also reduces surface free energy. Therefore, experimentally, it has been found that there is aggregation of particles in some cases. Thus, for reducing the surface free energy, Ostwald ripening and aggregation are competing processes. Fig. 6.12 shows Ostwald ripening and aggregation.

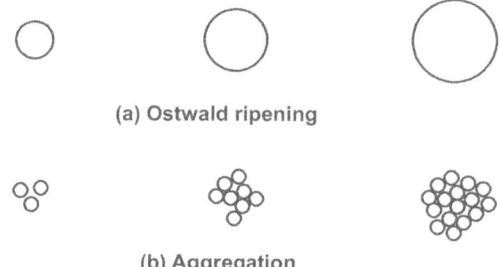

Fig. 6.11 : Growth of nanoparticles

6.7 SYNTHESIS OF METAL NANOPARTICLES BY COLLOIDAL ROUTE

The colloidal metal nanoparticles are synthesized by reduction of metal salt or acid. Highly stable gold particles can be obtained by reducing chloroauric acid ($HAuCl_4$) with trisodium citrate ($Na_3C_6H_5O_7$).

$$HAuCl_4 + Na_3C_6H_5O_7 \longrightarrow Au^+ + C_6H_5O_7^- + HCl + 3\ NaCl$$

The gold nanoparticles are formed by nucleation and condensation. The growth is bigger in size by reduction of more Au^+ ions on the surface. These atoms are stabilized by oppositely charged citrate ions. Fig. 6.13 shows formation of gold nanoparticles.

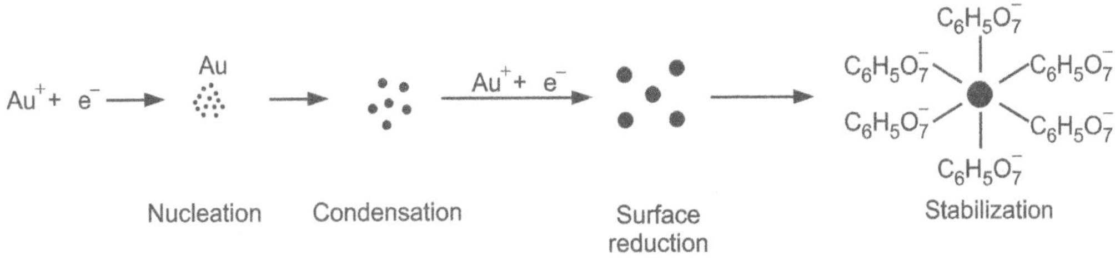

$Au^+ + e^- \longrightarrow Au \longrightarrow \cdots \xrightarrow{Au^+ + e^-} \cdots \longrightarrow$ [with $C_6H_5O_7^-$ groups around central particle]

Nucleation   Condensation   Surface reduction   Stabilization

Fig. 6.12 : Growth of gold nanoparticles

The reaction is carried out in aqueous (water) solution as explained earlier. The gold nanoparticles fabricated in above manner are stable by Coulomb force. It is also possible to use capping such as thiol to stabilize them. In the same way, nanoparticles of metals such as copper, silver etc. can be fabricated by using proper precursors, temperature, pH, duration of synthesis, etc. Also by controlling above parameters, particle parameters such as size, shape, distribution can be controlled.

The gold nanoparticles in colloidal form show different colours depending upon the size of nanoparticles.

6.8 APPLICATIONS OF NANOTECHNOLOGY

At nanoscale the materials change their physical properties such as colour, resistance, strength etc. drammatically. These special properties can be used in many fields for making new devices, instruments and consumer goods. These nanoscale devices are extremely small in dimensions and have unique features. Some of the applications are as mentioned below.

6.8.1 Electronics

The discovery of semiconductor transistor replaced the heavy and power consuming vacuum tubes. The transistors are power saving, small and light weight. The Integrated Circuits (ICs) made the instruments still smaller by fabricating a number of large components on a small chip. But the size of components cannot be reduced to atomic level, because after some level the properties of materials become size dependent. At this level, the **'nanoscience'** or **'nanotechnology'** comes into the picture.

Single Electron Transistor (SET). Spin Valves and Magnetic Tunnel Junctions (MTJ) are the new devices based on nanotechnology. These devices are small, faster and relatively cheaper. The spin valve type devices are used in personal computers to read disk, which have enabled to increase data storage capacity of hard disks. These are the devices based on charge and spin. Earlier, devices were based on charge only and spin was neglected. The spin-based electronics is called as **'spintronic'** or **'magnetoelectronics'**. Using an external magnetic field, spin transport can be controlled. The advantage with spin is that it cannot be easily destroyed by scattering from collisions with other charges, impurities or imperfections. Some of the spin-based devices are Spin FET, Spin LED, Spin RTD etc.

Nanotechnology can also be used in computers for designing **'nonvolatile memory'**, smaller and faster microprocessor and better quality monitors. The nanoparticle coating on screen of TV or monitors will improve quality and resolution.

6.8.2 Energy

Currently used energy sources are firewood, coal, oil and gas. These sources are limited in nature and large-scale use of these sources is damaging environment. So scientists have started searching some alternatives which will solve problems with conventional sources of energies. Some of the non-conventional sources of energies are solar energy, hydel energy, tidal energy, biomass energy etc.

The disadvantage of solar cells is that their efficiency is less (~ 30%) and hence require large surface area. Research is going on to use nanomaterials for making solar cells, which will reduce the size of the cells and increase the efficiency. Other source of energy is hydrogen fuel, which can be obtained by splitting water (H_2O) using sunlight in presence of nanomaterials. The nanomaterial will work as **'photocatalyst'**. The main problem with hydrogen is storage as it can catch fire easily. Materials like carbon nanotubes can be used as storage material without risk.

Portable electronic appliances such as mobile phones, laptops, calculators etc. require rechargeable, light-weight batteries. Such batteries require frequent replacement or recharging as their energy density is low. Attempts are being made to increase their energy density by replacing the electrode materials.

6.8.3 Automobiles

The body of a car is made up of steel and some alloys. The body structure should be strong and non-deformable. The nanotube composites have mechanical strength better than steel and attempts are made to make composites that can replace steel. Currently, manufacturing of nanotubes is expensive but scientists are trying to make it economical. Nanoparticle paints provide smooth, thin and attractive coating. Research is going on to change the colour of car by applying a small voltage.

Self-cleaning glass can be made by mixing small amount of titania (TiO_2) nanoparticles while manufacturing it. The titania is capable of dissociating organic dust in presence of UV light present in sunlight. Once dissociated it may fall down or evaporate. Water droplets on glass give hazy look, but titania glass can spread the water evenly giving clear sight. Such special glass can be used to make window glass of a car.

By using nanoparticles light weight and less rubber consuming, thinner tyres can be made. This will reduce the weight, price of the car and will increase the mileage as a result of reduced weight. Nanoparticles can be used as catalysts to convert harmful emissions into less harmful gases. With the help of nanocarbon tubes, hydrogen fuel can be stored safely and can be used for running a car. The hydrogen fuel is eco-friendly and ever lasting.

6.8.4 Space and Defence

In space and defence also, scientists are trying to replace the conventional materials by nanomaterials. A nanoporous material called **'aerogels'** have extremely low density ranging between 0.01 to 0.8 gm/cm^3. Aerogels have small nanosized pores in them and can be of various materials. Basically, aerogels are poor conductors of heat. Therefore, aerogels can be used in spacecrafts to reduce the weight. Even special light-weight suits and jackets can be made using aerogels.

In satellites or spacecrafts, we use solar energy. But solar cells have low efficiency resulting in large surface area and heavy weight. Nanoparticles can be used to reduce the size and weight of solar cells. Space vehicles also need materials which can withstand harsh and extreme conditions during launching and in space. Polymer composites using silica fibres and nanoparticles have larger Young's modulus, low temperature coefficient of expansion and high impact strength. The nanoparticles in polymer composites are better radiation protectors in comparison to microparticle-based composites.

6.8.5 Medical

The nanoparticles can be used for drug delivery, detection of cancer or tumor and treating them. As nanoparticles are very small in size, they can be injected easily and can be guided towards specific part in the body. Recently, gold nanorods which have strong scattering and absorption property in the infrared are used to detect and destroy cancer cells in rats. The infrared laser beam can be used to detect and destroy cancer cells without affecting the healthy cells. This is possible because healthy cells require twice the laser power as compared to cancer cell for destruction and infrared light can get easily transmitted through cells and muscles. Thus, by using low power infrared laser, only cancer cells can be killed without affecting the healthy cells.

Drugs can be encapsulated in nanocapsules and can be guided towards desired part of the body. Then drug can be delivered in controlled manner, fastly and slowly, by opening the capsule in desired way. The opening of capsule can be controlled externally by magnetic field, infrared light or physiologically. This will help in treating diabetic or HIV affected patients.

The scientists are also working to develop better body implants. The body implants should be strong and biocompatible. The body implant should be strong enough so that it does not get deformed easily. Also, it should be biocompatible so that once implanted body cells should be able to grow.

Some nanotechnology-based tests are developed which are simple and fast. These tests can be used for detection of viruses, DNA, proteins and antibodies. Porous silicon and carbon nanotubes-based sensors can also be used in medical field.

6.8.6 Environmental

Whenever a new technology emerges, there is always concern about its impact on social life, health and environment. Technology brings comfort in life but it also creates problems such as global climatic changes, pollution, new deceases, depletion of natural resources, etc. Therefore, the question arises whether the nanotechnology will solve or increase these problems. Although ill effects of nanoparticles are possible but they are not studied yet.

On the other hand, it is believed that nanomaterials themselves will reduce the pollution and environment related problems. Efficient production of nanomaterial by low temperature synthesis routes will help to reduce industrial pollution. Use of nanomaterials as hydrogen fuel storage and oil filters may reduce emission by vehicles. The nanomaterials are light weight and require only small quantity. This will bring down the prices of products making them affordable. Thus likely to solve problems of poor people.

The nanoparticle-based sensors are much sensitive than conventional sensors being used. These nanoparticle-based sensors will be capable to detect and rectify problems. Such sensors will be useful in water purification systems, detection of toxic ions, metal ions, pesticides etc. and their remediation on large scale.

6.8.7 Textile

The special threads and dyes used in textile industry are products of nanotechnology. Clothes produced with such technology will give pleasant look of synthetic fiber but comfort of cotton. These clothes will not require ironing or frequent cleaning. Some of the washing machine companies are trying to use silver nanoparticles in washing machines which will make the clothes germ-free.

6.8.8 Cosmetics

Nanoparticles are widely used in cosmetic industry. Due to their small size nanoparticle-based creams are better option as they can be used in small amount and do not leave any gaps between them. This gives a smooth appearance. Zinc oxide and titanium oxide nanoparticles of uniform size are able to absorb ultraviolet light and protect the skin from ultraviolet radiations. The small nanoparticles in some of the creams scatter light in such a way that the appearance of wrinkles is suppressed. Nanoparticle-based dyes and colours are harmless to skin and can be used in hair creams or gels. Some creams using nanoparticles are already in market and becoming quite popular.

SUMMARY

- The Greek word nano means one billionth.
- Nanoscience is the study of the fundamental principles of molecules and structures with at least one dimension of nanosize.
- The research and application of the nanostructures into nanoscale devices is called nanotechnology.

- Most of the physical properties of nanomaterials are different than when they are in bulk form.
- The colour of nanoparticles are different from the colour of bulk material.
- The resistivity of materials having nanosized grain is larger than polycrystalline materials.
- The nanoparticles having single domain do not show coercivity or hysteresis.
- The nanoparticles are not just the fragments of bulk material and have different structures.
- The nanocrystal line pellet have low density as some pores are left when the powder is compressed.
- The process by which the nanoparticles are obtained is called as nano-fabrication or nano-scale manufacturing or synthesis.
- In top-down nanofabrication, we start with large structure and is made smaller.
- In bottom-up nanofabrication, we start with individual atom and make nanostructures.
- In physical method, high energy ball milling or vapour deposition method is used to get nanostructures.
- In chemical method, the nanoparticles are obtained in colloidal form.
- In biological method, microorganisms are used for nanoparticle synthesis.
- Colloids are phase separated nanoparticles suspended in some host matrix.
- The growth of nanoparticles takes place either by Ostwald ripening or aggregation.
- The colloidal metal nanoparticles are synthesized by reduction of metal salt or acid.
- The nanoparticles have vast applications in almost all the fields.
- Most of the applications are still in trial stage and very few are commercially available.

EXERCISE

1. What is nanoscience ? Why classical mechanics cannot be applied to nanoparticles ?
2. Why properties of nanoparticles are different from what they are in bulk form ? Explain optical and electrical properties of nanoparticles.
3. State and explain any three properties of nanoparticles.
4. Explain the following properties of nanoparticles :
   (i) Magnetic properties.
   (ii) Mechanical properties.
5. What are different types of nano-fabrications ? Explain physical method for getting nanoparticles.
6. Write short notes on :
   (i) High energy ball milling.   (ii) Physical vapour deposition.

7. What are colloids ? Give advantages of chemical method.
8. Write a short note on biological methods for nanoparticle synthesis.
9. What are colloids ? How colloids can be synthesized ?
10. Explain different methods of nanoparticle growth with LaMer diagram.
11. Explain synthesis of metal nanoparticles by colloidal route.
12. Explain the applications of nanoparticles in the field of (a) automobile, (b) medical.
13. Give advantages of nanoparticles over bulk material in the field of (a) environment, (b) space and defence.
14. Nanoparticles will reduce environmental pollution. Justify.
15. Explain the optical and electrical properties of nanoparticles.
16. Classify the following properties of nano-particles into optical, electrical and mechanical ones :
    (a) Nano-particles exhibit change in colour, which changes with the change in their size.
    (b) When nano-particles are embedded in plastics, the strength is enhanced.
    (c) Gold, when synthesized in nano-particle form, appears red.
    (d) The I-V characteristics of nano-particles is not linear but is like a staircase.
    (e) Nano-particles may acquire superconducting state under some conditions.
    (f) When polycrystalline magnesium is converted into nano-crystalline magnesium, the Young's modulus decreases from 4100 N/m^2 to 3900 N/m^2.
17. Explain any two properties of nano-materials.
18. Explain optical and electrical properties of nano-particles.
19. Describe any two properties of nano-particles.
20. Explain optical and electrical properties of nano-particles.
21. Explain the synthesis of metal nanoparticles by colloidal route.
22. Explain briefly how colloids are synthesized by a chemical route.
23. Explain synthesis of metal nanoparticles by colloidal route.
24. Explain synthesis of metal nanoparticles by colloidal route.
25. Discuss any one application of nano technology.
26. Explain applications of nano particles in the field of medicine and electronics.
27. State any seven distinct applications of nano-technology.

✠ ✠ ✠

Unit - IV (OPTICS – I)

CHAPTER 7
INTERFERENCE

7.1 INTRODUCTION

The most common type of radiation which we come across in day to day life is electromagnetic wave or photon (the light quanta). Some of the electromagnetic waves can stimulate retina and some cannot. The part of the electromagnetic wave which can stimulate the retina is called **'light'**. The branch of physics which deals with light is called **'optics'**. Further, optics can be broadly classified as (a) **'geometrical optics'**, (b) **'physical or wave optics'** and (c) **'quantum optics'** depending upon the basic behaviour of light assumed for explaining the optical phenomena. In the current course our main focus will be on physical optics, where we assume the wave nature of light.

From basic optical phenomena such as interference and diffraction, we can conclude that the light has a wave nature. In this unit, we will be studying these two basic properties of light. But these properties fail to explain the type of oscillations involved i.e. polarisation. The polarisation of light will be studied in later part of the text.

The wave theory of light was proposed by Chritian Huygen in 1679 but interference was demonstrated by Thomas Young only in 1802. There are several examples of interference that can be observed in everyday life. Basically, oil is colourless but a film of oil floating on water shows bright colours and also keeps on changing colour. Similarly a soap bubble, a compact disc, a thin sheet of mica or cellophane appear coloured. All this is due to interference of light. In engineering too, interference has wide applications such as measurement of thickness and stress, testing flatness of a surface, anti-reflecting coating etc.

7.1.1 Interference of Waves

If two waves of same frequency travel in same direction with a constant phase difference with time, they combine so that their energy is not uniformly distributed in space, but is maximum at certain points and minimum (or zero) at other points. This phenomenon is called **interference**. In interference, energy is neither created (at maxima) nor destroyed (at minima) but is redistributed so that there is more energy at certain points (maxima) and less energy at other points (minima). Even after interference the total energy of the system remains constant.

Thus, interference is the redistribution of energy due to superposition of two or more waves.

7.1.2 Principle of Superposition

'The principle of superposition states that when two or more waves are superposed in space or a medium, the waves travel independently, through each other and the resultant displacement of each position is the algebraic/vector sum of the displacements due to each wave'.

Fig. 7.1 shows superposition of two waves.

In Fig. 7.1 (a), two crests, with amplitude a_1 and a_2, are approaching each other and the point where they meet the resultant amplitude ($a_1 + a_2$) is more than the individual amplitudes. After this, they pass through each other as though they have not interfered at all. Similarly, in Fig. 7.1 (b), one crest and one trough, with amplitude a_1 and $-a_2$, are approaching each other. At the point where they meet the resultant amplitude ($a_1 - a_2$) is less than the individual amplitudes. The first case is called **'constructive interference'** and the second case is called **'destructive interference'**.

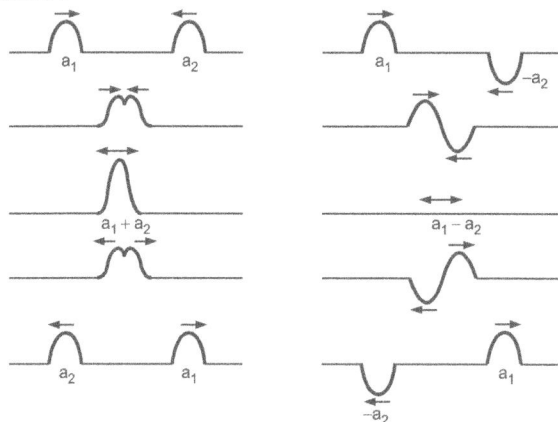

(a) Constructive interference (b) Destructive interference

Fig. 7.1 : Superposition

7.1.3 Constructive Interference

When the crest of one wave overlaps the crest of the other or the trough of one overlaps with the trough of the other, the displacement is maximum. This is called as **'constructive interference'**.

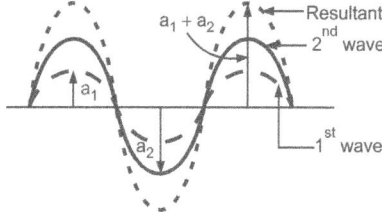

Fig. 7.2 : Constructive interference

In this case, the waves are in phase and the resultant amplitude equals the sum of the two component amplitudes.

i.e. $\qquad A = a_1 + a_2$ ... (1)

If $\qquad a_1 = a_2 = a$

then $\qquad A = 2a$ ... (2)

The resultant intensity will be $\quad I = A^2 = 4a^2$ ... (3)

Here the path difference between two waves is 0. Constructive interference will also take place when the path difference is λ or 2λ. In general, condition for constructive interference is,

$$\text{Path difference, } \Delta = n\lambda \quad \ldots(4)$$

where $n = 0, 1, 2, \ldots n$.

In terms of phase difference,

$$\text{Phase difference, } \delta = k\Delta, \text{ where } k = \frac{2\pi}{\lambda}$$

$$\therefore \quad \delta = \frac{2\pi}{\lambda} \cdot n\lambda$$

$$\delta = 2n\pi \quad \ldots(5)$$

7.1.4 Destructive Interference

In the other case, when the crest of one wave overlaps the trough of other or vice-versa, the displacement is minimum. This is called as **'destructive interference'**.

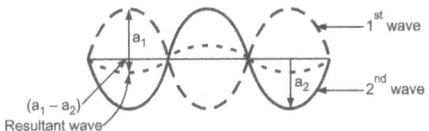

Fig. 7.3 : Destructive interference

In this case, the waves are 180° out of phase and the resultant amplitude is the difference of the two component amplitudes.

i.e. $\quad A = a_1 - a_2 \quad \ldots(6)$

If $\quad a_1 = a_2 = a$

then $\quad A = 0 \quad \ldots(7)$

The resultant intensity, $\quad I = A^2 = 0 \quad \ldots(8)$

Here the path difference between two waves is λ/2. The same thing will happen when the path difference is 3λ/2 or 5λ/2. In general, destructive interference will occur when

$$\text{Path difference, } \Delta = \left(n + \frac{1}{2}\right)\lambda \quad \ldots(9)$$

where $n = 0, 1, 2, \ldots, n$.

or $\quad$ Phase difference, $\delta = k \cdot \Delta$ where $k = \frac{2\pi}{\lambda}$

$$\delta = \frac{2\pi}{\lambda}\left(n + \frac{1}{2}\right)\lambda$$

$$\delta = (2n + 1)\pi \quad \ldots(10)$$

7.1.5 Conditions for Stable Interference

The Conditions Necessary for Stable Interference are
- The two interfering waves should emit light of **same wavelength or frequency**.
- The two interfering waves must be **coherent**.
- The interfering waves must have **equal amplitudes**.
- The two interfering waves must be propagated along **the same line**.
- The **separation between the two sources must be as small as possible** so that the path difference between the two interfering waves, reaching a particular point, is not very large.
- The source of two interfering wave must be **narrow**, as a broad source will be equivalent to many fine sources.

Intensity Distribution in the Fringe System

If the amplitude of interfering waves are a_1 and a_2, and the phase difference is δ, then the vector sum of these two amplitude vectors will be A, as shown in Fig. 7.4.

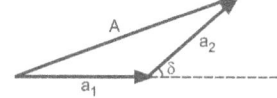

Fig. 7.4 : Addition of waves

The resultant amplitude A will depend upon the phase difference δ. For maxima, the angle δ is zero and the component amplitudes a_1 and a_2 will be parallel. So the resultant amplitude will be A = 2a (if $a_1 = a_2 = a$). For minima, a_1 and a_2 are in opposite directions (antiparallel) as the phase difference is 180°. The resultant amplitude is zero (if $a_1 = a_2 = a$). Thus, the intensity at a point will depend on the cosine of the angle made by two interfering waves.

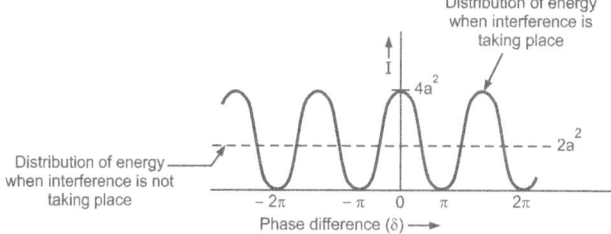

Fig. 7.5 : Intensity distribution

If the two waves of light arrive at a point on the screen exactly out of phase, then interference is destructive and the resultant intensity is zero. The energy which apparently disappears in minima is present in the maxima, where the intensity is greater than the intensity produced by two waves acting separately. In other words, the energy is not destroyed but redistributed in the interference pattern. The average intensity on the screen is exactly the same as what it would be in absence of interference. In interference pattern, the intensity varies between $4a^2$ and zero, whereas in absence of interference, we would have an uniform intensity of $2a^2$, as shown in Fig. 7.5.

7.1.6 Analytical Treatment of Interference

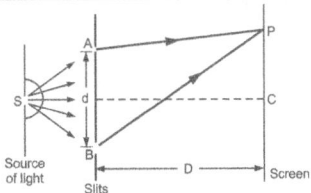

Fig. 7.6

Consider a monochromatic source S emitting light of wavelength λ. Points A and B are equidistant from S, acting as two virtual coherent sources separated by a distance d. Let 'a' be the amplitude of the emitted waves from each slit. The screen is at a distance D from the virtual source. Consider a point P on the screen where interference takes place. If δ is the phase difference between the two rays AP and BP reaching point P.

Then,
$$y_1 = a \sin \omega t$$
$$y_2 = a \sin (\omega t + \delta)$$

According to the principle of superposition the resultant displacement y will be sum of individual displacements y_1 and y_2.

$$y = y_1 + y_2$$
$$y = a \sin \omega t + a \sin (\omega t + \delta)$$
$$y = a \sin \omega t + a (\sin \omega t \cos \delta + \cos \omega t \sin \delta)$$
$$y = a \sin \omega t (1 + \cos \delta) + a \cos \omega t \sin \delta$$

Let,
$$a (1 + \cos \delta) = A \cos \theta \qquad \ldots (1)$$
and
$$a \sin \delta = A \sin \theta \qquad \ldots (2)$$

$\therefore$
$$y = A \sin \omega t \cos \theta + A \cos \omega t \sin \theta$$
$$y = A \sin (\omega t + \theta) \qquad \ldots (3)$$

This represents the equation of a simple harmonic vibration of amplitude A.

Squaring and adding (1) and (2),
$$A^2 \sin^2 \theta + A^2 \cos^2 \theta = a^2 \sin^2 \delta + a^2 (1 + \cos \delta)^2$$
$$A^2 = a^2 \sin^2 \delta + a^2 + a^2 \cos^2 \delta + 2a^2 \cos \delta$$
$$A^2 = 2a^2 + 2a^2 \cos \delta$$

$\therefore$
$$A^2 = 2a^2 (1 + \cos \delta)$$
$$A^2 = 2a^2 \left(\sin^2 \frac{\delta}{2} + \cos^2 \frac{\delta}{2} + \cos^2 \frac{\delta}{2} - \sin^2 \frac{\delta}{2} \right)$$
$$A^2 = 4a^2 \cos^2 \frac{\delta}{2}$$

As the intensity at any point is proportional to the square of the amplitude,
$$I = A^2 \text{ (constant of proportionality is taken as unity)}$$

$\therefore$
$$I = 4a^2 \cos^2 \delta/2$$

Condition for Maximum and Minimum

Case (i) Constructive Interference : When the phase difference $\delta = 0, 2\pi, 2(2\pi) \ldots n(2\pi)$ or path difference $\Delta = 0, \lambda, 2\lambda \ldots n\lambda$ then, $I = 4a^2$.

i.e., **intensity is maximum when phase difference is a whole number multiple of 2π or the path difference is a whole number multiple of λ.**

Case (ii) Destructive Interference : When the phase difference $\delta = \pi, 3\pi, \ldots (2n+1)\pi$ or the path difference $\Delta = \dfrac{\lambda}{2}, \dfrac{3\lambda}{2}, \ldots (2n+1)\dfrac{\lambda}{2}$ then, $I = 0$.

i.e. **intensity is minimum when phase difference is an odd integer multiple of π or the path difference is an odd integer multiple of $\lambda/2$.**

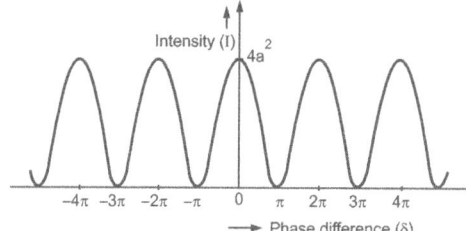

Fig. 7.7 : Energy distribution curve

7.1.7 Visibility of Fringes

Assume that the intensity of each wave is I. When the waves are incoherent, there is no interference and intensity will be (2I) uniform. When the light is coming from coherent sources, interference fringes appear on the screen with a maximum of 4I and minimum of zero.

If the light is partially coherent i.e. consists of a mixture of coherent and incoherent light, the maximum will not be 4I and minimum will not be zero.

Then the visibility of fringes, Visibility $= \dfrac{I_{max} - I_{min}}{I_{max} + I_{min}}$

The percentage of coherent light in partially coherent light is called degree of coherence, which decides the visibility.

7.2 CONCEPT OF THIN FILM

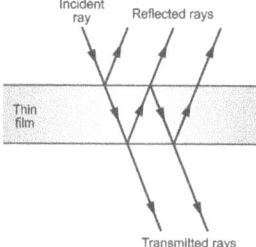

Fig. 7.8 : Multiple reflections in a transparent thin film

A film is said to be **'thin'** when its thickness is of the order of wavelength of visible light (taken to be 5500 A°, which is the centre of the visible spectrum). If the thickness of the film is about 10 μm to 50 μm, it is considered to be a thick film. A thin film may be a thin sheet of transparent material like glass, mica or an air film enclosed between two transparent sheets or a soap bubble.

A light ray incident on a thin transparent film undergo reflection from the upper and lower surfaces of the film. They travel along different paths and may be reunited to produce **'interference'**. In a thin film, a small portion gets reflected from the upper surface while a major portion is transmitted into the film. The lower surface reflects a small portion, of the transmitted component, back into the film while the rest of it emerges out of the film from other side. Hence, a small portion of light gets partially reflected in succession several times within the film (as shown in Fig. 7.8). In a transparent thin film, the two surfaces strongly transmit and weakly reflect the incident light. In such cases, only the first few reflection at the top surface and the first few reflection at the bottom surface will be of appreciable strength. Hence, only the first two rays will be considered in the discussion. At each reflection, the incident amplitude is divided into a reflected and transmitted component' Therefore, interference in thin films is called **'interference by division of amplitude'**. This phenomenon was first observed by Newton and Robert Hooke but was correctly explained by Thomas Young.

In the Ongoing Discussion, Following Facts are Assumed

- When a ray of light gets **'reflected'** from a **'denser medium'** into a **'rarer medium'**, it undergoes a **'phase change of π'** or a **'path change of $\lambda/2$'**
- A **distance 't'** traversed by light in a medium of **refractive index 'μ'** has an equivalent **optical path 'μ t'**.

7.3 INTERFERENCE DUE TO THIN FILMS OF UNIFORM THICKNESS

Consider a thin film of thickness 't' and refractive index 'μ'. Let XY and X'Y' be the faces of this parallel sided film. The film is surrounded by air on both the sides. A plane monochromatic light ray, which can be considered as a parallel beam, is incident on the upper surface of the film. Let AB represent one of the incident rays. The light ray travelling along AB is incident at an angle 'i' on the upper surface of the film. A part of the incident light is reflected at the upper face along BB' and a part is refracted at an angle 'r' along BC. At C, it is partly reflected back into the film along CD, while a major portion is transmitted along CC'. The ray along CD emerges along DD' parallel to BB'. Both rays BB' (ray 1) and DD' (ray 2) are obtained from the same incident ray. They are, therefore, coherent and can produce interference. The condition of interference depends on the optical path difference between rays 1 and 2.

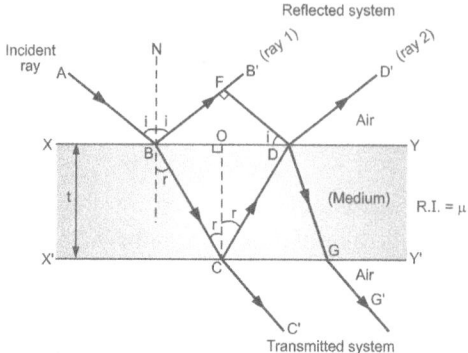

Fig. 7.9 : Reflection of light from a parallel thin film

To compute the optical path difference between the reflected ray BB' (ray 1) and the refracted ray DD' (ray 2), draw a normal DF from ray DD' on line BB'. Beyond points F and D, both rays travel equal distances. While ray BB' has covered a distance BF in air, the ray DD' has covered a distance BCD in the film of refractive index μ.

The geometric **'path difference'** between ray 1 and ray 2 is, BC + CD − BF.

∴ Optical path difference is, $\Delta = \mu(BC + CD) - BF$ ... (1)

(∵ distances BC and CD are travelled in medium of R.I. = μ)

From $\triangle$ BCO and $\triangle$ DCO, $\cos r = \dfrac{CO}{BC}$ and $\cos r = \dfrac{CO}{CD}$

∴ $\cos r = \dfrac{t}{BC}$ and $\cos r = \dfrac{t}{CD}$ (∵ CO = t)

∴ $BC = CD = \dfrac{t}{\cos r}$ ... (2)

and $BF = BD \sin i$ (from $\triangle$ BFD)

But $BO = OD = BC \sin r$ (from $\triangle$ BCO and $\triangle$ DCO)

∴ $BF = 2\, BC \sin r \sin i$ as BD = BO + OD

From equation (2), $BF = \dfrac{2t}{\cos r} \sin r \sin i$

Dividing and multiplying by $\sin r$,

$$BF = \dfrac{2t}{\cos r} \sin^2 r \, \dfrac{\sin i}{\sin r}$$

$$BF = \dfrac{2\mu t}{\cos r} \sin^2 r \qquad \left(\because \dfrac{\sin i}{\sin r} = \mu\right) \text{ ... (3)}$$

Substituting equations (2) and (3) in equation (1),

$$\Delta = \mu\left(\dfrac{t}{\cos r} + \dfrac{t}{\cos r}\right) - \dfrac{2\mu t}{\cos r} \sin^2 r$$

$$\Delta = \frac{2\mu t}{\cos r} - \frac{2\mu t}{\cos r} \sin^2 r$$

$$\Delta = (1 - \sin^2 r)\frac{2\mu t}{\cos r}$$

$$\Delta = \frac{2\mu t}{\cos r} \cos^2 r \qquad (\because \sin^2 r + \cos^2 r = 1)$$

$$\Delta = 2\mu t \cos r \qquad \dots (4)$$

7.3.1 In Reflected System

The path difference given by (4) is not the true optical path difference between rays 1 and 2. The phase change due to reflection is to be taken into account. At B, the reflection is in a rarer medium. So, a path change of $\lambda/2$ occurs in the reflected ray BB'. At C, reflection is in a denser medium, therefore no path change occurs in ray 2.

∴ Total path difference between rays 1 and 2 is given by,

Total path difference = Path difference due to thin film + Path difference due to reflections

$$\Delta = 2\mu t \cos r \pm \frac{\lambda}{2} \qquad \dots (5)$$

Condition for Constructive Interference

If the total path difference is equal to an integral multiple of λ then rays 1 and 2 meet in phase and undergo constructive interference.

i.e., $\quad \Delta = n\lambda$

∴ $\quad 2\mu t \cos r \pm \lambda/2 = n\lambda$

$$2\mu t \cos r = (2n \pm 1)\lambda/2 \quad \text{where } n = 0, 1, 2, 3 \dots \qquad \dots (6)$$

Condition for Destructive Interference

If the optical path difference is equal to an odd integral multiple of $\lambda/2$, then rays 1 and 2 meet in opposite phase and undergo destructive interference.

i.e. $\quad \Delta = (2n \pm 1)\frac{\lambda}{2}$

∴ $\quad 2\mu t \cos r \pm \frac{\lambda}{2} = (2n \pm 1)\frac{\lambda}{2}$

$$2\mu t \cos r = n\lambda \quad \text{where } n = 0, 1, 2 \dots \qquad \dots (7)$$

The **number n** is called the order of interference. The rays incident on the film at the same angle are divided into two rays which become parallel on reflection from the surfaces of the film. Parallel rays do not intersect at finite distances, hence fringes are not observed at finite distances. The rays are to be condensed by a lens and interference is observed in its focal plane. Else, it can be observed by the unaided eye focused at infinity. Therefore, these interference fringes are said to be **localized at infinity**.

Important Cases
- If the film is extremely thin i.e. $t \ll \lambda$ or $t \to 0$ then the path difference, $\Delta \approx \lambda/2$. The film will appear dark in reflected light.
- When monochromatic light is incident normal to the film then $\cos r = 1$.

$$2\mu t = (2n+1)\frac{\lambda}{2} \text{ for brightness}$$

and $\quad 2\mu t = n\lambda \quad$ for darkness.

This implies that the film will appear bright in reflected light if the film has thickness of $t = \dfrac{\lambda}{4\mu}, \dfrac{3\lambda}{4\mu}, \ldots\ldots$ and it will appear dark for a thickness of

$$t = \frac{\lambda}{2\mu}, \frac{2\lambda}{2\mu}, \frac{3\lambda}{2\mu} \ldots\ldots$$

- If the incident monochromatic light is parallel, the whole film will be uniformly bright or dark as film thickness 't' and angle of refraction 'r' are constant. For a given incident wavelength (say green) the condition of constructive interference causes the incident colour to intensify (intense green).
- A change in the angle of incidence of the rays causes a change in the path difference. The optical path difference decreases with increase in angle of incidence. Hence, as inclination of the film is changed, it will appear alternately dark and bright for incident monochromatic light.
- If white light is incident on the film, the optical path difference will vary from one colour to the other as λ is different. Hence, the film will appear coloured, the colour being that of the rays which interfered constructively. Further, as the inclination of the film is changed, the film will appear coloured.
- If the incident white light is not parallel, the optical path difference will change due to change in the incident angle. Hence, the film will show different colours when viewed from different directions.

7.3.2 In Transmitted System

When the film is observed in transmitted light, it can be shown that the path difference between rays CC' and GG' (Fig. 7.9) is equal to $2\mu t \cos r$. Reflections at C and D are in a denser medium. So, no additional path change will occur due to reflection.

Total path difference = Path difference due to thin film
+ Path difference due to reflections

$\therefore \qquad \qquad \Delta = 2\mu t \cos r + 0 \qquad \qquad \ldots (8)$

Condition for Constructive Interference

For constructive interference the total phase difference should be an integral multiple of λ.

i.e. $\qquad \qquad \Delta = n\lambda$

$\therefore \qquad \qquad 2\mu t \cos r = n\lambda \qquad \qquad \ldots (9)$

Condition for Destructive Interference

For destructive interference the total phase difference should be an odd integral multiple of $\lambda/2$.

i.e.
$$\Delta = (2n \pm 1)\frac{\lambda}{2}$$

$\therefore \qquad 2\mu t \cos r = (2n \pm 1)\dfrac{\lambda}{2}$ ... (10)

As is evident, the condition for brightness on reflection becomes the condition for darkness on transmission and vice versa.

7.4 INTERFERENCE IN FILMS OF NON-UNIFORM THICKNESS (WEDGE SHAPED FILM)

A **wedge** is a plate or film of varying thickness, having zero thickness at one end and progressively increasing to a particular thickness at the other end.

Consider two plane surfaces XY and X'Y' inclined at an angle α. The thickness of the film increases linearly from X to Y. When the wedge is illuminated by a parallel beam of monochromatic light, the rays reflected from its two surfaces will not be parallel. They appear to diverge from a point S near the film. When the film is viewed with reflected monochromatic light, **equidistant interference fringes** are observed which are parallel to the line of intersection of the two surfaces. The fringes are alternately bright and dark and are localised at the surface of the film. With incident white light, coloured fringes are observed.

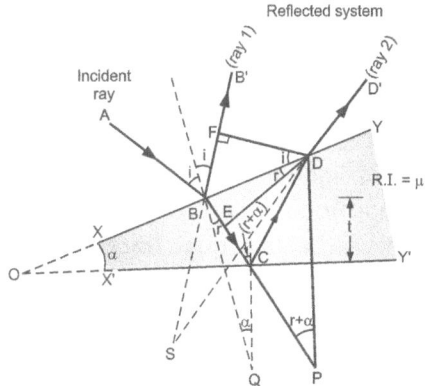

Fig. 7.10 : Wedge-shaped film

On illuminating the film with monochromatic light, one system of rays is reflected from the front surface XY and the other system of rays is obtained by transmission at the back surface X'Y' (not shown in Fig. 7.10) and consequent reflections at the front surface. As both rays are obtained from a single source, they are coherent and produce interference. The interfering rays BB' and DD' are not parallel but appear to diverge from a point S. The optical path difference between them is given by,

$$\Delta = 2\mu t \cos(r + \alpha)$$

[**Note** : Derivation not expected.]

In Reflected System

Due to reflection, an additional path change is introduced in the reflected system at point B.

∴ Total path difference = Path difference due to thin film
+ Path difference due to reflections

$$\Delta = 2\mu t \cos(r + \alpha) \pm \frac{\lambda}{2} \qquad \ldots (1)$$

Condition for Constructive Interference

For constructive interference the total phase difference should be an integral multiple of λ.

∴ $\Delta = n\lambda$

i.e. $2\mu t \cos(r + \alpha) \pm \frac{\lambda}{2} = n\lambda$

∴ $2\mu t \cos(r + \alpha) = (2n \pm 1)\frac{\lambda}{2} \qquad \ldots (2)$

Condition for Destructive Interference

For destructive interference the total phase difference should be an odd integral multiple of $\lambda/2$.

$$\Delta = (2n \pm 1)\frac{\lambda}{2}$$

i.e. $2\mu t \cos(r + \alpha) \pm \frac{\lambda}{2} = (2n \pm 1)\frac{\lambda}{2}$

∴ $2\mu t \cos(r + \alpha) = n\lambda \qquad \ldots (3)$

Nature of Interference Pattern

If the film is illuminated by parallel light, then 'i' is constant everywhere and so is 'r', the angle of refraction. In addition, if monochromatic light is used, the path change will occur only due to 't'. In this case, the fringes will be of **'equal thickness'**. For a wedge shaped film, 't' remains constant only in a direction parallel to the thin edge of the wedge. So, straight fringes parallel to the edge of the wedge are obtained. The fringes are alternately bright or dark for monochromatic light. For white light, coloured fringes are obtained.

**Fig. 7.11 : Interference pattern in wedge-shaped film.
Alternately bright and dark bands are parallel**

7.5 FRINGE WIDTH (β)

When a wedge film is illuminated by monochromatic light of wavelength λ, it gives fringes of equal thickness. Fringe width can be calculated by knowing the position of consecutive minima or maxima. Here, for mathematical simplicity, we will consider minima.

For n^{th} minimum, we have

$$2\mu t \cos(r + \alpha) = n\lambda$$

For normal incidence, $r = 0$

$$\therefore \quad 2t\mu \cos \alpha = n\lambda \quad \ldots (1)$$

Let this n^{th} dark band be formed at a distance x_n from the thin edge.

$$\therefore \quad t = x_n \tan \alpha \quad \text{(from Fig. 7.12)} \ldots (2)$$

From equations (1) and (2),

$$2\mu x_n \tan \alpha \cos \alpha = n\lambda$$

or $$2\mu x_n \sin \alpha = n\lambda \quad \ldots (3)$$

Fig. 7.12

Similarly, if the $(n + 1)^{th}$ minimum is obtained at a distance x_{n+1} from the thin edge, then

$$2\mu x_{n+1} \sin \alpha = (n + 1)\lambda \quad \ldots (4)$$

Subtracting equation (6) from equation (7), we get fringe width of a bright fringe.

$$2\mu (x_{n+1} - x_n) \sin \alpha = \lambda$$

$\therefore$ Fringe width, $$\beta = x_{n+1} - x_n = \frac{\lambda}{2\mu \sin \alpha}$$

$$\beta = \frac{\lambda}{2\mu \sin \alpha} \cong \frac{\lambda}{2\mu\alpha} \quad \text{(for small } \alpha \text{ and in radians)} \quad \ldots (5)$$

For an air film ($\mu = 1$), fringe width,

$$\beta = \frac{\lambda}{2 \sin \alpha} \approx \frac{\lambda}{2\alpha} \text{ (for small } \alpha) \quad \ldots (6)$$

Similarly, it can be shown that the fringe width for dark fringes is given by,

$$\beta = \frac{\lambda}{2\mu \sin \alpha} \quad \ldots (7)$$

which is the same as that of a bright fringe.

The width of a dark or bright fringe is however equal to half the fringe width.

In equation (5), as all quantities on the right side are constant, β is constant for a given wedge angle α. It means that the **interference fringes** are **equidistant** from each other. According to relation (6), as angle α increases, the fringes move closer. At $\alpha = 1°$, the interference pattern vanishes. If α is gradually decreased, the fringe separation increases and ultimately the fringes disappear as the faces of the film become parallel ($\alpha = 0°$).

7.6 FORMATION OF COLOURS IN THIN FILMS

From article 1.3 (equations 6, 7, 9, 10) it is clear that the conditions of interference are complementary i.e. the conditions of interference in the case of reflected and transmitted systems are opposite. For a given path difference if a bright fringe is observed in reflected system, a dark fringe will be observed in the transmitted system.

The condition for maxima in reflected system is $2\mu t \cos r = (n \pm 1/2) \lambda$. If white light is incident on the film the wavelength satisfying above relation will be present in reflected system and corresponding colour will be seen. The colour appearing on the film will change if μ, t and r are changed. So different colours in reflected (or transmitted) rays are seen if, one of the three parameters μ, t and r is changed.

When oil is dropped on water surface, it spreads slowly and a thin film is formed. The film itself is although **colourless** but **appears colourful** and keeps on changing colour, **due to interference**. The thin film keeps on changing colour as the oil film changes the thickness. The thickness changes as the oil spreads on the water surface and due to waves present in the water surface.

A soap bubble is water film which is basically colourless but appears colourful due to interference and the colour also keeps on changing. The colour changes due to change in the thickness of the bubble which is caused by the gravitational force. When the soap bubble is about to burst the thickness is negligible and total path difference is just $\lambda/2$. Due to which the waves interfere destructively and bubble becomes black. A soap bubble floating in air also changes the colour as the angle of incidence and hence angle of refraction r changes.

SOLVED EXAMPLES

Example 7.1 : In a certain region of interference we get 490th order maximum for sodium 5890 A° line. What will be the order of interference maximum at the same plane for sodium 5896 A° ?

Data : n = 490, λ = 5890 A°

Formula : $\Delta = n\lambda$

Solution :

Path difference for nth order maximum, $\Delta = n\lambda$

∴ Path difference for 490th order maximum when λ is 5890 A°

$$\Delta = 490 \times 5890 \times 10^{-8}$$

$$\Delta = 2.89 \times 10^{-2} \text{ cm}$$

For sodium light of wavelength λ_1 = 5896 A°, the order of interference is n_1. Then the

Path difference = $n_1 \lambda_1 = 2.89 \times 10^{-2}$

∴ $n_1 = \dfrac{2.89 \times 10^{-2}}{\lambda_1}$

$$\therefore \quad n_1 = \frac{2.89 \times 10^{-2}}{5896 \times 10^{-8}} = 489.5$$

∴ The order of interference maximum = $\boxed{489}$

Example 7.2 : Fringes are produced with monochromatic light of λ = 5450 A°. A thin glass plate of μ = 1.5 is then placed normally in the path of one of the interferring beams and the central band of the fringe system is found to move into the position previously occupied by the third bright band from the centre. Calculate the thickness of the glass plate.

Data : λ = 5450 A°, μ = 1.5, n = 3
Formula : $t(\mu - 1) = n\lambda$
Solution :

$$t = n \frac{\lambda}{(\mu - 1)}$$

Substituting,
$$t = \frac{3 \times 5450 \times 10^{-8}}{1.5 - 1}$$

$$\boxed{t = 0.000327 \text{ cm}}$$

Example 7.3 : When light falls normally on a soap film, whose thickness is 5×10^{-5} cm and whose refractive index is 1.33; which wavelength in the visible region will be reflected most strongly ?

Data : $t = 5 \times 10^{-5}$ cm, $\mu = 1.33$
Formula : $2\mu t \cos r = (2n + 1) \lambda/2$ where n = 0, 1, 2, 3, ... etc.
Solution :

For normal incidence,

$$\cos r = 1$$

$$\therefore \quad 2\mu t = (2n + 1) \frac{\lambda}{2}$$

$$\therefore \quad \lambda = \frac{2 \times 2\mu t}{2n + 1}$$

$$\lambda = \frac{4 \times 1.33 \times 5 \times 10^{-5}}{(2n + 1)}$$

For n = 0,
$$\lambda = \frac{4 \times 1.33 \times 5 \times 10^{-5}}{1} = 2.66 \times 10^{-4} \text{ cm}$$

$$\boxed{\lambda = 26{,}600 \text{ A°}}$$

For n = 1,

$$\lambda = \frac{4 \times 1.33 \times 5 \times 10^{-5}}{3} = 8.866 \times 10^{-5} \text{ cm}$$

$$\boxed{\lambda = 8866 \text{ A°}}$$

For n = 2,

$$\lambda = \frac{4 \times 1.33 \times 5 \times 10^{-5}}{5} = 5.32 \times 10^{-5} \text{ cm}$$

$$\boxed{\lambda = 5320 \text{ A}°}$$

For n = 3,

$$\lambda = \frac{4 \times 1.33 \times 5 \times 10^{-5}}{7} = 3.8 \times 10^{-5} \text{ cm}$$

$$\boxed{\lambda = 3800 \text{ A}°}$$

The wavelength 5320 A° will be most strongly reflected in the visible region.

Problem 7.4 : A parallel beam of sodium light λ = 5890 A° strikes a film of oil floating on water. When viewed at an angle of 30° from the normal, 8th dark band is seen. Determine the thickness of the film if refractive index of oil = 1.5

Data : λ = 5890 A°, ∠i = 30°, μ = 1.5, n = 8

Formulae : (i) $2\mu t \cos r = n\lambda$ or $t = \dfrac{n\lambda}{2\mu \cos r}$ ... (1)

(ii) $\mu = \dfrac{\sin i}{\sin r}$

Solution :

$$\sin r = \frac{\sin i}{\mu}$$

$$\cos r = \sqrt{1 - \sin^2 r}$$

∴ $\cos r = \sqrt{1 - \dfrac{\sin^2 i}{\mu^2}}$

∴ $\cos r = \sqrt{1 - \dfrac{\sin^2 30}{(1.5)^2}}$

$\cos r = 0.943$

Substituting in (1),

∴ $t = \dfrac{8 \times 5890 \times 10^{-8}}{2 \times 1.5 \times 0.943}$

$= \boxed{1.6302 \times 10^{-4} \text{ cm}}$

Example 7.5 : Two glass plates enclose a wedge-shaped air film, touching at one edge and are separated by a wire of 0.03 mm diameter at a distance of 15 cm from the edge. Monochromatic light of λ = 6000 A° from a broad source falls normally on the film. Calculate the fringe width of the fringes thus formed.

Data : λ = 6000 × 10^{-8} cm; For air film, μ = 1

Diameter = 0.03 mm = 0.003 cm

Distance of fringe from the edge = 15 cm

Formula : Fringe width,

$$\beta = \frac{\lambda}{2\mu \sin \alpha} \approx \frac{\lambda}{2\mu \tan \alpha}$$

Solution :

$$\beta = \frac{6000 \times 10^{-8}}{2 \times 1 \times \frac{0.003}{15}} = \boxed{0.15 \text{ cm}}$$

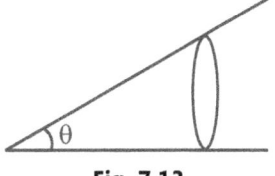

Fig. 7.13

Example 7.6 : Interference fringes are produced by monochromatic light falling normally on a wedge-shaped film of cellophane whose refractive index is 1.4. The angle of the wedge is 20 sec of an arc and the distance between the successive fringes is 0.25 cm. Calculate the wavelength of light.

Data : $\beta = 0.25$ cm, $\mu = 1.4$, $\theta = 20$ sec $= \frac{20}{60 \times 60} \times \frac{\pi}{180} = \frac{1}{180} \times \frac{\pi}{180}$ radians

Formula :
$$\beta = \frac{\lambda}{2\mu\alpha}$$

$$\therefore \quad \lambda = 2\mu\,\alpha \cdot \beta$$

Solution :

$$\lambda = 2 \times 1.4 \times \frac{\pi}{180 \times 180} \times 0.25$$

$$\boxed{\lambda = 6.79 \times 10^{-5} \text{ cm}}$$

Example 7.7 : Two plane rectangular pieces of glass are in contact at one edge and separated by a hair at opposite edge, so that a wedge is formed. When light of wavelength 6000 A° falls normally on the wedge, nine interference fringes are observed. What is the thickness of the hair ?

Data : $\lambda = 6000 \times 10^{-8}$ cm, $n = 9$, $r = 0$ for normal incidence

Formula : $2\mu t \cos(r + \alpha) = n\lambda$

Solution :

If the fringes are seen normally and the angle of wedge is very small, then $r = 0$, so that

$$\cos(r + \alpha) = \cos \alpha = 1$$

For air film, $\mu = 1$

$$\therefore \quad 2\mu t = n\lambda$$

$$2 \times 1 \times t = 9 \times 6000 \times 10^{-8}$$

$$\therefore \quad t = \frac{9 \times 6000 \times 10^{-8}}{2}$$

$$= \boxed{27 \times 10^{-5} \text{ cm}}$$

Example 7.8 : A square piece of cellophane film with index of refraction 1.5 has a wedge-shaped section, so that its thickness at two opposite sides is t_1 and t_2. If with light of $\lambda = 6000$ A°, the number of fringes appearing on the film is 10, calculate the difference $t_2 - t_1$.

Data : $\lambda = 6000 \times 10^{-8}$ cm, $\mu = 1.5$

Formula : $2 \mu t_1 \cos(r + \alpha) = n \lambda$ ... (1)

Solution :

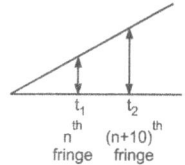

Fig. 7.14

For $(n + 10)^{th}$ dark fringe,

$$2 \mu t_2 \cos(r + \alpha) = (n + 10) \lambda \quad ... (2)$$

For normal incidence, $r = 0$ and if the angle of wedge is small,

$$\cos(r + \alpha) = \cos \alpha = 1$$

∴ Equations (1) and (2) become

$$2 \mu t_1 = n \lambda \quad ... (3)$$

$$2 \mu t_2 = (n + 10) \lambda \quad ... (4)$$

∴ Subtracting equation (3) from equation (4), we get

$$2 \mu (t_2 - t_1) = 10 \lambda$$

∴ $$t_2 - t_1 = \frac{10 \lambda}{2 \mu} = \frac{10 \times 6000 \times 10^{-8}}{2 \times 1.5}$$

i.e. $\boxed{t_2 - t_1 = 2 \times 10^{-4} \text{ cm}}$

Example 7.9 : A parallel beam of light of wavelength 5890 A° is incident on a thin film of refractive index 1.5, such that the angle of refraction into the film is 60°. Calculate the smallest thickness of the film which will make it appear dark by reflection.

Data : $\lambda = 5890$ A°, $r = 60°$, $\mu = 1.5$

Formula : For darkness,

$$2\mu t \cos r = n\lambda. \text{ Let } n = 1$$

Solution :

$$t = \frac{\lambda}{2\mu \cos r} = \frac{5890 \times 10^{-8}}{2 \times 1.5 \times \cos 60}$$

$\boxed{t = 3.926 \times 10^{-5} \text{ cm}}$

Example 7.10 : The optical path difference between two sets of similar waves from the same source arriving at a point on the screen is 199.5 λ. Is the point dark or bright ? If the path difference is 0.012 cm, find the wavelength of the light used.

Data : $\Delta_1 = 199.5 \lambda$, $\Delta_2 = 0.12$ cm

Formula : For 199.5 λ it is odd path difference, therefore point is a dark fringe and for darkness,

$$\Delta = (2n-1)\frac{\lambda}{2} \left(\because \left(\frac{2n-1}{2}\right) = 199.5 \right)$$

Solution :

$0.012 = 199.5\,\lambda$

$\lambda = \dfrac{0.012}{199.5}$

$\lambda = 6.015 \times 10^{-8}$ cm

$\boxed{\lambda = 6015\ \text{A}°}$

Example 7.11 : Two pieces of plane glass are placed together with a piece of paper between the two at one edge. Find the angle in seconds of the wedge shaped air film between the plate, if on viewing the film normally with monochromatic light of wavelength 4800 A°, there are 18 bands per cm.

Solution :

18 bands per cm

∴ Band width, $\beta = \dfrac{1}{18}$

$\beta = 0.0556$ cm

We know, $\beta = \dfrac{\lambda}{2\alpha}$

$\alpha = \dfrac{\lambda}{2\beta} = \dfrac{4800 \times 10^{-8}}{2 \times 0.0556}$

$\alpha = 4.3165 \times 10^{-4}$ rad

Note conversion of radians into seconds.

$\alpha = 4.3165 \times 10^{-4} \times \dfrac{180}{\pi} \times 60 \times 60$

$\boxed{\alpha = 89.02\ \text{seconds}}$

Example 7.12 : Two optically plane glass strips of length 10 cm are placed one over the other. A thin foil of thickness 0.010 mm is introduced between the plates at one end to form an air film. If the light used has wavelength 5900 A°, find the separation between consecutive bright fringes.

Solution :

$\tan \alpha = \dfrac{t}{x}$

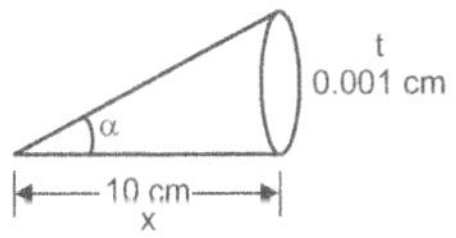

Fig. 7.15

As α is very small, tan α = α

$$\alpha = \frac{t}{x} = \frac{0.001}{10}$$

$$\alpha = 0.0001 \text{ rad}$$

$$\beta = \frac{\lambda}{2\alpha} = \frac{5.9 \times 10^{-5}}{2 \times 0.0001} \quad \boxed{\beta = 0.295 \text{ cm}}$$

Note while using α in calculation it must be all the time in radians. If it is given in seconds then convert it in rad.

Example 7.13 : Find the thickness of a wedge-shaped film at a point where fourth bright fringe is situated. λ for sodium light is 5893 A°.

Data : n = 4, λ = 5893 A°

Formula : For bright band and wedge-shaped film,

$$2\mu t \cos(r + \alpha) = (2n - 1)\frac{\lambda}{2}$$

Let normal incidence, r = 0 and α is very small ∴ cos (r + α) = 1, μ = 1

∴ $$2t = (2n - 1)\frac{\lambda}{2}$$

Solution :

$$2t = \frac{(2 \times 4 - 1) \lambda}{2}$$

$$t = \frac{7}{4} \times 5893 \times 10^{-8}$$

$$\boxed{t = 1.031275 \times 10^{-4} \text{ cm}}$$

Example 7.14 : Monochromatic light emitted by a broad source of light of wavelength 6×10^{-5} cm falls normally on two glass plates which enclose a thin wedge-shaped film of air. The plates touch at one end and are separated at a point 15 cm from the end by a wire 0.5 mm in diameter. Find the width between any two consecutive bright fringes.

Solution :

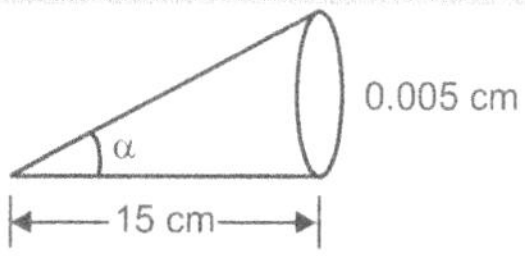

Fig. 7.16

$$\alpha = \frac{t}{x} = \frac{0.005}{15} = 3.333 \times 10^{-4} \text{ rad}$$

Bandwidth, $$\beta = \frac{\lambda}{2\alpha}$$

$$\beta = \frac{6 \times 10^{-5}}{2 \times 3.333 \times 10^{-4}}$$

$$\boxed{\beta = 0.09 \text{ cm}}$$

7.7 NEWTON'S RINGS

When a **plano-convex lens** of large focal length with its convex surface is placed in contact with a **plane glass plate**, an air film of gradually increasing thickness is formed between them. The thickness of the film at the point of contact is zero and increases gradually outwards. If monochromatic light is allowed to fall normally, and the film is viewed in reflected light, alternate **bright and dark rings** are observed. These rings are concentric around the point of contact between the lens and the glass plate. These fringes are called as **Newton's rings** as they were discovered by Newton. [See Fig. 7.17 (a)]

Experimental Arrangement

The experimental arrangement for obtaining Newton's rings is shown in Fig. 7.17 (b).

A plano-convex lens L of large radius of curvature is placed on a plane glass plate P. The point of contact between them is O. The light from an extended monochromatic source (sodium lamp) falls on a glass plate G held at an angle of 45° with the vertical.

The glass plate G reflects normally a part of the incident light towards the air film between the lens L and the glass plate P. A part of the incident light is reflected by the curved surface of the lens L and a part is transmitted which is reflected back from the plane surface of plate P (i.e. rays are reflected from the top and bottom surfaces of the air film). These two reflected rays interfere and produce an **interference pattern** in the form of **circular rings**. These rings are **localised** in the air film and can be seen with a microscope focused on the film.

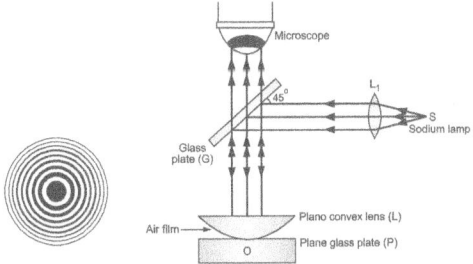

(a) Typical Newton's rings pattern observed in reflected light   (b) Experimental arrangement for observing Newton's rings

Fig. 7.17

Explanation of the Formation of Newton's Rings

Newton's rings are formed due to interference between the waves reflected from the top and bottom surfaces of the air film, formed between the lens and the glass plate.

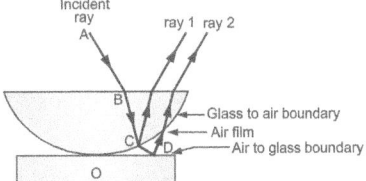

Fig. 7.18 : Formation of Newton's rings

When a monochromatic ray of light AB, is incident on the system, it gets partially reflected at C, the bottom of curved surface of the lens (glass-air boundary). This goes out in the form of ray 1 without any phase reversal. The other part is refracted along CD. At D, the top surface of the plane glass plate, it gets partially reflected to form ray 2. This ray has, a phase reversal as it is reflected from air to glass boundary. As the rays 1 and 2 are derived from the same source and are coherent, so they interfere to form fringes. Interference does not take place between rays reflected from the surfaces of lens and glass plate due to their thickness which is much larger than wavelength of light.

The radius of curvature of plano-convex lens is very large and the small section of the air film trapped between lens and the glass plate will be similar to a wedged air film. Therefore, the optical path difference will be same as that of wedged air film.

The optical path difference for wedge film is,

$$\Delta = 2\mu t \cos(r + \alpha) \qquad \ldots (1)$$

For air film, $\mu = 1$, for normal incidence $\cos r = 1$ and $\alpha \approx 0$

$$\therefore \quad \Delta = 2t \qquad \ldots (2)$$

In Reflected System

Total optical path difference = Path difference due to thin film
+ Path difference due to reflections

$$\therefore \quad \Delta = 2t \pm \frac{\lambda}{2} \qquad \ldots (3)$$

Condition for Constructive Interference

For constructive interference the total phase difference should be an integral multiple of λ.

$$\Delta = n\lambda$$

$$\therefore \quad 2t \pm \frac{\lambda}{2} = n\lambda$$

$$2t = \left(n \pm \frac{1}{2}\right)\lambda \qquad \ldots (4)$$

Condition for Destructive Interference

For destructive interference the total phase difference should be an odd integral multiple of $\lambda/2$.

$$\Delta = (2n \pm 1)\frac{\lambda}{2}$$

$$\therefore \quad 2t \pm \frac{\lambda}{2} = (2n \pm 1)\frac{\lambda}{2}$$

$$2t = n\lambda \qquad \ldots (5)$$

Radii of Bright Rings

The plano-convex lens LOL' is placed on a glass plate AB. The point C is the centre of the sphere of which LOL' is a part. Let R be the radius of curvature of the lens and r_n be the radius of the nth Newton's rings corresponding to the constant film thickness 't'.

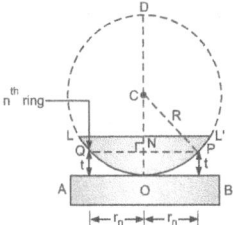

Fig. 7.19

By the property of circle (theorem of intersecting chords),

$$NP \times NQ = NO \times ND$$

i.e. $\quad r_n \times r_n = t(2R - t) = 2Rt - t^2 \approx 2Rt$ (as t^2 is very small)

∴ $\quad r_n^2 = 2Rt \qquad \qquad \ldots (6)$

or $\quad t = \dfrac{r_n^2}{2R} = \dfrac{D_n^2}{8R}$ (D_n being diameter of nth bright ring) $\quad \ldots (7)$

The condition for the formation of nth bright ring is

$$2t = (2n \pm 1)\dfrac{\lambda}{2} \qquad \ldots (8)$$

From equations (7) and (8),

$$2 \cdot \dfrac{D_n^2}{8R} = (2n \pm 1)\dfrac{\lambda}{2}$$

$$D_n^2 = (2n \pm 1) \cdot 2\lambda R$$

$$D_n = \sqrt{2\lambda R} \cdot \sqrt{2n \pm 1} \qquad \text{i.e. } D_n \propto \sqrt{2n \pm 1} \ldots (9)$$

Equation (9) shows that diameter of a bright ring is proportional to the square root of odd natural numbers.

Radii of Dark Rings

The condition for formation of dark Newton's ring is,

$$2t = n\lambda \qquad \ldots (10)$$

Substituting for t from (8),

$$2 \cdot \dfrac{D_n^2}{8R} = n\lambda$$

$$D_n^2 = 4n\lambda R \qquad \text{... (11)}$$

$$D_n = 2\sqrt{n\lambda R} \text{ i.e. } D_n \propto \sqrt{n} \qquad \text{... (12)}$$

Thus, the diameter of a dark ring is proportional to the square root of a natural number.

7.7.1 Properties of Newton's Rings

1. **Rings Get Closer Away from the Centre :** Consider equation (12) giving the diameter of a dark ring. We have

$$D_n \propto \sqrt{n} \text{ and } D_{n+1} \propto \sqrt{n+1}$$

$$\therefore \quad D_{n+1} - D_n \propto (\sqrt{n+1} - \sqrt{n})$$

If constant of proportionality is taken as 1, then

$$D_{n+1} - D_n = \sqrt{n+1} - \sqrt{n}$$

$$\therefore \quad D_2 - D_1 = \sqrt{2} - \sqrt{1} = 0.414$$

$$D_3 - D_2 = \sqrt{3} - \sqrt{2} = 0.317$$

Therefore, the **fringe width decreases** with the order of the fringe and the fringes get closer as the order increases. This can be shown for bright rings too.

This can also be explained in another way. The angle of the wedge increases as one moves away from the centre. From the equation for fringe spacing $\beta = \dfrac{\lambda}{2\mu\alpha}$, the fringe separation decreases as the wedge angle α increases. Hence, the rings come closer with increase in their radii.

2. **Dark Central Spot :** At the point of contact of the lens with the glass plate, the thickness of the air film t = 0. From equation (3), it can be seen that the path difference between rays reflected from the top and bottom surfaces of the film is $\lambda/2$. Hence, the interfering waves at the centre are opposite in phase and interfere destructively. Thus, a **dark spot** is produced at the centre.

3. **Fringes of Equal Thickness :** It can be seen from equations (4) and (5) that **maxima and minima occur alternately** due to variation in the thickness 't' of the film. Each maxima or minima is, therefore, a locus of constant film thickness. Hence, the fringes are called fringes of equal thickness.

4. **Circular Fringes :** The circular wedge of air film may be regarded as having an axis passing through the point of contact O. This film bulges from the point of contact to outward with gradually increasing thickness of air film. The locus of points having the same thickness falls on a circle having its centre at the point of contact. Thus the thickness of the air film is the same at all points on any circle having O as the centre. The fringes are therefore circular. If the thickness satisfies the condition for constructive interference, the **circular fringe** is bright; otherwise it is dark.

5. **Localised Fringes :** When the system is illuminated with a parallel light beam, the reflected rays are not parallel. They interfere near to the top surface of the film. When

viewed from the top, the rays appear to diverge. As the fringes are seen at the upper surface of the film, they are said to be localised in the film.

6. **White Light :** With white light, few **coloured fringes** are seen at centre. Away from centre they overlap.

Example 7.15 : A convex lens is placed on a plane glass slab and is illuminated by a monochromatic light. The diameter of the 10th dark ring is measured and is found to be 0.433 cm. The radius of curvature of the lower surface of the lens is 70 cm. Find the wavelength of the light used.

Data : R = 70 cm, n = 10, D_n = 0.433 cm

Formula : $D_n^2 = 4nR\lambda$

Solution :

$$(0.433)^2 = 4 \times 10 \times 70 \times \lambda$$

$$\therefore \lambda = \frac{(0.433)^2}{4 \times 10 \times 70}$$

$$\lambda = 6.696 \times 10^{-5} \text{ cm} = \boxed{6696 \text{ A}°}$$

Example 7.16 : In a Newton's rings experiment, the diameter of the 15th dark ring was found to be 0.590 cm and that of the 5th dark ring was 0.336 cm. If the radius of the plano-convex lens is 100 cm, calculate the wavelength of the light used.

Data : D_{15} = 0.590 cm, D_5 = 0.336 cm, R = 100 cm, m = 10

Formula : $\lambda = \dfrac{(D_{n+m})^2 - (D_n)^2}{4mR}$

Solution :

$$\lambda = \frac{D_{15}^2 - D_5^2}{4 \times 10 \times R} = \frac{(0.590)^2 - (0.336)^2}{4 \times 10 \times 100}$$

$$\lambda = 5.880 \times 10^{-5} \text{ cm}$$

$$\boxed{\lambda = 5880 \text{ A}°}$$

Example 7.17 : The diameter of a dark ring in Newton's rings experiment decreases from 1.4 cm to 1.2 cm when air is replaced by a liquid as medium between lens and flat surface. Calculate the refractive index of the liquid.

Data : D_{air} = 1.4 cm, D_{liquid} = 1.2 cm

Formula : $\mu = \dfrac{D_{air}^2}{D_{liquid}^2}$

Solution :

$$\mu = \frac{(1.4)^2}{(1.2)^2}$$

$$\boxed{\mu = 1.36}$$

Example 7.18 : The diameter of the tenth dark ring in Newton's rings experiment is 0.5 cm. Calculate the radius of curvature of the lens and the air thickness at the position of the ring. The wavelength of light used is 5000 A°.

Data : $D_{10} = 0.5$ cm, $n = 10$, $\lambda = 5000 \times 10^{-8}$ cm

Formulae : (i) $D_n^2 = 4nR\lambda$, (ii) $t = \dfrac{D_n^2}{8R}$

Solution :

(i) $$R = \frac{D_n^2}{4n\lambda} = \frac{0.5^2}{4 \times 10 \times 5000 \times 10^{-8}}$$

$$\boxed{R = 125 \text{ cm}}$$

(ii) Thickness is given by

$$t = \frac{D_n^2}{8R} = \frac{0.5^2}{8 \times 125} = \boxed{2.5 \times 10^{-4} \text{ cm}}$$

Example 7.19 : In a Newton's ring experiment, find the radius of curvature of the lens surface in contact with the glass plate when with a light of wavelength 5890 A°, the diameter of the third dark ring is 0.32 cm. The light is incident normally.

Data : $\lambda = 5890$ A°, $D_3 = 0.32$ cm, $n = 3$

Formula : $D_n^2 = 4Rn\lambda$

Solution : $R = \dfrac{D_n^2}{4n\lambda}$

$$R = \frac{(0.32)^2}{4 \times 3 \times 5890 \times 10^{-8}}$$

$$\boxed{R = 144.87 \text{ cm}}$$

Example 7.20 : In Newton's rings, the diameter of a certain bright ring is 0.65 and that of tenth ring beyond it is 0.95 cm. If $\lambda = 6000$ A°, calculate the radius of curvature of a convex lens surface in contact with the glass plate.

Data : $D_n = 0.65$ cm, $D_{n+p} = 0.95$ cm, $\lambda = 6 \times 10^{-5}$ cm

Formula : $\dfrac{(D_{n+p})^2 - D_n^2}{4m\lambda}$

Solution :

$$R = \frac{(0.95)^2 - (0.65)^2}{4 \times 10 \times 6 \times 10^{-5}}$$

$$\boxed{R = 200 \text{ cm}}$$

Example 7.21 : In a Newton's ring experiment, a drop of water $\left(\mu = \frac{4}{3}\right)$ is placed between the lens and the plate. In this case, the diameter of the 10th ring was found to be 0.6 cm. Calculate the radius of curvature of the face of the lens in contact with the plate.
Given : $\lambda = 6000$ A°.
Data : $\mu = 1.3333$, $D_{10} = 0.6$ cm, $\lambda = 6 \times 10^{-5}$ cm, $n = 10$
Formula : $D_n^2 = \dfrac{4n\lambda R}{\mu}$
Solution :
$$R = \dfrac{D_n^2 \times \mu}{4n\lambda} = \dfrac{(0.6)^2 \times 1.3333}{4 \times 10 \times 6 \times 10^{-5}}$$
$$\boxed{R = 200 \text{ cm}}$$

Example 7.22 : Newton's rings are observed in reflected length of $\lambda = 5900$ A°. The diameter of the 5th dark ring is 0.4 cm. Find the radius of curvature of the lens and thickness of the air film.
Data : $\lambda = 5.9 \times 10^{-5}$ cm, $n = 5$, $D_5 = 0.4$ cm, $\therefore r = 0.2$ cm
Formula : $D_n^2 = 4nR\lambda$
Solution :
$$R = \dfrac{(0.4)^2}{4 \times 5 \times 5.9 \times 10^{-5}}$$
$$R = 135.59 \text{ cm}$$
$$t = \dfrac{r^2}{2R} = \dfrac{(0.2)^2}{2 \times 135.59}$$
$$\boxed{t = 1.475 \times 10^{-4} \text{ cm}}$$

Example 7.23 : In a Newton's ring experiment, the diameters of 4th and 12th dark rings are 0.4 cm and 0.7 cm respectively. Calculate the diameter of 20th dark ring.
Data : $m = 12$, $n = 4$, $D_m = 0.7$ cm, $D_n = 0.4$ cm.
Formulae : (i) $R = \dfrac{D_{n+m}^2 - D_n^2}{4(m-n)\lambda}$
  (ii) $D_n^2 = 4nR\lambda$

$\therefore \quad D_n^2 = 4n \left(\dfrac{D_{n+m}^2 - D_n^2}{4(m-n)\lambda}\right) \cdot \lambda$

$$D_n^2 = \dfrac{4n(D_{n+m}^2 - D_n^2)}{4m}$$

Solution :

$$D_{20}^2 = 4 \times \frac{(0.7)^2 - (0.4)^2}{4(8)} \times 20$$

$$= \boxed{0.908 \text{ cm}}$$

Example 7.24 : If the diameter of nth dark ring in a Newton's ring experiment changes from 0.3 cm to 0.25 cm, as liquid is placed between the lens and the plate, calculate the value of μ of the liquid.

Data : $D_{air} = 0.3$ cm, $D_{liquid} = 0.25$ cm

Formula :
$$\mu = \frac{(D_n)^2_{air}}{(D_n)^2_{liquid}}$$

Solution :

$$\mu = \frac{(0.3)^2}{(0.25)^2}$$

$$= \boxed{1.44}$$

7.8 APPLICATIONS OF INTERFERENCE

7.8.1 Testing of Optical Flatness of Surfaces

Interference is now widely used for testing the quality of a surface finish. Even after machining, machine components retain certain surface irregularities. These act as sources of stress, leading to cracks thereby limiting the suitability of the components to certain applications. Therefore, the surfaces of components, which will be subjected to high stresses, are required to have a high surface finish. There are two ways in which the optical flatness or smoothness of a surface may be tested.

(a) The specimen surface is placed over the optically plane surface. If the surface is optically plane, no interference fringes will be observed. Because there will be no air film enclosed between the two planes and the path difference between the reflected pairs will be $\lambda/2$, which is the condition for destructive interference. If the given surface is not optically flat but has some imperfections, fringe pattern will be observed.

(b) If the specimen to be tested is placed inclined to an optically flat surface, a **wedge shaped air film** will be enclosed between them. The air wedge produces **straight** and **equidistant fringes** if the surface of the component is **smooth**. These fringes are parallel to the line of intersection of two surfaces. The fringes or bands are of equal thickness as each fringe is the locus of the points at which the thickness of the film has a constant value. If the fringes are curved towards the contact edge, the surface is concave and if the fringes curve away, it is convex.

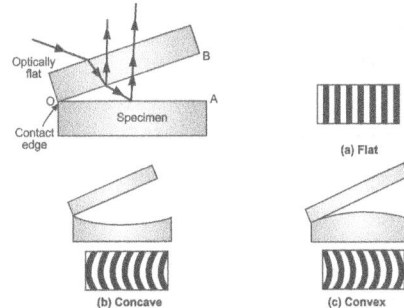

Fig. 7.20 : Testing of surfaces for optical flatness

7.8.2 Interference Filter

An interference filter is an optical filter that transmits one or more spectral lines and transmits others, while maintaining a nearly zero coefficient of absorption for all wavelengths of interest. An interference filter may be high-pass, low-pass band pass or band-rejection.

An interference filter uses the phenomenon of interference to transmit or reject a particular spectral range or line. To achieve this a number of thin coating with different refractive indices is applied to the glass. The incident rays at the boundaries of these layer will split and large number of reflected and refracted rays are generated as shown in Fig. 7.21. These rays will overlap and interfere constructively or destructively.

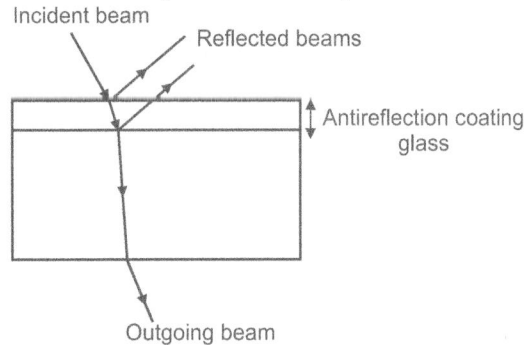

Fig. 7.21 : Interference filter

By adjusting angle of in credence, refractive index and thickness of coating, desired wavelengths can be made to interfere constructively. This beam of light will be available for further applications.

7.8.3 Antireflection or Non-reflecting Coatings

Optical instruments like telescopes, cameras, etc. use multicomponent glass lenses. When light is incident on these lenses, part of the light is reflected. Hence, the transmitted component has reduced intensity. When the number of reflections are large, the quality of the image produced will be poor. It was in 1935 that Alexander Smakula discovered that the phenomenon of interference could be used to reduce reflections from a surface by coating it with a thin transparent film. Such a film coated to reduce reflections is called **an antireflection film (AR coating) or non-reflecting film**. A thin film can act as an AR coating if the waves reflected from its top and bottom surfaces are exactly 180° out of phase and the waves have equal amplitudes. To achieve this, surfaces of lenses, prisms, etc. are coated with a thin layer or film of hard transparent material with refractive index intermediate between that of air and glass (less than that of glass). Light is reflected, from both surfaces of the layer, from a medium of greater refractive index than that in which it is travelling. So, the same phase change occurs in both reflections. If the film thickness is a quarter of the wavelength in the film, the total path difference is a half wavelength. Light reflected from the first surface is out of phase with light reflected from the second surface leading to destructive interference.

The path difference due to non-reflecting film,

Δ = path difference due to film + Path difference due to reflections.

$$\therefore \quad \Delta = 2\mu t \cos r + 0 \quad \ldots (1)$$

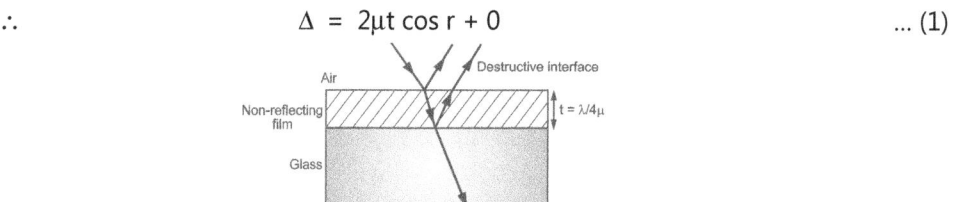

Fig. 7.22 : Anti-reflection film

Considering normal incidence, the condition for destructive interference is,

$$2\mu t = (2n \pm 1) \frac{\lambda}{2}$$

For n = 0, $\quad 2\mu t = \dfrac{\lambda}{2}$

or $\quad t = \dfrac{\lambda}{4\mu} \quad \ldots (2)$

This means that the optical thickness, μt, of the material that has to be coated for reducing reflections is a quarter of the wavelength.

For glass (μ = 1.5), the materials having refractive index nearer to this value are magnesium fluoride (μ = 1.38) and cryolite (μ = 1.36) are usually used. In addition, the materials should adhere well, should be durable, scratch proof and insoluble in ordinary solvents. The coating is obtained by evaporating magnesium fluoride on the surface in vacuum.

It is seen that condition (2) is satisfied only at a particular wavelength. This is usually chosen in the central yellow-green portion of the spectrum (λ = 5500 A°), where the eye is most sensitive. This leads to more reflection at both longer (red) and shorter (blue) wavelengths. The reflected light will therefore have a **'purple hue'**.

The overall reflection from a lens or a prism surface can be reduced, in this manner, from about 5% to 1%. This helps in increasing transmitted light. The same principle is used to minimize reflections from silicon photovoltaic cells (solar cells) by using a thin layer of silicon monoxide. This helps in increasing the amount of light actually reaching the solar cell.

7.8.4 Multilayer ARC

When the coating is anti-reflecting for the middle of the visible spectrum some reflection occurs at both the red and violet end of the spectrum. This gives the lens a purplish for cosmetic reasons, the color of appearance residual resident reflected light can be adjusted for eliminating wider.

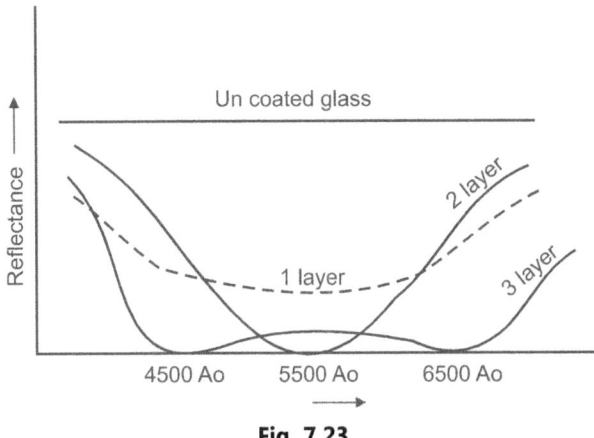

Fig. 7.23

An antireflection coated lens has an increased transmission for eliminating winder part of visible spectra, coating can be done for more than one wavelength. The Fig. 7.23. shows coating for wavelengths 4500A° and 6500A°. For better ARC more number of layers can be deposited.

Example 7.25 : MgF_2 of refractive index 1.38 is coated on a glass plate in order to reduce the reflection from the glass surface using interference. How thick is the coating needed to produce a minimum reflection at the centre of visible spectrum (5500 A°) ?

Data : $\mu = 1.38$, $\lambda = 5500 \times 10^{-8}$ cm

Considering normal incidence, $\cos r = 1$.

Formula : $$2\mu t = \frac{\lambda}{2}$$

∴ Thickness of coating, $$t = \frac{\lambda}{4\mu}$$

Solution :

$$t = \frac{5500 \times 10^{-8}}{4 \times 1.38}$$

$$\boxed{t = 996.37 \times 10^{-8} \text{ cm}}$$

Example 7.26 : Fringes of equal thickness are observed in a thin glass wedge of refractive index 1.52. The fringe spacing is 1 mm and the wavelength of light is 5893 A°. Calculate the angle of wedge in seconds of an arc.

Data :
$$\mu = 1.52$$
$$\lambda = 5893 \text{ A}°$$
$$\beta = 1 \text{ mm}$$

Formula : Fringe width is,
$$\beta = \frac{\lambda}{2\alpha}$$

Solution :

$$1 \times 10^{-1} = \frac{5893 \times 10^{-8}}{2\alpha}$$

$$\therefore \quad \alpha = \frac{5893 \times 10^{-8}}{2 \times 1 \times 10^{-1}}$$

$$\alpha = 2.9 \times 10^{-4} \text{ radian}$$

or $\quad \alpha = \dfrac{2.9 \times 10^{-4} \times 180 \times 60 \times 60}{3.14}$ of an arc = $\boxed{59.8 \text{ sec.}}$

Example 7.27 : A parallel beam of sodium light strikes a film of oil floating on water. When viewed at an angle 30° from the normal, in the reflected light, eighth dark band is seen. Determine the thickness of the film. Refractive index of oil is 1.46 and $\lambda = 5890$ A°.

Data :
$$i = 30°$$
$$\mu = 1.46$$
$$\lambda = 5890 \text{ A}°$$

Formulae : (i) By Snell's law,
$$\frac{\sin i}{\sin r} = \mu$$

(ii) $\quad 2\mu t \cos r = n\lambda$

Solution :

(i) $\quad \dfrac{\sin 30}{\sin r} = 1.46$

$$\sin r = \frac{0.5}{1.46} = 0.34247$$

$\therefore \quad \boxed{r = 20°}$

(ii) The thickness is given by relation (condition for minima)

$$2\mu t \cos r = n\lambda$$

$$t = \frac{8 \times 5890 \times 10^{-8}}{2 \times 1.46 \times \cos 20°}$$

$$\boxed{t = 1.7 \times 10^{-4} \text{ cm}}$$

Example 7.28 : In a Newton's rings experiment, the diameter of the 5th ring was 0.336 cm and that of 15th ring was 0.59 cm. Find the radius of curvature of the plano-convex lens, if the wavelength of light used is 5890 A°.

Data :
$$D_{15} = 0.59 \text{ cm}$$
$$D_5 = 0.336 \text{ cm}$$
$$\lambda = 5890 \text{ A°}$$
$$m = 10$$

Formula :
$$R = \frac{D_{n+m}^2 - D_n^2}{4 m \lambda}$$

Solution :
$$R = \frac{D_{15}^2 - D_5^2}{4 \times 10 \times \lambda}$$

$$R = \frac{(0.59)^2 - (0.336)^2}{4 \times 10 \times 5890 \times 10^{-8}}$$

$$\boxed{R = 99.83 \text{ cm}}$$

Example 7.29 : A soap film of refractive index 4/3 and thickness 1.5×10^{-4} cm is illuminated by white light incident at an angle of 45°. The light reflected by it is examined by a spectroscope in which is found a dark and corresponding to wavelength of 5×10^{-5} cm. Calculate the order of interference band.

Data :
$$\mu = 4/3 = 1.33$$
$$t = 1.5 \times 10^{-4} \text{ cm}$$
$$i = 45°$$
$$\lambda = 5 \times 10^{-5} \text{ cm}$$

Formulae : (i) By Snell's law,

$$\frac{\sin i}{\sin r} = \mu$$

(ii) $2\mu t \cos r = n\lambda$

Solution :

(i) $$\frac{\sin 45°}{\sin r} = 1.33$$

$$\sin r = \frac{0.707}{1.33}$$

sin r = 0.53038

or $r = 32°$

(ii) The order of interference will be given by (condition for dark band)

$$2\mu t \cos r = n\lambda$$

$$n = \frac{2 \times 1.33 \times 1.5 \times 10^{-4} \times \cos 32°}{5 \times 10^{-5}}$$

$$\boxed{n = 6.78}$$

The order of interference,

$$n = 6$$

Example 7.30 : A wedge shaped air film having an angle of 40 seconds is illuminated by monochromatic light and fringes in reflected system are observed through a microscope. The distance between the consecutive bright fringes was measured as 0.12 cm. Calculate the wavelength of light used.

Data :
$\alpha = 40$ sec.
$\beta = 0.12$ cm
$\alpha = 40$ sec
$\alpha = \dfrac{40 \times \pi}{60 \times 60 \times 180}$ radian
$\alpha = 1.9 \times 10^{-4}$ rad.

Formula :
The fringe width is given by,
$$\beta = \frac{\lambda}{2\alpha}$$
$$\lambda = 2\beta\alpha$$

Solution :
$$\lambda = 2 \times 0.12 \times 1.9 \times 10^{-4}$$
$$\lambda = 5 \times 10^{-5} \text{ cm}$$
$$\boxed{\lambda = 5000 \text{ A}°}$$

Example 7.31 : In Newton's rings experiment the diameters of nth and $(n+8)^{th}$ bright rings are 4.2 mm and 7.00 mm respectively. Radius of curvature of the lower surface of the lens is 2.00 m. Determine the wavelength of the light.

Data :
$D_n = 4.2$ mm
$D_{n+8} = 7$ mm
$R = 2$ m

Formula :
$$\lambda = \frac{D_{n+m}^2 - D_n^2}{4mR}$$

Solution :

$$\lambda = \frac{D_{n+8}^2 - D_n^2}{4(n+8-n)R}$$

$$\lambda = \frac{0.7^2 - 0.42^2}{4 \times 8 \times 200}$$

$$\lambda = 5 \times 10^{-5} \text{ cm}$$

$$\boxed{\lambda = 5000 \text{ A}°}$$

Example 7.32 : Newton's rings are formed by light reflected normally from a plano-convex lens and a plane glass plate with a liquid between them. The diameter of nth ring is 2.18 mm and that of $(n+10)^{th}$ ring is 4.51 mm. Calculate the refractive index of the liquid, given that the radius of curvature of the lens is 90 cm and wavelength of light is 5893 A°.

Data :
$$D'_n = 2.18 \text{ mm}$$
$$D'_{n+10} = 4.5 \text{ mm}$$
$$R = 90 \text{ cm}$$
$$\lambda = 5893 \text{ A}°$$

Formula :
$$R = \frac{\mu(D'^2_{n+m} - D'^2_n)}{4m\lambda}$$

$$\mu = \frac{4m\lambda R}{D'^2_{n+m} - D'^2_n}$$

Solution :

$$\mu = \frac{4 \times 10 \times 5893 \times 10^{-8} \times 90}{0.45^2 - 0.218^2}$$

$$\boxed{\mu = 1.368}$$

Example 7.33 : A parallel beam of monochromatic light of wavelength $\lambda = 5890$ A° is incident on a thin film of $\mu = 1.5$ such that the angle of refraction is 60°. Find the maximum thickness of the film so that it appears dark for normal incidence, what is the thickness required ?

Data :
$$\lambda = 5890 \text{ A}°$$
$$r = 60°$$
$$\mu = 1.5$$

Formula : For dark band,
$$2\mu t \cos r = n\lambda$$
$$t = \frac{n\lambda}{2\mu t \cos r}$$

Solution :

For maximum thickness, n = 1

$$t = \frac{1 \times 5890 \times 10^{-8}}{2 \times 1.5 \times \cos 60}$$

$$t = 4 \times 10^{-5} \text{ cm}$$

For normal incidence, r = 0 and hence cos r = 1.

∴ $$t = \frac{1 \times 5890 \times 10^{-8}}{2 \times 1.5 \times \cos 0}$$

$$\boxed{t = 2 \times 10^{-5} \text{ cm}}$$

Example 7.34 : An oil drop of volume 0.2 cc is dropped on the surface of a water tank of area 1 sq. m. The thin film spreads uniformly over the whole surface and white light reflected normally is observed through a spectrometer. The spectrum is seen to contain a first dark band whose centre has a wavelength of 5.5×10^{-5} cm. Find the refractive index of oil.

Data :
- V = 0.2 cc
- A = 1 sq. m.
- n = 1
- $\lambda = 5.5 \times 10^{-5}$ cm

Formulae : (i) Volume = Area × thickness (ii) $2\mu t \cos r = n\lambda$

Solution :

(i) $\quad 0.2 = 1 \times 10^4 \times t$

$\quad t = 2 \times 10^{-5}$ cm

(ii) For minima,

$$2\mu t \cos r = n\lambda$$

Let, $\quad r = 0$

$$\mu = \frac{n\lambda}{2t}$$

$$\mu = \frac{1 \times 5.5 \times 10^{-5}}{2 \times 2 \times 10^{-5}}$$

$$\boxed{\mu = 1.375}$$

Example 7.35 : A beam of monochromatic light of wavelength 5.82×10^{-7} m falls normally on a glass wedge of wedge angle of 20 seconds of an arc. If the refractive index of glass is 1.5, find the number of dark interference fringes per cm of the wedge length.

Data :
- $\lambda = 5.82 \times 10^{-7}$ m
- θ = 20 seconds
- μ = 1.5

The angle in degrees,

$$\theta = \frac{20}{60 \times 60} \times \frac{\pi}{180}$$

$$\theta = 9.69 \times 10^{-5}$$

Formula:

The fringe width, $\beta = \dfrac{\lambda}{2\mu\theta}$

Solution:

$$\beta = \frac{5.82 \times 10^{-7}}{2 \times 1.5 \times 9.69 \times 10^{-5}}$$

∴ $\beta = 0.2 \times 10^{-2}$ m $= 0.2$ cm

∴ Number of dark fringes/cm

$$= \frac{1}{\beta} = \frac{1}{0.2} = \boxed{5}$$

Example 7.36: A parallel beam of sodium light of wavelength 5890×10^{-8} cm is incident on a thin glass plate of refractive index 1.5, such that the angle of refration into the plate is 60°. Calculate the smallest thickness of the plate which will make it appear dark by reflection.

Data:
$\lambda = 5890 \times 10^{-8}$ cm
$\mu = 1.5$
$r = 60°$

Formula: The condition for dark fringe in reflected system is
$2\mu t \cos r = n\lambda$

Solution:

Taking $n = 1$

$2 \times 1.5 \times t \times \cos 60 = 5890 \times 10^{-8}$

∴ $t = 3.926 \times 10^{-3}$ cm $= \boxed{3.926 \times 10^{-5} \text{cm}}$

SUMMARY

- The superposition of two waves of equal amplitude, frequency and a constant phase difference is called as interference. The result is alternate dark and bright fringes.

    Conditions on path difference (x):

    (a) Constructive interference or bright fringe – Whole number multiple of λ.

    (b) Destructive interference or dark fringe – Odd integer multiple of $\dfrac{\lambda}{2}$.

- A film is said to be thin if its thickness is of the order of a few wavelengths.

- In a thin film of uniform thickness in reflected system, condition for

  (a) constructive interference : $\quad 2\mu t \cos r = (2n+1)\dfrac{\lambda}{2}$

  (b) destructive interference : $\quad 2\mu t \cos r = n\lambda$

  (c) in transmitted system, the conditions reverse.

- In a wedge-shaped film, the condition for

  (a) constructive interference : $\quad 2\mu t \cos(r+\alpha) = (2n+1)\dfrac{\lambda}{2}$

  (b) destructive interference : $\quad 2\mu t \cos(r+\alpha) = n\lambda$

  (c) fringe width : $\quad \beta \approx \dfrac{\lambda}{2\mu\alpha}$

  (d) fringes obtained are : equal in thickness, straight, parallel and equidistant.

- Newton's rings are : circular in shape, centre is dark for reflected light.

- Radius for

  (a) Bright ring (reflected light) $\quad D_n^2 = (2n \pm 1) \cdot 2\lambda R$

  (b) Dark ring (reflected light) $\quad D_n^2 = 4n\lambda R$

- Wavelength of monochromatic source of light $\quad \lambda = \dfrac{D_{n+p}^2 - D_n^2}{4pR}$

- Refractive index of liquid $\quad \mu = \dfrac{D'^{2}_{n+p} - D'^{2}_{n}}{D_{n+p}^2 - D_n^2}$

- Michelson's interferometer uses monochromatic light and is used for high precision measurement of wavelengths.

  (a) Wavelength of monochromatic source $\quad \lambda = \dfrac{2x}{N}$

  (b) Resolution of two spectral lines $\quad \Delta\lambda = \lambda_1 - \lambda_2 = \dfrac{\lambda_{avg}^2}{2x}$

  (c) Refractive index of material $\quad \mu = \dfrac{x}{t} + 1$

  (d) Thickness of plate $\quad t = \dfrac{x}{\mu - 1}$

- Interference is used to test optical flatness of a surface.
- Antireflection coatings are thin transparent coatings of quarter wave thickness

$$\mu t = \frac{\lambda}{4}$$

IMPORTANT FORMULAE

- Constructive interference, $x = n\lambda$, $n = 0, 1, 2 \ldots$
- Destructive interference, $x = (2n + 1)\frac{\lambda}{2}$, $n = 0, 1, 2 \ldots$
- $2\mu t \cos r = (2n \pm 1)\frac{\lambda}{2}$, $n = 0, 1, 2 \ldots$
- $2\mu t \cos r = n\lambda$, $n = 0, 1, 2 \ldots$
- $2\mu t \cos(r + \alpha) = (2n \pm 1)\frac{\lambda}{2}$, $n = 0, 1, 2 \ldots$
- $2\mu t \cos(r + \alpha) = n\lambda$, $n = 0, 1, 2 \ldots$
- $\beta = \dfrac{\lambda}{2\mu \sin \alpha}$
- $D_n^2 = \sqrt{2\lambda R} \cdot \sqrt{2n \pm 1}$ (bright)
- $D_n^2 = 4n\lambda R$
- $\lambda = \dfrac{D_{n+p}^2 - D_n^2}{4pR}$
- $\mu = \dfrac{D'^2_{n+p} - D'^2_n}{D^2_{n+p} - D^2_n}$
- $t = \dfrac{\lambda}{4\mu}$

EXERCISE

1. Explain the phenomena of interference.
2. What is constructive and destructive interference?
3. Derive the conditions for constructive and destructive interference.
4. Explain the phenomenon of interference in thin films in reflected light.

5. What are Newton's rings ? Explain how they are formed.
6. Explain the formation of colours in thin films.
7. Explain the phenomenon of interference in thin film in transmitted light.
8. How can Newton's rings be obtained in the laboratory ? How will you use them to measure the wavelength of sodium light ?
9. Explain the theory and the experimental arrangement of Newton's rings experiment.
10. What have you understood by non-reflecting films ? Explain.
11. Explain how the phenomenon of interference is utilized in testing the planeness of a surface.
12. In Newton's rings, show that the radii of dark rings are proportional to the square root of natural numbers.
13. When seen by reflected light, why does an excessively thin film appear to be perfectly black when illuminated by a white light ?
14. Explain, why colours are not observed in the case of a thick film when illuminated by a white light.
15. How can Newton's rings be used to determine the refractive index of a liquid ? Derive the formula used.
16. Prove that in reflected light Newton's rings, the diameters of bright rings are proportional to the square root of the odd natural numbers.
17. How can Newton's rings be obtained in the laboratory ? Prove that for Newton's rings in reflected light, the diameters of dark rings are proportional to the square root of natural numbers.
18. Explain how the principle of thin film interference can be used for measurement of thickness of thin film.
19. A thin film of uniform thickness is illuminated by monochromatic light. Obtain the conditions of darkness and brightness of the film as observed in reflected light.
20. Derive expression for path difference in reflected light and state the condition for constructive and destructive interference for a film of uniform thickness.
21. A thin film of uniform thickness is illuminated by a monochromatic light. Obtain the conditions of darkness and brightness of the film as observed in reflected light. Why does an excessively thin film appear dark in reflected light ?
22. Derive an expression of condition of maxima and minima for reflected light in case of thin transparent film of uniform thickness.
23. A thin film of uniform thickness is illuminated by a monochromatic light. Obtain the conditions of brightness and darkness of the film as observed in reflected light. When seen in reflected light, why does an excessively thin film appear to be perfectly black, when illuminated by white light ?

24. Explain the phenomenon of interference in parallel sided thin film in reflected light.
25. A wedge shaped film is illuminated with monochromatic light. Obtain an expression for number of dark bands per unit length.
26. Draw a diagram showing interference in reflected light in a thin wedge shaped film. Give the mathematical conditions for constructive and destructive interference. Explain how this type of interference pattern can be used for testing the optical flatness of surfaces.
27. When seen by reflected light, why does an excessively thin film appear to be perfectly black when illuminated by white light ?
28. An excessively thin film appears dark when observed in reflected light. Explain why.
29. A thin film illuminated by white light appears coloured when observed in reflected light. Explain why.
30. Explain the formation of Newton's rings. Prove that in Newton's rings by reflected light, the diameters of bright rings are proportional to square root of odd natural numbers.
31. Give the experimental set up for the formation of Newton's rings in the laboratory and explain the formation of rings there. How can this set up be used to determine the refractive index of a transparent liquid ? Derive the necessary expression.
32. Give experimental setup to obtain Newton's rings. Explain how interference takes place.
33. How can Newton's rings be obtained in the laboratory ? Prove that for the Newton's rings in the reflected light, the diameter of bright rings are proportional to the square root of odd natural numbers.
34. Explain how can Newton's rings be obtained in the laboratory and used for the determination of wavelength of monochromatic source of light.
35. Explain the formation of Newton's rings. Prove that for Newton's rings in reflected light, the diameters of dark rings are proportional to the square root of natural numbers.
36. Give experimental set up to obtain Newton's rings. Explain how interference takes place.
37. Explain the formation of Newton's rings. Prove that in Newton's rings by reflected light, the diameters of bright rings are directly proportional to the square root of odd natural number. Hence, explain how rings are getting closer with increase in their diameter with order.
38. How can Newton's rings be obtained in the laboratory ? Show that the diameter of nth dark ring is directly proportional to the square root of natural number.
39. Explain the formation of Newton's rings. Obtain an expression for the diameter of dark rings in reflected system. What will happen to the diameter of nth dark ring if air film is replaced by water film ? Explain.
40. Explain the use of thin film as anti-reflection coating.

41. Explain the following engineering application of interference:
    Non-reflecting coating.
42. Explain the use of thin film as anti-reflecting coating.
43. Explain the use of thin film as anti-reflection coating.
44. (i) Explain the use of thin film as anti-reflecting coating.
    (ii) Explain how interference pattern can be used for testing the optical flatness of surfaces.
45. Explain the working of non-reflecting coating.
46. Explain the use of thin film as antireflection coating.
47. Explain how the phenomenon of interference is utilised in:
    (i) testing the planeness of a surface
    (ii) anti-reflection coating.

UNSOLVED PROBLEMS

1. A parallel beam of light of wavelength 5890 A° is incident on a thin film of refractive index 1.5, such that the angle of refraction into the film is 60°. Calculate the smallest thickness of the film which will make it appear dark by reflection. **(Ans.** 3.926×10^{-5} cm**)**

2. Two pin holes separated by a distance of 0.5 mm are illuminated by a monochromatic light of wavelength 6000 A°. An interference pattern is obtained on a screen placed at a distance of 100 cm from the pin holes. Find the distance on the screen between the fifth and tenth dark fringes. **(Ans.** 0.6 cm**)**

3. An oil drop of volume 0.2 cc is dropped on the surface of a tank of water of area 1 sq. meter. The film spreads uniformly over the whole surface and white light reflected normally is observed through a spectrometer. The spectrum is seen to contain first dark band whose centre has wavelength of 5.5×10^{-5} cm. Find the refractive index of oil. **(Ans.** 1.375**)**

4. A soap film of refractive index $\frac{4}{3}$ and of thickness 1.5×10^{-4} cm is illuminated by white light incident at an angle of 60°. The light reflected by it is examined by a spectroscope in which is found a dark band corresponding to a wavelength of 5×10^{-5} cm. Calculate the order of interference of the dark band. **(Ans.** n = 6**)**

5. The optical path difference between two sets of similar waves from the same source arriving at a point on the screen is 199.5 λ. Is the point dark or bright? If the path difference is 0.012 cm, find the wavelength of the light used. **(Ans.** Dark, 6015 A°**)**

6. In a Newton's rings experiment, the diameter of the 5th ring is 0.336 cm and the diameter of the 15th ring is 0.590 cm. Find the radius of curvature of the plano convex lens, if the wavelength of light used is 5890 A°. **(Ans. 99.82 cm)**

7. In a Newton's rings experiment, find the radius of curvature of the lens surface in contact with the glass plate when with a light of wavelength 5890 A°, the diameter of the third dark ring is 0.32 cm. The light is incident normally. **(Ans. 144.9 cm)**

8. In Newton's rings, the diameter of a certain bright ring is 0.65 cm and that of tenth ring beyond it is 0.95 cm. If λ = 6000 A°, calculate the radius of curvature of a convex lens surface in contact with the glass plate. **(Ans. 200 cm)**

9. In a Newton's rings experiment, a drop of water $\left(\mu = \frac{4}{3}\right)$ is placed between the lens and the plate. In that case, the diameter of the 10th ring was found to be 0.6 cm. Calculate the radius of curvature of the face of the lens in contact with the plate, given λ = 6000 A°.

(Ans. 200 cm)

10. Newton's rings are observed in reflected light of λ = 5900 A°. The diameter of the 5th dark ring is 0.4 cm. Find the radius of curvature of the lens and the thickness of the air film. 35.59 cms, 0.000295 cm)

11. In a Newton's ring experiment, the diameters of 4th and 12th dark rings are 0.4 cm and 0.7 cm respectively. Calculate the diameter of 20th dark ring. **(Ans. 0.894 cm)**

12. In a Newton's rings experiment, the source emits two wavelengths λ_1 = 6000 A° and λ_2 = 4500 A°. It is found that nth dark ring due to λ_1 coincides with (n + 1)th dark ring due to λ_2. If the radius of curvature of the curved surface is 90 cm, find the diameter of nth dark ring for λ_1. **(Ans. 0.2538 cm)**

13. If the diameter of nth dark ring in a Newton's ring experiment changes from 0.3 cm to 0.25 cm, as a liquid is placed between the lens and the plate, calculate the value of μ of the liquid.

(Ans. μ = 1.44)

14. A wedge-shaped air film, having an angle of 45 seconds, is illuminated by monochromatic light and fringes are observed vertically through a microscope. The distance measured between the consecutive fringes is 0.12 cm, calculate the wavelength of light used.

(Ans. 5233 A°)

15. Two pieces of plane glass are placed together with a piece of paper between the two at one edge. Find the angle in seconds, of the wedge shaped air film between the plates, if on viewing the film normally with monochromatic light of wavelength 4800 A°, there are 18 bands per cm. **(Ans. 89.1 seconds)**

16. Two rectangular pieces of a plane glass are laid one upon the other and a thin wire is placed between them, so that a thin wedge shaped air film is formed between them. The plates are

illuminated with sodium light of λ = 5893 A° at normal incidence. Bright and dark bands are formed, there being 10 of each per cm length of the wedge measured normal to the edge in contact. Find the angle of the wedge. **(Ans.** 2.94×10^{-4} radians)

17. Two optically plane glass strips of length 10 cm are placed one over the other. A thin foil of thickness 0.010 mm is introduced between the plates at one end to form an air film. If the light used has wavelength 5900 A°, find the separation between consecutive bright fringes.

(Ans. 0.295 cm)

18. Find the thickness of a wedge-shaped film at a point where fourth bright fringe is situated. λ or sodium light is 5893 A°. **(Ans.** 1.03×10^{-4} cm)

REFERENCES

For better understanding of interference patterns from thin films :

- http://dev.physicslab.org/Document.aspx?doctype=3&filename=PhysicalOpticsThinFilmInterference.xml.

Animations of thin film interference patterns :

- http://www.wellesley.edu/Physics/Yhu/Animations/tfi.html

To understand physics behind antireflection coatings :

- http://mysite.verizon.net/vzeoacw1/thinfilm.html

Photographs of Newton's Rings pattern :

- http://www.fas.harvard.edu/~scdiroff/1ds/LightOptics/NewtonsRings/NewtonsRings.html

More information about Michelson's interferometer and photographs of fringes :

- http://www.phy.davidson.edu/StuHome/cabell_f/diffractionfinal/pages/Michelson.html.

✠ ✠ ✠

CHAPTER 8
DIFFRACTION

8.1 INTRODUCTION

Along with interference, diffraction is another phenomenon which supports the wave theory of light. Diffraction is responsible for the appearance of brilliant colours in a wide variety of natural phenomena. Diffraction with white light results into a beautiful rainbow like pattern. The flamboyant colours in the feathers of a peacock, the irridescent colours on the neck of pigeons, on the skins of snakes and on the back of beetles are due to diffraction of light.

In practical applications, the diffraction affects the resolution of optical instruments such as microscopes and telescopes. Thus diffraction decides the usefulness of these devices. Diffraction of X-rays from the crystals is used in understanding the crystal structure.

In engineering, diffraction is used for measurement of dimensions, stress, pressure etc.

Definition :

Diffraction is **bending of light** due to presence of an obstacle in the path of light. A diffraction pattern results from the interference of waves, diffracted by an obstacle, coming from the same source of light.

For visible diffraction pattern,
- The size of obstacle should be **comparable to the wavelength** of light.
- The source of light must be a **point source**.

Diffraction is also defined as the encroachment of light in the region of geometrical shadow.

According to Huygen's wave theory, each progressive wave produces secondary waves, the envelope of which produces the secondary wavefront.

OR

Every point of a wavefront may be considered as a source of secondary wavelets that spread out in all directions with a speed equal to the speed of propagation of waves.

In Fig. 8.1 (a), 'S' is a monochromatic source of light, MN is a small aperture, M'N' is the screen and AB is the illuminated portion on the screen in the absence of the aperture. Above A and below B, it is supposed to be a geometrically shadow region. But practically, the shadows formed are not sharp and light encroaches in the geometrical shadow region.

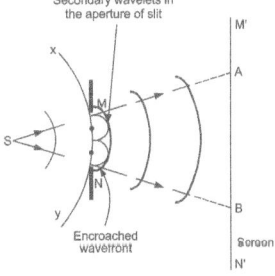

Fig. 8.1 (a)

This is because when the primary wavefront XY is incident on the aperture MN, every point within the aperture can be viewed as creating secondary waves which propagate outward from the aperture. The envelope of all these secondary waves gives a new circular wavefront, thus slit works as a new source of light. The centre of the wave has more intensity and it fades out at the edges in the geometrical shadow region. Thus light through the aperture does not create a perfect image of the aperture and the diffraction observed can be explained.

Similarly, if an opaque obstacle MN is placed in the path of light [See Fig. 8.1 (b)], the geometrical shadow region 'AB' is not sharp.

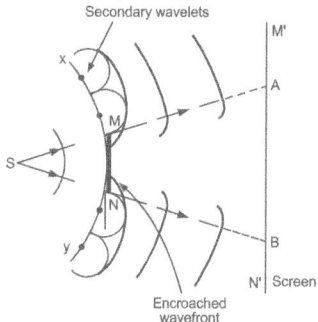

Fig. 8.1 (b)

This is because when the primary wavefront XY is incident on the aperture MN, it develops a secondary wavefront. The envelope of this secondary wavefront encroaches in the geometrical shadow region.

8.2 DIFFRACTION OF WAVES

In general, a diffraction situation requires a source of light, an obstacle and a screen to form the diffraction pattern as shown in Fig. 8.2.

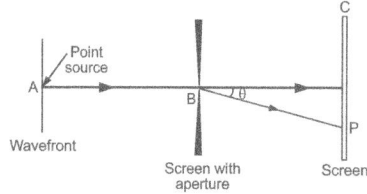

Fig. 8.2 : General Diffraction Situation

A plane wavefront A falls on an opaque screen B containing an aperture of arbitrary shape. The screen C receives the light that passes through this aperture. The light intensity pattern on the screen can be calculated by subdividing the wavefront into elementary areas **ds**, each of which becomes a source of expanding Huygen's wavelets. The light intensity at an arbitrary point P is found by superposing the wave disturbances caused by the wavelets reaching P, from all these elementary radiators. The wave disturbances reaching P differ in amplitude and phase because (i) the elementary radiators are at varying distances from P, (ii) areas of the radiators are different, and (iii) the light leaves the radiators at different angles to the normal to the wavefront.

Diffraction patterns are not often observed in everyday life. This is because, ordinary light sources are not monochromatic and are not point sources. If an ordinary light bulb is used instead of a point source, each wavelength of light, from every point of the bulb, forms its own diffraction pattern. These patterns overlap and no individual pattern is observed.

There is no fundamental difference between interference and diffraction. The term interference is used for effects involving waves from two sources. Diffraction involves a continuous distribution of secondary waves from a large number of sources or aperture. But, both phenomena are governed by the same basic superposition and Huygen's principle.

8.3 CLASSES OF DIFFRACTION

The diffraction involves a source, an obstacle and a screen. Depending upon the distances between source to obstacle and obstacle to the screen, diffraction is classified into two classes :

- Fraunhofer's diffraction.
- Fresnel's diffraction.

Fraunhofer's Diffraction	Fresnel's Diffraction
1. It is also called **far field** diffraction.	1. It is also called **near field** diffraction.
2. The source and screen are at **large distance** (infinite) from the obstacle.	2. The source and/or screen are at **small distance (finite)** from the obstacle.
3. The wavefronts incident on the obstacle and screen is a **plane wavefront** i.e. the rays are parallel.	3. The wavefronts incident on the obstacle are **spherical or cylindrical** i.e. rays are diverging.
4. The diffraction pattern is **not sensitive** to the distance.	4. The diffraction pattern is **sensitive** to the distance. (If distance is increased to large value it will be converted to Fraunhofer's diffraction.)
5. A **pair of convex lenses** are used for making the rays parallel.	5. The wavefront is directly allowed to fall on an obstacle or the screen.
6. Fig. 8.3 (a)	6. Fig. 8.3 (b)

7. The maximums and minimums are **well defined**. 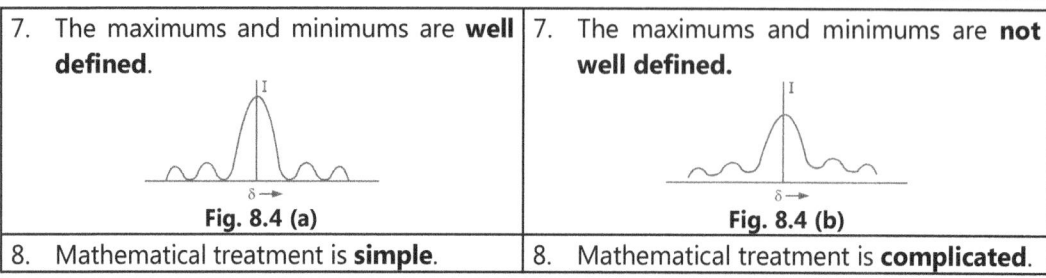 Fig. 8.4 (a)	7. The maximums and minimums are **not well defined**. Fig. 8.4 (b)
8. Mathematical treatment is **simple**.	8. Mathematical treatment is **complicated**.

8.4 FRAUNHOFER'S DIFFRACTION AT SINGLE SLIT GEOMETRICAL METHOD

For obtaining a Fraunhofer's diffraction pattern, the incident wavefront must be plane. Thus, **the source of light should either be at a large distance from the slit or a collimating lens must be used**.

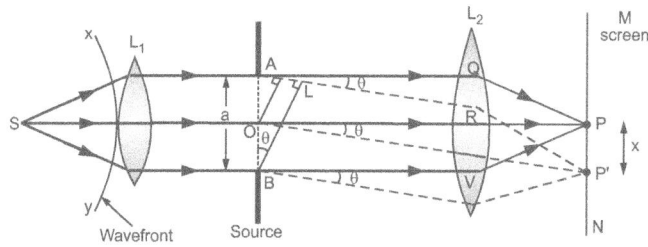

Fig. 8.5

In Fig. 8.5, 'S' is a narrow slit perpendicular to the plane of the paper and illuminated by a monochromatic light to act as a source of light. The wave coming from source S is made parallel by the collimating lens L_1. A plane wavefront is incident on the slit AB and each point on this wavefront is a source of the secondary wavefront. The secondary waves from points equidistant from O and situated in the upper and lower halves OA and OB of the wavefront, travel the same distance to reach P and hence the path difference is zero. The secondary waves interfere with one another and P will be a point of **maximum intensity**.

Now, consider that the secondary waves are travelling in the direction AR, inclined at an angle θ to the direction OP. All the secondary waves travelling in this direction reach the point P' on the screen. The point P' will be of **maximum** or **minimum intensity** depending on the path difference between the secondary waves originating from the corresponding points of the wavefront.

Phasor Method :

The diffraction pattern for a single slit can be found out by the phasor method. Our approach is as follows.

We divide the slit into a large number of narrow **pseudoslits N** of equal width, $\Delta x = \dfrac{a}{N}$, where 'a' is the width of the slit. The contribution of each pseudoslit will be represented by a phasor. To find the resultant wave amplitude, we add the N phasors.

For convenience in drawing, the slit of width 'a' in Fig. 8.6 (a) has been split into six pseudoslits. If we call the phase difference between the first and the last phasor as φ, it will be the angle labelled as φ in Fig. 8.6 (b).

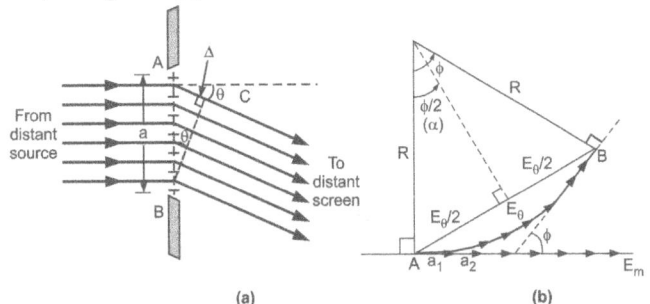

Fig. 8.6 : (a) Diffraction from singe slit   (b) Phasor diagram

The path difference between first and last wave is

$$\Delta = AC$$
$$\Delta = a \sin \theta \quad \text{[From Fig. 8.6 (a)]} \quad \ldots (1)$$

∴ Phase difference, $\phi = k \cdot \Delta$, where $k = \dfrac{2\pi}{\lambda}$

∴ $\phi = \dfrac{2\pi}{\lambda} \cdot \Delta = \dfrac{2\pi}{\lambda} (a \sin \theta)$ ... (2)

For simplicity we will define angle α, such that,

$$\alpha = \dfrac{\phi}{2} = \dfrac{\pi}{\lambda} (a \sin \theta) \quad \ldots (3)$$

The phase difference between the waves reaching at the point from adjacent slit is

$$\Delta\phi = \dfrac{2\pi}{\lambda} (\Delta x \sin \theta) \quad \ldots (4)$$

At point P, N wave vectors with the same amplitude, the same wavelength and the same phase difference between adjacent members combine to produce a resultant disturbance. Such wave vectors are called **phasors**. Thus, finding the resultant amplitude at P is equivalent to finding the vector sum of N phasors. The phasor diagram at any point P, away from the centre of the diffraction pattern is as shown in Fig. 8.6 (b).

The amplitude a_n contributed at a point on the screen by any one of the pseudoslit will be the same, since they are of equal width. But the phases of these amplitudes will be different at different points. Let δ be the phase difference between two adjacent amplitudes which is constant. So each amplitude is inclined at an angle δ with the preceding one and their vector sum E_θ is the resultant amplitude. If the wavefront is divided into large or infinite number of equal elements, the vector a_n will become shorter and δ will decrease by the same proportion. In this way, the vector diagram will approach **an arc of a circle**. The resultant amplitude E_θ is still the same and equal to **the length of the chord of arc**. The length of arc is just the amplitude E_m obtained when all of the amplitudes are in phase i.e. slit is not there and diffraction is absent. The radius of arc is R and a perpendicular has been dropped from the centre on the chord E_m. This will divide the apex angle and chord into two equal halves ($E_\theta/2$ and $E_\theta/2$)

In Fig. 8.6 (b), from the right triangle with apex angle $\phi/2$, we see that

$$\frac{E_\theta}{2} = R \sin \phi/2 \qquad \ldots (5)$$

$$\therefore \quad E_\theta = 2R \sin \alpha \qquad \left(\because \alpha = \frac{\phi}{2}\right)$$

Also,

$$\phi = \frac{\text{length of arc}}{\text{radius}} = \frac{E_m}{R}$$

This gives

$$E_m = R\phi \quad \text{or} \quad E_m = 2R\alpha \qquad \ldots (6)$$

Dividing (5) by (6)

$$\frac{E_\theta}{E_m} = \frac{2R \sin \alpha}{2R\alpha}$$

$$\therefore \quad E_\theta = E_m \frac{\sin \alpha}{\alpha} \qquad \ldots (7)$$

Equation (7) gives the amplitude for the single slit diffraction pattern at any angle θ.

The intensity I_θ is proportional to the square of the amplitude.

$$\therefore \quad I_\theta = I_m \left(\frac{\sin \alpha}{\alpha}\right)^2 \qquad \ldots (8)$$

where $I_m = E_m^2$ is the maximum amplitude.

8.5 CONDITIONS FOR MAXIMA AND MINIMA

(a) Principal Maximum

The resultant amplitude in diffraction pattern of a single slit is given by,

$$E_\theta = E_m \frac{\sin \alpha}{\alpha} = \frac{E_m}{\alpha} \left[\alpha - \frac{\alpha^3}{3!} + \frac{\alpha^5}{5!} - \frac{\alpha^7}{7!} + \ldots\right]$$

when $\sin \alpha$ is written in ascending powers of α, where $\alpha = \frac{\pi}{\lambda} a \sin \theta$.

$$\therefore \quad E_\theta = E_m \left[1 - \frac{\alpha^2}{3!} + \frac{\alpha^4}{5!} - \frac{\alpha^6}{7!} + \ldots\right]$$

For E_θ to be maximum, the negative terms in the bracket must vanish. This is possible only when $\alpha = 0$ i.e. $\alpha = \frac{\pi}{\lambda} a \sin \theta = 0$ or $\sin \theta = 0$ or $\theta = 0$.

Thus, the maximum value of E_θ is E_m and the principal maximum is formed at $\theta = 0$. The condition $\theta = 0$ simply means that this maximum is formed by parts of the secondary wavelets which travel normally to the slit. The position of principal maximum is directly opposite to the slit and it is bordered symmetrically by dark and bright bands.

(b) Minimum Intensity Positions (Minima)

The intensity $I_\theta = I_m \left(\dfrac{\sin \alpha}{\alpha}\right)^2$ will be zero in the diffraction pattern if,

$$\sin \alpha = 0 \text{ and } \alpha \neq 0.$$

The values of α which satisfy this condition are

$$\alpha = m\pi \qquad \text{where } m = \pm 1, \pm 2, \pm 3, \ldots$$

$\therefore \qquad \alpha = \dfrac{\pi}{\lambda} a \sin \theta = m\pi$

Thus, the condition for minima is

$$a \sin \theta = m\lambda \qquad \ldots (1)$$

where $m = 0$ is not possible, because then θ becomes zero, which corresponds to the principal maximum.

Equation (1) gives the positions of minima on either side of the principal maximum in the diffraction pattern of a single slit.

(c) Secondary Maxima

Analysis shows that the secondary maxima lie approximately half way between the two minima. They are found from

$$\alpha = \pm\left(m + \dfrac{1}{2}\right)\pi, \qquad m = 1, 2, 3, \ldots$$

or $\qquad a \sin \theta = (2m+1)\cdot\lambda/2$

Substituting this value of α in $I_\theta = I_m \left(\dfrac{\sin \alpha}{\alpha}\right)^2$, we get

$$\dfrac{I_\theta}{I_m} = \left\{\dfrac{\sin\left(m + \dfrac{1}{2}\right)\pi}{\left(m + \dfrac{1}{2}\right)\pi}\right\}^2 = \dfrac{1}{\left(m + \dfrac{1}{2}\right)^2 \cdot \pi^2}$$

For $m = 1, 2, 3, \ldots$

$$\dfrac{I_\theta}{I_m} = 0.045, 0.016, 0.0083 \ldots$$

The successive maxima decrease in intensity rapidly. The relative intensity distribution in the single slit diffraction pattern for $\dfrac{a}{\lambda} = 10$ is shown in Fig. 8.7.

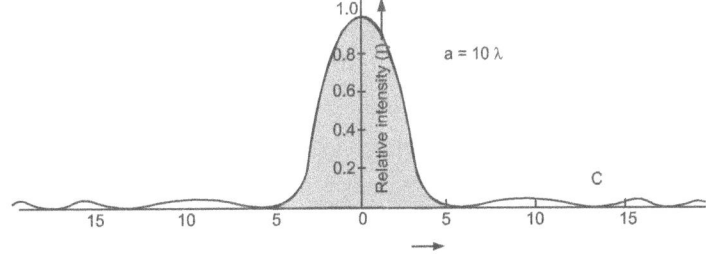

Fig. 8.7 : Intensity distribution in diffraction pattern due to a single slit

8.6 INTENSITY PATTERN DUE TO A SINGLE SLIT

Consider monochromatic plane waves incident on a single slit of width 'a'. When aperture is very small, only one secondary wavelet comes through and the wavefront is spherical. Suppose the slit width is such that several secondary wavelets pass through the slit. At the distance screen, these secondary wavelets superpose giving a rippled intensity distribution which is called **the single-slit diffraction pattern** as shown in Fig. 8.8.

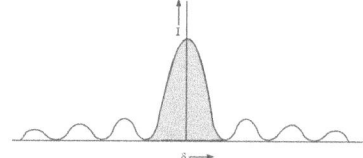

Fig. 8.8

The intensity in the pattern has a central maximum and then falls to zero (the first minimum), past the first minimum the intensity rises to a relatively small secondary maximum before again dropping to zero (the second minimum). The rippling continues with each secondary maximum having less magnitude than the previous secondary maximum.

Dependence of Spectrum on Width and Wavelength

The position of the minimum is given by, $a \sin \theta = m\lambda$. Therefore, the angular width of the spectrum will depend upon the slit width a, wavelength λ and order of interference m.

The width of spectrum inversely depends upon the slit width, hence **smaller the slit width, wider will be the spectrum**. Fig. 8.9 shows spectrum width for different slit width.

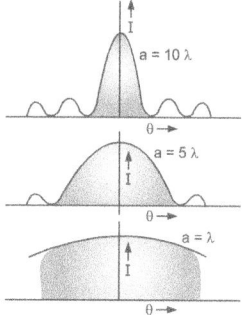

Fig. 8.9

Fig. 8.9 shows the variation of single slit diffraction pattern as the slit width varies. Decreasing the aperture size from 10λ to 5λ causes the diffraction pattern to spread out about twice as far.

The wavelength directly decides the spectrum width. If the slit is illuminated by white light, the light of different wavelengths will form a spectrum of different angular width. All this will overlap giving a colourful spectrum.

The spectrum width directly depends on the order 'm'. But for higher order, the intensity decreases.

8.7 DIFFRACTION AT CIRCULAR APERTURE

The diffraction pattern formed by a plane wave from a point source passing through a circular aperture is of considerable importance as it is applied to the resolving power of optical instruments such as telescopes, microscopes etc. The geometric optics assumes that the image of a point source will be a point. The geometrical optics does not consider the wave nature of light and hence diffraction at the edges of aperture of the instrument is neglected. But in practice the image is not a point image but a diffraction pattern formed by circular aperture. The diffraction pattern consists of a bright central maxima, corresponding to the image in geometrical optics, surrounded by fainter secondary maxima and minima. Fig. 8.10 shows diffraction pattern at a single slit.

(a) Intensity pattern   (b) Intensity distribution
Fig. 8.10 : Diffraction pattern

The diffraction pattern consists of a bright central disc, known as Airy's disc, surrounded by a number of fainter rings. Neither the disc nor rings are sharply limited but shade off gradually at the edges, being separated by circle of zero intensity (minima).

The condition for minima for a single slit is given by

$$a \sin \theta = m\lambda \text{ where } m = 0, 1, 2 \ldots \qquad \ldots (I)$$

In case of circular aperture, m is not an integer but can have fractional values such as m = 0, 1.22, 1.635 ... .

The value $\theta = 0$ gives principal maxima while m = 1.22 gives first minima. The position of first minima decides the diameter of principal maxima, hence the resolving power of the instrument.

Therefore, equation for first minima becomes

$$a \sin \theta = 1.22\lambda \qquad \ldots (II)$$

If d is the diameter of circular aperture then,

$$d \sin \theta = 1.22\lambda \qquad \ldots (III)$$

For small values of θ, $\sin \theta \approx \theta$.

$$\therefore \qquad \theta = \frac{1.22\lambda}{d} \qquad \ldots (IV)$$

8.8 PLANE DIFFRACTION GRATING

Grating : An arrangement consisting of a **large number of parallel** slits of the same width and separated by equal opaque spaces is known as **diffraction grating**.

A grating is prepared by ruling equidistant parallel lines on a plane glass plate with the help of a diamond point. The lines act as opaque spaces and the incident light cannot pass through them. The space between any two lines acts as a slit and is transparent to light.

A plane transmission grating generally contains 15,000 to 20,000 lines per inch. It was first constructed by Fraunhofer. If the lines are drawn on a silvered surface, it acts as a **reflection grating**.

Theory of Plane Diffraction Grating :

Consider the diffraction pattern of N parallel slits each of width 'a' and separated by equal opaque spaces 'b'. The distance between the centres of adjacent slits is d = (a + b) and it is called the **grating element**. The grating element is defined as the reciprocal of number of lines per cm i.e.

$$(a + b) = \frac{1}{N}, \text{ where N is lines per cm}$$

or
$$(a + b) = 2.54/N \text{ where N is lines per inch.}$$

Let a plane wavefront of wavelength λ be incident normally on the slits. According to Huygen's principle every point in the slit is regarded as the origin of secondary wavelets which spread out in all directions. Therefore, rays are diffracted from each slit in all directions. The resultant amplitude of light from a single slit of width 'a' in a direction making angle θ with the normal is given by

$$E_N = E_m \left(\frac{\sin \alpha}{\alpha}\right) \qquad \ldots (1)$$

where
$$\alpha = \frac{\pi}{\lambda} a \sin \theta \qquad \ldots (2)$$

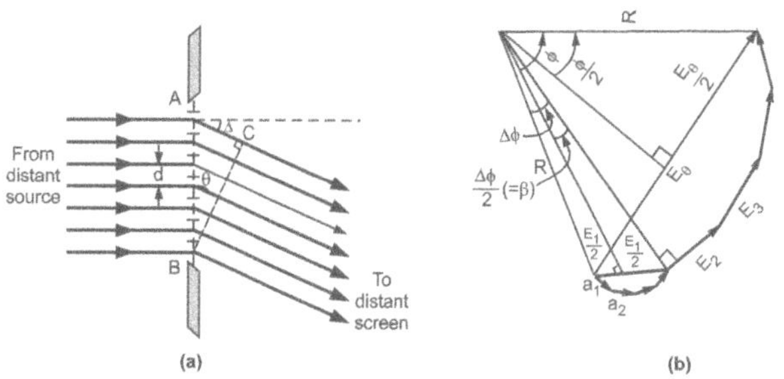

Fig. 8.11 : (a) Diffraction at N Slits, (b) Phasor Diagram

We can replace all the secondary wavelets in each slit by a single wave of amplitude $E_m \frac{\sin \alpha}{\alpha}$, starting from its mid-point and travelling at an angle θ with the normal.

We need, therefore, find only the N-slit interference pattern and multiply it by $E_m \frac{\sin \alpha}{\alpha}$ to obtain the complete pattern.

To find the interference pattern for N slits, we make use of phasors. Assuming each phasor to have amplitude E_N and at an angle $\Delta \phi$ the phasor diagram is as shown in Fig. 8.11 (b).

The phase angle $\Delta \phi$ is the phase difference between the waves coming from adjacent slits and is given by

$$\Delta \phi = k \cdot (\text{path difference between consecutive slits})$$

$$\Delta\phi = \frac{2\pi}{\lambda}(a+b)\sin\theta$$

$$\Delta\phi = \frac{2\pi}{\lambda} d \sin\theta \qquad \ldots (3)$$

We will define angle β such that

$$\beta = \frac{\Delta\phi}{2} = \frac{\pi}{\lambda}(a+b)\sin\theta \qquad \ldots (4)$$

The total phase difference between first and last wave will simply be sum of the phase differences added by each slit individually.

$$\therefore \quad \phi = N\Delta\phi$$

$$\phi = N\frac{2\pi}{\lambda}(a+b)\sin\theta \qquad \ldots (5)$$

or $\qquad \phi = 2N\beta \qquad$ [from equation (4)] ... (6)

As the slits of a grating are of equal width, the amplitude of light diffracted from each slit will be same. The amplitude of diffracted wave will be,

$$E_1 = E_2 = \ldots = E_N = E_m\left(\frac{\sin\alpha}{\alpha}\right) \qquad \ldots (7)$$

Mathematically, it can be proved that the resultant amplitude is,

$$E_\theta = E_m \frac{\sin\alpha}{\alpha} \cdot \frac{\sin N\beta}{\sin\beta} \qquad \ldots (8)$$

Intensity is square of the amplitude.

$$\therefore \quad I_\theta = I_m \left(\frac{\sin\alpha}{\alpha}\right)^2 \cdot \frac{\sin^2 N\beta}{\sin^2 \beta} \qquad \ldots (9)$$

The first factor $\left(\frac{\sin\alpha}{\alpha}\right)^2$ in equation (9) gives the intensity distribution in the **diffraction pattern due to a single slit**. The second factor $\frac{\sin^2 N\beta}{\sin^2 \beta}$ may be said to give the interference pattern for N slits.

Thus, we can say that each of the N slits gives rise to a diffracted beam in which the intensity distribution depends on the width of the slit. These diffracted beams then interfere with one another to produce the final diffraction pattern.

8.9 CONDITIONS FOR MAXIMA AND MINIMA

8.9.1 Principal Maxima

The condition for principal maxima is that, the path difference between the waves from adjacent slits must be an integer multiple of λ. Therefore, the condition for principal maxima is

$$(a+b)\sin\theta = m\lambda, \text{ where, } m = 0, 1, 2, 3, \ldots m \qquad \ldots (1)$$

Here m is called the **order of interference**.
This is equivalent to saying that,

$$\beta = \frac{\pi}{\lambda}(a+b)\sin\theta$$

$$\beta = \frac{\pi}{\lambda}(m\lambda) = m\pi \qquad \text{... (2)}$$

For these values of β, $\dfrac{\sin N\beta}{\sin \beta}$ becomes indeterminate.

But by L'Hospital's rule,

$$\lim_{\beta \to m\pi} \frac{\sin N\beta}{\sin \beta} = \lim_{\beta \to m\pi} \frac{N\cos N\beta}{\cos \beta} = \frac{N\cos Nm\pi}{\cos m\pi} = \pm N$$

∴ The intensity of the principal maxima is given as

$$I_\theta = N^2 \left(I_m \frac{\sin^2\alpha}{\alpha^2} \right) \qquad \text{... (3)}$$

Thus, the intensity of principal maxima increases with increasing N. The intensity of the principal maximum is greatest while on either side of it, the intensities of other maxima go on decreasing.

8.9.2 Minima

The intensity is given by,
$$I_\theta = \left(I_m \frac{\sin\alpha}{\alpha} \right)^2 \cdot \frac{\sin^2 N\beta}{\sin^2 \beta}$$

For minima, $\sin N\beta = 0$ but $\sin \beta \neq 0$. i.e. $N\beta = m\pi$, where m has any integral value except N, 2N, 3N .... etc., because for these values of m, $\beta = 0, \pi, 2\pi$.... etc. and these correspond to principal maxima.

Thus, for minima,
$$N\beta = m\pi$$

$$\text{or} \quad \beta = \frac{m\pi}{N} \qquad \text{But} \quad \beta = \frac{\pi}{\lambda}(a+b)\sin\theta$$

∴ The condition for minima becomes

$$\frac{\pi}{\lambda}(a+b)\sin\theta = \frac{m\pi}{N}$$

or $\qquad (a+b)\sin\theta = \dfrac{m}{N}\lambda$, but $m \neq nN$ ... (4)

where n = 0, 1, 2, 3, ...

Hence, the positions of minima are given by

$$(a+b)\sin\theta = \frac{\lambda}{N}, \frac{2\lambda}{N}, \frac{3\lambda}{N} \ldots\ldots \qquad \text{... (5)}$$

There are (N – 1) minima between any two consecutive principal maxima.

(c) Secondary Maxima

As there are (N – 1) minima between two consecutive principal maxima, there must be (N – 2) other maxima coming alternatively with the minima between two consecutive principal maxima. These maxima are called the secondary maxima. The positions of secondary maxima are obtained by differentiating the expression for intensity with respect to β and equating to zero.

8.10 INTENSITY PATTERN

A diffraction pattern due to diffraction grating consists of m principal maximum, one each for integer value of m. But the intensity of the principal maxima goes on decreasing with order. In between any two principal maxima there are minima and secondary. The intensity of secondary maxima is negligible in comparison with the intensity of principal maxima. The intensity from maxima to minima or minima to maxima changes gradually as a function of sine.

The number of minima and secondary maxima in between principal maxima is not fixed but depends upon the number of slits in grating. If the number of slits in grating are N, then the number of minima will be (N – 1) and secondary maxima will be (N – 2).

Fig. 8.12 shows diffraction pattern for N = 5, which has (N – 1 = 4) minima and (N – 2 = 3) secondary maxima.

Diffraction pattern for N = 5 :

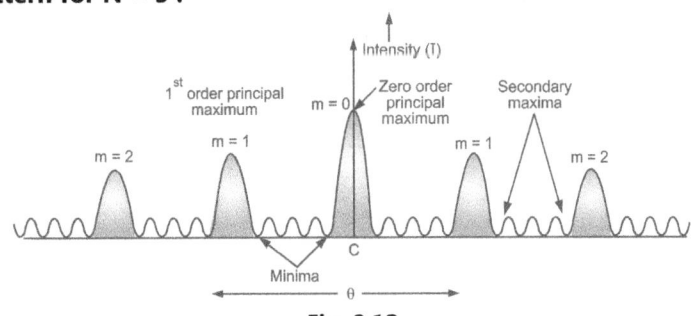

Fig. 8.12

Fig. 8.12 represents the diffraction pattern for a grating.

8.11 RAYLEIGH'S CRITERION FOR RESOLUTION

According to Rayleigh's criterion, two point sources or two spectral lines of equal intensity are just resolved by an optical instrument if the central maximum of the diffraction pattern due to one falls on the first minimum of the diffraction pattern of the other.

Let us consider the intensity distribution pattern of two wavelengths λ and $\lambda + d\lambda$.

The separation between their central maxima will depend upon $d\lambda$. If $d\lambda$ is considerably large, two wavelengths will be quite apart [See Fig. 8.13 (a)] and the two spectral lines will be well resolved.

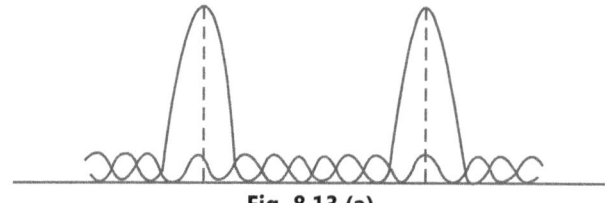

Fig. 8.13 (a)

But $d\lambda$ will have a limiting value in which case the angular separation between their maxima is such that the central maxima of one (λ) coincides with the first minimum of the other (λ and $d\lambda$) and vice versa [See Fig. 8.13 (b)].

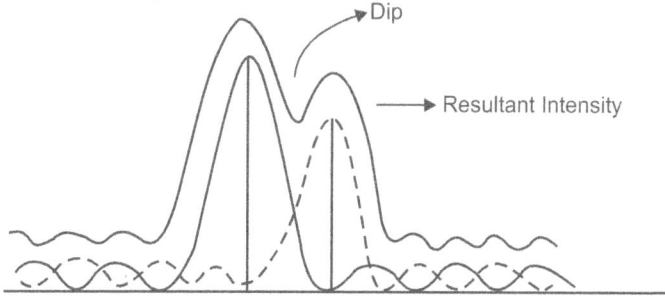

Fig. 8.13 (b) : Rayleigh's criterion for resolution

In Fig. 8.13 (b), two spectral lines of wavelengths λ and $\lambda + d\lambda$ are shown. The central maximum in the diffraction pattern for λ is shown to occur at angle θ and the first minimum at $\theta + d\theta$. If the central maximum in the diffraction pattern for ($\lambda + d\lambda$) is also found to occur at ($\theta + d\theta$), where the first minimum for λ occurs, then only the two spectral lines will be been, just as separate or resolved.

If $d\lambda$ is lesser then the limiting value satisfying the condition of Rayleigh's criterion, the two spectral lines will overlap and the resultant intensity pattern is as shown in Fig. 8.13 (c). Hence, in this case, the spectral lines are not resolved.

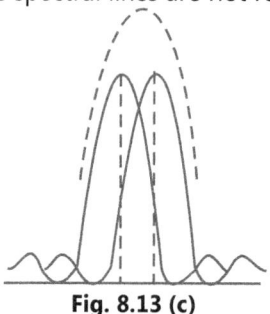

Fig. 8.13 (c)

8.12 RESOLVING POWER OF A GRATING

Method - I :

The angular separation between two spectral lines may be very small indeed. However, a grating is capable of resolving the images of the slit formed by the two spectral lines of wavelengths λ and ($\lambda + d\lambda$).

The resolving power of a grating is defined as, the smallest wavelength difference $d\lambda$ for which the spectral lines can be just resolved at the wavelength λ, and is mathematically expressed as

$$R = \frac{\lambda}{d\lambda} \qquad \ldots (1)$$

Let $(a + b)$ be the grating element and N the number of slits in the grating. If a plane wavefront of wavelength λ is incident on the grating and if the mth order maximum in the diffraction pattern is formed at angle θ_m then, the condition for this maximum to be formed is that, the path difference between the waves from adjacent slits must be

$$(a + b) \sin \theta_m = m \lambda \qquad \ldots (2)$$

If the mth order maximum for $(\lambda + d\lambda)$ is formed at $(\theta_m + d\theta_m)$, the angular separation $d\theta_m$ between the mth order maxima for wavelengths λ and $(\lambda + d\lambda)$ is obtained by differentiating equation (2). We have

$$(a + b) \cos \theta_m \, d\theta_m = m \cdot d\lambda$$

i.e.
$$d\theta_m = \frac{m \cdot d\lambda}{(a + b) \cos \theta_m} \qquad \ldots (3)$$

By Rayleigh's criterion of resolution, these two spectral lines can be just resolved, if the first minimum adjacent to the mth order maximum for λ in the diffraction pattern is also formed at $(\theta_m + d\theta_m)$. Then, the condition for this first minimum adjacent to m^{th} order maximum for λ to occur at $(\theta_m + d\theta_m)$ is,

$$(a + b) \sin (\theta_m + d\theta_m) = m \lambda + \frac{\lambda}{N} \qquad \ldots (4)$$

because the path difference between a maximum and its adjacent minimum is $\frac{\lambda}{N}$.

Now, $\sin (\theta_m + d\theta_m) = \sin \theta_m \cos d\theta_m + \sin d\theta_m \cos \theta_m$

i.e. $\sin (\theta_m + d\theta_m) = \sin \theta_m \cdot 1 + d\theta_m \cos \theta_m \qquad \ldots (5)$

since, $\cos d\theta_m = 1$ and $\sin d\theta_m = d\theta_m$ if $d\theta_m$ is small.

∴ From (4) and (5),

$$(a + b) (\sin \theta_m + d\theta_m \cos \theta_m) = m \lambda + \frac{\lambda}{N}$$

By equation (1), this gives

$$(a + b) \cos \theta_m \cdot d\theta_m = \frac{\lambda}{N}$$

or
$$d\theta_m = \frac{1}{(a + b) \cos \theta_m} \cdot \frac{\lambda}{N} \qquad \ldots (6)$$

From equations (3) and (6), we have

$$\frac{m \cdot d\lambda}{(a + b) \cos \theta_m} - \frac{\lambda}{(a + b) \cos \theta_m \, N}$$

or $\dfrac{\lambda}{d\lambda} = m \cdot N$

∴ $R = \dfrac{\lambda}{d\lambda} = m \cdot N$ ... (7)

Equation (7) gives the resolving power of a grating.

It is seen that, the resolving power is independent of the grating element (a + b). It increases with the order of the spectrum m, and also with the number of lines on the grating surface.

Method - II :

Resolving power of a grating can also be found as follows :

By definition, $R = \dfrac{\lambda}{d\lambda}$ ... (1)

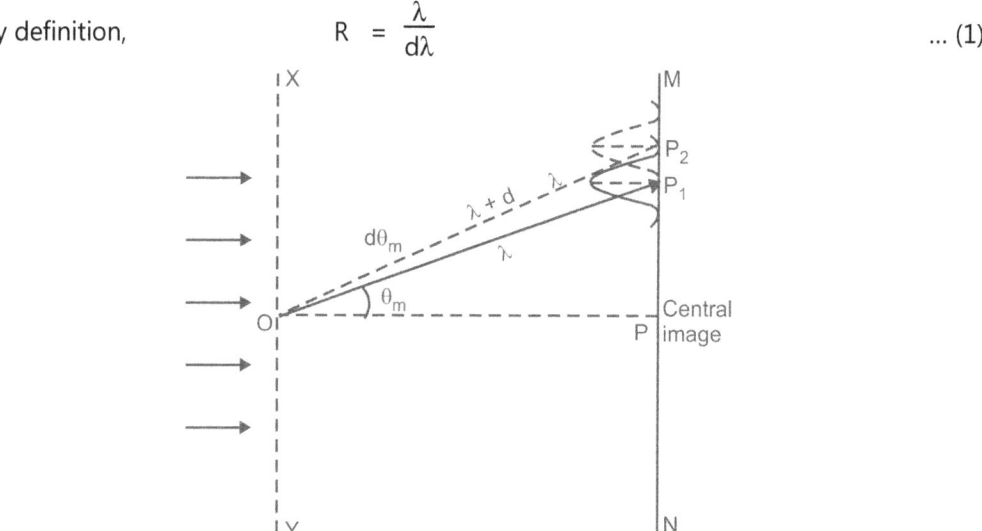

Fig. 8.14

In Fig. 8.14, **XY** is the grating surface and MN is the field of view of the telescope. P_1 is the mth primary maximum of a spectral line of wavelength λ at angle of diffraction θ_m. P_2 is the mth primary maximum of a second spectral line of wavelength $\lambda + d\lambda$ at a diffracting angle $\theta_m + d\theta_m$.

P_1 and P_2 are the spectral lines in the mth order. These two spectral lines according to Rayleigh's criterion, will appear resolved, if the position of P_2 also corresponds to the first minimum of P_1.

The direction of the mth primary maximum for a wavelength λ is given by

$(a + b) \sin \theta_m = m\lambda$ ... (2)

The direction of the mth primary maximum for a wavelength $(\lambda + d\lambda)$ is given by

$(a + b) \sin(\theta_m + d\theta_m) = m(\lambda + d\lambda)$ ... (3)

The two lines will appear just resolved if the angle of diffraction $(\theta_m + d\theta_m)$ also corresponds to the direction of first minimum after the mth primary maximum at P_1 (corresponding to λ).

This is possible, if the extra path difference introduced is λ/N, where N is the total number of lines on the grating surface.

$\therefore \quad (a+b) \sin(\theta_m + d\theta_m) = m\lambda + \lambda/N$ ... (4)

From equations (3) and (4),

$$m(\lambda + d\lambda) = m\lambda + \frac{\lambda}{N}$$

or $$m \, d\lambda = \frac{\lambda}{N}$$

$\therefore \quad R = \dfrac{\lambda}{d\lambda} = mN$ ... (5)

Equation (5) gives the resolving power of a grating.

The resolving power of a grating is independent of the grating element. The resolving power is directly proportional to (i) the order of the spectrum, and (ii) the total number of lines on the grating surface.

8.13 RESOLVING POWER OF A TELESCOPE

A telescope is used to see distant objects with clarity. The details it reveals, depend on the angle the two point objects make at the objective rather than on the linear separation between them.

The resolving power of a telescope is defined as the reciprocal of the least angle subtended at the objective by two distant point objects which can be distinguished just as separate in the focal plane of the telescope.

The ring holding the objective lens acts as the circular aperture. The diffraction pattern due to a circular aperture consists of a central bright disc surrounded by concentric dark and bright rings.

Extending Rayleigh's criterion for the resolution of diffraction patterns to the circular aperture, we say that, two patterns are resolved when the central maximum of one falls on the first dark ring of the other.

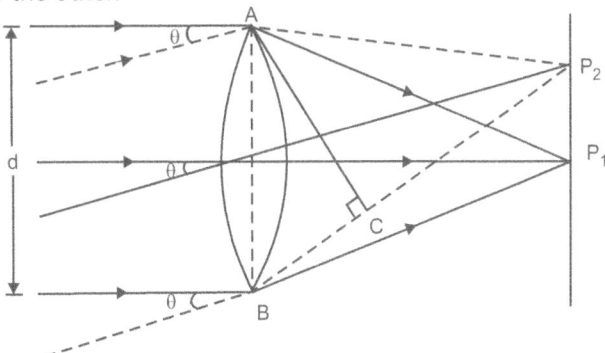

Fig. 8.15 : Resolving power of a telescope

Let 'd' be the diameter of the objective AB of the telescope. Consider the incident rays of light from two neighbouring points of a distant object. The full lines show rays of light from one point object and the dotted lines show the rays of light from the neighbouring point object. The image of each point object is a Fraunhofer diffraction pattern. The diffraction pattern of the first object consists of a central bright disc surrounded by concentric dark and bright rings with centre at P_1. The diffraction pattern of the second object is also a similar diffraction pattern with centre at P_2.

According to Rayleigh, these two images are said to be resolved, if the position of the central maximum of the second image coincides with the first dark ring of the first image and vice versa.

The path difference between the secondary waves travelling in the directions AP_1 and BP_1 is zero and hence, they reinforce with one another at P_1. Similarly, all the secondary waves, from the corresponding points between A and B will have zero path difference. Thus, P_1 corresponds to the central maximum of the first image.

The secondary waves travelling in the directions AP_2 and BP_2 will meet at P_2. The path difference between the secondary waves travelling in the directions BP_2 and AP_2 is equal to BC (See Fig. 8.15).

From the $\triangle$ ABC, $\qquad$ BC = AB sin θ = AB · θ = d · θ $\qquad$ (for small angles)

If this path difference d · θ = λ, the position of P_2 corresponds to the first minimum of the first image. But P_2 is also the position of the central maximum of the second image. Thus, Rayleigh's criterion of resolution is satisfied, if

$$d \cdot \theta = \lambda$$

i.e. $\qquad \theta = \dfrac{\lambda}{d} \qquad \qquad \ldots (1)$

Equation (1) holds good for rectangular aperture. For circular aperture, according to Airy, this equation becomes

$$\theta = 1.22 \dfrac{\lambda}{d} \qquad \ldots (2)$$

Equation (2) gives the least angle the two distant point objects should subtend at the objective for their resolution. Hence, resolving power of the telescope is given by

$$R = \dfrac{1}{\theta} = \dfrac{d}{1.22 \lambda} \qquad \ldots (3)$$

Equation (3) shows that resolving power of a telescope depends on wavelength λ and diameter d of the aperture.

SOLVED EXAMPLES

Example 8.1 : A slit of width 0.16 mm is illuminated by a light of wavelength 5600 A°. Find the half angular width of the central maximum.

Data : a = 0.016 cm, $\lambda = 5600 \times 10^{-8}$ cm, n = 1.

Formula : a sin θ = nλ.

Solution :

$$a \sin \theta = n \lambda$$
$$\text{but} \quad n = 1$$

$$\therefore \quad \sin\theta = \frac{\lambda}{a}$$

$$\theta = \sin^{-1}\frac{\lambda}{a}$$

Substituting,
$$\theta = \sin^{-1}\left(\frac{5600\times 10^{-8}}{0.016}\right)$$

$$\therefore \quad \boxed{\theta = 12'}$$

Example 8.2 : A slit of variable width is illuminated by red light of λ = 6500 A°. At what width of the slit, the first minimum will fall at $\theta = 30°$?

Data : $\lambda = 6500\times 10^{-8}$ cm, $\theta = 30°$, n = 1

Formula : a sin θ = nλ.

Solution :

$$a\sin\theta = n\lambda$$
$$\text{but } n = 1$$
$$a = \frac{\lambda}{\sin\theta}$$

Substituting,
$$a = \frac{6500\times 10^{-8}}{\sin 30}$$

$$\therefore \quad \boxed{a = 0.13\times 10^{-3} \text{ cm}}$$

Example 8.3 : A light of λ = 6000 A° falls on a screen at a distance of 200 cm from a narrow slit. Find the width of the slit, if the first minimum lies 5 mm on either side of the central maximum.

Data : $\lambda = 6000\times 10^{-8}$ cm, f = 200 cm, x = 0.5 cm, n = 1.

Formula : a sin θ = nλ, tan $\theta = \frac{x}{f} \approx \sin\theta$

Solution :

$$\sin\theta = \frac{\lambda}{a} = \frac{x}{f} \qquad \because n = 1$$

$$\frac{\lambda}{a} = \frac{x}{f}$$

$$a = \frac{\lambda f}{x}$$

Substituting,
$$a = \frac{6000\times 10^{-8}\times 200}{0.5}$$

$$\boxed{a = 0.024 \text{ cm}}$$

Example 8.4 : A lens whose focal length is 40 cm forms a Fraunhofer diffraction pattern of a slit 0.3 mm wide. Calculate the distance of the first dark band and of the next bright band from the axis. Given $\lambda = 5890$ A°.

Data : $\lambda = 5890 \times 10^{-8}$ cm, f = 40 cm, a = 0.03 cm

Formula : $a \sin \theta = n\lambda$

$$\sin \theta = \frac{x}{f} \qquad a \sin \theta = (2n+1)\frac{\lambda}{2}$$

Solution :

For n = 1, $\sin \theta = \frac{\lambda}{a}$

For first dark band, $\sin \theta = \frac{x}{f}$

$\therefore \quad \frac{\lambda}{a} = \frac{x}{f}$

$\therefore \quad x = \frac{\lambda f}{a}$

Substituting, $x = \frac{5890 \times 10^{-8} \times 40}{0.03}$

$\therefore \quad \boxed{x = 0.0785 \text{ cm}}$

For bright band, n = 1

$$a \sin \theta = (2n+1)\frac{\lambda}{2} \qquad \ldots (1)$$

$$\sin \theta = \frac{x_1}{f} \qquad \ldots (2)$$

From (1) and (2), $\frac{x_1}{f} = (2n+1)\frac{\lambda}{2a}$

$x_1 = \frac{3}{2}\frac{\lambda}{a}f$

Substituting, $x_1 = \frac{3}{2} \frac{5890 \times 10^{-8}}{0.03} \times 40$

$\boxed{x_1 = 0.11775 \text{ cm}}$

Example 8.5 : A lens of focal length 100 cm forms Fraunhofer's diffraction pattern of a single slit of width 0.04 cm in its focal plane. The incident light contains two wavelengths λ_1 and λ_2. It is found that, fourth minimum corresponding to λ_1 and the fifth minimum corresponding to λ_2 occur at the same point 0.5 cm from the central maximum. Calculate λ_1 and λ_2.

Data : f = 100 cm, a = 0.04 cm, x = 0.5 cm

Formula : $a \sin \theta = n\lambda$, $\sin \theta = \frac{x}{f}$.

Solution :

Condition for fourth minimum

$$a \sin \theta_1 = 4 \lambda_1$$

$\therefore \qquad \sin \theta_1 = \dfrac{4 \lambda_1}{a} \qquad \qquad \ldots (1)$

Also, $\qquad \sin \theta_1 = \dfrac{x}{f} \qquad \qquad \ldots (2)$

From (1) and (2), $\qquad \dfrac{x}{f} = 4 \dfrac{\lambda_1}{a}$

$\therefore \qquad \lambda_1 = \dfrac{x}{f} \cdot \dfrac{a}{4}$

$$\lambda_1 = \dfrac{0.5}{100} \times \dfrac{0.04}{4}$$

$$\boxed{\lambda_1 = 5 \times 10^{-5} \text{ cm}}$$

It is given that fourth minimum of λ_1 coincides with fifth minimum of λ_2. In that case, $\theta_1 = \theta_2 = \theta$, where θ_1 and θ_2 are the angular deviations for the fourth and fifth minimum respectively, then

$$a \sin \theta_1 = 4 \lambda_1 = 5 \lambda_2$$

or $\qquad 5 \lambda_2 = 4 \lambda_1$

$$\lambda_2 = \dfrac{4}{5} \lambda_1$$

$\therefore \qquad \lambda_2 = \dfrac{4}{5} \times 5 \times 10^{-5}$

$$\boxed{\lambda_2 = 4 \times 10^{-5} \text{ cm}}$$

Example 8.6 : In Fraunhofer's diffraction pattern due to a single slit, the screen is at a distance of 100 cm from the slit and the slit is illuminated by a monochromatic light of wavelength 5893 A°. The width of the slit is 0.1 mm. Calculate the separation between the central maximum and the first minimum.

Data : f = 100 cm, λ = 5893 × 10^{-8} cm, a = 0.1 mm = 0.01 cm

Formula : $a \sin \theta = n\lambda$, $\tan \theta = \dfrac{x}{f} \approx \sin \theta$

Solution :

$$x = f \dfrac{\lambda}{a}$$

$$x = \dfrac{100 \times 5893 \times 10^{-8}}{0.01}$$

$$\boxed{x = 0.5893 \text{ cm}}$$

Example 8.7 : Calculate the angular position of the first minimum in Fraunhofer's diffraction pattern of a slit 10^{-4} cm wide, if it is illuminated by light of wavelength 5000 A°.

Data : λ = 5000 A°, a = 10^{-4} cm, n = 1

Formula : a sin θ = nλ.

Solution :

$$a \sin \theta = n\lambda$$

$$\sin \theta = \frac{n\lambda}{a}$$

$$\theta = \sin^{-1}\left(\frac{n\lambda}{a}\right)$$

$$\theta = \sin^{-1}\left(\frac{1 \times 5000 \times 10^{-8}}{10^{-4}}\right)$$

$$\boxed{\theta = 30°}$$

Example 8.8 : A light of wavelength 5×10^{-5} cm is incident normally on the plane transmission grating of width 3 cm and having 15000 lines. Find the angle of diffraction in the first order.

Data : $\lambda = 5 \times 10^{-5}$ cm, $(a + b) = \frac{3}{15000}$, n = 1

Formula : (a + b) sin θ = nλ.

Solution :

$$(a + b) \sin \theta = n\lambda$$

$$\sin \theta = \frac{n\lambda}{a + b}$$

$$\theta = \sin^{-1}\left(\frac{\lambda}{a + b}\right)$$

Substituting,

$$\theta = \sin^{-1}\left(\frac{5 \times 10^{-5}}{3} \times 15000\right)$$

$$\boxed{\theta = 14° \ 29'}$$

Example 8.9 : The limits of a visible spectrum are approximately 400×10^{-7} cm to 700×10^{-7} cm. Find the angular width of the first order visible spectrum produced by a plane grating having 15000 lines/inch when light is incident normally on the grating.

Data : $\lambda_1 = 400 \times 10^{-7}$ cm, $\lambda_2 = 700 \times 10^{-7}$ cm, $a + b = \frac{1}{\frac{15000}{2.54}} = \frac{2.54}{15000}$ cm

Formula : (a + b) sin θ = nλ.

Solution :

Let θ_1 and θ_2 be the angles corresponding to λ_1 and λ_2.

Here, $\quad n = 1$

$\therefore \quad \sin \theta_1 = \dfrac{\lambda}{a+b}$

or $\quad \theta_1 = \sin^{-1} \dfrac{\lambda_1}{(a+b)}$

$\sin \theta_2 = \dfrac{\lambda_2}{a+b}$

$\theta_2 = \sin^{-1}\left(\dfrac{\lambda_2}{(a+b)}\right)$

$\therefore$ Angular width of first order visible spectrum will be $\theta_2 - \theta_1$.

Substituting, $\quad \theta_1 = \sin^{-1}\left(\dfrac{400 \times 10^{-7} \times 15000}{2.54}\right)$

$\theta_1 = 13° \, 40'$

$\theta_2 = \sin^{-1} \dfrac{700 \times 10^{-7} \times 15000}{2.54}$

$\theta_2 = 24° \, 30'$

$\therefore \quad \theta_2 - \theta_1 = 24° \, 30' - 13° \, 40'$

$= \boxed{10° \, 50'}$

Example 8.10 : A parallel beam of sodium light is allowed to be incident normally on a plane grating having 4250 lines per cm and a second order spectral line is observed to be deviated through 30°. Calculate the wavelength of the spectral line.

Data : $\theta = 30°$, $a + b = \dfrac{1}{4250}$, $n = 2$.

Formula : $(a + b) \sin \theta = n\lambda$.

Solution :

$(a + b) \sin \theta = n \lambda$

but $\quad n = 2$

$\therefore \quad \lambda = \dfrac{(a+b)}{2} \sin \theta$

Substituting, $\quad \lambda = \dfrac{1}{4250} \times \dfrac{1}{2 \times 2}$

$\lambda = 5.880 \times 10^{-5} \, \text{cm}$

$= \boxed{5880 \, \text{A}°}$

Example 8.11 : How many orders will be visible, if the wavelength of the incident radiation is 5000 A° and the number of lines on the grating is 2620 in one inch ?

Data : $\lambda = 5000 \times 10^{-8}$ cm, $(a + b) = \dfrac{2.54}{2620}$ cm

Formula : $(a + b) \sin \theta = n\lambda$.

Solution :

$$(a + b) \sin \theta = n\lambda$$

To have maximum order, the maximum possible value of $\sin \theta = 1$

∴ $\quad n = \dfrac{(a+b)}{\lambda}$

Substituting, $\quad n = \dfrac{2.54}{2620} \times \dfrac{1}{5 \times 10^{-5}}$

∴ $\quad \boxed{n = 19.38}$

Hence, the highest order of the spectrum which can be seen is 19.

Example 8.12 : In a plane transmission grating, the angle of diffraction for the second order principal maximum for the wavelength 5×10^{-5} cm is 30°. Calculate the number of lines in one cm of the grating surface.

Data : $\lambda = 5 \times 10^{-5}$ cm, $\theta = 30°$, $n = 2$.

Formula : $(a + b) \sin \theta = n\lambda$.

Solution :

$$(a + b) \sin \theta = n\lambda$$
$$\text{but, } n = 2$$

∴ $\quad (a + b) = \dfrac{n\lambda}{\sin \theta}$

Substituting, $\quad (a + b) = \dfrac{2 \times 5 \times 10^{-5}}{1/2}$

∴ $\quad (a + b) = 20 \times 10^{-5}$ cm

But $\quad (a + b) = \dfrac{1}{\text{no. of lines/cm}}$

∴ $\quad$ No. of lines/cm $= \dfrac{1}{a+b} = \dfrac{1}{20 \times 10^{-5}} = \boxed{5000 \text{ lines/cm}}$

Example 8.13 : Monochromatic light of wavelength 6×10^{-5} cm falls normally on a slit of width 0.001 cm. Calculate the angular width of the central bright maximum.

Data : $\lambda = 6 \times 10^{-5}$ cm, $a = 0.001$ cm

Formula : $a \sin \theta = n\lambda$.

Solution :

$$a \sin \theta = n\lambda$$
$$\text{but, } n = 1$$

∴ $\quad \sin \theta = \dfrac{\lambda}{a}$

$$\theta = \sin^{-1}\frac{\lambda}{a}$$

$$\theta = \sin^{-1}\frac{6 \times 10^{-5}}{0.001} = 3° 26'$$

∴ The angular width of the central bright maximum = 2θ = $\boxed{6° 52'}$

Example 8.14 : Monochromatic light of wavelength 6.56×10^{-5} cm falls normally on a grating 2 cm wide. The first order spectrum is produced at an angle of 18° 14' from the normal. What is the total number of lines on the grating ?

Data : $\lambda = 6.56 \times 10^{-5}$ cm, $\theta = 18° 14'$, $n = 1$.
Total width of the grating = 2 cm

Formula : $(a + b)\sin\theta = n\lambda$.

Solution :

$$(a + b)\sin\theta = n\lambda$$

As $n = 1$

∴ $(a + b) = \dfrac{\lambda}{\sin\theta}$

Substituting, $(a + b) = \dfrac{6.56 \times 10^{-5}}{\sin 18° 14'} = \dfrac{6.56 \times 10^{-5}}{0.3123}$

$(a + b) = 21.005 \times 10^{-5}$ cm

But $(a + b) = \dfrac{1}{\text{No. of lines/cm}}$

$21.005 \times 10^{-5} = \dfrac{1}{\text{No. of lines/cm}}$

∴ No. of lines/cm = $\dfrac{1}{21.005 \times 10^{-5}}$

= $\boxed{4761 \text{ lines/cm}}$

Since, the grating has 2 cm width, total number of lines on the grating is $4761 \times 2 = \boxed{9{,}522}$

Example 8.15 : A grating has 6000 lines/cm. Find the angular separation of two yellow lines of mercury of wavelengths 5770 A° and 5791 A° in the second order.

Data : $a + b = \dfrac{1}{6000}$ cm. $\quad \lambda_1 = 5770 \times 10^{-8}$ cm

$\lambda_2 = 5791 \times 10^{-8}$ cm

$n = 2$

Formula : $(a + b)\sin\theta = n\lambda$.

Solution :

$(a + b)\sin\theta_n = n\lambda$

For λ_1, $(a + b)\sin\theta_2 = n\lambda_1$

$\sin\theta_2 = \dfrac{n\lambda_1}{(a + b)} = 2 \times 5770 \times 10^{-8} \times 6000 = 0.6924$

$\theta_2 = 43.82°$

For λ_2, $(a + b) \sin \theta_2 = n \lambda_2$

$\sin \theta_2 = \dfrac{n \lambda_2}{(a + b)} = 2 \times 5791 \times 10^{-8} \times 6000 = 0.6949$

$\theta_2 = 44.02°$

Angular separation between the two yellow lines = $\theta_2' - \theta_2$

= 44.02 − 43.82 = $\boxed{0.2° \text{ or } 12'}$

Example 8.16 : Calculate the angles at which the first dark band and the next bright band are formed in Fraunhofer's diffraction pattern of a slit of 0.2 mm wide. Given λ = 5890 A°.

Data : a = 0.2 mm, λ = 5890 A°.

Formulae : (i) $a \sin \theta = n\lambda$ **(ii)** $a \sin \theta' = \left(n + \dfrac{1}{2}\right)\lambda$

Solution :

(i) For n = 1 ⇒ $\sin \theta = \dfrac{n\lambda}{a} = \dfrac{5890 \times 10^{-10}}{0.2 \times 10^{-3}} = 2.945 \times 10^{-3}$

$\theta = \sin^{-1}(2.945 \times 10^{-3}) = 0.1687° = \boxed{10.12°}$

(ii) For n = 2 ⇒ $a \sin \theta' = \left(n + \dfrac{1}{2}\right)\lambda$; $\sin \theta' = \left(n + \dfrac{1}{2}\right)\dfrac{\lambda}{a} = \dfrac{3\lambda}{2a}$

$\sin \theta' = 4.4175 \times 10^{-3}$; $\theta' = 0.2531° = \boxed{15.18°}$

Example 8.17 : Examine if two spectral lines of wavelengths 5890 A° and 5896 A° can be clearly resolved in the (i) first order and (ii) second order by a diffraction grating 2 cm wide and having 425 lines per cm.

Data : λ_1 = 5890 A°, λ_2 = 5896 A°, w = 2 cm, N = 425 lines/cm

Formula : $(a + b) \sin \theta = m\lambda$

Solution :

$(a + b) = \dfrac{2}{425} = 4.7 \times 10^{-3}$ cm, n = 1

In first order :

$\sin \theta_1 = \dfrac{n\lambda_1}{a + b} = \dfrac{1 \times 5890 \times 10^{-8}}{4.7 \times 10^{-3}}$

$\sin \theta_1 = 0.0125$

$\theta_1 = 0.71°$

$\sin \theta_1 = \dfrac{n\lambda_2}{a + b} = \dfrac{1 \times 5896 \times 10^{-8}}{4.7 \times 10^{-3}}$

$\sin \theta_1 = 0.01254$

$$\boxed{\theta_1 = 0.71°}$$

In second order: $\sin\theta_2 = \dfrac{n\lambda_1}{a+b} = \dfrac{2 \times 5890 \times 10^{-8}}{4.7 \times 10^{-3}}$

$\sin\theta_2 = 0.02506$
$\sin\theta_2 = 1.44°$
$\sin\theta_2 = 0.02508$

$$\boxed{\theta_2 = 1.4376}$$

θ_2 both values slightly differ means slightly resolved.

Example 8.18 : Calculate the wavelength of light whose diffraction maximum in the diffraction pattern due to a single slit falls at $\theta = 30°$ and coincides with the first minimum for red light of wavelength 6500 A°.

Data : $\theta = 30°$, $\lambda = 6500$ A°

Formulae : (i) $a \sin\theta = n\lambda_1$,

(ii) $a \sin\theta = \left(n + \dfrac{1}{2}\right)\lambda_2$ for bright band 'a' is constant, θ is constant order.

Solution :

(i) $n\lambda_1 = \left(n + \dfrac{1}{2}\right)\lambda_2$ here $n = 1$

(ii) $\lambda_2 = \dfrac{n\lambda_1}{\left(n + \dfrac{1}{2}\right)} = \dfrac{\lambda_1}{3/2} = \boxed{4333.33 \text{ A°}}$

Example 8.19 : Monochromatic light of wavelength $\lambda = 6560$ A° falls normally on a grating. The spectral line is diffracted at an angle of 19° 9' from the normal in the first order. Find the grating element.

Data : $\lambda = 6560$ A°, $\theta = 19° 9'$, $n = 1$

Formula : $(a + b) \sin\theta = m\lambda$

Solution :

$(a + b) = \dfrac{m\lambda}{\sin\theta} = \dfrac{1 \times 6560 \times 10^{-8}}{\sin(19° 9')}$

$= \dfrac{6560 \times 10^{-8}}{0.340} = 1.9 \times 10^{-4} = \boxed{2 \times 10^{-4} \text{ cm}}$

Example 8.20 : Light is incident normally on a grating 0.5 cm wide with 2500 lines. Find the angles of diffraction for the principal maxima of the two sodium lines in the first order spectrum $\lambda_1 = 5890$ A° and $\lambda_2 = 5896$ A°.

Data : w = 0.5 cm, Total lines = 2500 lines, $\lambda_1 = 5890$ A°, $\lambda_2 = 5896$ A°.

Solution :

In 1 cm = 2500 × 2 = 5000 lines ∴ (a + b) = $\dfrac{1}{5000}$ = 2×10^{-4} cm, order n = 1.

For wavelength λ_1 = 5890,

$$\sin \theta_1 = \dfrac{n\lambda_1}{a+b} = \dfrac{1 \times 5890 \times 10^{-8}}{2 \times 10^{-4}}$$

$$\sin \theta_1 = 0.2945$$

$$\boxed{\theta_1 = 17.12°}$$

$$\sin \theta_2 = \dfrac{n\lambda_2}{a+b} = \dfrac{1 \times 5896 \times 10^{-8}}{2 \times 10^{-4}}$$

$$\sin \theta_2 = 0.2948$$

$$\boxed{\theta_2 = 17.2°}$$

Example 8.21 : What is the highest order spectrum that is visible with light of wavelength 6000 A° by means of a grating having 5000 lines per cm ?

Data : λ = 6000 A°

N = 5000 lines per cm, a + b = $\dfrac{1}{5000}$ cm

Formula : (a + b) sin θ = n λ

Solution :

Take, sin θ = 1

∴ a + b = nλ $\dfrac{1}{5000}$ = n × 6000 × 10^{-8}

$$\boxed{n = 3.3}$$

The highest order is n = 3.

Example 8.22 : Light of wavelength 5460 A° falls on a diffraction grating normal to its surface. The grating is ruled with 7500 lines per cm. What is the angle corresponding to the first bright fringe produced by the grating ?

Data : λ = 5460 A°

N = 7500 lines per cm

n = 1

a + b = $\dfrac{1}{7500}$ cm

Formula : (a + b) sin θ = n λ

Solution :

$$\dfrac{1}{7500} \sin \theta = 1 \times 5460 \times 10^{-8}$$

$$\sin \theta = 0.4095$$

$$\boxed{\theta = 24.17°}$$

Example 8.23 : Calculate the angular separation between the first order minima on either side of the central bright maxima when slit is 6×10^{-4} cm wide and $\lambda = 6000$ A°.

Data : $\quad a = 6 \times 10^{-4}$ cm

$\quad\quad\quad\quad \lambda = 6000$ A°

Formula : $\quad a \sin \alpha = n \lambda$

Solution :

Take $\quad n = 1$

$$\sin \theta = \frac{1 \times 6000 \times 10^{-8}}{6 \times 10^{-4}}$$

$$\sin \theta = 0.1$$

$$\theta = 5.739° = \boxed{5° \, 44'}$$

Example 8.24 : How many orders will be visible if the wavelength of the incident light is 6000 A° and the number of lines on the grating is 5.0×10^3 lines per cm ?

Data : $\quad \lambda = 6000$ A°

$\quad\quad\quad N = 5.0 \times 10^3$ lines per cm

Solution :

$$(a + b) \sin \theta = n \lambda$$

Take $\quad \sin \theta = 1$

$$\frac{1}{N} = n\lambda$$

$$n = \frac{1}{5 \times 10^3 \times 6000 \times 10^{-8}}$$

$$\boxed{n = 3.33}$$

The number of order, $\quad n = 3$

Example 8.25 : What is the longest wavelength that can be observed in the third order for a transmission grating having 7000 lines per cm ? Assume normal incidence.

Data : $\quad n = 3$

$\quad N = 7000$ lines per cm, $(a + b) = \dfrac{1}{7000}$ cm

Formula : $\quad (a + b) \sin \theta = n \lambda$

Solution :

Take $\quad \sin \theta = 1$

$$\frac{1}{N} = n \lambda$$

$$\lambda = \frac{1}{7000 \times 3}$$

$$\lambda = 4.761 \times 10^{-5} \text{ cm}$$

$$\boxed{\lambda = 4761 \text{ A°}}$$

Example 8.26 : What is the highest order of spectrum which may be seen with the light of wavlength 6328 A° by means of a grating with 3000 lines km ?

Data : N = 3000 lines /cm

λ = 6328 A°, $(a + b) = \dfrac{1}{3000}$ cm

Formula : $(a + b) \sin \theta = n \lambda$

Solution :

Take $\sin \theta = 1$

$\dfrac{1}{N} = n \lambda$

$n = \dfrac{1}{3000 \times 6328 \times 10^{-8}}$

$\boxed{n = 5.26}$

The highest order, n = 5

Example 8.27 : A grating has 6000 lines per cm. How many orders of light of wavelength 4500 A° can be seen ?

Data : N = 6000 lines per cm

λ = 4500 A°, $(a + b) = \dfrac{1}{6000}$ cm

Formulae : (i) $(a + b) = \dfrac{1}{N}$ cm (ii) $(a + b) \sin \theta = m\lambda$

Solution :

(i) $(a + b) = \dfrac{1}{6000} = 1.666 \times 10^{-4}$ cm

(ii) $(a + b) \sin \theta = m\lambda$

Take $\sin \theta = 1$

$m = \dfrac{1.666 \times 10^{-4}}{4500 \times 10^{-8}}$

∴ $\boxed{m = 3.7}$

Hence, highest order visible = 3

Example 8.28 : A single slit diffraction pattern is formed using white light. For what wavelength of light does the second minimum coincide with the third minimum for the wavelength 4000 A° ?

Data : λ_1 = 4000 A°

$n_1 = 3$

$n_2 = 2$

Formula : For single slit minima,
$$a \sin \theta = n\lambda$$

Solution : $a \sin \theta = 2 \times \lambda_2$
and $a \sin \theta = 3\lambda_1$
∴ $2\lambda_2 = 3\lambda_1$
∴ $2 \times \lambda_2 = 3 \times 4000\ \text{A}°$
∴ $\boxed{\lambda_2 = 6000\ \text{A}°}$

Example 8.29 : A light of wavelength 5.8×10^{-7} m is incident on a slit having a width of 0.3×10^{-3} m. The viewing screen is 2.00 m from the slit. Find the position of the first dark fringes and the width of the central bright fringe. What happens to the diffraction pattern if the slit width is increased ?

Data :
$\lambda = 5.8 \times 10^{-7}$ m
$a = 0.3 \times 10^{-3}$ m
$D = 2.00$ m
$n = 1$

Formulae : (i) For single slit,
$$a \sin \theta = n\lambda$$
(ii) From Fig. 8.16, $\sin \theta \approx \dfrac{d}{D}$ (for large D)

Solution :
From (1) and (2),

∴ $\quad a\dfrac{d}{D} = \lambda$

∴ $\quad d = \dfrac{D\lambda}{a}$

$\quad d = 3.87 \times 10^{-3}$ m

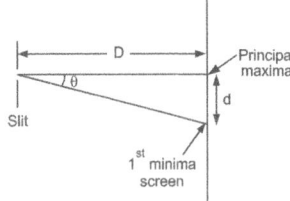

Fig. 8.16

The width of central bright fringe
$= 2d$
$= \boxed{7.74 \times 10^{-3}\ \text{m}}$

If the slit width is increased, width of principal maxima decreases.

Example 8.30 : A monochromatic light from a helium-neon laser (λ = 623.8 nm) is incident normally on a diffraction grating containing 6000 lines/cm. Find the angles at which the first and second order maxima are obtained.

Data : λ = 623.8 nm = 623.8 × 10^{-7} cm

N = 6000 lines/cm, $(a+b) = \dfrac{1}{6000}$ cm

Formulae : (i) $(a+b) = \dfrac{1}{N}$ cm, (ii) $(a+b)\sin\theta = n\lambda$

Solution :

(i) $(a+b) = \dfrac{1}{6000} = 1.66 \times 10^{-4}$ cm

(ii) $(a+b)\sin\theta = n\lambda$

For n = 1, $\theta_1 = \sin^{-1}\left(\dfrac{1 \times 623.8 \times 10^{-7}}{1.66 \times 10^{-4}}\right) = \boxed{22.31°}$

For n = 2, $\theta_2 = \sin^{-1}\left(\dfrac{2 \times 623.8 \times 10^{-7}}{1.66 \times 10^{-4}}\right) = \boxed{49.39°}$

SUMMARY

- The bending of waves around the corners of the obstacle and their encroachment into the region of geometrical shadow is called "diffraction of waves".
- Three elements of diffraction : source, obstacle or aperture and the screen.
- Diffraction phenomenon can be observed only when the size of the obstacle or aperture is comparable to the wavelength of incident waves.
- Fraunhofer's diffraction pattern due to a single rectangular slit consists of a central bright maximum.
- The intensities of the secondary maxima lying on either side of central maxima go on decreasing away from the central maxima.
- The intensity for a single slit diffraction pattern at any angle θ is

$$I_\theta = I_m \dfrac{\sin^2\alpha}{\alpha^2}$$

- Condition for maxima in the single slit diffraction pattern is

$$\alpha = 0, \quad \theta = 0.$$

- Condition for minima in the single slit diffraction pattern is

$$\alpha = \pm m\pi$$
$$a\sin\theta = m\lambda$$

- Condition for secondary maxima in the single slit diffraction pattern is

$$\alpha = \pm\left(m + \dfrac{1}{2}\right)\pi$$

$$a \sin \theta = (2m + 1) \frac{\lambda}{2}$$

- A plane diffraction grating is a device having N narrow slits side by side separated by opaque spaces.
- Grating is an application of multiple slit diffraction.
- The intensity for diffraction grating is

$$I_\theta = I_m \frac{\sin^2 \alpha}{\alpha^2} \cdot \frac{\sin^2 N\beta}{\sin^2 \beta}$$

- Condition for principal maxima in the intensity pattern of a grating,

$$(a + b) \sin \theta = m\lambda$$

- Condition for minima,

$$(a + b) \sin \theta = \frac{m}{N} \lambda$$

IMPORTANT FORMULAE

- $a \sin \theta = n\lambda$
- $\sin \theta = \frac{\lambda}{a}$ if $n = 1$
- $\sin \theta = \frac{x}{f}$
- $a \sin \theta = (2n + 1) \frac{\lambda}{2}$
- $(a + b) \sin \theta = n\lambda$
- $(a + b) \sin \theta = \frac{m}{N} \lambda$
- $a + b = \frac{1}{N \text{ lines/cm}}$

EXERCISE

1. Distinguish between Fresnel and Fraunhofer diffraction.
2. Explain the phenomenon of diffraction of light. State its types and distinguish between them.
3. Explain : (i) Diffraction of light (ii) Diffraction grating.
4. Explain the difference between interference and diffraction.
5. Describe the phenomenon observed when a monochromatic light falls on a single slit.
6. Derive an expression for the intensity at a point in the Fraunhofer's type of diffraction produced by a single slit.

7. Explain the formation of spectra by a plane transmission grating.
8. Obtain the conditions for maxima and minima in Fraunhofer diffraction due to a single slit.
9. What is plane transmission grating ? Explain how it can be used for determining the wavelength of given monochromatic light.
10. Give the theory of plane transmission grating.
11. Discuss Fraunhofer's diffraction at a single slit and derive the condition for obtaining secondary minimum intensity positions.
12. What is diffraction of light ? What are the types of diffractions ? Distinguish between them.
13. What is diffraction ? What are its types ? Distinguish between them.
14. What is diffraction of light ? What are the types of diffraction ? Distinguish between them.
15. A beam of monochromatic light of wavelength λ passes through a slit of width 'a'. The rays after undergoing the Fraunhofer's diffraction through an angle θ, produced a resultant disturbance at some point P given by,

$$E_\theta = E_m \frac{\sin \alpha}{\alpha}$$

where E_m = Maximum amplitude of disturbance for the undiffracted rays, $\alpha = \frac{\pi}{\lambda} a \sin \theta$.

Assuming this expression for E_θ, obtain the condition for principal maxima, minima and secondary maxima. Draw the intensity distribution curve.

16. Discuss the Fraunhofer's diffraction at a single slit and obtain the conditions for principal maxima and minima. Draw the intensity distribution curve.
17. Discuss the Fraunhofer's diffraction at a single slit and derive the condition for secondary maximum intensity positions.
18. Obtain the condition for maxima in Fraunhofer's diffraction due to a single slit.
19. Obtain the condition for minima in Fraunhofer's diffraction due to a single slit.
20. Discuss the Fraunhofer's diffraction at a single slit. Draw the intensity distribution curve.
21. Discuss the Fraunhofer's diffraction at a single slit. Obtain the condition for principal maximum and minimum.
22. Explain Fraunhofer's diffraction due to a single slit and obtain an expression for resultant amplitude of diffraction pattern. Obtain the conditions of principal maxima and minima.
23. Obtain the condition for maxima and minima in the Fraunhofer's diffraction due to single slit.
24. Give the theory of plane diffraction grating. Obtain the conditions for the formation of principal maxima and minima.
25. What is diffraction grating ? How it is obtained ?

26. Give the theory of plane diffraction grating and obtain the condition for n^{th} order maxima.
27. Give the theory of plane diffraction grating. Obtain the condition for the formation of nth order maximum.

UNSOLVED PROBLEMS

1. Light is incident normally on a grating 0.5 cm wide with 2500 lines. Find the angles of diffraction for the principal maxima of the two sodium lines in the first order spectrum λ_1 = 5890 A° and λ_2 = 5896 A°. **(Ans.** θ_1 = 17.1°, θ_2 = 17.2°)
2. What is the highest order spectrum which can be seen with monochromatic light of wavelength 6000 A° by means of a diffraction grating with 5000 lines/cm ? **(Ans.** n = 3)
3. A plane grating has 15000 lines per inch. Find the angle of separation of 5408 A° and 5016 A° lines of helium in the second order spectrum. **(Ans.** $(\theta_2 - \theta_1)$ = 16')
4. A diffraction grating used at normal incidence gives a line λ_1 = 6000 A° in a certain order superimposed on another line, λ_2 = 4500 A° of the next highest order. If the angle of diffraction is 30°, how many lines are there in a cm in the grating ? **(Ans.** 2778 lines/cm)
5. What is the highest order spectrum which may be seen with light of wavelength 5000 A° by means of a grating with 3000 lines/cm ? **(Ans.** n = 6)
6. A plane diffraction grating has the value of grating constant equal to 15×10^{-4} cm. Calculate the position of third order maximum for $\lambda = 2.4 \times 10^{-4}$ cm. **(Ans.** θ_3 = 28.7°)
7. Monochromatic light of wavelength λ = 6560 A° falls normally on a grating. The spectral line is diffracted at an angle of 19° 9' from the normal in the first order. Find the grating element. **(Ans.** 2×10^{-4} cm)
8. A single slit Fraunhofer's diffraction pattern is formed using white light. For what wavelength of light does the second minimum coincide with the third minimum for the wavelength 4000 A° ? **(Ans.** 6000 A°)
9. In a plane transmission grating with 5000 lines/cm and for wavelength 6000 A°, if the opaque spaces are exactly 2.0 lines the transparent spaces, which order of spectra will be absent ? **(Ans.** 3rd, 6th, 9th etc. orders)
10. Light of wavelength 6×10^{-5} cm falls on a screen at a distance of 100 cm from a narrow slit. Find the width of the slit if the first minimum has 1 mm on either side of the central maximum. **(Ans.** 0.06 cm)
11. Calculate the angles at which the first dark band and the next bright band are formed in Fraunhofer diffraction pattern of a slit of 0.3 mm wide, given λ = 5890 A°. **(Ans.** 6.7', 10')
12. Calculate the angular separation between the first order minima on either side of central bright maximum, when slit is 6×10^{-4} cm wide and λ = 6000 A°. **(Ans.** 73° 4')
13. Light of wavelength 5500 A° falls normally on slit of width 22×10^{-5} cm. Calculate the angular position of the first two minima from the central bright maximum. **(Ans.** 14° 29', 30°)

14. Plane waves of λ = 6000 A° fall normally on a single slit of width 0.2 mm. Calculate the total angular width of the central bright maximum and also the linear width as observed on a screen placed 2 m away. (**Ans.** 20', 1.2 cm)

REFERENCES

Animation of single slit diffraction pattern :
- http://www.walter-fendt.de/ph14e/singleslit/htm

An interactive animation of diffraction pattern with a grating :
- http://www.physics.uq.edu.au/people/mcintype/php/laboratories/index.php?e=14.

More information about resolving power :
- http://www.astronomynotes.com/telescop/s6.htm

More information about X-ray diffraction :
- http://www.eserc.stonybrook.edu/ProjectJava/Bragg/

✠ ✠ ✠

Unit - V (OPTICS – II)

CHAPTER 9
POLARIZATION

9.1 INTRODUCTION

The phenomena like interference or diffraction prove the wave nature of light. But it does not tell us whether the light waves are longitudinal or transverse. Because even longitudinal waves, like sound waves, show the phenomena of interference and diffraction. The phenomenon of polarization can be explained only by considering the transverse nature of light. And it has been proved by electromagnetic theory that the light is transverse wave.

In longitudinal waves, the particles of the medium vibrate to and fro in the direction of propagation of the wave.

But in the transverse waves, the particles of the medium vibrate up and down at right angles to the direction of propagation of the wave. But the important difference between longitudinal and transverse wave is that the transverse waves can be polarized. Hence the following experiments are considered to explain what polarization is.

9.2 POLARIZATION OF WAVES

The transverse nature of waves leads to the characteristic phenomenon called **polarization**. The characteristic, polarization is not exhibited by longitudinal waves. Thus only transverse waves could be polarized. In a transverse wave, if the directions of all the vibrations at all the points are restricted to one particular plane, then the wave is called **polarized**, more specific plane polarized. A plane polarized wave is the simplest of a transverse wave, which is also termed as linearly polarized wave.

9.3 POLARIZATION OF LIGHT

9.3.1 Mechanical Experiment

Consider a string AB passing through slits S_1 and S_2. The end B of the string is fixed while the end A is free. The free end A is given up and down motion rapidly such that transverse waves are set up in the string. These transverse waves travel towards the end B. In this case the particles of string vibrate along the direction parallel to S_1 therefore, passes through S_1. Since S_2 is parallel to S_1, these transverse vibrations pass through S_2 also, to reach the end B. If the end A is given motion in all possible directions instead of the up and down motion, the particle of the string will vibrate in all directions. When these vibrations reach vertical slit S_1, they are restricted to the vertical plane only. These vertical vibrations will reach the end B if S_2 is parallel to S_1. If on the other hand, S_2 is perpendicular to S_1, the vibrations of the string are completely stopped by S_2. This is because the displacement of the particles are now at right angles to the slit S_2. Thus, the string does not vibrate between S_2 and B.

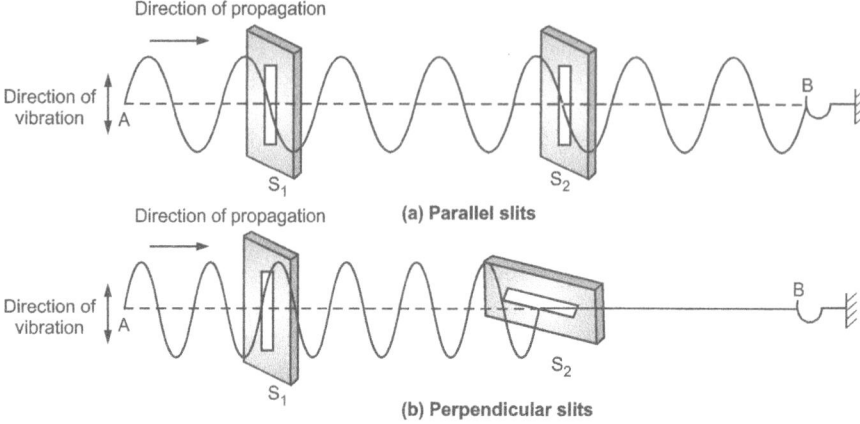

(a) Parallel slits

(b) Perpendicular slits

Fig. 9.1

If longitudinal waves are produced by moving the string forward and backward along it's length, then the waves will freely pass through S_1 and S_2 irrespective of their positions.

9.3.2 Optical Experiment

Light from a source is allowed to fall normally on the flat surface of a thin plate of tourmaline crystal, cut parallel to it's axis.

The crystal A is rotated and the intensity of light transmitted through A is noted. No change is observed. Now, another crystal B is placed with it's axis parallel to A. On observing the intensity of the light transmitted through B, no change is observed.

If now the crystal A is kept fixed and B is gradually rotated, it is seen that the intensity of light emerging out of B decreases. It becomes zero when the axis of B is perpendicular to that of A. If B is further rotated, the intensity increases and becomes maximum when the axes of A and B are again parallel.

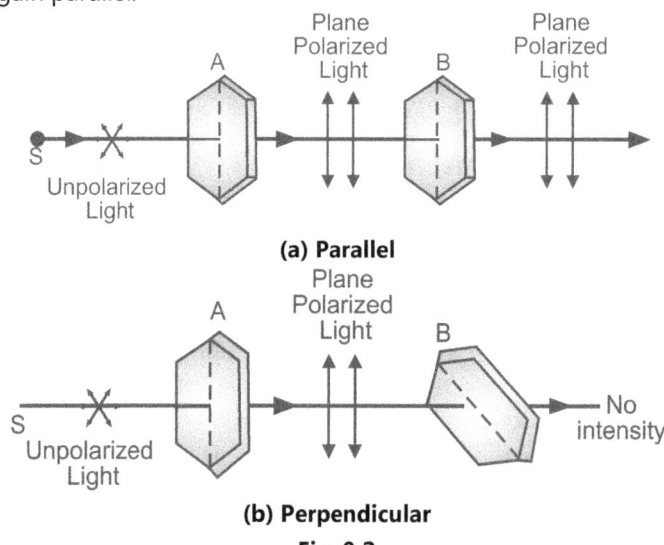

(a) Parallel

(b) Perpendicular

Fig. 9.2

Thus the intensity of transmitted light is maximum when axes of A and B are parallel, and zero when they are perpendicular.

From these experiments, it is clear that light waves are transverse. If they were longitudinal, then the rotation of crystal B would not have produced any change in the intensity of light.

9.3.3 Polarization

Thus, light from the source S consists of transverse waves having vibrations in all directions in a plane perpendicular to the direction of propagation of light. When such a beam reaches the crystal A, vibrations parallel to it's axis are only allowed to pass. Thus, the light coming out of crystal A is not symmetrical about the direction of propagation of light. It's vibrations are confined only to a single plane, in a plane perpendicular to the direction of propagation. Such a light is called a **plane polarized light**, the crystal A is called **polarizer** and crystal B which detects these vibrations is known as **analyzer**. The phenomenon is called as **polarization**.

9.4 REPRESENTATION OF PLANE POLARIZED LIGHT (PPL), UNPOLARIZED LIGHT (UPL) AND PARTIALLY POLARIZED LIGHT

According to the electromagnetic theory, light consists of electric and magnetic vectors vibrating continuously with time in a plane, transverse to the direction of propagation of light and to each other. However, **in explaining polarization only the vibrations of the electric vector are considered**. It does not mean that magnetic field vectors are absent, they are present. But for drawing simplicity they are not shown in the diagram.

9.4.1 Unpolarized Light

The light having vibrations along all possible directions perpendicular to the direction of propagation of light, is called an **unpolarized light**. It is symmetrical about it's direction of propagation.

Fig. 9.3 : Unpolarized light

It can be considered to consist an infinite number of waves each having its own vibration. Therefore, for any position of the crystal there will be one vibration parallel to its axes, so when such a light is passed through a single tourmaline crystal and is rotated no change in the intensity of the emergent light is observed.

Since unpolarized light has vibrations along all possible directions, at right angles to the directions of propagation of light, it is represented by a star.

9.4.2 Polarized Light

The light having vibration only along a single plane perpendicular to the direction of propagation of light is called a **polarized light**. It's vibrations are one sided, therefore it is dissymmetrical about the direction of propagation of light. When polarized light is passed through a single rotating crystal, a change in the intensity of emergent light is observed.

According to the electromagnetic theory, a plane polarized light can be defined as follows :

A light wave is said to be **plane polarized** if the electric vector (E) or magnetic vector (H) at any point is vibrating along the same plane perpendicular to the direction of propagation of light wave.

The polarized beam of light has vibrations along a single plane. If they are parallel to the plane of the paper, they are represented by arrows [See Fig. 9.4 (a)]. If they are perpendicular to the plane of the paper, they are represented by dots on a ray of light. [See Fig. 9.4 (b)].

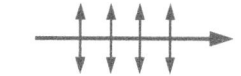

(a) Parallel to plane of paper

(b) Perpendicular to plane of paper

Fig. 9.4 : Plane polarized light

9.4.3 Partially Polarized Light

A partially polarized light is a mixture of plane polarized and unpolarized light. It is represented as shown in Fig. 9.5.

In partially polarized light the vibrations in the plane of plane polarized light dominate over the vibrations in other directions.

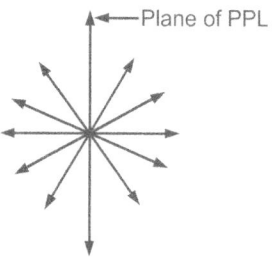

Fig. 9.5 : Partially polarized light

9.5 DOUBLE REFRACTION

Calcite Crystal

Calcite or Iceland spar is crystallised calcium carbonate ($CaCO_3$). It is found in large quantities in Iceland as a large transparent crystal. It crystallises in many forms and readily breaks into simple rhombohedron.

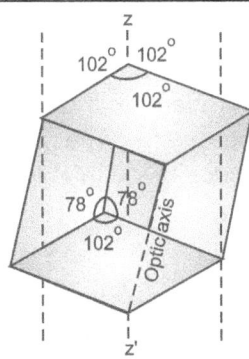

Fig. 9.6 : Calcite crystal form
The direction of the optic axis is indicated by broken lines

For a point in calcite, there are **three principal sections**, one for each pair of opposite faces. The principal section does not always suffice in describing the direction of vibrations. Here, we make use of the two other planes, **the principal plane of the ordinary ray**, a plane containing the ordinary ray and the optic axis, and **the principal plane of the extraordinary ray** or a plane containing the E-ray and the optic axis. The O-ray always lies in the plane of incidence. This is not generally true for the E-ray. The principal planes of the two refracted rays do not coincide except in special cases. The special cases are those for which the plane of incidence is a principal section as shown in Fig. 9.9. Under these conditions, the plane of incidence, the principal section and the principal planes of the O and E rays all coincide.

Optic Axis

The **optic axis** is the direction of symmetry of unisotropic media along which double refraction does not take place.

A line drawn through any of the blunt corners making equal angles with each of the three edges gives the direction of the optic axis. In fact any line parallel to this line is also an optic axis. Therefore, optic axis is not a line but **it is a direction** (as shown in Fig. 9.9).

Principal Section

A plane containing **the optic axis** and **perpendicular to the opposite faces** of the crystal is called the **principal section of the crystal**. The principal section cuts the surfaces of a calcite crystal in a parallelogram with angles 109° and 71°.

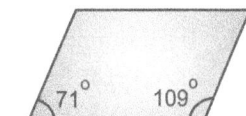

Fig. 9.7 : Principal section of calcite crystal

Principal Plane

The plane containing **the optic axis** and **the ordinary ray** is called **principal plane of the ordinary ray**. Similarly the plane containing **the optic axis** and **the extraordinary ray** is called **the principal plane of the extraordinary ray**.

Experiments revealed that the vibrations of the ordinary rays are perpendicular to the principal section of the crystal while the vibrations of the extraordinary rays are parallel to the principal section of the crystal. Thus, the two rays are plane polarized, their vibrations being at right angles to each other.

Double Refraction

The phenomenon of double refraction was discovered by Erasmus Bartholinus in 1669 during his studies on calcite. When light is incident on a calcite crystal, it is found to produce two refracted rays which are different in properties. The phenomenon of causing **two refracted rays** by a crystal is called **birefringence** or **double refraction**. The crystals are said to be **birefringent**.

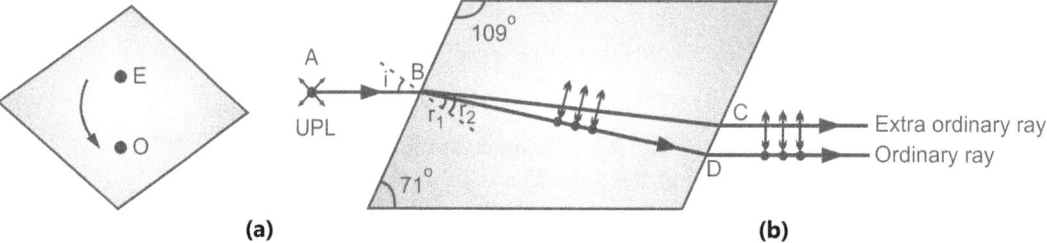

(a)   (b)

Fig. 9.8 : Double reflection

All anisotropic materials exhibit double refraction. The two rays formed in double refraction are linearly polarized in mutually perpendicular directions. One of the rays **obeys Snell's law** of refraction and hence is called **an ordinary ray or O-ray**. The other ray **does not obey Snell's law** and is called an **extraordinary ray or E-ray.** If one of the rays is eliminated, the light transmitted by the crystal will be a linearly polarized light.

When a ray of light AB is incident on the calcite crystal making an angle of incidence i, it is refracted along two paths inside the crystal : (i) along BC making an angle of refraction r_2, (ii) along BD making an angle of refraction r_1. These two rays emerge out along DO and CE which are parallel as the crystal faces are parallel.

9.6 LAW OF MALUS

Statement : The law states that, the intensity of polarized light emerging from the analyzer is proportional to the **square of the cosine** of the angle between the plane of the transmission for the analyzer and the plane of the polarizer.

Proof : Let A_o be the amplitude of the incident plane polarized light. Let θ be the angle between the planes of transmissions of the analyzer and the polarizer. The amplitude A_o may be resolved into two components **$A_o \cos \theta$** and **$A_o \sin \theta$**. The vibrations of the former are parallel to the plane of the transmission of the analyzer, while the vibrations of latter are perpendicular to this i.e. **$A_o \cos \theta$** is **transmitted** by the analyzer while **$A_o \sin \theta$** is **eliminated**.

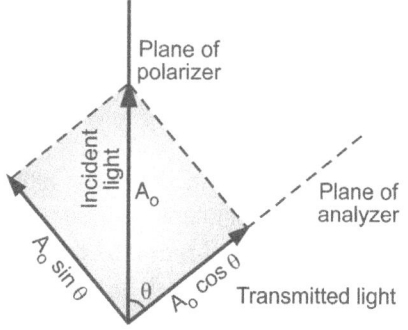

Fig. 9.9

The amplitude of the transmitted beam,

$$A = A_o \cos\theta$$

Therefore, the intensity of the transmitted beam, $I = A^2$ but $A = A_o \cos^2\theta$

$$\therefore \quad I = A_o^2 \cos^2\theta$$
$$I = I_o \cos^2\theta$$

The intensity of incident beam I_o is constant, therefore,

$$I \propto \cos^2\theta$$

This is called as **law of Malus**.

Note : In the case of incident unpolarized light, the law of Malus is $I = \frac{1}{2}I_0$. Because unpolarized light vibrates in all possible directions in a plane perpendicular to the direction of propagation. Therefore, the average value of $\cos^2\theta$ will have to be considered.

Then the intensity of the transmitted light is

$$I = I_0 \cos^2\theta = \frac{1}{2}I_0$$

since the average value of $\cos^2\theta$ over all possible values of θ is $\frac{1}{2}$ (i.e. $\cos^2\theta = \frac{1}{2}$) i.e. an ideal polarizer will be one which will transmit 50 % of the incident unpolarized light as plane polarized light.

9.7 HUYGEN'S THEORY OF DOUBLE REFRACTION

Huygen explained the phenomenon of double refraction on the basis of the principle of secondary wavelets.

He assumed :

1. When a beam of ordinary unpolarized light strikes a doubly refracting crystal, each point on the surface sends out **two wavefronts**, one for ordinary ray and the other for extraordinary ray.
2. The **ordinary-ray** travels with the **same speed** v_o in all directions and the crystal has a single refractive index $\mu_o = \frac{c}{v_o}$ for this wave. Thus, the O-ray has a **spherical wavefront**.
3. The **speed of extra-ordinary ray v_e varies with direction**. So, the refractive index, $\mu_e = \frac{c}{v_e}$ also varies with direction for the E-ray. Therefore, the extra-ordinary ray develops a wavefront which is **ellipsoidal**.
4. The velocity v_e measured is perpendicular to the optic axis.
5. The velocities of the O-ray and E-ray are the same along the optic axis.
6. When rays are incident along the optic axis, the spherical and ellipsoidal wavefronts touch each other at points of intersection with the optic axis and double refraction does not take place.

7. If $v_o > v_e$ or $\mu_o < \mu_e$, the spherical wavefront lies outside the elliptical wavefront. Such crystals are called **positive crystals**. The examples of positive crystal are quartz, ice etc.

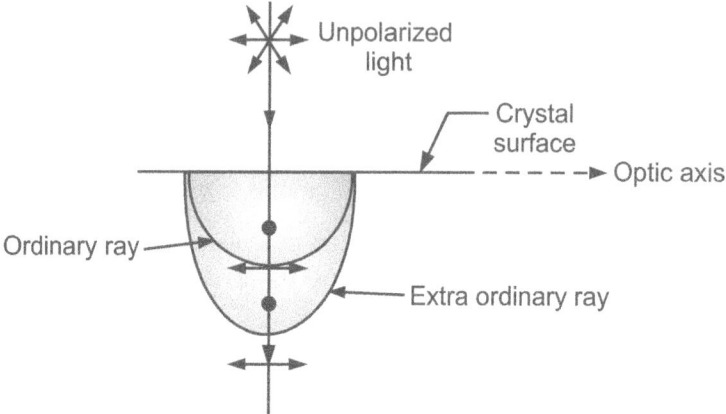

Fig. 9.10 : Double refraction

8. If $v_e > v_o$ or $\mu_e < \mu_o$, the elliptical wavefront lies outside the spherical wavefront. Such crystals are called **negative crystals**. The examples of negative crystals are calcite, tourmaline, etc.

9.7.1 Cases of Double Refraction of Crystal Cut with Optic Axis Lying in the Plane of Incidence

1. Parallel to the Surface

Fig. 9.11 shows unpolarized plane wavefront AB incident normally on the crystal surface XY. The optic axis lies along XY and is in the plane of incidence. At the points A and B, it develops two wavefronts, one spherical for O-ray and one elliptical for E-ray. The envelope of O-ray and E-ray gives the corresponding wavefront which is plane polarized. It should be noted that both O-ray and E-ray are plane polarized light.

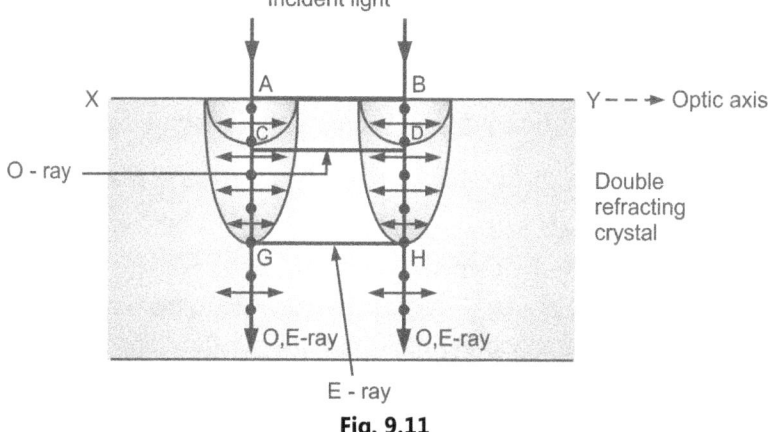

Fig. 9.11

Here both O-ray and E-ray travel along the same direction with different velocities. As O-ray and E-ray travel along the same direction with different velocities, a path difference is introduced between them. This principle is used in **the construction of quarter and half-wave plates**.

2. Perpendicular to the Surface

Fig. 9.12 shows unpolarized plane wavefront AB incident normally on the crystal surface XY. Optic axis lies in the plane of incidence and perpendicular to the crystal surface. As the light is incident in the direction of optic axis, O-ray and E-ray travel with the same speed along the optic axis. As a result O-ray and E-ray travel along the same directions with same velocity. Hence the phenomenon of **double refraction is absent** in this case. Ordinary and extraordinary wavefronts CD and GH coincide at all instants.

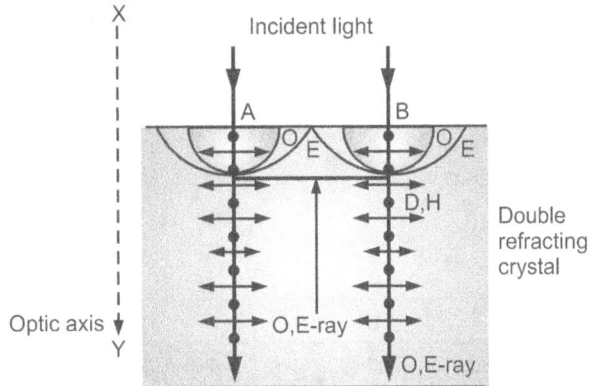

Fig. 9.12

3. Inclined to the Surface

Fig. 9.19 shows an unpolarized plane wavefront incident normally on the crystal surface so that the optic axis makes an angle with the crystal surface. O-ray and E-ray travel with different velocities in different direction in the crystal. Hence double refraction is seen in this case and both O-ray and E-ray are separated by an angle depending upon the distance travelled in crystal.

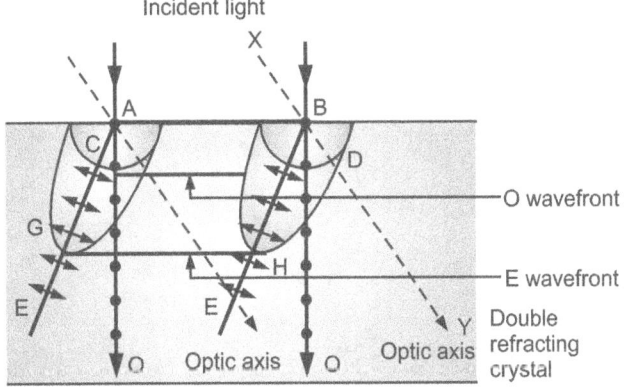

Fig. 9.13

9.8 POSITIVE AND NEGATIVE CRYSTALS

Positive Crystals	Negative Crystals
1. For positive crystals, $v_o > v_e$ and $\mu_o < \mu_e$.	1. For negative crystals, $v_o < v_e$ and $\mu_o > \mu_e$.
2. The velocity of O-ray is same in all directions.	2. The velocity of O-ray is same in all directions.
3. The wavefront of O-ray lies outside the wavefront of E-ray.	3. The wavefront of O-ray lies inside the wavefront of E-ray.
4. Examples : Quartz, Ice.	4. Examples : Calcite, Tourmaline.

Fig. 9.14 (a)   Fig. 9.14 (b)

9.9 POLARIZATION BY DOUBLE REFRACTION - NICOL PRISM

Nicol prism is an optical device used for **producing and analysing plane polarised light**.

Principle :

The Nicol prism is made in such a way that it eliminates one of the refracted rays by total internal reflection i.e. O-ray is eliminated and only E-ray is transmitted through the prism.

Construction :

A **calcite crystal** whose length is three times it's breadth is taken. Let ABCD be the principal section of the crystal with ∠ BAD = 71°. The end faces of the crystal are cut in such a way that they make angles 68° and 112° in the principal section instead of 71° and 109°.

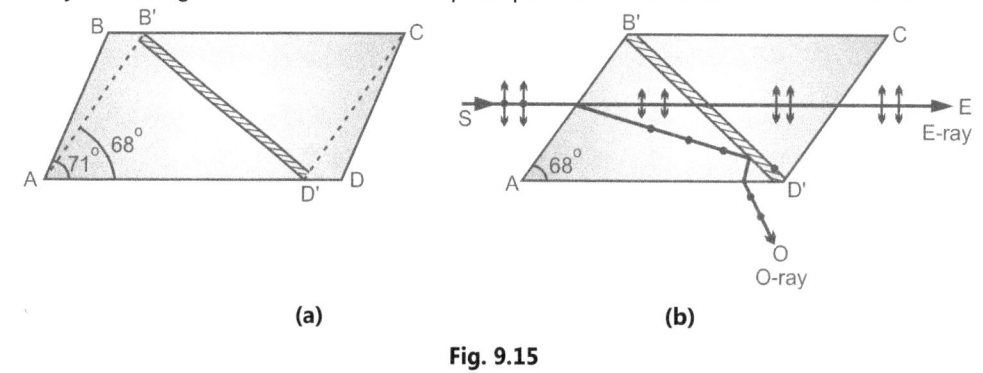

(a)   (b)

Fig. 9.15

The crystal is then cut into two pieces from one blunt corner to the other along a plane perpendicular to the principal section. The two cut faces are grounded and polished optically flat. It is then cemented together by Canada balsam whose refractive index lies between the refractive indices for the O-ray and E-ray for calcite.

Refractive index of Calcite for O-ray
$$\mu_o = 1.658$$

Refractive index of Canada Balsam
$$\mu_c = 1.55 \quad \text{Using sodium light of } \lambda = 5893 \text{ A}°,$$

Refractive index of Calcite for E-ray
$$\mu_e = 1.486$$

Canada balsam layer acts as a rarer medium for O-ray and as a denser medium for E-ray. Except the end faces, the sides of the crystal are blackened.

Working :

When a ray of unpolarized light is incident on the prism surface, it splits into O-ray and E-ray. Both the rays are polarized having vibrations at right angles to each other.

When the O-ray passes from a portion of the crystal into the layer of Canada balsam, it passes from a denser medium to rarer medium. When the angle of incidence is greater than the critical angle, the O-ray is totally internally reflected and is not transmitted.

When the E-ray passes from calcite to the Canada Balsam layer, it enters in rarer medium. Therefore, the E-ray is not affected and is transmitted through the prism. Refractive index for O-ray with respect to Canada balsam,

$$\mu = \frac{1.658}{1.55}$$

If C is the critical angle,

$$\therefore \quad \mu = \frac{1}{\sin C}$$

$$\sin C = \frac{1}{\mu} = \frac{1.55}{1.658}$$

$$C = 69°$$

As the length of the crystal is large, the angle of incidence at Canada balsam surface for the O-ray is greater than the critical angle. Thus, it suffers total internal reflection while E-ray is transmitted which is plane polarized having vibrations in the principal section.

Special Cases :
- If the angle of incidence is less than the critical angle for O-ray, it is not reflected and is transmitted through the prism.
  In this position, both the O-ray and E-ray are transmitted through the prism.
- The E-ray also has a limit beyond which it is totally internally reflected by Canada balsam surface. If E-ray travels along the optic axis, its refractive index is the same as that of O-ray i.e. 1.658. But it is 1.486 for all other directions of E-ray.

Therefore depending on the direction of propagation of E-ray, μ_e lies between 1.486 and 1.658.

Therefore for a particular case, μ_e may be more than 1.55 and the angle of incidence will be more than the critical angle. Then E-ray will also be totally internally reflected.

9.10 PRODUCTION OF PLANE POLARIZED LIGHT BY SELECTIVE ABSORPTION (DICHROISM)

There are certain crystals and minerals which are doubly refracting and have the property of absorbing one of the doubly refracting beams to a greater extent than the other. The crystals showing this property are termed as **Dichroic Crystals** and the phenomenon is known as **Dichroism**.

This phenomenon of selective absorption is shown by a number of substances but the most notable and outstanding is Tourmaline. Tourmaline absorbs ordinary ray much more strongly than the extraordinary ray. When a plate of tourmaline is cut with the face parallel to the optic axis and unpolarized light is allowed to incident on it, the light splits into ordinary and extraordinary rays. Both the rays are plane polarized and travel through the crystal in the same direction. When the plate is sufficiently thick, the ordinary ray is almost completely absorbed and the extraordinary ray is partly absorbed and it emerges out. In this way, a plane polarized light with vibrations in the plane of incidence is obtained.

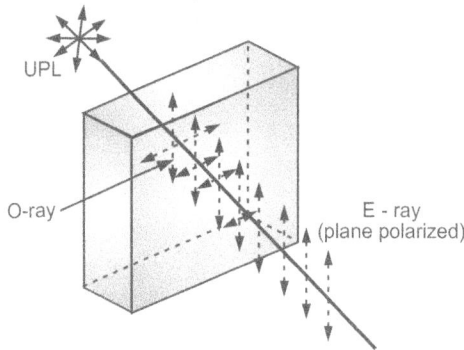

Fig. 9.16

Thus, plane polarized light is obtained by the property of selective absorption.

Polaroids

A polaroid is a polarizing film which produces polarized light from ordinary unpolarized light by the method of selective absorption. Crystals of iodosulphate of Quinine (Heraphite) show dichroism. But individually they are of no use due to their tiny size. Hence, Land developed a polarizing film in which these crystals are embedded in a volatile viscous medium with their optic axis parallel to each other. This is achieved by making a paste of the crystals in nitrocellulose. This is then forced to pass through a narrow slit. On the other side, a ribbon-like film is obtained. The axes of the crystals in the film are parallel, because only those molecules pass through the slit whose axes are parallel to the length of the slit. This film enclosed between two glass plates is a polaroid. When ordinary light is incident on such a polaroid, the emergent light will be plane polarized.

Applications of Polaroids
- They are used to produce and analyze plane polarized light.
- They are used in head lights and screens of motor cars.
- They are used in the windows of trains and airplanes to control the intensity of light.
- They are used as polarized sun glasses in goggles.

9.11 RETARDATION PLATES

When an unpolarized light is incident normally on the crystal it develops two wavefronts one spherical and one elliptical. Both the wavefronts travel along the same direction but with different speeds if the optic axis is parallel to the crystal surface. In a negative crystal, the sphere lies inside the ellipse. i.e. E-ray travels faster than O-ray. Due to this a path difference is introduced. This path difference depends on the thickness of the crystal i.e. the distance which it travels in denser medium, because after coming out of the medium both will travel with the same speed.

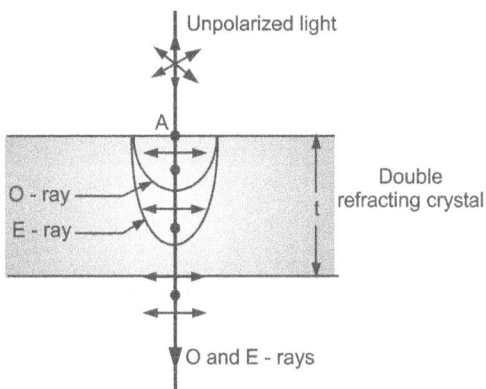

Fig. 9.17 : Double refraction

If the refractive index for O-ray is μ_o and thickness of crystal is t, then optical path will be given by $\mu_o t$. Similarly, for E-ray optical path will be $\mu_e t$.

∴ The optical path difference for negative crystal,

$$\Delta = \mu_o t - \mu_e t$$
$$\Delta = (\mu_o - \mu_e) t$$

Or phase difference

$$\delta = k \cdot \Delta = \frac{2\pi}{\lambda} (\mu_o - \mu_e) t$$

Similarly, for positive crystal,

$$\Delta = (\mu_e - \mu_o) t$$

and
$$\delta = \frac{2\pi}{\lambda}(\mu_e - \mu_o) t$$

If the thickness t and wavelength λ is constant, the plate will add definite amount of phase difference. Generally, wavelength λ is taken 5893 A° for calculating the thickness. So by using plates of fixed thickness one can add definite amount of phase difference. Such plates are called **retardation plates** and are used for producing and detecting polarized light.

Retardation Plate :

A plate of proper thickness cut from a double-refracting crystal with its faces, parallel to optic axis so as to produce a desired and definite value of phase difference between O and E-ray of polarized light emerging out of the plate is called a retardation plate.

Depending upon the phase difference they add, retardation plates are of two types :

(i) Quarter Wave Plate (QWP).
(ii) Half Wave Plate (HWP).

9.11.1 Quarter Wave Plate (QWP)

The simplest device for producing and detecting circularly polarized light is a quarter wave (λ/4) plate. Such plates are made of thin sheet of quartz or calcite cut parallel to the optic axis. The thickness is adjusted, so as to introduce a 90° (or π/2) phase or λ/4 path difference between O and E-ray. The correct thickness can be calculated by equation of phase difference,

$$\delta = \frac{2\pi}{\lambda}(\mu_o - \mu_e) t$$

For QWP, $\delta = \pi/2$

∴ $$\frac{\pi}{2} = \frac{2\pi}{\lambda}(\mu_o - \mu_e) t$$

∴ $$t = \frac{\lambda}{4(\mu_o - \mu_e)} \text{ for negative crystal.}$$

Similarly for positive crystal,

$$t = \frac{\lambda}{4(\mu_e - \mu_o)}$$

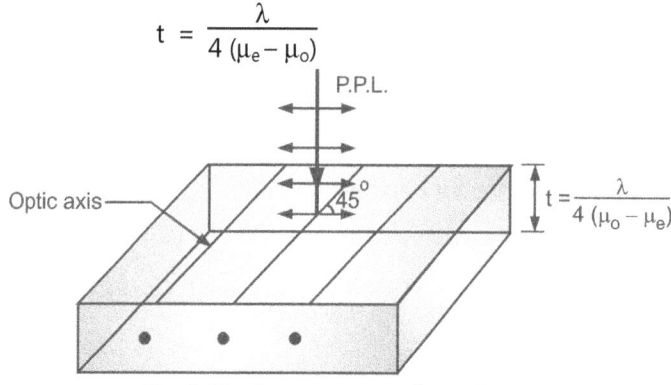

Fig. 9.18 : Quarter wave plate (QWP)

When a QWP is oriented at an angle of 45° with the plate of incident plane polarized light as shown in Fig. 9.21, the emerging light is circularly polarized light. For any other angle, other than 0°, 45°, 90°, between 0 to 90° the emerging light is elliptically polarized light.

9.11.2 Half Wave Plate (HWP)

The thickness of half wave plate is selected such that the O-ray and E-ray have a phase difference π or path difference of $\lambda/2$ on passing through the crystal.

The thickness can be calculated by equation of phase difference

$$\delta = \frac{2\pi}{\lambda}(\mu_o - \mu_e)t$$

For HWP, $\delta = \pi$

$$\therefore \pi = \frac{2\pi}{\lambda}(\mu_o - \mu_e)t$$

$$t = \frac{\lambda}{2(\mu_o - \mu_e)} \quad \text{for negative crystal.}$$

The equation for positive crystal will be

$$t = \frac{\lambda}{2(\mu_e - \mu_o)}$$

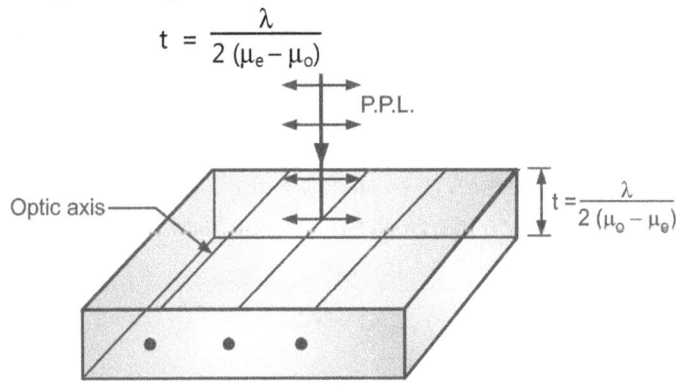

Fig. 9.19

The half wave plate merely alters the plane of polarization of plane polarized light by an angle 2θ, where θ is the angle between the plane of polarization of incident light and principal section.

9.12 ANALYTICAL TREATMENT FOR CIRCULARLY AND ELLIPTICALLY POLARISED LIGHT

When an unpolarized monochromatic light is incident on a Nicol prism, the emergent beam is plane polarised. If this plane polarized light is incident normally on a thin plate of a doubly refracting crystal cut with faces parallel to the optic axis, it is split up into O-ray and E-ray. Both of these rays are polarized at right angles and travel along the same direction, but with different velocities. Hence, there will be a phase difference δ between the two rays depending on the thickness 't' of the crystal.

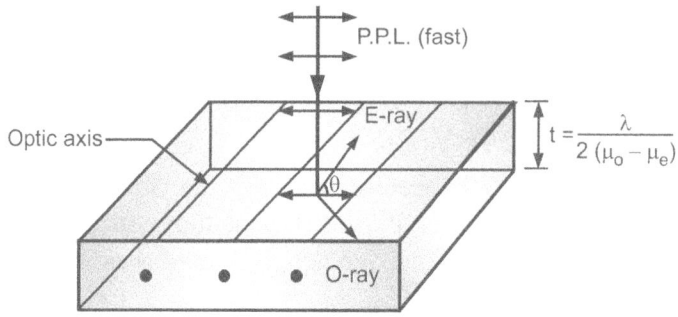

Fig. 9.20

Let the linear vibrations in the incident plane polarized light be along MN inclined at an along θ with the optic axis. Let A be the amplitude of vibration of the incident light. On entering the calcite crystal, the incident polarized light is split up into two components.

1. E-ray having vibrations parallel to the optic axis of amplitude A cos θ.
2. O-ray having vibrations perpendicular to the optic axis of amplitude A sin θ.

These waves travel in the same direction with different velocities, hence a phase difference δ is introduced between them. Thus, the waves emerging from the crystal may be represented by two simple harmonic vibrations of different amplitude and having a phase difference δ between them.

The displacement of E-ray, along the optic axis

$$x = A \cos\theta \sin(\omega t + \delta) \qquad \ldots (1)$$

and the displacement of O-ray, perpendicular to the optic axis

$$y = A \sin\theta \sin\omega t \qquad \ldots (2)$$

Let
$$A \cos\theta = a$$
$$A \sin\theta = b$$

∴
$$x = a \sin(\omega t + \delta)$$
$$y = b \sin\omega t$$

Rearranging, we get

$$\frac{x}{a} = \sin\omega t \cos\delta + \cos\omega t \sin\delta \qquad \ldots (3)$$

$$\frac{y}{b} = \sin\omega t \qquad \ldots (4)$$

From equation (3),

$$\frac{x}{a} = \sin\omega t \cos\delta + \sqrt{1 - \sin^2\omega t}\, \sin\delta$$

substituting for sin ωt from equation (4)

$$\frac{x}{a} = \frac{y}{b} \cos\delta + \sqrt{1 + \frac{y^2}{b^2}}\, \sin\delta$$

$$\frac{x}{a} - \frac{y}{b}\cos\delta = \sqrt{1 - \frac{y^2}{b^2}}\sin\delta$$

Squaring

$$\left(\frac{x}{a} - \frac{y}{b}\cos\delta\right)^2 = \left(1 - \frac{y^2}{b^2}\right)\sin^2\delta$$

$$\frac{x^2}{a^2} + \frac{y^2}{b^2}\cos^2\delta - \frac{2xy}{ab}\cos\delta = \left(1 - \frac{y^2}{b^2}\right)\sin^2\delta$$

$$\frac{x^2}{a^2} + \frac{y^2}{b^2} - \frac{2xy}{ab}\cos\delta = \sin^2\delta \qquad \ldots (5)$$

This is an equation of an ellipse inclined to the co-ordinate axes.
Hence, the emergent light is elliptically polarized. But the exact nature of the resultant depends on the value of δ which in turn depends on the thickness 't' of the crystal.

(a) Elliptically Polarised Light : When the thickness of the plate is such that

$$\delta = \frac{\pi}{2} \text{ and } a \neq b \text{ i.e. } A\cos\theta \neq A\sin\theta \text{ or } \theta \neq 45°$$

∴ Equation (5) becomes

$$\frac{x^2}{a^2} + \frac{y^2}{b^2} = 1$$

This is the equation of **an ellipse** with its axes coinciding with the co-ordinate axes. Thus, the emergent light is **elliptically polarized**.

(b) Circularly Polarised Light : When the thickness of the plate is such that

$$\delta = \frac{\pi}{2}, \text{ and when } a = b \text{ i.e. } A\cos\theta = A\sin\theta \text{ or } \theta = 45°$$

Equation (5) becomes

$$x^2 + y^2 = a^2$$

This is the equation of a circle of radius 'a'. Under these conditions, the emergent beam is **circularly polarized**.

9.13 PRODUCTION OF CIRCULARLY AND ELLIPTICALLY POLARISED LIGHT

9.13.1 Circularly Polarized Light

To produce circularly polarized light, the two waves vibrating at right angles to each other having the same amplitude and time period should have a phase difference of $\frac{\pi}{2}$ or a path difference of $\frac{\lambda}{4}$.

To achieve this a parallel beam of monochromatic light is allowed to fall on a Nicol prism N1. The beam coming out the prism N_1 is plane polarized. This plane polarized light is then allowed to fall normally on a quarter wave plate is split up into O and E components having amplitude and period. The light emerging from the quarter wave plate is circularly polarized as shown in Fig. 9.21.

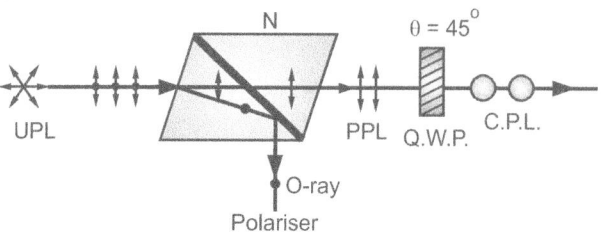

Fig. 9.21 : Production of CPL

9.13.2 Elliptically Polarised Light

Elliptically polarised light is produced if the amplitude of the O-ray and E-ray are unequal and there is phase difference of $\frac{\pi}{2}$ or a path difference of $\frac{\lambda}{4}$ between them.

A monochromatic beam of light is passed through a Nicol prism. The light emerging from the Nicol prism is plane polarized. This plane polarized light is allowed to fall on a quarter wave plate normally such that the vibrations in the incident plane polarized light make an angle θ (θ ≠ 0°, 44°, 90°) with the optic axis of the plate. When is condition is satisfied, the plane polarized light on entering the quarter wave plate is split up into O and E components having unequal amplitude and equal periods.

The light emerging from the quarter wave plate will be elliptically polarized.

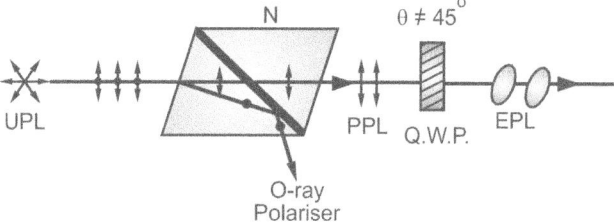

Fig. 9.22 : Production of EPL

9.14 ANALYSIS OF POLARISED LIGHT

In practice, light may be unpolarized, partially polarized or polarized (plane, circularly and elliptically). The unaided eye is unable to distinguish the different types of polarization. The actual type of polarization of a beam may be determined by using an analyzer and a quarter wave plate or a compensator.

Steps Used in the Analysis of Polarization :

Step 1 :

1. The light (of unknown type of polarization) is allowed to fall on an analyzer. If the intensity of the transmitted light varies from **0 to maximum**, twice in one full rotation of the analyzer then the incident light is **plane polarized (PPL)**.

2. If the intensity of transmitted light varies between maximum and minimum, but does not become extinguished in any position of the analyzer, then the incident light is either **practically plane polarized (partially PL)** or **elliptically polarized light (EPL).**
3. If the intensity of transmitted light **does not vary** (remains constant) then the incident light is either **unpolarized (UPL)** or **circularly polarized light (CPL).**

Step 2 :

To distinguish between elliptically polarized and partially polarized light or circularly polarized and unpolarized light, a quarter wave plate (QWP) is used. Light is made incident first on the QWP and then allowed to pass through the analyzer.

1. If the incident light is **EPL**, the QWP converts it into PPL. Therefore, the intensity of this beam will vary between **0 to maximum** twice in one full rotation. On the other hand, if the light intensity varies from minimum to maximum without becoming zero then the incident light is **partially plane polarized**.
2. If the incident light is **CPL**, the QWP converts it into a PPL. Therefore, the intensity of this beam will vary between **0 to maximum** twice in one full rotation. On the other hand, if the light intensity **remains constant**, then the incident light is **unpolarized**.

9.14.1 Detection of Various Types of Light

1. Unpolarised light (UPL) : When unpolarized beam of light is passed through a Nicol prism (analyzer) the emergent beam is plane polarised. As the Nicol prism is rotated about the direction of the incident beam, the intensity of transmitted beam remains unaltered. This is due to the fact that for any orientation of the Nicol prism, the vibration of unpolarized incident beam will be transmitted which is parallel to the principal section as shown in Fig. 9.23.

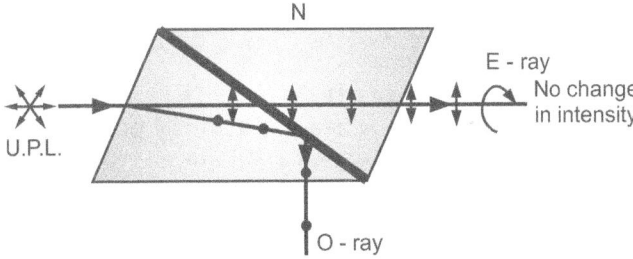

Fig. 9.23 : Analysis of UPL

2. Circularly Polarised Light (CPL) : When circularly polarised light is incident on a Nicol prism and Nicol prism is rotated about the direction of the incident light, the intensity of the transmitted beam will remain unchanged. This is because at any instant of time if CPL is resolved into its components, we will get two equal components. The component along the transmission axis will be transmitted, hence upon rotation intensity does not change which is a situation similar to UPL.

However, if a QWP is introduced in the path of CPL before the analyzer it will be converted into PPL as shown in Fig. 9.24. The CPL has a phase difference of $\pi/2$ and introduction of QWP adds another phase difference of $\pi/2$, thus, having a total phase of π. This gives a PPL.

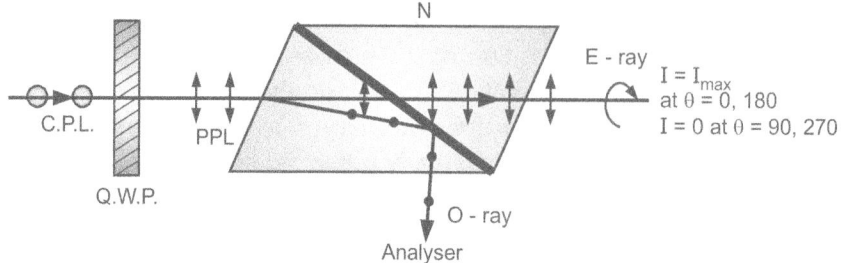

Fig. 9.24 : Analyzer of CPL

Now, as the analyzer is rotated the light transmitted through it will be completely absent for two positions 180° apart and will be maximum for two positions during one compete rotation. But for unpolarized light the intensity will still remain unchanged.

3. Plane Polarised Light (PPL) : When plane polarised light is incident on a Nicol prism only E-ray is transmitted which is also PPL. So, as the Nicol prism is rotated about the direction of the incident beam, the intensity of the transmitted light will change and a position is reached when the transmitted light is absent. If the Nicol is rotated further the intensity will increases gradually and becomes maximum after rotation of 90°. During one complete rotation, there will be two positions 180° apart for which transmitted light is absent or maximum as shown in Fig. 9.25.

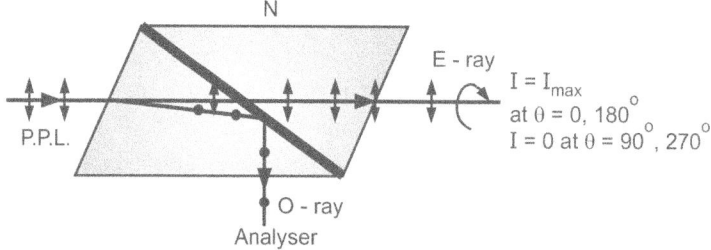

Fig. 9.25 : Analyzer of PPL

4. Partially Polarised Light (Par PL) : A beam of partially polarised light consists of UPL and PPL. When it is resolved into its components, we get two unequal components. If thus beam of light is passed through analyzer and the analyzer is rotated, at one particular position one component is absorbed and the other component is transmitted. So the intensity will vary between maximum (for bigger component) and minimum (for smaller component). During one compete rotation, there will be two positions 180° apart, for which transmitted light is maximum or minimum.

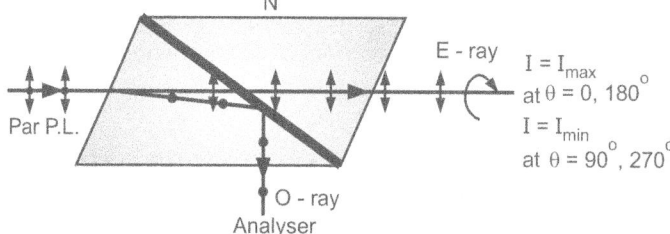

Fig. 9.26 : Analysis of Par PL

5. Elliptically Polarised Light (EPL): An elliptically polarised light has two components of unequal length. So depending upon the orientation of the analyzer one of the components is transmitted and other is eliminated. Hence, when EPL is passed through an analyzer of the transmitted light will vary between a maximum (for bigger component) and minimum (for smaller component) value but the beam will never disappear. This is case similar to the case of Par PL. For overcoming this problem a QWP is introduced in the path of the ray before the analyzer as shown in Fig. 9.27.

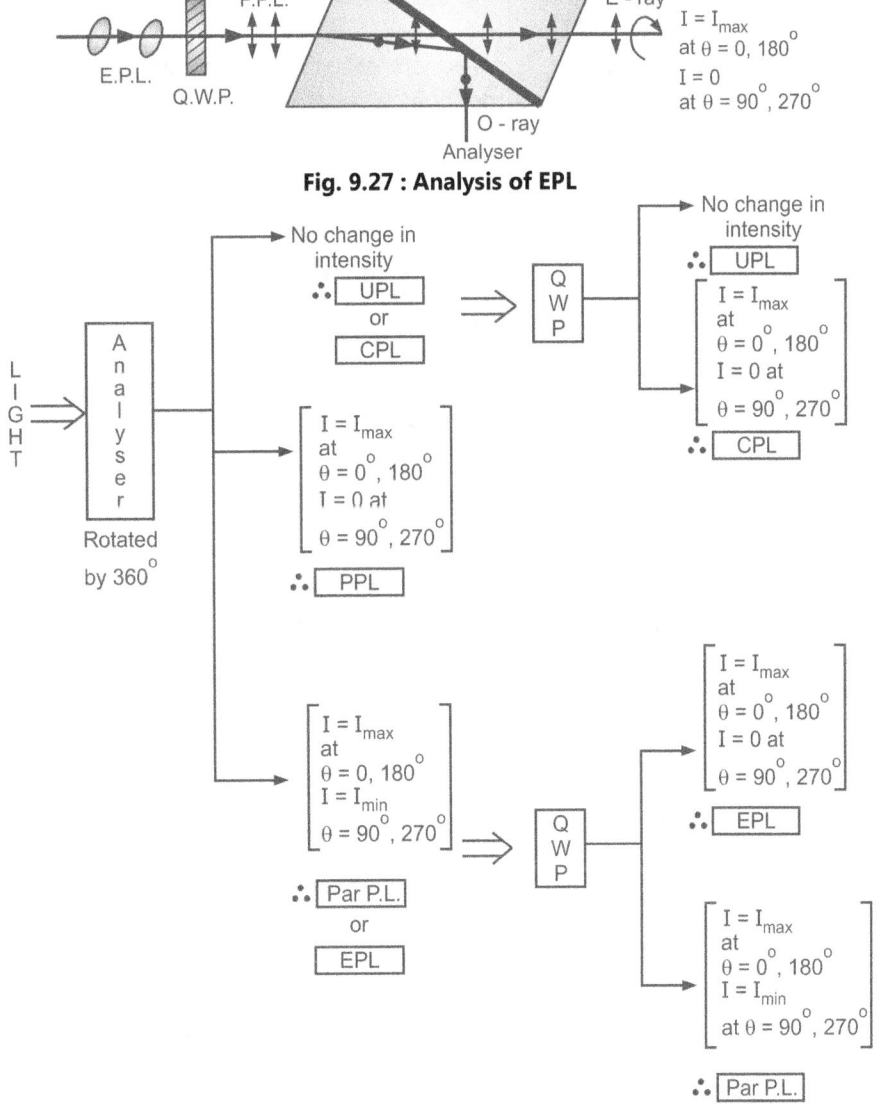

Fig. 9.27 : Analysis of EPL

Fig. 9.28 : Analysis of polarised light

Note : QWP is introduced before analyzer.

This will convert EPL into PPL, which can be analyzed as mentioned earlier. An EPL has a phase of π/2 and QWP introduces another phase of π/2, giving a total phase of π. The phase difference of π gives a PPL.

9.15 OPTICAL ACTIVITY

When a beam of a plane polarized light is directed along the optic axis of quartz, the plane of polarization turns steadily about the direction of the beam and the beam emerges vibrating in some other plane than that at which it has entered. The amount of rotation depends upon the distance travelled in the medium and wavelength of the light. This phenomenon of rotation of the plane of polarization is called **optical activity**. The substances which show optical activity are sodium chlorate, turpentine, sugar crystal etc. Fig. 9.29 shows optical activity.

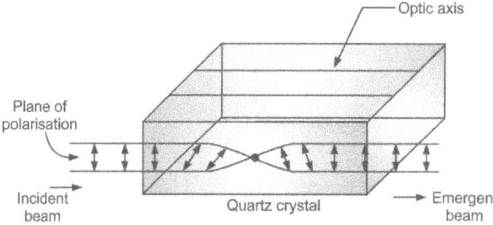

Fig. 9.29 : Optical activity

Some crystals rotate the plane of vibration to the right and some to the left. The substances which rotate to the right are called **right handed or dextrorotatory** and those which rotate to the left are called **left handed** or **laevorotatory**.

9.15.1 Specific Rotation

A striking feature of optical activity is that different colours are rotated by different amount. This rotation is nearly proportional to the inverse square of the wavelength. This gives a **rotatory dispersion**, violet being rotated nearly four times as much as red light. Fig. 9.30 shows rotatory dispersion.

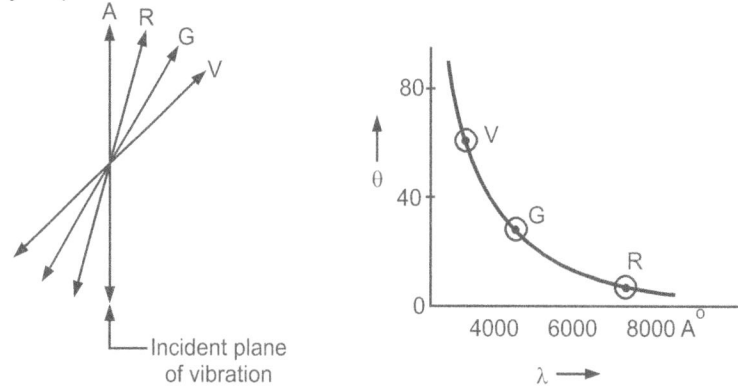

Fig. 9.30 : Rotatory dispersion

The rotation for a 1 mm thick plate is called **the specific rotation**.

9.15.2 Optically Active Materials

Optical activity is exhibited by organic compounds whose molecular arrangement lacks in symmetry. Therefore, upon entering in the material, the plane polarized light changes the plane of polarization depending upon the molecular arrangement of the material. Most of the petroleum exhibits optical activity which are organic in nature. The optical activity is not exhibited by synthetic materials as they are mixture of left handed and right handed molecules in equal quantity, thus giving net zero rotation.

9.16 LAURENT'S HALF SHADE POLARIMETER

Polarimeters are instruments, used for finding the optical rotation of different solutions. When they are calibrated to read directly the percentage of cane sugar in a solution, they are named as saccharimeters. Polarimeters can be used to find the specific rotation of sugar solution or if the specific rotation is known, they can be used to find its concentration.

Construction : The essential parts of a polarimeter are as shown in Fig. 9.31. Light from a monochromatioc source S is rendered parallel by a collimating lens L. N_1 and N_2 are two Nicol prisms, N_1 acts as a polarizer while N_2 acts as a analyzer. N_2 is capable of rotation about a common axis of N_1 and N_2. The rotation of N_2 can be read on a graduated circular scale S.C. The light after passing through the polarizer N_1 becomes plane polarized with its vibrations in the principal plane of the Nicol N_1. The plane polarized light now passes through a half shade device HS and then through a glass tube BC containing the optically active substance. The tube is closed at the end by metal covers. The light emergent from the analyzer N_2 is viewed through a telescope T. The telescope is focused on the half shade.

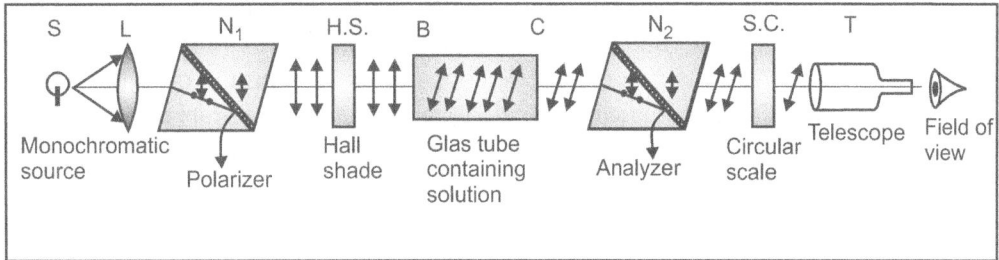

Fig. 9.31 : Laurent's half shade polarimeter

9.16.1 Action of Half Shade

When an optically active substance is placed in between two crossed Nicols, the field of view is not dark. In order to make it dark the analyzer is rotated. It is observed that, when the analyzer is rotated, the field of view is not dark for a considerable region. Hence the measurement of optical is not accurate. To avoid this difficulty, a half-shade device is used. Laurent's half-shade plate consists of a semi-circular half wave plate ACB of quartz. The thickness of the quartz is so chosen that it introduces a phase difference of π between the ordinary and extraordinary ray passing through it. The other half ADB is made of glass and its thickness is such that is absorbs and transmits the same amount of light as done by the quartz half-plate. The two plates are cemented along the diameter AB. The optic axis of the quarts plate lies along the line AB.

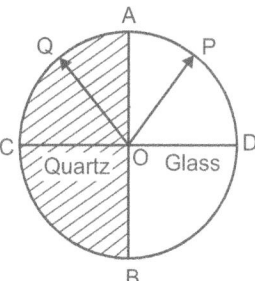

Fig. 9.32 : Laurent's half shade plate

Let the plane polarized light coming from the polarizer be incident normally on the half shade the plate with its vibrations parallel to OP. Here OP makes an angle θ with AB. The vibrations emerge from glass plate along the plane OP. Inside the quartz plate, the incident ray would be split up into two ordinary and extraordinary components. One having vibrations along OA and the other along OD. These rays travel with unequal velocities throiugh the quartz plate which introduces a phase difference of π between them. Hence on emerging from the plate, the vibrations will be along OA and PC and their resultant vibrations along OQ, where ∠ AOOP = ∠ AOQ. If the initial position of ordinary components is represented by OD then the final position is represented by OC. If the principal plane of the analyzing Nicol is parallel to OP, then the light emerging from glass portion will pass unobstructed while light from quartz will be partly obstructed. Due to this fact, the glass half will appear brighter then the quartz half. On the other hand, if the principal plane of the analyzer is parallel to OQ, the light from quartz portion will be unobstructed while light from glass will be partly obstructed. Thus, the quartz half will appear brighter than the glass half. The two halves will look equally illuminated when the analyzer is so turned that its principal plane is exactly parallel to AB. Any slight rotation in either direction produces a sharp difference in the illumination of the two halves.

9.16.2 Determination of Specific Rotation

Specific rotation S is given by

$$S = \frac{\theta}{l \times c}$$

Where θ is the angle of rotation in degrees, l, is the length of the solution in decimeters and c is the concentration of solution in gm/cc. Hence, to determine the specific rotation of a substance, a solution of known concentration is prepared. The length of the solution is measured directly. The value of θ is determined as follows :

The experimental tube is filled with distilled water and placed in its position. The telescope is focused on the half-shade plane and the analyzer is rotated till equally bright position is observed in the field of view. The readings of two verniers on the circular scale is noted. Now, the tube is filled with the optically active solution and placed in its position. The analyzer is rotated and is brought to a position so that the whole field of view is equally bright. The new positions of the two verniers are again noted on the circular scale. The difference in the two readings of the same vernier gives the angle of rotation, θ produced by the solution. Thus knowing θ, l and c the specific rotation S can be calculated by the given formula.

9.17 LCD (AS AN EXAMPLE OF POLARIZATION)

Liquid crystal display (LCD) is a passive device i.e. does not emit light of its own, and works on the principle of polarization. The common applications of LCD are wrist watch calculator, clock and general displays. Recently, LCDs have also replaced Cathode Ray Tube (CRT) in the displays of computers, laptops and TVs.

A LCD display consists of liquid crystal sandwiched between two thin glass plates with transparent conducting coating on the inner faces. The conducting plate is etched in the form of 7-segment display (to display a digit or alphabet) as shown in Fig. 9.33 (b). The whole assembly is then placed between two polaroid sheets with crossed plane of polarization.

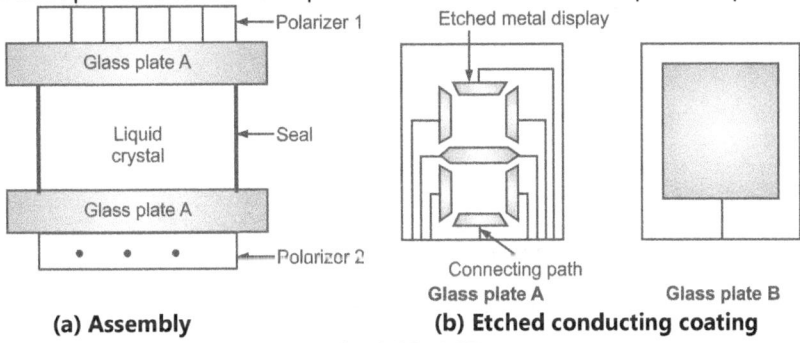

(a) Assembly (b) Etched conducting coating

Fig. 9.33 : LCD

Basically, liquid crystals are optically active, which rotates the plane of polarization of plane polarized light. Therefore, the thickness of liquid crystal is selected in such a way that it rotates the plane of polarization by 90°.

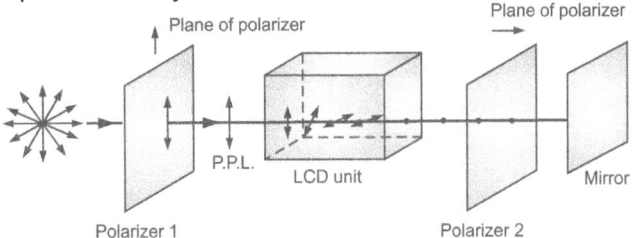

Fig. 9.34 : Working of LCD

Fig. 9.34 shows the schematic working of LCD. When the unpolarized light is incident on polarizer 1, it gets linearly polarized. Upon passing through the liquid crystal it gets rotated by 90° and therefore passes through the polarizer 2 whose transmission axis is perpendicular to that of front polarizer. The mirror on back, reflects back the liquid which emerges unobstructed from the front polarizer. This gives impression of uniform illumination.

When an external voltage is applied the molecules within the electrodes will get aligned in the direction of the field. Therefore, the plane of polarization will not change in this region and will be absorbed by the polarizer. This gives a dark digit or alphabet.

SOLVED EXAMPLES

Example 9.1 : Two polarizing plates have polarizing directions parallel so as to transmit maximum intensity of light. Through what angle must either plate be turned if the intensity of the transmitted beam is to drop to one third ?

Data : $I = \dfrac{I_0}{3}$

Formula :
From Law of Malus, $I = I_0 \cos^2 \theta$

Solution :

Substituting, $\dfrac{I_0}{3} = I_0 \cos^2 \theta$

$$\cos^2 \theta = \dfrac{1}{3}$$

Or $\cos \theta = \pm \dfrac{1}{\sqrt{3}}$

$$\boxed{\theta = 54° 41' \text{ or } \pm 144° 40'}$$

Example 9.2 : At a certain temperature, the critical angle of incidence of water for total internal reflection is 48° for a certain wavelength. What is the polarizing angle and the angle of refraction for light incident on the water that gives maximum polarization of the reflected light ?

Data : Critical angle C = 48°

Formulae : (i) $\mu = \dfrac{1}{\sin C}$, **(ii)** $\mu = \tan i_p$

Solution :

(i) Substituting, $\mu = \dfrac{1}{\sin 48°}$

$$\boxed{\mu = 1.345}$$

(ii) From Brewster's law,

$$\mu = \tan i_p$$
$$1.345 = \tan i_p$$
$$i_p = \tan^{-1}(1.345)$$

But $i_p = 53°\,22'$
$i_p + r = 90°$
∴ $r = 90° - i_p$
$90° - 53°\,22' = r$
∴ $\boxed{r = 36°\,38'}$

Example 9.3 : Calculate the thickness of a quarter wave plate for which $\mu_0 = 1.544$ and $\mu_e = 1.553$ for light of wavelength 5893 A°.

Data : $\lambda = 5893 \times 10^{-8}$ cm; $\mu_0 = 1.544$, $\mu_e = 1.553$

Formula :

For quartz, $t = \dfrac{\lambda}{4(\mu_e - \mu_0)}$

Solution :

Substituting, $t = \dfrac{5893 \times 10^{-8}}{4(0.009)}$

∴ $\boxed{t = 0.001637 \text{ cm}}$

Example 9.4 : Two Nicol prisms are oriented with their principal planes making an angle of 60°. What percentage of incident unpolarized light will pass through the system ?

Data : $\theta = 60°$

Formulae : (i) For unpolarized light,

$$I = \dfrac{I_0}{2}$$

(ii) For plane polarized light,

$$I_T = I \cos^2\theta = \dfrac{I_0}{2}\cos^2\theta$$

Solution :

$$I_T = \dfrac{I_0}{2}\cos^2 60°$$

$$I_T = 0.125\, I_0$$

∴ The percentage of incident unpolarized light transmitted through the system is

$\%\, I_T = 0.125 \times 100$

∴ $\boxed{\%\, I_T = 12.5\%}$

Example 9.5 : A polarizer and an analyzer are oriented so that the amount of light transmitted is maximum. How can the analyzer be oriented so that the transmitted light is reduced to (1) 0.75, (2) 0.25 ?

Data : (1) $I = 0.75\, I_0$, (2) $I = 0.25\, I_0$

Formula : $I = I_0 \cos^2\theta$

Solution :

Substituting $\quad 0.75\ I_0 = I_0 \cos^2 \theta$

$$\frac{3}{4} = \cos^2 \theta$$

$$\pm \frac{\sqrt{3}}{2} = \cos \theta$$

$\therefore \quad \boxed{\theta = \pm 30°, \pm 120°}$

$$0.25\ I_0 = I_0 \cos^2 \theta$$

$$\frac{1}{4} = \cos^2 \theta$$

$$\pm \frac{1}{2} = \cos \theta$$

$\therefore \quad \boxed{\theta = \pm 60°, \pm 150°}$

Example 9.6 : A quarter wave plate of thickness 2.275×10^{-3} cm is cut with its faces parallel to the optic axis. If the emergent beam of light is elliptically polarized, find the wavelength of monochromatic light made incident normally on the plate. Given that $\mu_o = 1.586$, $\mu_e = 1.592$.

Data : $\quad \mu_o = 1.586;\ \mu_e = 1.592;\ t = 2.275 \times 10^{-3}$ cm

Formula : For a QWP, $\quad t = \dfrac{\lambda}{4(\mu_e - \mu_o)}$

Solution :

$$\lambda = 4t(\mu_e - \mu_o) = 4 \times 2.275 \times 10^{-3} (1.592 - 1.586)$$
$$= 0.0546 \times 10^{-3} \text{ cm}$$
$$= \boxed{5460\ \text{A}°}$$

Example 9.7 : Calculate the thickness of mica plate required to make a quarter wave plate and a half wave plate for light of wavelength 5890 A°. The refractive indices for ordinary and extra-ordinary beams are 1.586 and 1.592 respectively.

Data : $\lambda = 5890$ A°, $\mu_o = 1.586$, $\mu_e = 1.592$

Formulae : (i) $t = \dfrac{\lambda}{4(\mu_e - \mu_o)}$, **(ii)** $t = \dfrac{\lambda}{2(\mu_e - \mu_o)}$

Solution :

(i) For QWP :
$$t = \frac{5890 \times 10^{-8}}{4(1.592 - 1.586)} = \boxed{2.45 \times 10^{-3} \text{ cm}}$$

(ii) For HWP :
$$t = \frac{5890 \times 10^{-8}}{2(1.592 - 1.586)}$$
$$= \boxed{4.90 \times 10^{-3} \text{ cm}}$$

Example 9.8 : A polarizer and an anlayzer are oriented so that the maximum of light is transmitted. To what fraction of its maximum value and intensity of transmitted light reduced when the analyzer is rotated through (i) 30°, (ii) 45° and (iii) 60° ?

Solution :

Law of Malus : $\quad I = I_m \cos^2 \theta \quad \therefore \quad \dfrac{I}{I_m} = \cos^2 \theta$

(i) $\theta = 30°$, $\quad \dfrac{I}{I_m} = (\cos^2 30°) = 0.75$

(ii) $\theta = 45°$; $\quad \dfrac{I}{I_m} = (\cos^2 45°) = 0.50$

(iii) $\theta = 60°$, $\quad \dfrac{I}{I_m} = (\cos^2 60°) = 0.25$

Example 9.9 : Find the specific rotation of cane sugar solution. If the plane of polarization is turned through 26.4°, the length of the tube containing 20% sugar solution is 20 cm.

Data : $\theta = 26.4°$, $l = 20$ cm $= 2$ dm; $c = 20\% = \dfrac{20}{100} = 0.20$ gm/cc

Formula : $\quad s = \dfrac{\theta}{l \times c}$

Solution :

$$s = \dfrac{26.4°}{2 \times 0.20} = \boxed{66° \text{ (as 10 cm = 1 dm)}}$$

Example 9.10 : Plane polarized light is incident on a piece of quartz cut parallel to the axis. Find the least thickness for which the ordinary and extra-ordinary rays combine to form plane polarized light. Given : $\mu_o = 1.5442$, $\mu_e = 1.5633$, $\lambda = 5 \times 10^{-5}$ cm.

Data : $\mu_o = 1.5442$, $\mu_e = 1.5633$, $\lambda = 5 \times 10^{-5}$ cm.

Formula : The half wave plate combines O and E rays to produce plane polarized light.

$$t = \dfrac{\lambda}{2(\mu_e - \mu_o)}$$

Solution :

$$t = \dfrac{5 \times 10^{-5}}{2(1.5633 - 1.5442)} = \boxed{1.3 \times 10^{-3} \text{ cm}}$$

Example 9.11 : If the plane of vibration of incident beam makes an angle of 30° with the optic axis, compare the intensities of the extra-ordinary and ordinary light.

[**Hint :** Amplitude of E-ray = A cos θ, Amplitude of O-ray = A sin θ).

Solution :

We know, $\quad I \propto A^2$ and according to law of Malus, $I \propto \cos^2 \theta$

For E-ray : $\quad I_E = A^2 \cos^2 \theta = A^2 \cos^2 30° = 0.75 \, A^2$

For O-ray : $I_O = A^2 \sin^2 \theta = A^2 \sin^2 30° = 0.25\,A^2$

$\therefore \quad \dfrac{I_E}{I_O} = \dfrac{0.75}{0.25} = 3$

$$\boxed{I_E = 3 I_O}$$

Example 9.12 : A beam of linearly polarized light is changed into circularly polarized light by passing it through a slice of crystal 0.003 cm thick. Calculate the difference in the refractive indices of the two rays in the crystal assuming this to be the minimum thickness that produces the effect and that the wavelength is 6×10^{-5} cm.

Data : t = 0.003 cm = 6×10^{-5} cm.

Formula : A circularly polarized light is produced with the help of a QWP.

$\therefore$ **For QWP;** $\quad t = \dfrac{\lambda}{4(\mu_o - \mu_e)}$

Solution :

$$(\mu_o - \mu_e) = \dfrac{\lambda}{4t} = \dfrac{6 \times 10^{-5}}{4 \times 0.003} = \boxed{0.005}$$

Example 9.13 : Polarizer and analyzer are set with their polarizing directions parallel so that the intensity of transmitted light is maximum. Through what angle should either be turned so that the intensity is reduced to (i) 1/2 and (ii) 25% of the maximum intensity ?

Data : (i) I = 0.5 I_o, (ii) I = 0.25 I_o

Formula : $\quad I = I0 \cos 2\theta$

Solution :

(i) $\quad I = I_o \cos^2 \theta$

$0.5\, I_o = I_o \cos^2 \theta$

$\cos^2 \theta = \dfrac{1}{2}$

$\cos \theta = 0.707$

$\boxed{\theta = 45°}$

(ii) $\quad 0.25\, I_o = I_o \cos^2 \theta$

$\cos^2 \theta = 0.25$

$\cos \theta = 0.5$

$\boxed{\theta = 60°}$

Example 9.14 : A quarter wave plate of thickness 2.275×10^{-3} cm is cut with its faces parallel to the optic axis. The emergent beam is elliptically polarized. Find the wavelength of monochromatic light made incident normally on the plate.

Given : $\mu_o = 1.586$, $\mu_e = 1.592$

Data : $t = 2.275 \times 10^{-3}$ cm, $\mu_o = 1.586$, $\mu_e = 1.592$

Formula : $\quad t = \dfrac{\lambda}{4(\mu_e - \mu_o)}$ or $\lambda = 4t(\mu_e - \mu_o)$

Solution :

$$\lambda = 2.275 \times 10^{-3} \times 4 (1.592 - 1.586)$$

$\therefore \qquad \lambda = 5.46 \times 10^{-5}$ cm $= \boxed{5460 \text{ A}°}$

Example 9.15 : Calculate the thickness of a quarter wave plate and a half wave plate, given that $\mu_e = 1.553$, $\mu_o = 1.544$ and $\lambda = 5000$ A°.

Data :
$\mu_e = 1.553$
$\mu_o = 1.544$
$\lambda = 5000$ A°

Formulae : (i) For QWP, $\quad t = \dfrac{\lambda}{4(\mu_e - \mu_o)}$

(ii) For HWP, $\quad t = \dfrac{\lambda}{2(\mu_e - \mu_o)}$

Solution :

(i) For QWP, $\quad t = \dfrac{5000 \times 10^{-8}}{4(1.553 - 1.544)}$

$\boxed{t = 1.388 \times 10^{-3} \text{ cm}}$

(ii) For HWP, $\quad t = \dfrac{5000 \times 10^{-8}}{2(1.553 - 1.544)}$

$\boxed{t = 2.77 \times 10^{-3} \text{ cm}}$

Example 9.16 : Calculate the thickness of a half wave plate of quartz for green light of wavelength 5000 A°. Given that $\mu_e = 1.5553$ and $\mu_o = 1.544$.

Data : $\lambda = 5000$ A°, $\mu_e = 1.5553$, $\mu_o = 1.544$

Formula : For HWP, $\quad t = \dfrac{\lambda}{2(\mu_e - \mu_o)}$

Solution :

$$t = \dfrac{5000 \times 10^{-8}}{2(1.5553 - 1.544)}$$

$\boxed{t = 2.2 \times 10^{-3} \text{ cm}}$

Example 9.17 : A polarizer and analyzer are oriented so that the amount of transmitted light is maximum. Through what angle should either be turned so that the intensity of transmitted light is reduced to (i) 0.75 and (ii) 0.25 times the maximum intensity ?

Solution : See Example 9.4.

Example 9.18 : A 20 cm long tube containing 48 c.c. of sugar solution rotates the plane of polarization by 11°. If the specific rotation of sugar is 66°, calculate the mass of sugar in the solution.

Data :
$$l = 20 \text{ cm}$$
$$s = 66°$$
$$\theta = 11°$$

Formula : Specific rotation
$$s = \frac{10\theta}{l \times c}$$
$$\therefore c = \frac{10\theta}{l \times s}$$

Solution :
$$c = \frac{10 \times 11}{20 \times 66} = \frac{1}{12} \text{ gm/cc}$$

∴ 1 c.c. of sugar solution contains 1/12 gm of sugar.

∴ 48 c.c. of sugar solution will contain,
$$\frac{1}{12} \times 48 = \boxed{4 \text{ gm}}$$

Example 9.19 : Calculate the thickness of
(i) Quarter wave plate.
(ii) Half wave plate.

Given : $\mu_e = 1.553$, $\mu_0 = 1.544$, $\lambda = 5000$ A°.

Solution : See problem 9.8.

UNIVERSITY QUESTIONS

1. Define the following terms : (i) Dichroism, (ii) Law of Malus.
2. Explain the phenomenon of double refraction on the basis of Huygen's wave theory.
3. Explain double refraction using Huygen's wave theory.
4. Explain the term 'Double refraction' and hence explain the phenomenon of it on the basis of Huygen's wave theory.
5. Give Huygen's theory of double refraction.
6. Explain the phenomena of double refraction on the basis of Huygen's wave theory of light.
7. What is a quarter wave plate ? Deduce the expression for its thickness in terms of the refractive indices of the quartz crystal.
8. What do you mean by quarter wave plate ? Deduce the expression for its thickness in terms of the refractive indices of the quartz crystal.

9. Explain giving diagram, the nature of refraction observed in case of a calcite crystal when
   (i) Optic axis is parallel to the refracting surface and lying in the plane of incidence (normal incidence).
   (ii) Optic axis is perpendicular to the refracting surface and lying in the plane of incidence (normal incidence).
10. Explain the principle, construction and working of half wave plate.
11. What are retardation plates ? Obtain an expression for the thickness of a QWP. Giving the necessary analytical treatment explain how the QWP can be used for production of circularly polarized light.
12. What is quarter wave plate ?
13. What are retardation plates ? Explain the working of half wave plate.
14. Explain the term : Optical activity.

SUMMARY

- Light from a natural source like the sun is unpolarized.
- Unpolarized light has the electric vector vibrating along all possible directions at right angles to the direction of propagation of light.
- There are three types of polarization (plane, circular and elliptical).
- Mixture of plane polarized light and unpolarized light is partially polarized light.
- If the vibrations of the electric vector in a light wave are confined to a single plane, then the light wave is plane polarized or linearly polarized.
- The phenomenon of confining vibrations of the light beam to a particular plane is called as polarization.
- Plane of vibration is that plane which contains the direction of vibration.
- Plane of polarization is that plane which contains no vibration. It is perpendicular to the plane of vibration.
- Plane polarized light can be produced from unpolarized light by reflection, refraction, scattering, selective absorption and double refraction.
- Brewster's law states that, tangent of the angle of polarization is proportional to the refractive index of the medium i.e. $\mu = \tan i_p$.
- Polarizing angle is that angle of incidence for which the reflected light is completely plane polarized.
- Law of Malus states that the intensity of the transmitted light is proportional to the square of the cosine of the angle between the plane of transmission of the analyzer and that of the polarizer i.e. $I = I_0 \cos^2 \theta$.

- When light passes through anisotropic crystals, it splits up into two rays, O-ray and E-ray. This phenomenon is known as double refraction or birefringence.
- Birefringence of the crystal is given by, $\Delta\mu = \mu_e - \mu_o$.
- If the velocity of ordinary ray is greater than that of the extraordinary ray ($\mu_e > \mu_o$) then the crystals are positive.
- If the velocity of extraordinary ray is greater than that of the ordinary ray ($\mu_o > \mu_e$) then the crystals are negative.
- Along the optic axis, O-ray and E-ray travel with the same velocity.
- A polaroid is a device that uses selective absorption for obtaining plane polarized light.
- Nicol prism is an optical device used for producing and analyzing plane polarized light.
- QWP and HWP are plates of doubly refracting uniaxial crystals of calcite or quartz of suitable thickness, whose refracting surface is cut parallel to the direction of optic axis.
- QWP introduces a path difference of $\frac{\lambda}{4}$ between the O-ray and E-ray.

$$\frac{\lambda}{4} = (\mu_o - \mu_e)\, t \qquad \text{for negative crystals}$$

$$\frac{\lambda}{4} = (\mu_e - \mu_o)\, t \qquad \text{for positive crystals}$$

- HWP introduces a path difference of $\frac{\lambda}{2}$ between the O-ray and E-ray.

$$\frac{\lambda}{2} = (\mu_o - \mu_e)\, t \qquad \text{for negative crystals}$$

$$\frac{\lambda}{2} = (\mu_e - \mu_o)\, t \qquad \text{for positive crystals}$$

- Using QWP and an analyzer, the state of polarization of any light can be determined.

IMPORTANT FORMULAE

- $\mu = \tan i_p$
- $i_p + r = \frac{\pi}{2}$
- $I = I_o \cos^2\theta$
- $\mu = \frac{1}{\sin c}$
- $\mu_o = \frac{\sin i}{\sin r_o} = \frac{c}{v_o}$
- $\mu_e = \frac{\sin i}{\sin r_e} = \frac{c}{v_e}$
- $t_{QWP} = \frac{\lambda}{4(\mu_o - \mu_e)}$
- $t_{HWP} = \frac{\lambda}{2(\mu_o - \mu_e)}$

EXERCISE

1. Explain the term polarization of light.
2. Define plane of polarization and plane of vibration. Explain a method to show that light waves are transverse.
3. Distinguish between polarized and unpolarized light.
4. State Brewster's law and use it to prove that when light is incident on a transparent substance at the polarizing angle, the reflected and refracted rays are at right angles to each other.
5. Explain how you would obtain plane polarized light by reflection.
6. What is pile of plates ? Explain how it can be used for producing plane polarized light.
7. What is polarizing angle ? Explain.
8. State and explain the law of Malus.
9. Explain the phenomenon of double refraction in calcite.
10. Describe the construction and working of a Nicol prism.
11. What is a Nicol prism ? Explain how a Nicol prism can be used as an analyzer and polarizer.
12. Explain giving diagrams the nature of refraction observed in the case of calcite crystal when :
    (a) optic axis is parallel to the refractive surface and lying in the plane of incidence (normal incidence).
    (b) optic axis is perpendicular to the refracting surface and lying in the plane of incidence (normal incidence).
13. Give Huygen's construction for ordinary and extraordinary wavefronts when the beam of light is refracted through a doubly refracting crystal when the optic axis is inclined to the crystal surface and lying in the plane of incidence (normal incidence).
14. What do you mean by selective absorption ? Explain.
15. What are polaroids ? Describe its construction and mention its uses.
16. What do you understand by retardation plates ? Give a short note on quarter wave plate and half wave plate.
17. How can elliptically polarized light and circularly polarized light be produced ?
18. How can you detect an elliptically and circularly polarized light ?
19. How will you distinguish circularly polarized light from unpolarized light and elliptically polarized light from partially plane polarized light ?
20. Mention the different methods of producing plane polarized light. Describe any one of them.
21. What is the basic principle of LCD ? Explain the working of LCD displays.

UNSOLVED PROBLEMS

1. If the plane of vibrations of the incident beam makes an angle of $30°$ with the optic axis, compare the intensities of extraordinary and ordinary light. **(Ans.** $\frac{I_e}{I_o} = 3$)

2. Calculate the thickness of (i) quarter wave plate, (ii) half wave plate, given that $\mu_e = 1.553$, $\mu_o = 1.544$ and $\lambda = 5000$ A°. **(Ans.** 1.39×10^{-3} cm, 2.78×10^{-3} cm)

3. A beam of light travelling in water strikes a glass plate which is also immersed in water. When the angle of incidence is 51°, the reflected beam is found to be polarized. Calculate the refractive index of glass. **(Ans. 1.233)**

4. A glass plate is used as a polarizer. Find the angle of polarization for it. Also find the angle of refraction, given μ for glass = 1.54. **(Ans. 57°, 33°)**

5. Two polarizing sheets have their polarizing directions parallel so that the intensity of the transmitted light is maximum. Through what angle must either sheet be turned so that the intensity becomes one half the initial value? **(Ans. 45°, 135°)**

6. The refractive index for plastic is 1.25. Calculate the angle of refraction for a ray of light inclined at polarizing angle. **(Ans. 38.6°)**

7. Plane polarized light of $\lambda = 6000\ A°$ is incident on a thin quartz plate cut with face parallel to the optic axis. Calculate,
   (i) the minimum thickness of the plate which introduces phase difference of 60° between O and E rays,
   (ii) the minimum thickness of the plate for which the O and E rays will combine to produce plane polarized light.
   Given $\mu_o = 1.544$ and $\mu_e = 1.553$ **(Ans. 0.011 cm, 0.00333 cm)**

8. A beam of light is passed through two Nicol prisms in series. In a particular setting, maximum light is passed by the system and it is 500 units. If one of the Nicols is now rotated by 20°, calculate the intensity of transmitted light. **(Ans. 441.5 units)**

9. Two Nicol prisms are oriented with their principal planes making an angle of 30°. What percentage of incident unpolarized light will pass through the system? **(Ans. 37.5 %)**

10. A polarizer and an analyzer are oriented so that the amount of light transmitted is maximum. To what fraction of its maximum value is the intensity of the transmitted light reduced when the analyzer is rotated through (i) 45°, (ii) 90°? **(Ans. 0.5, 0)**

REFERENCES

Better understanding of polarization with some animations :
- http://www.colorado.edu/physics/2000/polarization/index.html

Animation of double refraction :
- http://www.olympusmicro.com/primer/java/polarizedlight/icelandspar/index.html

Three dimensional diagram showing different types of polarization :
- http://hyperphysics.phy-astr.gsu.edu/hbase/phyopt/polclas.html

✠ ✠ ✠

CHAPTER 10
LASER

10.1 INTRODUCTION

The term laser stands for **'light amplification by stimulated emission of radiation'**. Laser is a light source which is highly coherent i.e. radiation emitted by all the emitters (atoms or molecules) in source agree in phase, direction of emission, polarisation and are essentially of one wavelength or colour (monochromatic). Due to coherence, a beam of laser light can travel many miles with only a negligible divergence. This makes it different from the conventional light sources which emit many wavelengths with phase and direction widely varying. Around 1917, Einstein first predicted the existence of two different kinds of processes by which an atom can emit radiation by (i) spontaneous emission, (ii) stimulated emission. In a laser, the process of stimulated emission is used for amplifying the light waves. The fact that stimulated emission process could be used in the construction of coherent optical sources was first put forward by Townes and Schawlow. The energy of an atom in any atomic system can change by (i) absorption, (ii) spontaneous emission, (iii) stimulated emission.

10.2 ABSORPTION

When a photon of energy $h\upsilon$ is incident on an atomic system, the atom gets excited from a lower energy E_1 to a higher energy E_2, if the energy of photon equals the difference in the energy levels i.e. $h\upsilon = E_2 - E_1$. In this process, the photon gets absorbed and the atom is said to be excited.

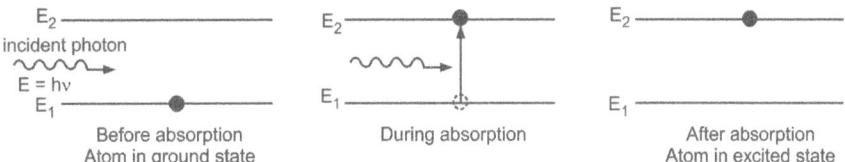

Fig. 10.1 : Absorption

10.3 SPONTANEOUS EMISSION

When a photon of energy $E = h\upsilon$ is incident on an atom, the atom absorbs the energy to rise to an excited state. The difference of the energy levels should be equal to the absorbed energy ($E_2 - E_1 = h\upsilon$). Though the electron stays in the ground state for an infinite amount of time (being a stable state), but it remains in the excited state for a short time called the **'life time'** of the excited state ($\approx 10^{-8}$ sec). Energy levels for which the life time is greater than 10^{-8} sec are called as **'metastable states'**.

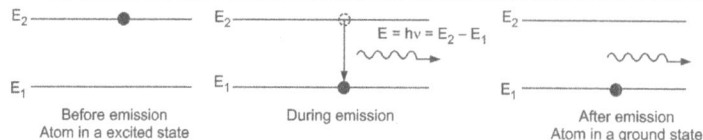

Fig. 10.2 : Spontaneous emission

The electron which is in an excited state E_2, spontaneously decays back to the lower energy level and radiates an energy equal to $E_2 - E_1$ in the form of photon of energy $h\upsilon$. Such an emission which is random in behaviour, depending only on the type of atom and the type of transition is known as **'spontaneous emission'**. The emitted radiations are not coherent and have a large range of wavelengths. Only those transitions occur which are permitted by selection rules.

10.4 STIMULATED EMISSION

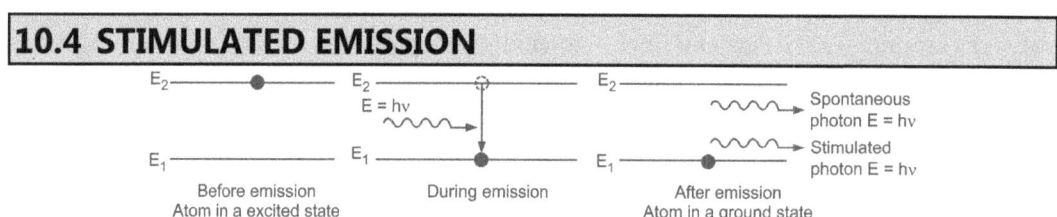

Fig. 10.3 : Stimulated emission

Consider Fig. 10.3 where the electrons are initially in the excited energy level and emission is stimulated before the spontaneous emission occurs. The excited atom is stimulated by a photon of exactly the same energy as the photon to be emitted. In such a case, two photons are emitted, one by the stimulated emission and the other stimulating photon. Both the photons travel in the same direction, have the same frequency and are in phase i.e. they are coherent. The emission of two photons with an input of only one photon implies amplification. The occurrence of spontaneous emission is directly proportional to the number of atoms in the specified energy level, whereas in stimulated emission, the rate of occurrence is proportional not only to the number of atoms in the excited state but also to the number of incident stimulating photons.

10.5 POPULATION INVERSION

The process of getting a large percentage of atoms into an excited state is called as **'population inversion'**. If a large number of atoms can be excited to upper energy levels, then the probability of stimulated emission and hence light amplification becomes greater. The states of the system, in which the population of the higher energy state is more than the population of the lower energy state, are called as **'negative temperature states'** (negative indicates a non-equilibrium state, not the physical state of the system).

In any atomic system, the number of particles in a higher energy state is normally less than the number of particles in a lower energy state. If N_2 denotes the number of particles in higher energy level E_2, and N_1 denotes the number of particles in lower energy level E_1, then

$N_2 < N_1$ i.e. the population of higher energy level is less than the population of lower energy level. This means that under normal conditions, the ground state E_1 is heavily populated than the excited state E_2. If photons of energy $h\upsilon = E_2 - E_1$ are incident on the atoms, a few of the incident photons get absorbed and some of the atoms get excited to the state E_2. This process of stimulated absorption depopulates level E_1. The rate at which this process occurs is expressed as

$$R_{12} = P_a N_1$$

where P_a is the probability of stimulated absorption and N_1 is the population of state E_1.
Similarly, the stimulated emission depopulates energy level E_2 resulting in the emission of photons.
The rate at which this process occurs is expressed as

$$R_{21} = P_e N_2$$

where P_e is the probability of the process of stimulated emission and N_2 is the population of state E_2.
At thermal equilibrium, these probabilities are equal i.e. $P_a = P_e$. Then, on comparing the two rates, it is observed that more energy is absorbed than emitted.
i.e. from (1) and (2),

$P_a N_1 > P_e N_2$ because $N_1 > N_2$.

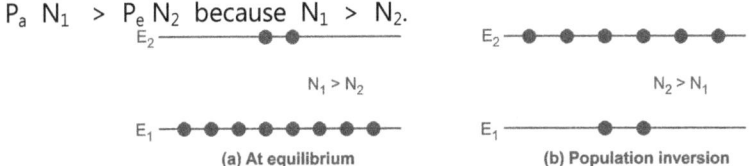

(a) At equilibrium (b) Population inversion

Fig. 10.4

To produce more emission, it is essential to have $N_2 > N_1$ i.e. the number of particles in higher energy level must be made more than the number of particles in lower energy level. This is called as **'population inversion'**. If this inversion is achieved, there can be more emission and incoming light will be amplified coherently. A system in which population inversion is achieved is called an **'active system'**. The method of raising atoms from lower energy levels to higher energy levels is called as **'pumping'**. It can be done by subjecting the atoms to a non-uniform electric field, flooding the gas with high intensity light, etc. A more common method of pumping is **'optical pumping'**.

10.6 METASTABLE STATE

The electron in an excited state has certain probability to decay or jump to a lower energy level. Generally, these probabilities are such that the jump occurs within 10^{-8} sec of excitation. However, there are some excited states, called **'metastable states'**, which have a very low probability of decay i.e. electrons stay for longer time. Electrons may stay in the metastable excited states for seconds, minutes or even hours. In stimulated emission, the electrons must remain in excited level and wait for stimulating photon. Therefore, the active medium must have a metastable state. The population inversion can be obtained by using metastable states as the electrons rest in metastable state for long time.

10.7 ACTIVE MEDIUM

A medium in which the population inversion takes place is called the **active medium**. The active medium is responsible for the light amplification and hence LASER. The active medium may be a solid, liquid or gas and accordingly the lasers are classified as solid state or gas lasers. Out of the total active medium, only small number of atoms are responsible for lasing action and remaining atoms help only in hosting active atoms or in population inversion. The atoms which particulate in stimulated emission are called **active centres**.

10.8 RESONANT CAVITY

A cavity can be constructed using mirrors such that the light rays return to their original position after travelling through the cavity for a certain number of times. Such cavities are known as **resonant cavities**. Fig. 10.5 shows cavity formed by two parallel mirrors M_1 and M_2. One of the mirrors is completely silvered (M_1) and the other is partially silvered (M_2). The laser beam emerges from the resonant cavity through the partially silvered mirror M_2.

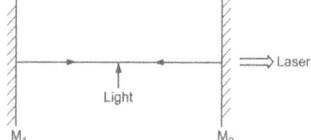

Fig. 10.5 : Resonant cavity

The active system is placed in the resonant cavity, the photon emitted will keep on reflecting back and forth within the cavity. The light which is incident parallel to the axis of optical cavity will only leak out as a laser. That is why, laser is highly directional.

10.9 PUMPING

The method of raising atoms from lower energy levels to higher energy levels is called as **'pumping'**. The pumping is used for achieving population inversion which is necessary for optical amplification to take place. There are several methods for pumping electrons. They are as follows :

10.9.1 Optical Pumping

In optical pumping, an external light source (flash lamp) is used to produce a high population in some particular energy level E_2 (say) by selective absorption as shown in Fig. 10.6.

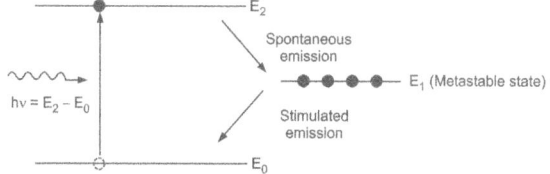

Fig. 10.6 : Optical pumping

When a flash of light falls on electrons in ground state, they absorb incident photons and get excited. After staying there for some time, some of the atoms make spontaneous transition to metastable state E_1. As the probability of spontaneous decay is less in metastable state, a large population accumulates in this level. This results in a population inversion between E_0 and E_1. Generally, this method is used in solid-state lasers, such as ruby laser.

10.9.2 Inelastic Atom-Atom Collisions

Here suitable mixtures of gases are used. The gases are selected in such a way that their excited states are almost same. This makes the energy exchange possible between the atoms of the gases. If two gases A and B have same excited state, A^* and B^* then,

$$A^* + B \rightarrow A + B^*$$

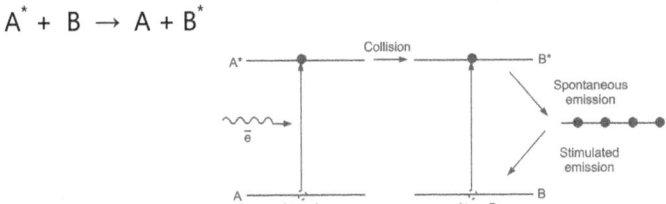

Fig. 10.7 : Inelastic atom-atom collision

The atom of gas A is excited by electric discharge. In collision with B, the energy is transferred to B. As a result, the excited level of atom B becomes more populated than lower level to which B can decay, as shown in Fig. 10.7. The best example is the He-Ne gas laser.

10.9.3 Forward Biasing of a P-N Junction

If a p-n junction is formed with degenerate (heavily doped) semiconductors, the bands under forward bias appear as shown in Fig. 10.8.

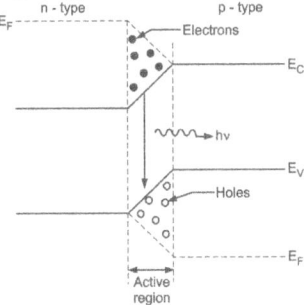

Fig. 10.8 : Forward biasing of a P-N junction diode

If the bias voltage is large enough, electrons and holes are injected into the active region. As a result, the depletion layer now contains a large number of electrons in conduction band and holes in valence band. If the population density is high enough, it gives population inversion. For a population inversion, the applied voltage should be selected in such a way that $eV > h\upsilon\ (= E_g)$.

The other methods of pumping are electron excitation, chemical reactions, etc. These methods will not be discussed in detail as they are beyond the scope of the text.

10.10 RUBY LASER

A ruby laser is a solid-state laser that uses a synthetic ruby crystal. Typical ruby laser is a pulsed laser of intense red colour.

Construction :

The laser consists of a ruby rod surrounded by a flash tube. One end of the rod is highly silvered while the other end is semi-silvered. The flash tube surrounds the ruby rod in the form of a spiral. Synthetic ruby consists of a crystal of aluminium oxide (Al_2O_3) in which a few of the aluminium atoms (Al^{3+}) are replaced by chromium atoms (Cr^{3+}). These atoms have the property of absorbing green light. The chromium impurity is the active atom of the laser. Doping of chromium gives ruby its characteristic red colour.

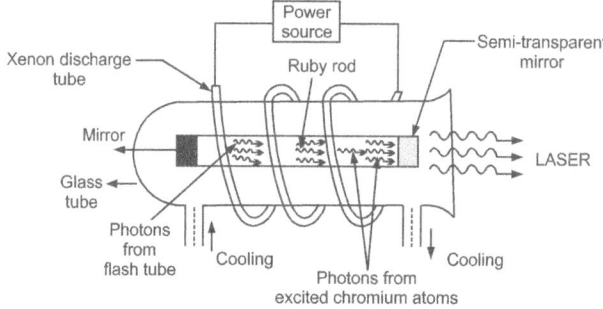

Fig. 10.9

(a) Pumping and Energy Levels of Chromium :

When ruby is in a steady magnetic field, chromium acquires energy states, of which three are represented schematically as shown in Fig. 10.9 (a).

As is clear from the figure, this is a three-level laser system. Level M actually consists of a pair of levels corresponding to wavelengths of 6943 A° and 6929 A°. However, laser action takes place only on 6943 A° line due to higher population inversion. The pumping of chromium atoms is performed with a Xenon or Krypton flash lamp. The chromium atoms in the ground state absorb radiation around wavelengths 5500 A° and 4000 A° and are excited to the levels marked E_1 and E_2.

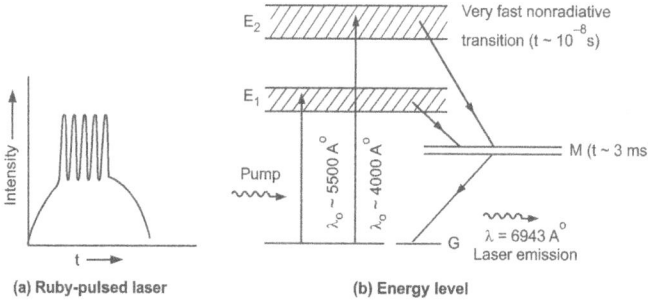

Fig. 10.10

(b) Assembly of Chromium Atoms to Metastable State :

The chromium atoms excited to these levels, relax rapidly through a non-radiative transition (in a time 10^{-8} to 10^{-9} sec) to the metastable state M, which has a life time of ~3 m secs. Laser emission occurs between level M and the ground state G at an output wavelength of 6943 A°.

(c) Operation :

The operational sequence starts with the ignition of the Xenon flash tube. Chromium atoms in the ruby rod are energized by absorption of the energetic photons from the flash tube. When the excited electrons in the chromium atoms fall back to their normal states, photons are given off by spontaneous emission emitting red light (hence ruby has a natural red colour). Some of these photons escape from the rod but many oscillate or bounce back and forth along the length of the rod with the help of the mirror at the two ends. When the electrons in the excited state are exposed to these radiations of the same frequency which they are about to emit, the emission process is triggered. Radiation is now emitted, which is exactly in phase with the exposed radiation. This cumulative process of flash tube photons exciting chromium atoms which in turn emit photons in the same direction and phase, continues until the coherent laser beam penetrates through the partially reflecting mirror on one end of the rod to give a powerful beam of red light.

(d) Pulsed Output :

A certain stage is reached when the population inversion caused by one flash of Xenon tube is used up. As soon as the flash lamp stops operating, the population of the upper level is depleted very rapidly and laser action ceases until the arrival of the next flash. Refer Fig. 10.10 (b). Thus, ruby is a **'pulsed laser'**. The output beam has a principal wavelength of 6943 A° equal to 4.3×10^{14} Hz frequency (lies in the visible spectrum). The duration of the output flash is about 300 μsec.

During the operation of a ruby laser, a very high temperature is produced. To prevent any damage to the ruby rod, it is surrounded by a liquid nitrogen container and is operated to give out the beam only in pulses. This laser is used in many applications as its output lies in the visible region where photographic emulsions and photo detectors are more sensitive than they are in the infrared region. Ruby lasers also find application in laser holography, laser ranging, etc.

10.11 HELIUM-NEON LASER – FOUR LEVEL LASER SYSTEM

This is a **'continuous laser'** unlike the ruby laser. In this laser, the vapours of metal are used as the media. It is an extremely popular form of laser as it is simple, inexpensive and has an extremely broad range of emission wavelengths (0.6 to 100 μm depending on the type of gas used). The first gas laser to be operated successfully was the He - Ne laser. In solid-state lasers, pumping is usually done by using a flash lamp or a continuous high power lamp. Such a technique is efficient if the laser system has broad absorption bands. In gas lasers, as the atoms are characterized by sharp energy levels, an electrical discharge is generally used to pump the atoms.

Construction :

It consists of a quartz tube with a diameter of about 2-8 mm and a length of 10-100 cm. It is filled with helium and neon. The pressure of helium is approximately 10 times that of neon. The neon atoms provide energy states for the transitions while helium provides a mechanism for efficiently exciting neon atoms to upper metastable states i.e. helium serves merely as an energy transfer agent. At one end of the tube is a total reflector while at the other is a partial reflector. The gas is excited by means of a high frequency generator.

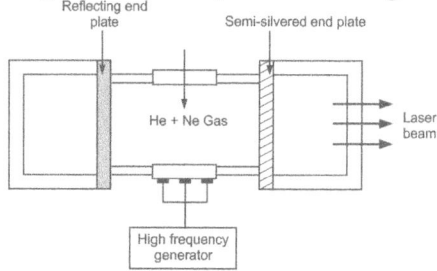

Fig. 10.11 : He-Ne laser

Principle :

In He-Ne laser, population inversion is produced through inelastic collisions between excited He atoms and Ne atoms in the ground state. The process can be expressed as

$$He^* + Ne \rightarrow He + Ne^* \quad (* \text{ shows an excited state})$$

This is possible, because the levels Ne_4 and Ne_6 of neon atoms have almost the same energy as the levels He_2 and He_3 of helium atoms as shown in the energy level diagram.

Working :

(a) Electric Discharge and Excitation of Helium :

When an electrical discharge is passed through the gas, the electrons which are accelerated down the tube collide with helium and neon atoms and excite them to higher energy levels. The helium atoms tend to accumulate at the levels He_2 and He_3 due to their long life times of $\approx 10^{-4}$ secs and 10^{-6} secs respectively.

(b) Transfer of Energy from Helium to Neon and Pumping :

As the levels Ne_4 and Ne_6 of neon atoms have almost the same energy as He_2 and He_3, excited helium atoms colliding with neon atoms in the ground state can excite the neon atoms to Ne_4 and Ne_6 states. As the pressure of helium is ten times that of neon, the levels Ne_4 and Ne_6 of neon are selectively populated as compared to other levels of neon.

i.e. $He^* + Ne \rightarrow He + Ne^*$ (* indicates excited state)

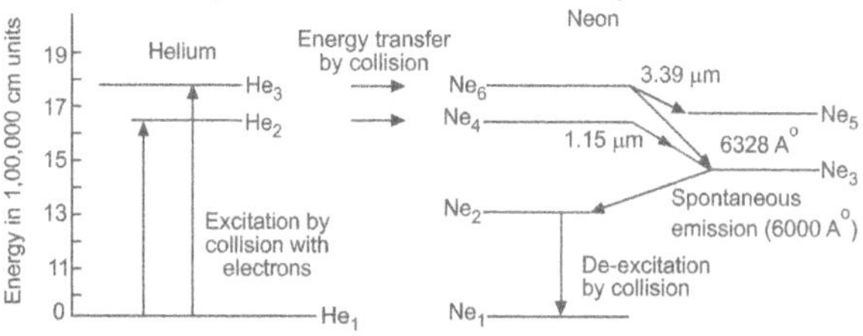

Fig. 10.12

(c) Population Inversion for Neon :

Transition between Ne_6 and Ne_3 produces the popular 6328 A° (632.8 nm) line of He - Ne laser. Neon atoms de-excite through spontaneous emission from Ne_3 to Ne_2 (life time $\sim 10^{-8}$ sec.). As this time is shorter than the life time of level Ne_6 ($\sim 10^{-7}$ sec.), steady state population inversion can be achieved between Ne_6 and Ne_3. Level Ne_2 is metastable and thus tends to collect atoms. The atoms from this level fall back to the ground level mainly through collisions with the walls of the tube. As Ne_2 is metastable, it is possible for the atoms in this level to absorb the spontaneously emitted radiation in $Ne_3 \rightarrow Ne_2$ transition to be re-excited to Ne_3. This tends to reduce the effect of inversion. It is for this reason that the gain in this laser transition is found to increase with decreasing tube diameter.

(d) Transition within Neon and Continuous Output :

The other two important wavelengths from the He - Ne laser correspond to the $Ne_4 \rightarrow Ne_3$ (1.15 µm) and $Ne_6 \rightarrow Ne_5$ (3.39 µm) transitions. The laser can be made to oscillate at 6328 A° by using optical elements (multilayer coated mirrors) in the path. These lasers are continuous, because the collision process maintains the energy states Ne_6 and Ne_4 at larger population densities than the lower states. This continued population inversion gives a continuous lasing action.

A typical He - Ne laser operates with a current of 10 mA at a D.C. voltage of 2500 V and gives an optical output of 5 mW. It's efficiency is then $\dfrac{5 \times 10^{-3}}{2500 \times 10^{-2}}$ = 0.02 %.

This is the only laser radiating in far infrared region. Hence, mostly used in laser '**Raman spectroscopy**'.

10.12 SEMICONDUCTOR LASER – TWO LEVEL LASER SYSTEM

A semiconductor diode laser is a p-n junction device that emits coherent light when forward biased. A p-n junction laser is also called '**injection laser**' as the charge carriers are injected into depletion region. The diode lasers are preferred over other lasers as they are compact, reliable and low cost.

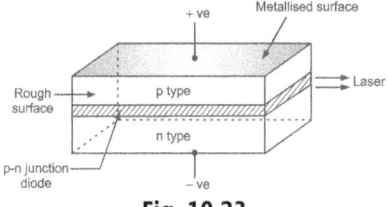

Fig. 10.23

Construction :

A laser diode is extremely small in size with sides of the order of 1 mm. The p-n junction of the diode lies in the horizontal plane. The top and bottom faces are metallised for making electrical contacts. Two plane mirrors are placed at front and back surface to form optical cavity. Sometimes the faces itself are polished to form optical cavity. The other two faces are roughened to prevent lasing action in that direction.

Working :

(a) Under Equilibrium :

In semiconductor diode laser, the p-n semiconductor is heavily doped (degenerate semiconductor). Fig. 10.10 shows the energy band of highly doped p-region and n-region. Due to very high doping on n-side, the donor level as well as a portion of conduction band is occupied by electrons. Hence, the Fermi level lies within the conduction band. Similarly, on the heavily doped p-side, holes exist in the valence band and hence the Fermi level lies in the valence band.

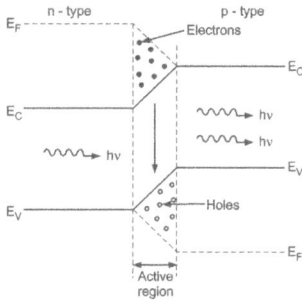

Fig. 10.14

(b) Forward Bias, Pumping and Recombination :

At low forward current, the electron-hole recombinations cause spontaneous emission of photons and the junction acts as an LED. As the current is increased, the intensity of light increases. When the current reaches a threshold value, the carrier concentration in the depletion region reaches a very high value i.e. a large concentration of electrons in the conduction band and a large concentration of holes in the valence band. As a result, the higher energy levels in the depletion region are having high population density of electrons while the lower levels are vacant. This is a state of population inversion. The region where the population inversion is achieved is called as **active region**. The forward bias acts as the pumping agent.

(c) Built-Up of Laser :

Due to forward bias, the band gap is very small and therefore electrons in the conduction band can recombine with holes in the valence band. During this process of recombination of electrons and holes, electrons loose their energy emitting a photon of energy equal to band gap. Some of the photons emitted during the process of recombination are reflected back from the polished ends and stimulate the electrons initiating the laser process. The highly polished ends continuously reflect the light back and forth. The photons parallel to the axis of resonator will leak out as laser beam.

The frequency of radiated photon is $\upsilon = E_g/h$, where E_g is band gap and h is Planck's constant. The wavelength of laser beam depends upon the material used, for GaAs laser wavelength is 9000 A° in IR region and GaAsP it is 6500 A° in visible region at room temperature.

Advantages of Semiconductor Laser :

Very less power required, simple, compact, highly efficient, more divergent, less monochromatic and highly temperature sensitive.

10.13 PROPERTIES OF LASER

Laser is basically a light source, but many of its properties are special or extreme. These properties make it different from ordinary sources. The basic properties of lasers which make different from ordinary light source are :

10.13.1 Monochromaticity

When the laser produces only one wavelength then it is fully monochromatic. This is impossible, in principle and in practice also. If $\Delta\lambda$ is the range of wavelengths included in a laser beam of wavelength λ, then $\Delta\upsilon$ is the corresponding frequency. This frequency band $\Delta\upsilon$ is called the **'line width'**. For white light consisting of all visible frequencies, the line width is $\sim 10^{14}$ Hz, while for a good laser it is about 10^2 Hz.

10.13.2 Coherence

The light emerging from a laser is coherent both in space and time. The existence of finite bandwidth $\Delta\upsilon$ means that the different frequencies present in laser can get out of phase width each other. If two waves differ by frequency $\Delta\upsilon$, the time required to get out of phase by a full cycle is $1/\Delta\upsilon$. This is called as **'coherence time'** of a beam and is denoted by $\Delta\tau$.

i.e.
$$\Delta\tau = \frac{1}{\Delta\upsilon}$$

For a laser with $\Delta\upsilon = 1$ MHz, $\Delta\tau = 1$ μs. On the other hand, sunlight has a bandwidth $\Delta\upsilon = 10^{14}$ Hz, therefore, $\Delta\tau = 10^{-14}$ s which is much smaller than laser.

The speed of light is so large that it travels a very large distance for a short coherence time. The distance $\Delta L = c\Delta\tau$ is called **'coherence length'** of the beam. For a laser beam with $\Delta\upsilon = 1$ MHz, the coherence length $\Delta L = 300$ m. Only the portions of the same beam, separated by a distance less than coherence length are capable of producing stable interference pattern.

10.13.3 Directionality

A laser has high degree of directionality and can travel very large distances without deviation. For a typical laser, the divergence is about 10^{-3} radians. This means that the laser beam diverges by ~ 1 mm for every meter that it travels. The reason is that the active material is placed in a resonant cavity. The light is reflected back and forth in the cavity and light travelling parallel to the axis gets emitted as the laser beam. The light travelling in the other direction is reflected back in the cavity.

10.13.4 Brightness

A laser radiates light into a narrow beam and its energy is concentrated in a small region. This is due to the fact that the divergence is very less. This results into extremely high intensity. Even a 1 W laser appears more intense than a ordinary 100 W lamp. This high concentration is used in many applications such as drilling, welding and cutting.

10.14 APPLICATION OF LASER

10.14.1 Engineering / Industry

Laser can be focussed to a very high energy density into a small image (≈ 1 micron in diameter) with the help of suitable lenses. Due to the small size of the image and the control over the energy, lasers are used extensively for cutting, welding and drilling circuits.

- **Drilling :** A laser beam is also used to drill holes of micron dimensions on printed circuit boards (PCBs). It is also used in resistance trimming in electric components industries. One can drill holes of the diameter of 10 μm through very hard substances like diamond. YAG laser is found to be very useful in such applications.

- **Welding :** Lasers are used as a heat source in welding the joints of the metals. This type of precise welding is extremely important in micro-electronics in which thin films are used. Thermocouple wires can easily be welded with the help of high power laser beam.

- **Micromachining :** Lasers are used for machining a surface in a slow and accurate manner to achieve an extraordinarily smooth finish.

- **Cutting :** Another important industrial application is metal or fabric cutting. A finely focussed laser beam can cut thick and hard metal sheets with high precision and accuracy. It is also used in tailoring industries to cut thousands of layers of cloth at one instant.

- Due to its intensity and directionality, laser is used in surveying. When tunnels are to be constructed, engineers use the laser beam as a reference, to check that it is being constructed along a straight line. Similarly, it can be used to dig a ditch to a certain prescribed depth. Its most interesting use in surveying has been in measuring the distance from the earth to the moon. This distance was measured to an accuracy of 600 ft, and with the aid of reflectors to within six inches. This accuracy will allow to determine the location of the north pole to within six inches. It is further believed that a laser could be used to check whether the gravitational constant is actually a constant.

- A laser beam can determine precisely the distance, velocity and direction as well as the size and form of distant objects by means of the reflected signal as in radar. A Lidar (Laser radar), which sends out beams of laser light and detects echoes even from atmospheric layers has been developed.

10.14.2 Medicine

- Bloodless cancer surgeries can be performed as the beam can be focussed on a small area, so that only the harmful tissue can be destroyed without damaging the surrounding region.
- Laser has been successfully used in ophthalmology, in the treatment of detached retinas, in welding cornea, etc. At the command of the physician, laser produces a beam of light which is directed onto the eye under treatment, to produce a minute coagulation. A series of these lesions weld the detached retina.
- Laser is used as a tool in the study of genetics. Lasers have been built into or are devised to be attached to microscopes. As a high density energy is achieved, it can be used in micro-surgery, micro-burning, etc. Such a microscopic laser can concentrate millions of watts of power per square millimeter into a selected area. For example, a focussed microscope laser can be used to make tiny openings (of 25 μ in diameter) in the cell walls, of say the nervous system, heart, retina, etc. without causing irreversible damage.
- Laser microprobes can be used as dental drills giving an advantage of no heating, no anaesthetic and no pain to the patient. They have also been successfully used for localized treatment of skin growths and blemishes in human beings. A large amount of energy can be transmitted through the skin to interact with deeper different biological materials or structures which are damaged.

10.14.3 Communication

In this technology, optical energy is transferred through a guided media, called the **'glass fibre'**. When a beam of light enters at one end of a transparent rod (glass rod say), the light beam is totally internally reflected and gets trapped within the rod. A similar behaviour is exhibited by a bundle of fine fibres. A beam enters at one end and is transmitted through the wire to the other end, even when the fibre is curved. A bundle may consist of thousands of individual fibres with diameters in the range of 2×10^{-4} cm to 1×10^{-3} cm. The study of the properties of such a bundle is known as **'fibre optics'**. One of the most important areas of application of fibre optics is in telecommunication. Optical frequencies are extremely large (~10^{15} Hz) as compared to conventional radio waves (~10^{6} Hz) and microwaves (~10^{10} Hz). Due to the high optical frequency, a light beam acting as a carrier wave is capable of carrying far more information in comparison to radiowaves and microwaves. In addition to the capability of carrying a huge amount of information, recently developed fibres are characterized by extremely low losses. Today fibre optic cable is the most promising signal transmitting media.

Optical Fibre

Optical fibre is a very thin and flexible medium having a cylindrical shape consisting of three sections : (i) the core, (ii) the cladding and (iii) the outer jacket.

Principle of Light Transmission :

The principle of light transmission through optical fibre is total internal reflection. For total internal reflection to take place at the fibre wall, the following conditions should be satisfied :

(i) The refractive index of the core material (μ_1) must be greater than that of the cladding (μ_2).

(ii) At the core-cladding interface, the angle of incidence θ must be greater than the critical angle, where $\theta_c = \sin^{-1}\left(\dfrac{\mu 2}{\mu 1}\right)$.

When a light ray travels from a denser to a rarer medium, the angle of refraction is greater than the angle of incidence. As the angle of incidence increases, the angle of refraction also increases and for a particular angle of incidence, the refracted ray grazes the interface between the core and the cladding. This angle of incidence is called as the **'critical angle θ_c'**. If angle of incidence is greater than θ_c, the ray will be reflected back into the core, i.e. it suffers **'total internal reflection'**. For angles equal to or greater than the critical angle the light will be totally reflected and no light will be refracted. Fig. 10.16 shows total internal reflection.

When light is incident on core of the fibre optics, it will be refracted and will travel in the core. After some time it will strike one of the core-cladding interface say upper surface. If the angle of incidene is greater than critical angle, it will be totally reflected and remain in the core. Now, the reflected light will travel to the lower surface. It is then incident on the lower surface where the same process is repeated and light gets transmitted from one end to the other end as shown in Fig. 10.15.

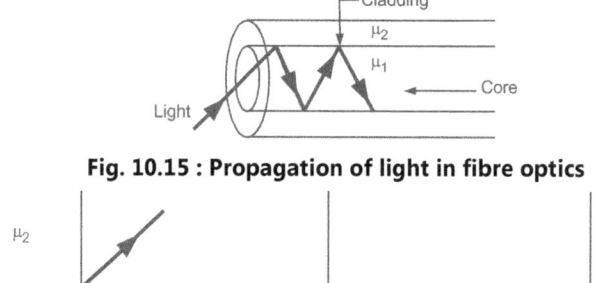

Fig. 10.15 : Propagation of light in fibre optics

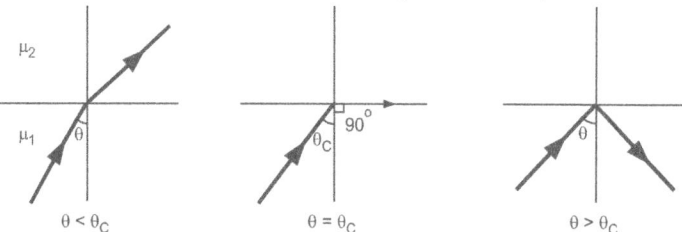

Fig. 10.16 : Total internal reflection

Communication Kit :

One of the most important areas of application of fibre optics is in telecommunication. The communication kit consists of a transmitter, optical fibre and the receiver. The block diagram is as shown in Fig. 10.17.

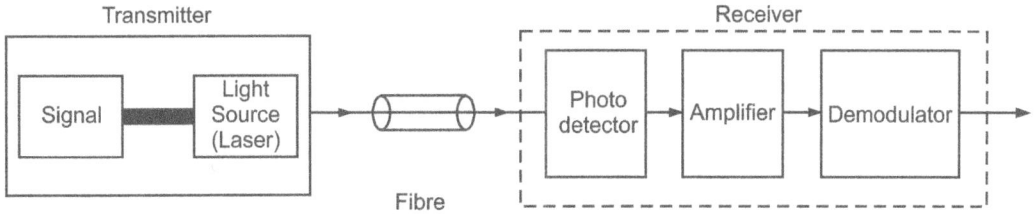

Fig. 10.17 : Communication kit

The transmitter consists of a light source, either LED or laser diode, with a signal. The light beam from the source is connected to the fibre, through optical connections. The carrier and signal frequency propagate through the fibre. At the other end, it is detected with the help of a photodetector. The received signal is demodulated and the information is stored or displayed by electronic circuits.

Advantages of Optical Fibre
- The optical frequencies are extremely high, of the order of 10^{14} Hz, the information carrying capacity is much higher than radio waves.
- The optical fibres are made of dielectric material, which offers electrical isolation between the transmitting and receiving circuits.
- The material used in fibres is silica glass (SiO_2), which is easily available and its cost is less.
- The fibres are very thin (few μm), light and occupy less space.
- As the transmission is due to total internal reflection, therefore losses are less.
- Does not form standing waves when the impedance of transmitter and receiver do not match.

10.14.4 Computer

CD Writer Devices : In the compact disk (CD), the pick-device or writing-device does not come into contact with the disc surface, therefore there is no degradation of the sound (data) while recording or reproduction. The recording of information on CD is done in binary form, i.e. in 1s and 0s with a laser beam and reading of the recorded information is also done by a low-powered laser beam. During reproduction, the stream of bits picked up by the laser beam flow at a constant rate of 4 million bits per second. The disk rotates at 480 rpm when reading the track near the centre, which gradually changes to 210 rpm when the track on the outer edge is read. This constant change in speed ensures that the tracks travel at a constant speed over the laser diode and the photo diode. The data is recorded in the form of a spiral track.

A laser beam is used to write data on the disk in digital form as tiny '**pits**' and '**lands**' ('**lands**' are reflective sections between pits). The laser beam starts from the innermost spiral of the disk and travels outwards as the disk rotates. The speed of the laser beam along the tracks is kept unchanged. The data to be recorded on the CD is given to a diode laser and the intensity of laser beam is controlled accordingly. The laser beams is focused on the disk surface which is coated on a special material. Depending on the material used, the laser beam either burns tiny holes or creates microscopic bubble in the place of 1s. Fig. 10.18 shows recording of CD.

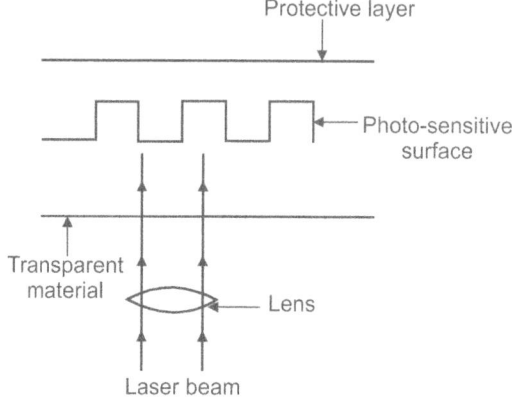

Fig. 10.18

While reading a laser beam of lower intensity is focused on the track and the reflected beam is sensed by a photodiode. As the holes or bubbles scatter the laser beam, very little light is reflected from these positions thereby detecting 1s.

Laser Printers : In case of laser printers, the image (data to be printed) is produced on the photo-sensitive drum with a laser beam. A laser beam is made 'on' or 'off' and swept back and forth across the drum with the help of a rotating mirror. The process is similar to the technique of image formation on CRT monitor. The laser beam is electronically controlled by a microcomputer. In second step powered ink, known as 'toner' is applied on the drum. Then the image is electro-statically transferred to the paper. Finally, the linked image on the paper is fused by a suitable technique, usually by heat. The laser printers provide very good quality printing at a moderately fast rate of 30 pages per minute or so.

10.15 HOLOGRAPHY

Holography :

This is a technique of producing an interference pattern between a direct laser beam and a laser beam reflected from an object on a photographic plate. This pattern on the developed photographic plate, when illuminated with laser in a proper manner, produces a three-dimensional image of the object called a **'hologram'**. It is used in microscopic investigations.

Holography deals with three-dimensional image of the object whereas photography is a two-dimensional effect. In photography, the photographic plate records only the intensity of light due to the image formed on it. In holography, both the intensity and phase distribution are recorded simultaneously using interference technique. Due to this the image produced by the technique of holography has a true three-dimensional form and is as true as the object itself.

Basic Technique :

The basic technique in holography is as follows :

- **Hologram Recording :**

The recording of hologram is achieved by superposition of **'the object wave'** with another wave called **'the reference wave'**. The reference wave is usually a plane wave. The resulting interference pattern is recorded on a photographic plate. As the shape of the object is very irregular, it results in complicated fringe pattern. Thus a hologram is a record of complicated interference fringe pattern.

Fig. 10.19 shows a typical configuration used for recording a hologram. A portion of a coherent beam (e.g. laser) is allowed to be scattered by the object and the other portion is reflected by a mirror. The former corresponds to the object wave and the latter to the reference wave. The object wave and the reference wave interfere and the resultant interference pattern is recorded on a photographic plate. When the photographic plate which has recorded the intensity variation is developed, one obtains a hologram of the object.

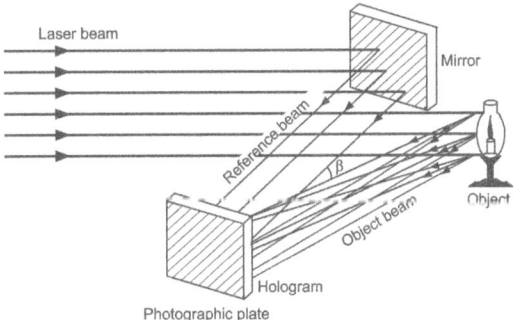

Fig. 10.19

The recorded interference pattern forms the hologram and contains information not only about the amplitude but also about the phase of the object wave. Unlike a photograph, the hologram bears little resemblance to the object.

- **Hologram Reconstruction :**

To see the reconstructed image, the hologram is illuminated by the reference beam alone, maintaining the original alignment and orientation. This process is called as **'reconstruction'**.

The developed photographic film (hologram) will have alternate transparent and opaque part of very irregular shape. Thus, it will serve as a diffraction grating when illuminated by the light source. The light from the hologram will be diffracted inward and outward. One set of diffracted rays will converge to form real image while one set will diverge to form virtual image as shown in Fig. 10.20. Thus, the hologram can form real as well as virtual images. The geometry of construction can be changed, so as to give more emphasis on real or virtual image.

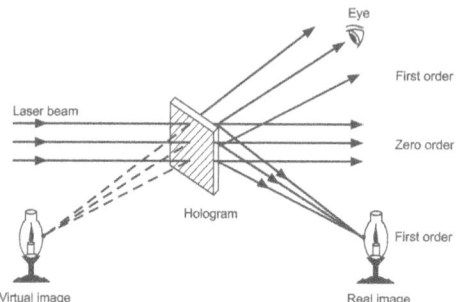

Fig. 10.20

UNIVERSITY QUESTIONS

1. Explain the process of spontaneous emission and stimulated emission.
2. Define and explain the terms : (i) pumping, (ii) active system.
3. Explain :
   (1) Stimulated emission (2) Optical pumping
   (3) Population inversion, (4) Metastable state.
4. Define the following terms :
   (1) Spontaneous emission (2) Stimulated emission
   (3) Pumping (4) Population inversion.
5. Explain the terms (a) Stimulated emission, (b) Population inversion.
6. Explain the terms : Optical pumping and Resonant cavity.
7. Explain the terms : Optical pumping, Population inversion.
8. Explain the terms : (i) Optical pumping, (ii) Population inversion.
9. Define the following concepts (any three) :
   (a) Spontaneous emission (b) Stimulated emission
   (c) Metastable state (d) Population inversion (e) Lasing.
10. State the important properties of lasers.
11. Explain :
    (i) population inversion, (ii) optical pumping,
    (iii) active system. Explain the properties of lasers.
12. Explain in brief the working of a semiconductor laser.
13. What are the special properties of laser? Hence explain the working of semiconductor laser.

14. With the help of energy band diagram, explain construction and working of semiconductor laser.
15. Explain :

    (i) stimulated emission, (ii) optical pumping,

    (iii) metastable state.

    Explain in brief the working of a semiconductor laser with diagram.
16. Explain the operation of solid ruby laser with neat labelled diagram.
17. State important characteristics of laser. With the help of neat labelled diagram, explain the operation of Ruby laser.
18. Explain : (i) spontaneous emission, (ii) stimulated emission. Draw a neat diagram and give the construction and working of a Ruby laser.
19. State important characteristics of laser. With the help of neat labelled diagram, explain the operation of Ruby laser.
20. State the important characteristics of lasers. With the help of a neat labelled diagram, explain the operation of Ruby laser.
21. State four important characteristics of laser. Explain construction and working of ruby laser.
22. Explain construction, working and energy level diagram of Ruby laser.
23. Explain the operation of Ruby laser with neat labelled diagram.
24. With the help of neat diagram explain construction and working of Ruby laser. Also comment on Ruby laser is a pulsed laser.
25. Explain construction and working principle of Ruby laser.
26. Explain construction and working of Ruby laser.
27. Explain construction and working of He-Ne low power gas laser with neat labelled diagram.
28. State important characteristics of LASER and write a short note on He-Ne LASER.
29. Draw a neat diagram and give the construction and working of He-Ne laser.
30. Draw a neat diagram and explain the construction and working of He-Ne laser.
31. Explain the construction and working of He-Ne laser. Explain its energy level diagram also.
32. With the help of neat energy level diagram explain the technique used to achieve population inversion in He-Ne laser.
33. Explain construction and working of He-Ne laser.
34. State and explain advantages of diode/semiconductor laser over He-Ne laser.

ENGG. PHYSICS (F.Y. B. TECH. B.V.)   LASER

35. Give advantages of using fibre optic media of communication.
36. State advantages of communication through fibre optic.
37. Explain communication through optical fibre. Give any five advantages of optical fibres for communication purpose.
38. Write a note on holography recording.
39. What is holography ? Explain the process of holography recording and reconstruction.
40. Explain how lasers are used in communication systems and in information technology.
41. What is holography ? Explain the process of holography recording and reconstruction.
42. What is holography ? Explain the process of hologram recording and reconstruction.
43. State any six applications of Laser.
44. Explain any one application of Laser in brief.
45. Explain any one application of Laser.
46. Describe propagation mechanism of light wave in optical fibres.
47. Draw a block diagram of the fibre optics communication system and explain the role of any four components in the system.

SUMMARY

- The term LASER stands for light amplification by stimulated emission of radiation. It is an intense, coherent, monochromatic beam.
- **Absorption :** Absorption is a process in which a photon, of energy $h\upsilon$, gets absorbed by an atom and it goes from a lower energy state E_1 to a higher energy state E_2.
- **Emission :**

   (i) Spontaneous emission : An electron which is raised to an excited state E_2 (due to absorption), spontaneously decays back to a lower energy level E_1 and radiates an energy equal to $E_2 - E_1$. Such an emission is called as spontaneous emission. This emission is random in nature and depends only on the type of atom and type of transition.

   (ii) Stimulated emission : A photon of energy $h\upsilon = E_2 - E_1$ triggers an excited atom to drop to the lower energy state giving up a photon. This phenomenon of forced emission of photons is called as stimulated emission.

- **Population inversion :** The process of getting a large percentage of atoms into an excited state is called as population inversion.
- **Active system :** A system in which population inversion is achieved is called an active system.

- **Pumping :** A method of raising atoms from lower energy levels to higher energy levels is called as pumping. It can be done by subjecting the atoms to a non-uniform electric field, flooding the gas with high intensity light (optical pumping) etc.

- **Metastable states :** Ordinary energy levels have a life time of 10^{-8} to 10^{-9} secs. Energy levels having a life time greater than ordinary energy levels (~10^{-6} to 10^{-3} secs) are called as metastable states.

- **Types of lasers :** Lasers are mainly divided into the following categories : (i) solid state laser, (ii) gas laser, (iii) semiconductor laser.

    They can be operated in two modes : (a) continuous, (b) pulsed.

- **Solid-state laser :** Ruby laser is an example of solid-state laser. It produces an intense red beam using a three-level system with a wavelength of 6943 A°. It is a pulsed laser.

- **Gas laser :** He-Ne laser is an example of a gas laser. It employs a four-level pumping scheme and operates in continuous mode. It produces a beam of wavelength 6328 A°.

- **Semiconductor laser :** A semiconductor laser is a specially fabricated pn junction that emits coherent light when it is forward biased. The basic mechanism of producing laser in a semiconductor diode laser, is the electron-hole recombination at the pn junction when a current is passed through the diode.

- Light from a laser is different from light from other sources in four basic ways :

    (i) directionality, (ii) monochromaticity, (iii) coherence, (iv) polarizability.

- Due to its unique properties, lasers are used in a variety of fields like welding, machining, surveying, communication, holography, cutting, drilling, information processing, surgery and related medical fields, in CD players, printers, etc.

IMPORTANT FORMULAE

- Rate of absorption, $R_{12} = P_a N_1$.
- Rate of stimulated emission, $R_{21} = P_e N_2$.
- At equilibrium, $P_a = P_e$.
- Population inversion, $N_2 > N_1$.
- Frequency of photons emitted, $\upsilon = \dfrac{E_2 - E_1}{h}$.
- For light transmission in fibre optics, $\theta_c = \sin^{-1} \dfrac{n^2}{n^1}$.

EXERCISE

1. Explain the operation of Ruby laser with a neat labelled diagram.
2. Explain the following terms :
   (i) Spontaneous emission, (ii) Stimulated emission,
   (iii) Population inversion.
3. Explain action of gas laser. How does stimulated emission take place with exchange of energy between Helium and Neon atoms ?
4. What is population inversion ? Explain the operation of He - Ne laser.
5. Define and explain the terms :
   (i) pumping (ii) active systems.
6. What are the different uses to which laser beams are put in industry, medicine ?
7. What are the properties of laser ?
8. Write a note on use of lasers in fibre communication systems and information technology.
9. Write a note on semiconductor laser.

✠ ✠ ✠

Unit - VI

CHAPTER 11
ARCHITECTURAL ACOUSTICS

11.1 INTRODUCTION

The word **acoustics** originated from a Greek word meaning to hear. Hence, acoustics is defined as the **Science of Sound**. It deals with the scientific study of sound and sound waves i.e. production, transmission and reception of sound. The sound wave is produced when the air in contact with the vibrating body is suddenly compressed. Due to the elastic nature of air, these compressions travel away from the source. Thus, the vibrating body sets up waves of compressions and rarefactions in the medium. When these waves come near ear drums, we feel a sensation of hearing. When the sound waves are periodic and harmonic, they give a pleasing effect. Such sound is called a **musical sound**. On the other hand, if they are non-periodic and non-harmonic, they give unpleasant effect. Such sound is known as **noise**.

The musical sound wave is periodic, harmonic and free of irregularities and discontinuities. On the other hand, noise wave is distorted with discontinuities and irregularities. Fig. 11.1 shows waveform of musical sound and noise.

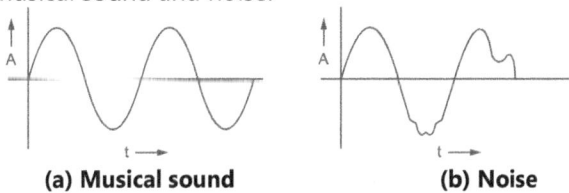

(a) Musical sound   (b) Noise

Fig. 11.1 : Sound

The human ear is sensitive to the waves in the range from 20 Hz to 20 kHz. But the word acoustics is applied to the similar waves with frequencies outside the range of human audibility i.e. ultrasonics and subsonics. Ultrasonics have frequencies above 20 kHz and subsonics below 20 Hz. One more parameter which decides the audibility along with frequency is the intensity. The minimum intensity that can be heard by human being is 10^{-12} W/m² and is called **threshold of hearing**. At one particular intensity it starts giving painful effect. The intensity at which this happens is called **threshold of feeling** and the value is 10 W/m².

11.2 ELEMENTARY ACOUSTICS

11.2.1 Velocity

The velocity of sound v is defined as the velocity with which a sound wave travels in a given medium. In a particular medium, the velocity of sound remains the same. But when the medium changes, the velocity also changes. In fluids i.e. air and liquid the velocity is mainly function of density of medium and temperature. As these features are different for different materials, the velocity of sound is also different. In gases, the velocity is given by

$$v = \sqrt{\frac{\gamma P_o}{\rho_o}} \qquad \ldots (11.1)$$

where, γ = Ratio of the specific heat of the gas at constant pressure to that at constant volume
P_o = Pressure
ρ_o = Density

For most gases the ratio P_o/ρ_o is nearly independent of pressure i.e. doubling the pressure is accompanied by doubling of the density of gas. If the atmosphere is homogeneous and isothermal the velocity remains independent of altitude. In practice, the change in velocity is significant with change in temperature in comparison with the change due to inhomogeneity. The relation of change in velocity with the temperature is given by

$$v = v_o + 0.6t \qquad \ldots (11.2)$$

where, v_o = 331.6 m/sec = velocity of sound at 0°C
and t = temperature in °C

The behaviour of velocity of sound in solids is more complicated and is given by the equation

$$v = \sqrt{\frac{\upsilon B_T}{\rho_o}} \qquad \ldots (11.3)$$

where B_T is the isothermal bulk modulus.

As all the above parameters depend upon temperature and pressure of liquid, therefore they will decide the velocity of sound in liquid. The empirical formula giving the velocity of sound in distilled water as a function of temperature at a pressure is given by

$$v = 1403 + 5t - 0.06t^2 + 0.0003t^3 \qquad \ldots (11.4)$$

where t is in °C.

The following table gives velocity of sound in different materials at 20°C.

Table 11.1

Sr. No.	Medium	Velocity, m/s
1.	Hydrogen	1305
2.	Air	344
3.	Pure water	1480
4.	Soft wood	3350
5.	Concrete	3400
6.	Mild steel	5050
7.	Glass	5200
8.	Granite	6400

11.2.2 Frequency

A sound wave is produced by a vibrating body, which sets the medium molecules into vibrations. These oscillating molecules transfer the energy from source to listener. In the process, the molecules maintain their position and only transfer the energy.

The number of vibrations or cycles completed in second is termed as frequency. Mathematically,

$$\text{frequency} = \frac{1}{\text{period}} \text{ Hz or cycles/sec.}$$

i.e. $f = \dfrac{1}{T}$

11.2.3 Wavelength

A sound wave travels in the form of periodic wave i.e. the wave repeats itself in equal intervals of time.

For a sinusoidal wave, the wavelength is the spatial period of the wave, the distance over which the wave's shape repeats. The wavelength is determined by considering the distance between consecutive corresponding points of the same phase such as crests, troughs or zero crossings as shown in Fig. 11.2.

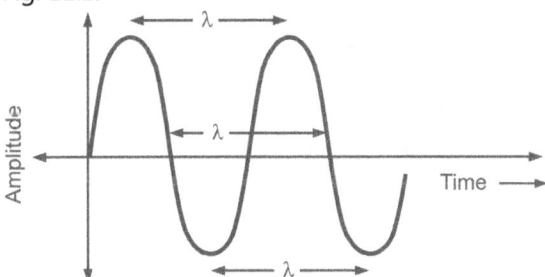

Fig. 11.2 : Wavelength of wave

The wavelength is a characteristic of travelling waves as well as standing waves. The common notation for wavelength is **lambda** (λ).

11.2.4 Intensity

The sound coming from different sources have different loudness, which is decided by the intensity of the sound along with the sensitivity of ears. The difference in loudness gives the information about the sources from which the sound is coming.

The sound waves transport energy from source to listener and the amount of energy that flows per second across the unit area in the direction of propagation is called the **intensity** of the wave.

i.e. $\quad \text{Intensity} = \dfrac{\text{Energy}}{\text{Area} \times \text{Time}} = \dfrac{E}{A \times t} \quad \ldots (11.5)$

But, $\dfrac{\text{Energy}}{\text{Time}}$ = Power

∴ Intensity = $\dfrac{\text{Power}}{\text{Area}} = \dfrac{P}{A}$ ... (11.6)

The unit used for intensity is W/m² or W/cm². The lower limit of sound intensity which can be heard by humans is 10^{-12} W/m² or 10^{-16} W/cm² while the upper limit is 10 W/m² or 10^{-4} W/cm².

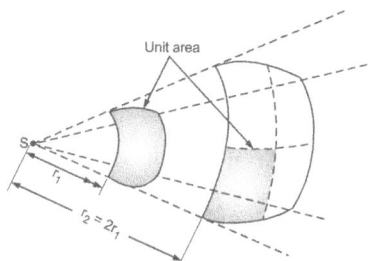

Fig. 11.3 : Intensity

The sound waves produce variation in the pressure of medium as they cause compression and rarefaction as they travel through the medium. Thus the intensity is related to the pressure by the following relation

$$I = \dfrac{P^2}{2\rho_0 v} \quad \text{... (11.7)}$$

where, P^2 = Square of pressure amplitude
ρ_0 = Density of medium
v = Velocity of sound

A point source in homogeneous medium produces spherical wavefront and the intensity will decrease with the distance from source to listener. For two listeners L_1 and L_2 at distances r_1 and r_2, the intensities received will be I_1 and I_2 respectively.

The relation between I_1 and I_2 is given by equation

$$\dfrac{I_1}{I_2} = \dfrac{r_2^2}{r_1^2} \quad \text{... (11.8)}$$

11.2.5 Intensity Level

In accordance with the Weber - Frechner law in Psychology, the loudness of a sound 'L' as judged by the law is proportional to the logarithm of the intensity.

i.e. $L \propto \log I$

One reason for using logarithmic scales is that it compresses the range of numbers required to describe the wide range of sound intensity and pressure. e.g. audible intensities range from 10^{-12} to 10 watts/m². Second reason is that human ear judges the relative loudness of two sounds not by direct ratio, but by the logarithms of the ratio of their intensities.

It is customary to describe acoustical intensity and acoustic pressure on a logarithmic scale as logarithm to the base ten of the ratio of two intensities and two pressures in experimental work. This is known as **sound intensity level** (denoted by SIL) or **sound pressure level** (denoted by SPL). The unit of sound level or SPL is Bel but the unit decibels is more frequently used. 1 decibel (dB) is $\frac{1}{10}$th of a Bel.

If I_1 and I_0 represent the intensities of two sounds of a particular frequency, and L_1 and L_0 the corresponding measures of loudness, then,

$$L_1 \propto \log_{10} I_1$$
$$L_1 = K \log_{10} I_1$$

Similarly,
$$L_0 = K \log_{10} I_0$$

The difference in loudness of the two is technically known as intensity level I.L.

∴ $\quad$ I.L. $= L_1 - L_0 = K [\log_{10} I_1 - \log_{10} I_0]$

i.e. $\quad$ I.L. $= K \log_{10} \dfrac{I_1}{I_0}$ ... (11.9)

where K is a constant that depends on the units. I_0 is the standard reference intensity taken as 10^{-16} watts/cm² or 10^{-12} watts/m². This corresponds to the intensity of sound, which can be just heard at a frequency of about 1000 hertz. This is taken as the **threshold of audibility** of a normal ear.

In the above equation, when K = 1 (unity), the difference in loudness (intensity level) is expressed in "Bels", a unit named after Alexander Graham Bell, inventor of telephone.

i.e. $\quad$ I.L. $= 1 \log_{10} \dfrac{I_1}{I_0}$

If $\quad I_1 = 10 I_0$

then $\quad$ I.L. $= 1 \log_{10} 10 = 1$ Bel

This unit is rather too large, hence one tenth of it, the decibel (dB) has become the standard, so that to express the intensity level of a sound of intensity I in decibels, equation (11.9) should be written as

$$\text{I.L.} = 10 \log_{10} \dfrac{I_1}{I_0} \text{ dB}$$

It can be seen from equation (11.9) that if $I_1 = 100 I_0$

$\quad$ I.L. $= 10 \log_{10} 100$ dB
$\quad$ I.L. $= 10 \log_{10} 10^2$ dB
$\quad$ I.L. $= 20$ dB

If $\quad$ I.L. $= 1000 I_0$
$\quad$ I.L. $= 10 \log_{10} 1000$ dB
$\quad$ I.L. $= 30$ dB

Thus when two sounds differ by 20 dB, the louder of them is 100 times more intense and when they differ by 30 dB, the louder one is 1000 times more intense. The loudness corresponding to the threshold is taken as zero. This occurs when the intensity of sound wave equals I_0 or 10^{-16} watts/cm², then its intensity level is zero. The maximum intensity which the ear can tolerate without sensation of pain is about 10^{-4} watts/cm². This corresponds to an intensity level,

$$I.L. = 10 \log_{10} \left(\frac{10^{-4}}{10^{-16}}\right)$$
$$= 10 \log_{10} (10^{12}) = 120 \text{ dB}$$

The following table gives the approximate values of some intensity of sounds measured in decibels.

Table 11.2

Source	Intensity level in dB
Threshold of hearing	0
Rustle of leaves	10
Whisper	20
Ordinary conversation	60
Heavy traffic	80
Thunder	110
Painful sounds	130 and above

Now, acoustical intensity and acoustic pressure are related as $I = \frac{P_e^2}{\rho c}$, where P_e is the measured effective pressure of the sound wave, ρ is the density of the medium and c is the velocity of sound. Since the intensity is proportional to the square of pressure, the sound pressure level (SPL) or intensity level (I.L.) is given by $SPL = 20 \log_{10} \left(\frac{P_e}{P_0}\right)$ dB. P_0 is the reference standard pressure = 2×10^{-5} newton/m².

11.2.6 Loudness (Weber and Frechner's Law)

Loudness is the characteristic of all sound. It is associated with the intensity of sound which is a definite physical quantity. But there is a marked difference between the loudness and the intensity of sound. Loudness of a sound is the **degree of sensation** depending on the intensity of sound and the sensitiveness of the ear. Loudness does not increase proportionally with intensity but as its logarithm.

According to Weber and Frechner's law,

$$L \propto \log I \qquad \ldots (11.10)$$

where L represents the sensation of loudness and I the intensity of sound. Since loudness is the degree of sensation and depends on the ear of the listener, it cannot be measured by physical apparatus. However, greater the intensity of sound, greater is its loudness. Loudness of sound depends on all the factors on which the intensity of sound depends.

The loudness depends on sensitivity of ears and ears are more sensitive to high frequencies than low frequencies. Therefore, it needs higher intensity at low frequencies than at high frequencies to give the sensation of the same loudness. The intensity of 60 dB at 40 Hz and of 0 dB at 1000 Hz gives the same loudness. The loudness of intensity of sound in dB over threshold of hearing as sensed by the ear at 1000 Hz is called **phon**. If the intensity of sound at 1000 Hz is 0 dB, it is 0 phon loudness. If it is 40 dB, the loudness is 40 dB. If an intensity of 60 dB at 40 Hz gives the same loudness as 0 dB intensity at 1000 Hz, then loudness at 40 Hz is zero phon, not 60 phon. Thus, loudness in phons at 1000 Hz is always equal to the intensity of sound in dB. But at any other frequency, the level of loudness can be found out only by determining the intensity of sound in 0 dB required at 1000 Hz to give the same loudness.

While phon is used to compare the loudness level for different frequencies, another unit **sone** is used to determine the increase in loudness. Loudness sensation produced by 1000 Hz sound of 40 dB is called 1 sone.

11.2.7 Timbre of Sound

The sound waves produced by speech and musical instruments are not pure sine waves, but are complex waves containing the fundamental frequencies and their harmonics. The fundamental frequency is called **tone** and other than the fundamental are called **overtones**. The proportion of tones and overtones in a sound form the special characteristics by which a particular sound can be recognized, even if all the sources produce the same fundamental frequency. This quality of sound is called **timbre**.

This quality of sound helps us to recognize a person even if he is not visible.

11.2.8 Reflection of Sound

Whenever sound waves are incident on an obstacle whose dimensions are much larger than the wavelength of wave, a part is reflected and a part is absorbed. The reflected wave makes same angle as that of angle of incidence.

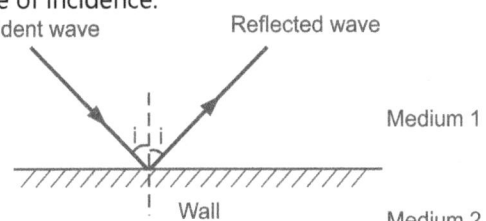

Fig. 11.4 : Reflection of sound wave

The amount of sound energy reflected or absorbed depends upon the nature of the surface while the amount of energy transmitted outside the room depends upon the sound insulation properties of the surface.

A concave surface leads to the concentration of reflected waves at certain points. Hence concave surfaces may be used to work as a **reflector**. A convex surface tends to spread the reflected waves. Hence, convex surfaces may be used to **spread** the sound throughout the room. Fig. 11.5 shows reflection of sound from different types of surfaces. The laws of reflection of sound help in deciding the shape of the room and its surfaces.

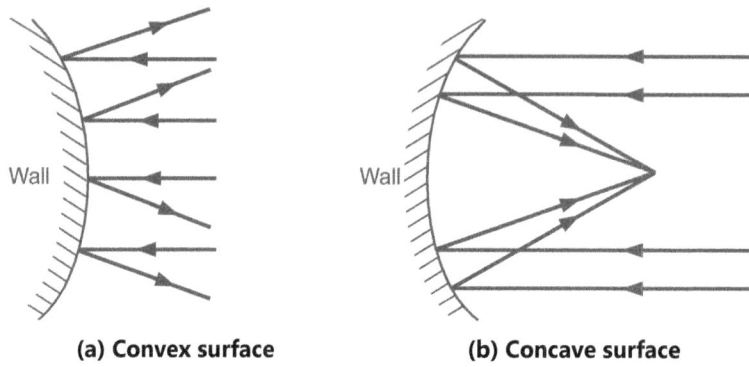

(a) Convex surface (b) Concave surface

Fig. 11.5 : Reflection of sound waves

The behaviour of reflected sound plays an important role in architectural acoustics. The main defects that are caused by reflection of sound are echo, reverberation, focussing and echelon.

11.2.9 Echo

An echo is produced when the reflected sound waves reach the ear just when the original direct sound from the same source has already been heard. Thus, echo is the repetition of same sound due to reflections from an obstacle.

The sensation of sound persists on human ear for 0.1 sec after the sound is heard. So, if the reflected sound reaches the listener with delay more than 0.1 sec, the reflected sound (of diminished intensity) is clearly distinguished from the original sound. Taking the velocity of sound as 340 m/s the reflected sound must travel a total distance of 340 × 0.1 = 34 m (to and fro) before reaching the listener for a clear echo. If the source and listener are same the distance between the source to obstacle should be 17 m or more for echo. In this case, the distance between the source and the obstacle will be calculated by formula $t = \dfrac{2d}{v}$, where d is the distance between the source and the obstacle.

11.3 REVERBERATION

Whenever sound is produced in a hall, it lasts for quite sometime. This is because sound waves keep on reaching the listener a number of times. Initially the listener receives sound waves directly from the source. Thereafter he receives the sound reflected from walls, ceilings, floor of the hall, etc. Thus, the sound lingers in the hall even when the source has been stopped or the listener continues to receive series of sound of decreasing energy. But due to reflection, at every stage, some energy is lost. Therefore, some interval of time is required for the sound energy to die out completely. The loss of sound energy is brought about by friction between the sound waves and air particles and also between sound waves and the surfaces with which it come in contact. The more the friction, the quicker will be the sound energy loss. This gradual process of loss of sound energy over a certain interval of time is known as **reverberation** or reverberation can be defined as **the persistence or prolongation of sound in the hall even after the sound source has been stopped**. If the reverberation of a syllable prolongs even after the utterance of another syllable, then a condition of unintelligibility will arise. This may lead to a bad acoustical condition.

11.3.1 Reverberation Time

The time during which sound persists in the hall is called **reverberation time**. This time is measured from the instant the source stops emitting sound.

In an auditorium when the sound source is switched on the intensity starts increasing with time. Because at any given instant, the total intensity will be sum of the intensity due to sound source (which is fixed) and due to reflections from the boundary (which increases with the number of reflections and hence with time). But the intensity cannot increase above a critical value as at some instant amount of sound reflected and absorbed will be same. When the sound source is switched off, the intensity due to sound source becomes zero and sound due to reflections decays exponentially resulting in reverberation. Fig. 11.6 shows rise and decay of sound in an auditorium.

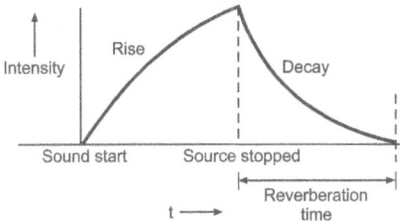

Fig. 11.6

The time of reverberation is also defined as the time taken for the sound to fall below the minimum audibility measured from the instant when the source stopped sounding. Professor Sabine by using an organ pipe of 512 vibrations per second found that its sound became inaudible when its intensity fell to one millionth of its intensity just before stopping the organ pipe. Hence, Sabine defined the standard reverberation time as the time taken by sound to fall to one millionth of its intensity just before the source is cut off. He also found that the time of reverberation depends upon the size of the hall, loudness of sound and the kind of music for which the hall is used.

There are several **factors which control the reverberation time**.

- The reverberation depends on the reflecting properties of the walls, floor and ceiling. If they are good reflectors, then sound would take long time to die away. Hence, reverberation time would be large.
- The reverberation depends on the coefficient of absorption of various surfaces such as carpets, cushions, curtains and furniture present in the room. Greater the absorption, lesser is the time of reverberation.
- The reverberation time depends on the frequency of the note.

Importance of Reverberation Time :
- If a building is to be acoustically good, it is very important that its reverberation time must be optimum. It should neither be too short nor too long. A very short reverberation time makes a room sound **dead**. Sensation of speaking in such a room is similar to that experienced when speaking from the top of an isolated building. The absorbing powers of materials are different at different frequencies. For higher frequencies, the absorbing power is greater. Hence, the material chosen in a room should be such that, it makes the reverberation time short for high notes and long for short notes. This will make the music sound pleasing.
- A **long reverberation time** is more undesirable than a short one. It causes confusion and renders speech unintelligible and music dissonant.
  The best value for reverberation time depends on the use for which a building is designed. For a listener a time of 0.5 seconds was found to be optimum. For music, the value is between 1 and 2 seconds. The optimum value of reverberation time for auditoriums varies with volume. It varies from 1.1 to 2.3 seconds.
- A certain amount of reverberation is desirable. Because this adds pleasing characteristics to the acoustical qualities of a room. Too much reverberation is undesirable, while too small reverberation has a deadening effect on the sound. Hence, obtaining the right amount of reverberation is the secret of good acoustics.

11.3.2 Sabine's Formula

Prof. W. C. Sabine of Harward University studied the subject of architectural acoustics. He used an organ pipe of frequency 512 Hertz to produce an average audible sound in an empty closed hall. He then measured the time interval for which the audible sound was present in the hall after the source of sound was shut off. This was termed as **reverberation time**. In a similar manner, he found the reverberation time for the hall full of furniture and audience. From his experiments carried out in halls of different sizes, he concluded that
- the reverberation time of a room varies inversely as the effective surface area of different surfaces and directly as the volume of the room,
- the reverberation time is independent of the position of the source and the listener and the shape of the room.

Mathematically, $$T \propto \frac{V}{A}$$

i.e. $$T = K \frac{V}{A}$$

where A is the total sound energy absorbed by the various sound absorbing materials in the hall.

V is the volume of the room.

K is the proportionality constant.

For auditorium having large number of absorbing materials having different surface area, the total absorption will be the sum of absorptions due to individual absorbing material.

i.e.
$$A = \sum_{1}^{n} aS = a_1 S_1 + a_2 S_2 + ... + a_n S_n$$

where $a_1, a_2, a_3, ..., a_n$ are the coefficients of absorption of materials and $S_1, S_2, ..., S_n$ are the surface areas of materials respectively.

$$\therefore T = \frac{V}{\sum a_n S_n}$$

If V is in cubic meters and S is in square meters, K = 0.165. If V is in cubic feet and S is in square feet, K = 0.05.

$$T = 0.165 \frac{V}{A} \text{ in M.K.S. system.}$$

Or
$$T = 0.05 \frac{V}{A} \text{ in British system.}$$

This equation is called **Sabine's formula** for reverberation time. It is an experimentally found empirical relation.

11.3.3 Remedies Over Reverberation

The reverberation time of an auditorium should be optimum, i.e. neither too less nor too large. The factors which decide the reverberation time are volume of auditorium, absorption coefficient and surface area. But once the auditorium is constructed, the volume cannot be changed easily.

For reducing the reverberation time, the easiest method is to use sound absorbent materials whose absorption coefficient is large. Depending upon the requirement, sound absorbing material and their surface area (dimensions) can be selected. The surface area also can be increased by making pyramid or conical shape on the wall, which helps in increasing the surface area. The common absorbent materials used are thick rugs, wooden furniture, thick curtain with folds. Even presence of audiences and windows decreases the reverberation significantly.

The reverberation can be increased by coating the walls of the auditorium with good reflecting materials. Metals, glasses and polished wooden surfaces are good reflecting surfaces.

11.4 SOUND ABSORPTION

When a sound wave strikes a surface, the total sound energy is distributed in three ways. A part of its energy is transmitted across the surface, a part of its energy is absorbed by friction and the remaining of its energy is reflected back by the surface. The property of a material which converts the sound energy into other form of energy is known as **absorption**.

The sound generated in an auditorium or hall is absorbed in four ways (i) by air, (ii) by the audience, (iii) by furniture and furnishings and (iv) at the boundary surfaces such as floors, ceilings, walls, etc.

(i) Absorption by Air : The absorption of sound in air is mainly due to the friction between the oscillating molecules when sound wave travels through it.

(ii) Absorption by Audience : Sound energy is absorbed by the clothing of the audience. Room acoustics change appreciably by the number of audience present. Absorption being more in winter than in summer due to heavy clothing.

(iii) Absorption by Furniture and Furnishings : Furniture, curtains, carpets etc. also absorb sound energy.

(iv) Absorption by Boundary Surface : When sound waves strike the boundary surface such as walls, floors, ceilings, absorption takes place due to the following factors : (a) Penetration of sound into porous materials. This causes resonance within air pockets in the pores until energy is dissipated. (b) Resonant vibration of panel materials. (c) Molecular damping in soft absorbing materials. (d) Transmission through structures.

11.5 ABSORPTION COEFFICIENT

When sound energy is incident on a surface, a part of the energy is absorbed by the surface. Different surfaces have different sound absorption capacity. This capacity depends upon the nature of the surface.

The **coefficient of absorption** of a surface is defined as **the ratio of the sound energy absorbed by it to that of the total sound energy incident on the surface**.

i.e. Absorption coefficient 'a' = $\dfrac{\text{Sound energy absorbed by the surface}}{\text{Total sound energy incident on the surface}}$

An open window allows all sound energy incident on it to pass through and it reflects none of the sound energy incident on it. Hence an open window is considered as a perfect sound absorber and an open window of unit area is chosen as the standard for expressing absorption of sound. Thus, the absorption coefficient of a material is defined as **the ratio of sound energy absorbed by a certain area of the surface to the sound energy absorbed by the same area of an open window**.

i.e. Absorption coefficient 'a' = $\dfrac{\text{Sound energy absorbed by a centain area of surface in a given time}}{\text{Sound energy absorbed by same area of an open window in same time}}$

The unit of absorption coefficient is written as O.W.U. i.e. open window units or Sabines.
Total absorption by material = Absorption coefficient × Area of material.

11.6 ABSORBENT MATERIALS

Most of the common building materials absorb sound to a small extent. Hence for providing better acoustical requirement, some other materials are to be incorporated on the surface of the room which absorb the sound significantly. Such materials are known as **absorbent materials**.

A good absorbent material should be water-proof, fire-proof, strong and good in appearance. The absorbent materials are found to be soft and porous. They work on the principle that sound waves penetrate into the pores and in this process they are converted into other form of energy by friction. The absorbing capacity of the absorbent materials depends on the thickness of the material, its density and frequency of sound. The acoustic properties of the absorbent materials are considerably changed by their modes of fixing. Some of the common types of absorbent materials are hairfelt, quilts and mats, acoustic plaster, acoustical tiles, strawboard, pulp boards, perforated plywood, wood particle board etc.

11.7 DIFFERENT TYPES OF NOISE AND THEIR REMEDIES

Noise can be defined as **unwanted sound**. As noise is unwanted, it either reduces the unintelligibility of sound or gives unpleasant effect. Therefore, in good hall, noise should be reduced by blocking the unwanted sound coming from outside as well as generated inside. Basically, there are three types of noises :

(a) Air-borne noise, (b) Structure borne noise and (c) Inside noise.

The prevention of the noise inside or outside the hall is known as **sound insulation** or **sound proofing**. The method employed for sound proofing depends on the type of noise to be treated.

(a) Air-Borne Noise : The noise which reaches the hall from outside through air is called **air-borne noise**. In this the noise is transported by air through open vent, window, door etc. The air-borne noise can be reduced by

(i) avoiding ventilators facing the streets,

(ii) placing doors and windows at proper place,

(iii) using heavy glass doors, windows and ventilators,

(iv) having double wall construction.

(b) Structure-Borne Noise : The noise which is conveyed through the structure of building is known as **structural noise**. This noise is caused by structural vibrations due to construction activities like hammering, drilling, operating machinery etc. The structure-borne noise can be reduced by

(i) breaking the continuity of the structure,

(ii) using double wall,

(iii) using anti-vibration mounts like rubber pad.

(c) Inside Noise : The noise which is produced inside the hall is called inside **noise**. They are produced by equipments and machineries used in the hall itself. This can be reduced by

(i) placing machineries on insulating pods,

(ii) covering floor with carpets,

(iii) sound absorbing materials should be placed close to noise producing source.

11.8 BASIC REQUIREMENT FOR ACOUSTIALLY GOOD HALL

Basically, acoustics is classified into three branches (i) architectural acoustics, (ii) electro acoustics and (iii) musical acoustics. In architectural acoustics, we deal with the behaviour of sound in an auditorium. Many times it is found that in an auditorium, sound cannot be heard clearly. Either intensity at some places is not high enough or repeated speeches are heard. For making a hall acoustically good, it should have following features.

- The sound must be **loud enough** in every part of hall.
- There should not be repeated speeches heard in the hall. i.e. **free of echo**.
- There should not be overlapping of speeches, i.e. **reverberation time** should have optimum value.
- **Focussing** of sound should not be there.
- Should be free of **echelon effect**.
- Should be **free of resonance**.
- **External sound** (noise) should be minimum.

11.9 FACTORS AFFECTING THE ARCHITECTURAL ACOUSTICS AND THEIR REMEDIES

An acoustically good hall is the one in which every syllable or musical note reaches the audience is audible and legible and then decays quickly to make space for the next syllable or note. If this aspect is not achieved, the hall is acoustically defective. The following factors affect the architectural acoustics :

(1) Reverberation : In a hall, when the reverberation is large, there is overlapping of sound. This will lead to lack of clarity in hearing. If the reverberation is small, there is a deadening effect on sound. As a result, the loudness becomes inadequate. Thus the time of reverberation for a hall should neither be too large nor too small. It should have an optimum value. This value can be calculated by a formula given by Prof. W. C. Sabine.

$$T = K\frac{V}{A} = 0.165\frac{V}{A}$$

where A is the total effective absorption of the hall and V is its volume.

Reverberation time can be controlled in the following ways :

(a) By providing sound absorbing materials on the walls and using carpets on floor.
(b) Using curtains and providing acoustic tiles.
(c) Providing windows and ventilators.
(d) Having furniture and audience.

(2) Echoes : An echo is heard when reflected waves from the same source reach the listener with a time delay of $1/10^{th}$ of a second. The reflected sound arriving earlier than this helps in raising the loudness while that arriving later produces echoes and causes confusion. Echoes can be reduced or avoided by covering long distant walls and high ceilings with absorbent materials like felt, perforated card boards, coarse cloth etc.

(3) Loudness : The control of reverberation may lead to the reduction in the intensity of sound. Hence the level of intelligible hearing goes down. For satisfactory hearing, sufficient loudness in every part of the hall is very important.

The loudness can be increased by (a) providing loud speakers, (b) providing sounding boards behind the speaker and facing towards the audience, (c) providing wooden reflectors above the speaker.

(4) Focusing due to Walls and Ceiling : Focusing surfaces like curved surfaces on the walls or ceiling produce concentration of sound in particular regions, while in some other parts, no sound is heard at all. This leads to poor and uneven sound intensity distribution. Uniform sound distribution can be achieved by (a) allowing no curved surfaces or covering the curved surfaces with sound absorbent materials, (b) having low ceiling, (c) providing parabolic reflectors behind the speaker with the speaker at the focus. This will help in sending a uniform reflected beam of sound in the hall.

(5) Echelon Effect : Regular succession of echoes occur when sound is reflected from equally spaced reflecting surfaces like staircase or a set of railings. This effect is known as **Echelon effect**. This makes the original sound confusing or unintelligible.

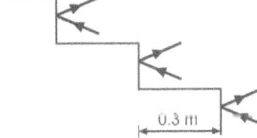

Fig. 11.7

This effect can be reduced by : (a) Covering the stairs with thick carpets. (b) Breaking the regularity of spacing of the steps.

(6) Resonance : Sometimes window panes and other parts of the structures which are not rigid are thrown into vibrations and they create other sounds. If some note of the audio frequency and the frequencies of new sounds are the same, then resonance occurs. Due to the interference between original sound and the created sound, the original sound is distorted. Thus the intensity of the note is entirely different from the original one. Also enclosed air in the hall causes resonance. Such resonant vibrations should be suitably damped.

(7) Seating Arrangement : The speaker or source of sound should be at the focus of a parabolic reflecting surface. The seats should be arranged such that they are perpendicular to the direction of sound. The seats should be gradually elevated. This arrangement ensures uniform distribution of sound.

(8) Balconies : The balconies should have shallow depths and high openings. They should have railing bars instead of walls. This allows sound energy to flow readily into space of the balcony.

(9) Noise : An external noise makes speech or music makes the sound unintelligible. The noise may come to room by air or structure. The noise could be reduced by sound insulations. The noise in the hall should be minimum so that the sound is heard clearly.

SOLVED EXAMPLE

Example 11.1 : A loud speaker emits energy equally in all directions at the rate of 1.5 joules/sec. What is the intensity level at a distance of 20 m ? ($I_0 = 10^{-6}$ watt/cm²)
Data : Rate of power = 1.5 J/sec = 1.5 watt, Distance (radius r) = 20 m = 2000 cm
Solution :

$$I_1 = \frac{Power}{Area} = \frac{P}{4\pi r^2} = \frac{1.5}{4\pi (2000)^2} \text{ watt/cm}^2$$

$$I_0 = 10^{-16} \text{ watt/cm}^2$$

∴ The intensity level

$$I.L. = 10 \log_{10}\left(\frac{I_1}{I_0}\right) = 10 \log_{10} \frac{\frac{1.5}{4\pi (2000)^2}}{10^{-16}}$$

$$= 10 \log_{10} \frac{1.5}{4\pi (2000)^2} \times 10^{-16}$$

$$= 10 \log_{10} \frac{1.5 \times 10^{10}}{16\pi} = \boxed{85 \text{ dB}}$$

Example 11.2 : A cinema hall has a volume of 7500 m³. It is required to have reverberation time of 1.5 sec. What will be the total absorption in the hall ?
Data : Volume V = 7500 m³, Reverberation time t = 1.5 sec
Solution :

$$\text{Reverberation time } t = \frac{0.165 \, V}{A}$$

$$\text{Substituting } 1.5 = \frac{0.165 \times 7500}{A}$$

∴ $$A = \frac{0.165 \times 7500}{1.5}$$

∴ $$\boxed{A = 825 \text{ O.W.U.}}$$

Example 11.3 : The volume of a hall is 3398.4 m³ and its total absorption equals 92.90 m² of open window. Entry of people inside the hall raises the absorption by 185.50 m². Calculate the change in the reverberation time.
Data : Volume V = 3398.4 m³, Total absorption A = $\sum a S$ = 92.90 m²,
Total absorption (hall + people) = $\sum a S + \sum a_1 S_1$
= 185.50 m²

Solution :

For hall, reverberation time is

$$t = \frac{0.165\,V}{\Sigma\,aS} = \frac{0.165 \times 3398.4}{92.90} = 6.04 \text{ sec.}$$

For (hall + people),

$$t_1 = \frac{0.165\,V}{\Sigma\,aS + \Sigma\,a_1 S_1} = \frac{0.165 \times 3398.4}{92.90 + 185.5} = 2.04 \text{ sec.}$$

∴ Change in reverberation time = 6.04 − 2.04 = **4 sec.**

Example 11.4 : A hall of volume 5000 m³ has a reverberation time of 3 sec. The surface area of the sound absorbing surface is 3500 m². Calculate the average coefficient of absorption.

Data : Volume V = 5000 m³, Reverberation time t = 3 sec., Surface area S = 3500 m²

Solution :

$$t = \frac{0.165 \times V}{\Sigma\,aS}$$

$$3 = \frac{0.165 \times 5000}{a \times \Sigma\,S}$$

∴ $$a = \frac{0.165 \times 5000}{3 \times 3500} = \boxed{0.076 \text{ OWU}}$$

Example 11.5 : A hall of 1500 m³ has a seating capacity for 120 persons. Calculate the reverberation time of the hall when (i) the hall is empty, (ii) the hall is full to its capacity, using the following data :

Data : Volume V = 1500 m³

Absorption due to plastered walls = 112 × 0.03 = 3.36 OWU

Absorption due to wooden floor = 130 × 0.0678 = 7.8 OWU

Absorption due to wooden ceiling = 170 × 0.04 = 6.8 OWU

Absorption due to wooden floor = 20 × 0.06 = 1.2 OWU

Absorption due to cushioned chairs = 100 × 1 = 100 OWU

∴ Total absorption = 119.16 OWU

Average absorption of one human being = 4.7 OWU

Solution :

Reverberation time $t = \dfrac{0.165\,V}{A}$

$$= \frac{0.165 \times 1500}{119.6}$$

$$= 2.04 \text{ sec.}$$

Absorption due to audience = 120 × 4.7

$$= 564 \text{ OWU}$$

$$\text{Reverberation time } t = \frac{0.165 \, V}{A}$$

$$= \frac{0.165 \times 1500}{119.16 + 564}$$

$$= \frac{0.165 \times 1500}{683.16}$$

$$= \boxed{0.117 \text{ sec.}}$$

Example 11.6 : A window, whose area is 1.4 m^2, opens on a street where the street noise result in an intensity level (at the window) of 80 deciBels. How much acoustic power enters the window via the sound waves ? Given : $I_0 = 10^{-12}$ watt/m^2.

Data : Area = 1.4 m^2, Intensity level = I.L. = 80 dB

Solution :

$$\text{Intensity level I.L.} = 10 \log_{10} \frac{I_1}{I_0}$$

Substituting,

$$80 = 10 \log_{10} \frac{I_1}{10^{-12}}$$

$$\text{Antilog} \left(\frac{80}{10}\right) = \frac{I_1}{10^{-12}}$$

$$\therefore \quad I_1 = 10^{-12} \times 10^8$$

$$I_1 = 10^{-4} \text{ watt/m}^2$$

$$\therefore \quad \text{Power} = I \times \text{area}$$

$$= 10^{-4} \times 1.4$$

$$\therefore \quad \boxed{\text{Power} = 1.4 \times 10^{-4} \text{ watt.}}$$

Example 11.7 : A lecture hall of 15 × 12 × 5 m dimensions has an average absorption coefficient 0.10. Calculate the reverberation time.

Solution :

$$\text{Volume of the hall } V = 15 \times 12 \times 5 = 900 \text{ m}^3$$

$$\text{Area of inside surfaces } S = 2(15 \times 12 + 12 \times 5 + 5 \times 15) = 630 \text{ m}^2$$

$$\text{Total absorption } A = 0.1 \times 630 = 63 \text{ OWU}$$

$$\text{Reverberation time } t = 0.165 \frac{V}{A}$$

$$= \frac{0.165 \times 900}{63}$$

$$= \boxed{2.354 \text{ sec.}}$$

Example 11.8 : A hall of length 20 m, breadth 15 m and height 10 m has average coefficient of absorption 0.10. If 20 micro watt source is used in the hall, calculate the reverberation time and ultimate intensity.

Solution :

$$\text{Volume of the hall} = 20 \times 15 \times 70 = 3000 \text{ m}^3$$

$$\text{Area of inside surfaces} = 2(20 \times 15 + 15 \times 10 + 10 \times 20) = 1300 \text{ m}^2$$

$$\text{Total absorption } A = 0.1 \times 1300$$

$$= 130 \text{ OWU}$$

$$\text{Reverberation time } t = 0.165 \frac{V}{A}$$

$$= \frac{0.165 \times 3000}{130}$$

$$= \boxed{3.715 \text{ sec.}}$$

$$\text{Ultimate intensity } I = \frac{P}{A}$$

$$= \frac{20}{1300}$$

$$= \boxed{0.0154 \text{ microwatt/m}^2}$$

Example 11.9 : A hall of volume 5000 m³ has a reverberation time of 2 seconds. If the absorbing surface of the hall has the area 3600 m², calculate the average coefficient of absorption.

Solution :

$$t = \frac{0.165 \, V}{\Sigma \, a \, S} = \frac{0.165 \, V}{a \, \Sigma \, S}$$

$$\therefore \quad a = \frac{0.165 \, V}{t \times \Sigma \, S} = \frac{0.165 \times 5000}{2 \times 3600} = \boxed{0.1118 \text{ OWU}}$$

SUMMARY

- **Reverberation :** Prolongation or persistance of sound in a closed hall even after sound source has been stopped.
- **Reverberation time :** Time for which sound persists in a hall.
- **Sabine's formula :** $T = K \frac{V}{A}$.

- **Absorption coefficient :** The ratio of the sound energy absorbed by any surface to that of the total sound energy incident on the surface.
- **Factors affecting architectural acoustics of a hall :**

    (a) Reverberation (b) Echo

    (c) Loudness (d) Focussing

    (e) Echelon (f) Resonance

    (g) Seating arrangement

    (h) Balconies

IMPORTANT FORMULAE

- $L \propto \log I$
- $SIL = 10 \log_{10} \dfrac{I}{I_o}$
- $T = 0.165 \dfrac{V}{A} = 0.165 \dfrac{V}{\Sigma\, aS}$

EXERCISE

1. Write two points of difference between :

    (a) Echo and reverberation

    (b) Intensity and intensity level.

2. Explain remedies for acoustical planning of a hall.
3. What do you mean by absorption coefficient ? Explain.
4. Explain absorption of sound waves.
5. Define and explain :

    (a) Intensity of sound, (b) Loudness, (c) Intensity level, (d) Echo.

6. Explain limits of audibility.
7. What is reverberation ? Explain.
8. What are the essential features that an acoustically good hall should have ?
9. Give Sabine's formula for standard reverberation time, and give the importance of reverberation time.
10. What are the factors which affect the architectural acoustics ?

UNSOLVED PROBLEMS

1. A man shouts standing infront of a mountain, hears an echo after 0.9 seconds later. Calculate the distance between the man and the mountain if the velocity of sound in air is 340 m/sec. **(Ans.** 153 m**)**

2. A man standing between two mountain ranges fires a gun and hears the sound of the firing again after a lapse of $1\frac{1}{2}$ secs., $2\frac{1}{2}$ sec and 4 sec. Explain how these repeated echoes are heard.

3. What is the intensity level in deciBels of a sound wave whose intensity is 10^{-10} watt/cm^2 ? **(Ans.** 60 dB**)**
   Given : $I_0 = 10^{-16}$ watt/cm^2.

4. Show that if the reference level of intensity is $I_o = 10^{-16}$ watts/cm^2, the intensity level of sound of intensity I is I.L. = 160 + 10 $\log_{10}$ I.

5. A lecture hall with a volume of 4,55,000 cubic feet is found to have a reverberation time of 1.5 seconds. What is the total absorption of the hall ? If the area of the sound absorbing surface is 8000 sq. ft. calculate the average absorption coefficient.

   (Ans. 1500 OWU, 1.90 OWU**)**

6. A hall has a volume of 80,000 cu. ft. It's total absorption is equivalent to 1000 sq. ft. of open window. What will be the effect on the reverberation time if the total absorption increases by another 1000 sq. ft. due to the presence of audience ?

   (Ans. Reverberation time changes from 4 sec. to 2 sec.**)**

7. 10^{-16} and 10^{-10} watts/cm^2 are the sound intensities of two sounds having same frequency. What will be the difference in the intensity levels of these sounds ?

   (Ans. 60 dB**)**

8. An open window whose area is 2 m^2 allows an intensity level of 70 dB to enter. Calculate the acoustic power that has entered through the window. **(Ans.** 2×10^{-5} watt**)**

9. A boy, standing between two parallel high mountains shouts for his mother. He hears his own echo twice one after 3 sec. and the other after 5 sec. If the velocity of sound in air is 340 m/sec., calculate the distance between the two mountains. **(Ans.** 1360 m**)**

10. The volume of a room is 600 m^3. The wall area of room is 220 m^2, the floor area is 120 m^2 and the area of ceiling is 120 m^2. The average absorption coefficient for wall is 0.03, for the floor is 0.06 and for ceiling is 0.8. Calculate the reverberation time.

    (Ans. 0.901 sec.**)**

11. A lecture hall 15 × 12 × 10 m has a reverberation time of 3.0 sec. Calculate the total absorption of its surfaces and the average absorption coefficient. **(Ans.** 0.11 OWU)

12. The dimensions of an auditorium are 17 m long, 13 m wide and 8 m high. The mean absorption coefficient is 0.1. What is the reverberation time ? **(Ans.** 3.16 secs.)

13. A lecture hall has a volume of 1,20,000 m^3. It has reverberation time of 1.5 sec. What is the mean absorption coefficient of the surfaces if the total sound absorbing surface is 25,000 m^2 ? **(Ans.** 0.528 OWU)

REFERENCES

Ultrasonic Images

- http://www.drgdiaz.com/pat/images.shtml

✠ ✠ ✠

CHAPTER 12
QUANTUM MECHANICS

12.1 INTRODUCTION

The most outstanding development in modern science is the conception of quantum mechanics. The quantum mechanics is better than Newtonian classical mechanics in explaining the fundamental physics. There was big development in physics between the time of Newton and the time of quantum mechanics. Newton showed that the motion of planets and the free fall of an object on earth is governed by the same law. Thus, he unified terrestrial and celestial mechanics. This was in contrast to ancient belief that the world of the earth and heaven is governed by different laws. It was earlier believed that the heat is some peculiar substance called **'caloric'**, which flows from a hot object to a cold object. But latter it was proved that the heat is the random motion or vibration of constituents of matter. Thus, thermodynamics and mechanics were unified.

For a long time, the phenomena of electricity, magnetism and light were treated as independent branches and were unconnected. But in nineteenth century, Faraday and Maxwell along with others unified these independent branches of physics. They proved that all three phenomena are manifestations of electromagnetic field. The simplest example is the electric field of an electric charge that exerts a force an another charge when it comes in the range. An electric current produces a magnetic field that exerts a force on magnetic materials. Such fields can travel through space, independent of charge and magnet, in the form of electromagnetic wave. The best example of electromagnetic wave is light. Finally, Einstein unified space, time and gravity in his theory of relativity.

Quantum mechanics also unified two branches of science : physics and chemistry. In previous developments in physics, fundamental concepts were not different from those of everyday experience, such as particle, position, speed, mass, force, energy and even field. These concepts are referred as **'classical'**. The world of atoms cannot be described and understood with these concepts. For atoms and molecules, the ideas and concepts used in dealing with objects in day to day life is not sufficient. Thus, it needed new concepts to understand the properties of atoms. A group of scientists W. Heisenberg, E. Schrodinger, P.A.M. Dirac, W. Pauli, M. Born and Neils Bohr, conceived and formulated these new ideas in the beginning of 20th century. This new formulation, a branch of physics, was named as **quantum mechanics**.

12.1.1 Limitations of Classical Mechanics

The classical physics is complete and beautiful in explaining daily experiences where big bodies are involved. But it breaks down severely at subatomic level and failed to explain some of the phenomenon totally. The phenomenas which classical physics failed to explain are black body radiation, photoelectric effect, emission of X-rays, etc.

In classical physics, a body which is very small in comparison with other body is termed as **'particle'**. Whereas in quantum mechanics, the body which cannot be divided further is termed as **'particle'**. The other main difference is the quantized energy state. In classical physics, an oscillating body can assume any possible energy. On the contrary, quantum mechanics says that it can have only descrete non-zero energy.

12.1.2 Need of Quantum Mechanics

Classical mechanics successfully explained the motions of object which are observable directly or by instruments like microscope. But when classical mechanics is applied to the particles of atomic levels, it fails to explain actual behaviour. Therefore, the classical mechanics cannot be applied to atomic level, e.g. motion of an electron in an atom. The other phenomenas, which classical mechanics failed to explain, are black body radiation, photoelectric effect, emission of X-rays, etc. The above problems were solved by Max Planck in 1900 by the introduction of the formula

$$E = nh\upsilon \quad \ldots (1)$$

where, $n = 0, 1, 2, \ldots$,

h = Planck's constant = 6.63×10^{-34} J/s

This is known as **'quantum hypothesis'** and marked the beginning of modern physics. The whole microscopic world obeys the above formula.

12.2 WAVE PARTICLE DUALITY OF RADIATION AND MATTER

The wave and particle duality of radiation can be easily understood by knowing what is a wave and what is a particle.

Wave : A **wave** originates due to vibrations, and it is spread out over a large region of space. A wave cannot be located at a particular place and mass cannot be attached to a wave. Actually, a wave is a spread out disturbance specified by its amplitude a, frequency υ, wavelength λ, phase δ and intensity I.

Particle : A **particle** is located at some definite point and it has mass. It can move from place to place. A particle gains energy when it is accelerated and it loses energy when it is slowed down. A particle is characterized by mass m, velocity v, momentum p, and energy E.

Looking at the above facts, it might appear difficult to accept wave particle duality of radiation, i.e. radiation is a wave which is spread out over all space and that it is also a particle which is localised at a point in space. But this wave particle duality of radiation has to be accepted because, sometimes radiation has to be assigned the behaviour of a wave and at other times radiation is to be assigned particle nature as discussed below.

The phenomena of interference, diffraction and polarisation require the presence of two or more waves at the same time and at the same position. It is very clear that two or more particles cannot occupy the same position at the same time. So one has to conclude that radiation behaves like waves.

Spectra of black body radiation, production and scattering of X-rays, Compton effect, photoelectric effect, etc. could not be explained on wave nature of radiation. These phenomena established that radiant energy interacts with matter in the form of photons or quanta. With this, Planck's quantum theory came into being to conclude that radiation behaves like particles.

Thus, radiation sometimes behaves as a wave and at some other times as a particle. It is to be noted that radiation cannot simultaneously exhibit its wave and particle properties. Now, wave-particle duality of radiation is universally accepted.

12.3 DE BROGLIE'S CONCEPT OF MATTER WAVES

Discrete particle nature of matter is very well established and now it is known that matter is composed of atoms and that electrons, protons and neutrons are the building blocks of all types of atoms.

The electromagnetic wave theory explained the phenomena of interference, diffraction and polarisation. The quantum theory provided both qualitative and quantitative explanation of spectra of black body radiation, scattering of X-rays and Compton effect, emission of line spectra, photoelectric effect, etc. These two theories coupled together established wave-particle duality of radiation. But inspite of the success of this duality of radiation, the two fundamental postulates of Bohr's theory of atomic structure remained unexplained for a long time. In the mean time Einstein's mass-energy relation, $E = mc^2$, had been verified, establishing that radiation and mass are mutually convertible.

On this background, in 1924 De Broglie extended the idea of dual nature of radiation to matter and proposed that matter possesses particle as well as wave characteristics. **He believed that motion of electron within an atom is guided by a peculiar kind of waves called 'Pilot waves'.**

While adverting the concept of matter waves, De Broglie was guided by wave - particle duality of radiation and the way in which nature manifests herself.

While proposing wave nature for matter, particle nature of matter being beyond any doubt, **De Broglie put forth following arguments** :

- Nature manifests herself mainly as matter and radiation, and nature loves symmetry. So wave particle duality of radiation points to similar duality of matter.
- The principle of least action in mechanics and the principle of least time in optics imply similar conditions. This close analogy of these two principles from two different branches of physics, shows the probability of the behaviour of matter as a wave like entity under suitable circumstances. This close parallelism between mechanics and optics also indicates similarity between matter and radiation, i.e. if radiation has dual nature then matter must also have similar wave-particle duality.
- Bohr orbits are of definite size and are selected by quantum rules. The radii of these quantum orbits are proportional to the square of integral numbers

$\left[r_n = \dfrac{h^2 \epsilon_0}{\pi m e^2}, n^2 \right]$ and electrons stay in these orbits for a considerable time without radiating energy. Thus, the stable non-radiating orbits of electrons in an atom are governed by integer rules. Now the only phenomena involving integers in physics are those of interference and modes of vibration of a stretched string, and both of them imply wave motion. So there must be a latent relationship between Bohr orbits and integers associated with them. This latent relationship can be understood by considering the length of a Bohr orbit as consisting of integral number of wavelengths (equal to the principal quantum number of the orbit) of the waves associated with electrons moving in that orbit (See Fig. 12.1).

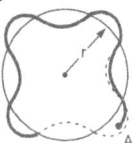

Fig. 12.1 : If the orbit length $2\pi r$ is an integral number of wavelengths, the wave will reinforce itself when it returns to the starting point A. In the case shown, $2\pi r = 4\lambda$

Now, the quantum condition for Bohr orbits is $mvr = n\dfrac{h}{2\pi}$. So the principal quantum number $n = \dfrac{2\pi mvr}{h}$, and **'De Broglie wavelength'** can be obtained by dividing the circumference $2\pi r$ of the nth permissible orbit by its principal quantum number n.

So,
$$\lambda = \dfrac{2\pi r}{n}$$

$$\lambda = \dfrac{2\pi r}{(2\pi mvr/h)}$$

$$\lambda = \dfrac{h}{mv}$$

This expression for De Broglie wavelength, agrees with the one he postulated, namely $\lambda = \dfrac{\text{Planck's constant}}{\text{momentum of the particle}}$, on the basis of his hypothesis of matter waves.

According to wave mechanics, electrons move around the nucleus as wave-packets which are formed in a somewhat similar manner as standing waves are formed.

12.3.1 Wavelength of Matter Waves or De Broglie Wavelength

By De Broglie's hypothesis, a moving material particle is associated with a wave whose wavelength is called **De Broglie wavelength** and it is given by the ratio of Planck's constant to the momentum of the particle.

$$\lambda = \dfrac{h}{p} = \dfrac{h}{mv}$$

where p is the momentum of the particle, m its mass, and v the velocity.

We can arrive at this expression for De Broglie wavelength, (1) by analogy with radiation and (2) by relativistic considerations.

12.3.2 De Broglie Wavelength by Analogy with Radiation

By Einstein's mass-energy relation, we have

$$E = mc^2 \qquad \ldots (1)$$

where E is the energy equivalent of mass m, and c is the velocity of light.

By Planck's quantum theory of radiation, the energy of a photon is given by

$$E = h\upsilon \qquad \ldots (2)$$

where h is Planck's constant and υ is the frequency of oscillations.

From equations (1) and (2), we get

$$h\upsilon = mc^2$$

But $\upsilon = \dfrac{c}{\lambda}$, (Since velocity = frequency × wavelength)

∴ $$h \cdot \dfrac{c}{\lambda} = mc^2$$

or $$\lambda = \dfrac{h}{mc} = \dfrac{h}{p} \qquad \ldots (3)$$

where p = mc is the momentum associated with the photon and λ is its wavelength.

12.3.3 De Broglie Wavelength in Terms of K.E. of the Particle

The momentum of a particle of mass m moving with velocity v is given by p = mv; and the De Broglie wavelength associated with the particle is given by

$$\lambda = \dfrac{h}{mv} = \dfrac{h}{p} \qquad \ldots (1)$$

The K.E. of the particle is given by

$$E = \dfrac{1}{2}mv^2$$

$$E = \dfrac{m^2 v^2}{2m} = \dfrac{p^2}{2m}$$

∴ $$p = \sqrt{2mE} \qquad \ldots (2)$$

From equations (1) and (2), we have

$$\lambda = \dfrac{h}{p} = \dfrac{h}{\sqrt{2mE}} \qquad \ldots (3)$$

In equation (3), De Broglie wavelength λ of a moving particle has been expressed in terms of K.E. of the particle.

12.3.4 De Broglie Wavelength for an Electron in Terms of Potential Difference

If an electron acquires velocity v on accelerating it through a potential difference of V volts, then the work done on the electron is eV, e being charge of the electron. This work is converted into kinetic energy of the electron,

i.e. $$E = \frac{1}{2}mv^2 = eV \qquad \ldots (1)$$

If e is in coulombs, m in kg, V in volts, then velocity v will be in m/s.

But $$\lambda = \frac{h}{\sqrt{2mE}}$$

From equation (1), $$\lambda = \frac{h}{\sqrt{2meV}} \qquad \ldots (2)$$

Ignoring relativistic correction, we can take $m = m_o$

$$\therefore \quad \lambda = \frac{h}{\sqrt{2 m_o eV}} \qquad \ldots (3)$$

Now, h, m_o and e are universal constants with values

$$h = 6.625 \times 10^{-34} \text{ J-s}$$
$$e = 1.6 \times 10^{-19} \text{ C}$$
$$m_o = 9.1 \times 10^{-31} \text{ kg}.$$

Substituting these values in equation (3), we get

$$\lambda = \frac{6.625 \times 10^{-34}}{\sqrt{2 \times 9.1 \times 10^{-31} \times 1.6 \times 10^{-19} \times V}} \text{ metres}$$

$$= \frac{12.27 \times 10^{-10}}{\sqrt{V}} \text{ metres}$$

$$\therefore \quad \lambda = \frac{12.27}{\sqrt{V}} \text{ A}° \qquad \ldots (4)$$

12.4 PROPERTIES OF MATTER WAVES

Matter waves are generated by a moving matter particle. If a particle of mass m moves with velocity v, then the wavelength of matter waves associated with it is given by $\lambda = \frac{h}{mv}$ and these waves travel with velocity $u = \frac{c^2}{v}$.

From this, properties of matter waves can be stated as :

- Lighter the particle, greater would be the wavelength of the matter waves associated with it. $\left(\lambda \propto \frac{1}{m}, \text{ for v constant}\right)$.

- Smaller the velocity of the particle, greater would be the wavelength of the matter waves. $\left(\lambda \propto \dfrac{1}{v}, \text{ for m constant}\right)$.
- For $v = \infty$, λ becomes zero and for $v = 0$, λ becomes infinity i.e. the wave becomes indeterminate when $v = 0$. This simply means that matter waves are produced by particles moving with finite velocities.
- Matter waves are different from electromagnetic waves, because matter waves can be produced by a moving particle which may be charged or uncharged, whereas electromagnetic waves are produced only by a moving charged particle. As the De Broglie wavelength $\lambda = \dfrac{h}{mv}$ is independent of charge, it is evident that matter waves are not electromagnetic waves.
- The velocity of matter waves depends on the velocity of the particle generating them $\left(u = \dfrac{c^2}{v}\right)$ and it is not constant.
- Matter waves travel faster than light, because the particle velocity v cannot exceed the velocity of light c. So the velocity of matter waves $u = \dfrac{c^2}{v}$ is greater than c.
- A wave is spread out in space and it cannot be localised at any point. So the wave nature of matter introduces a certain uncertainty in the position of the particle.

12.5 DAVISSON AND GERMER'S EXPERIMENT

This experiment on electron diffraction provided an experimental evidence for De Broglie's hypothesis of matter waves and also enabled experimental determination of De Broglie wavelength of matter waves associated with moving electrons.

Davisson and Germer directed a beam of electrons normally onto a nickel crystal and measured the intensity of the diffracted electrons in different directions by using an ionisation chamber detector. They found that quite a large number of scattered electrons passed through maximum and minimum intensity values, indicating that electron diffraction was taking place from the nickel crystal.

An ordinary nickel crystal is a face-centred cube with distance between nearest atoms in a unit cell equal to 3.51 A°. If the crystal is cut at right angles to a diagonal, the distance between two adjacent parallel planes of atoms in the triangular surface ABC (See Fig. 12.1) is found from X-ray crystallographic data to be 2.15 A°. Davisson - Germer used these planes for electron wave diffraction studies.

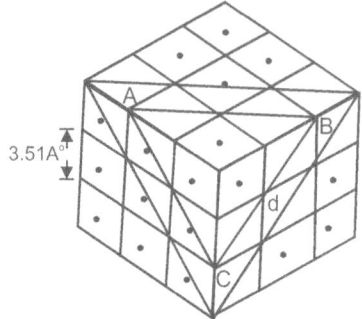

Fig. 12.2 : Face centred nickel crystal

Davisson - Germer's experimental arrangement for electron diffraction is shown in Fig. 12.3. They accelerated the electrons from a hot tungsten filament F by maintaining a steady potential difference between the filament and the plate P. Electrons then emerged through a fine opening 'O' in the plate in the form of a beam. The electron beam then fells normally on the surface of a nickel crystal N. The electrons were scattered in all directions and the intensity of scattered beam in any direction was measured by allowing the beam to enter the ionisation chamber I, set at the appropriate angle, and noting the deflection in a galvanometer connected to I.

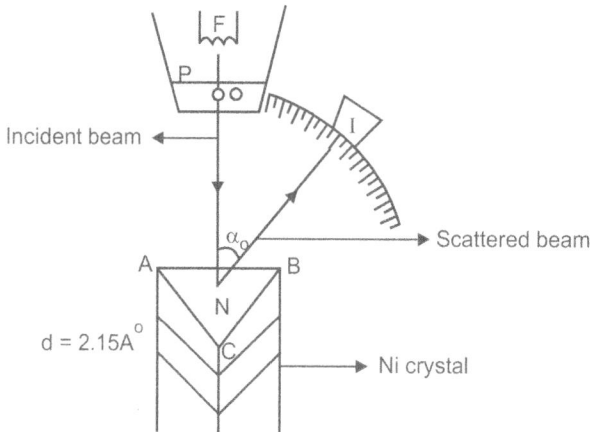

Fig. 12.3 : Davisson - Germer's experimental arrangement

The crystal is held in a fixed position throughout the measurements.

The incident beam is scattered in all directions and the angle between the incident beam and the scattered beam is taken as the scattering angle. A line perpendicular to the face of the crystal and passing through the point of incidence of the electron is taken as the axis about which the ionisation chamber I can be rotated. The intensity of scattered beam is determined as a function of the scattering angle, varying accelerating potential between filament and plate in steps, from 40 V to 68 V. The intensity of the scattered beam is then plotted as a function of the scattering angle for different accelerating voltages used. The experimental curves so obtained are as shown in Fig. 12.3.

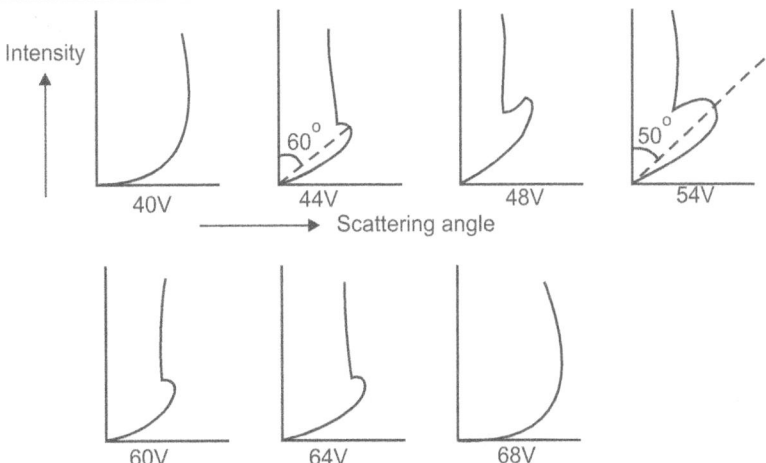

Fig. 12.4 : Davisson - Germer's experimental curves

It is seen from the experimental curves of Fig. 12.4 that the graph remains fairly smooth till the potential difference between the filament and the plate becomes 44 V, when a spur (bulging portion) appears on the curve at an angle of 60°. As this potential difference is increased, the length of the spur increases, till it reaches a maximum at an angle of 50° for 54 V electrons. With further increase in p.d. the spur decreases in length and finally disappears at an angle of about 40° for 68 V electrons.

The occurrence of a maximum spur at 50° for 54 V electrons can be explained as due to the constructive interference of the electron waves scattered in this direction from the regularly spaced parallel atomic planes in the crystal. These parallel atomic planes act as rulings of a diffraction grating. (See Fig. 12.5). The diffraction produced by electrons indicates that electrons have matter waves or De Broglie waves associated with them and experimental value of the wavelength of these electron waves can be found using Bragg's law equation $2 d' \sin \theta' = n\lambda'$ where d' is interplanar - separation of parallel atomic planes in the crystal, θ' is the glancing angle of incidence, λ' is the wavelength of incident waves and n is the order of reflection.

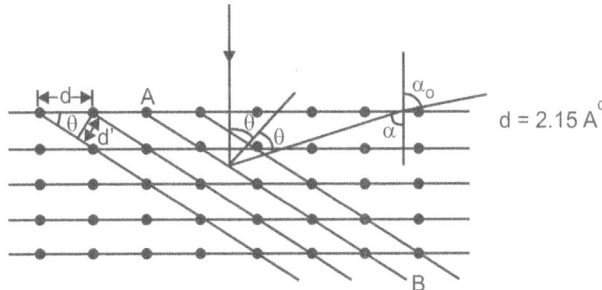

Fig. 12.5 : Electron scattering from parallel atomic planes in the crystal

Setting accelerating potential between the filament and the plate at 54 V, the intensity of diffracted electron beam was measured for different positions of the ionisation chamber. On plotting intensity versus α_o, a curve as shown in Fig. 12.6 was obtained, showing a pronounced scattering in the direction of $\alpha_o = 50°$.

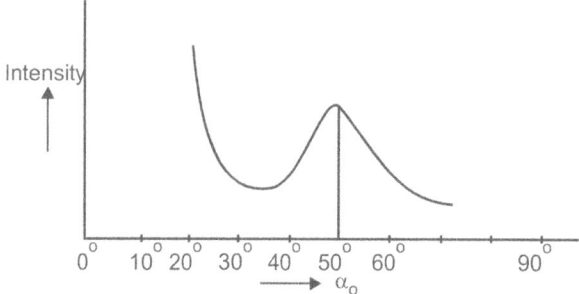

Fig. 12.6 : Intensity of scattered beam as a function of scattering angle for 54 V electron

The pronounced scattering at 50° for 54 V electrons can be understood as follows. As in Fig. 12.6, the electron beam incident normally on the crystal enters it without deviation, but the reflected beam, say from atomic plane AB, is incident obliquely on the crystal surface and is refracted on emergence from the crystal.

The experiment is performed in vacuum. So if λ is the wavelength in vacuum of the electron waves incident on the crystal and λ' their wavelength in the crystal, then the refractive index μ of the crystal is given by

$$\mu = \frac{\lambda}{\lambda'}$$

$$= \frac{\sin \alpha_0}{\sin \alpha} = \frac{\sin \alpha_0}{\sin 2\theta} \quad \ldots (1)$$

The waves in the crystal should satisfy Bragg's law for constructive interference. Using this law, we get from Fig. 12.6 for first order reflection,

$$2 d' \sin (90 - \theta) = 1 \cdot \lambda' \quad (\theta' = 90 - \theta)$$

$$\therefore \quad \lambda' = 2 d' \cos \theta \quad \ldots (2)$$

But from equation (1),

$$\lambda = \mu \lambda' \quad \ldots (3)$$

From equations (2) and (3), we have

$$\lambda = \mu (2 d' \cos \theta) \quad \ldots (4)$$

Substituting for μ from equation (1) in equation (4), we get

$$\lambda = \frac{\sin \alpha_0}{\sin 2\theta} \times 2 d' \cos \theta$$

$$= \frac{d'}{\sin \theta} \cdot \sin \alpha_0 \quad \ldots (5)$$

From Fig. 12.6, we see that $\frac{d'}{d} = \sin \theta$

∴ Equation (5) becomes

$$\lambda = d \sin \alpha_0$$

Now, for the nickel crystal using d = 2.15 A° and the experimental value of $\alpha_0 = 50°$

∴ The experimental value of the DeBroglie wavelength for a 54 V electron is

$$\lambda_{expt.} = d \sin \alpha_0$$
$$= 2.15 \times \sin 50° = 1.65 \text{ A°}$$

The theoretical value of the DeBroglie wavelength for these electrons can be found by using the equation $\lambda = \dfrac{12.27}{\sqrt{V}}$ A°, taking V = 54 volts.

Thus, $\lambda_{Theo.} = \dfrac{12.27}{\sqrt{54}}$ A° = 1.67 A°

This excellent agreement between the experimental and theoretical value of DeBroglie wavelength for 54 V electrons proves that DeBroglie's hypothesis of matter waves is confirmed experimentally by Davisson - Germer's experiment on electron diffraction.

SOLVED EXAMPLES

Example 12.1 : What is the De Broglie wavelength of an electron when accelerated through a p.d. of 10,000 volts ?

Data : V = 10,000 volts

Formula : $\lambda = \dfrac{12.27}{\sqrt{V}}$ A°

Solution :

$$\lambda = \dfrac{12.27}{\sqrt{10,000}}$$
$$= \boxed{0.1227 \text{ A°}}$$

Example 12.2 : Compute the wavelength of the De Broglie waves associated with a proton moving with 5 % of the velocity of light. Proton has 1836 times the mass of one electron.

Data : m = 1836 × 9.1 × 10^{-31} kg, h = 6.63 × 10^{-34} Joule-sec.,

$v = \dfrac{5}{100} \times 3 \times 10^8$ m/sec.

Formula : $\lambda = h/mv$

Solution :

$$\lambda = \dfrac{6.63 \times 10^{-34}}{1836 \times 9.1 \times 10^{-31} \times \dfrac{5}{100} \times 3 \times 10^8}$$

$$= \boxed{2.65 \times 10^{-14} \text{ m}}$$

Example 12.3 : Compute the kinetic energy and velocity of an electron in terms of those of a neutron, when their De Broglie wavelengths are equal to 1 A°. Take neutron mass as 1835 times the mass of electron.

Data : $\lambda_n = \lambda_e = 1$ A°; $m_n = 1835 \, m_e$

Formula: $$\lambda = \frac{h}{mv} = \frac{h}{\sqrt{2mE}}$$

Solution:

For electron, $\lambda_e = \dfrac{h}{m_e v_e} = \dfrac{h}{\sqrt{2 m_e E_e}}$

For neutron, $\lambda_n = \dfrac{h}{m_n v_n} = \dfrac{h}{\sqrt{2 m_n E_n}}$

Taking ratios $\dfrac{\lambda_n}{\lambda_e} = \dfrac{m_n v_n}{m_e v_e} = 1$ (given)

We have, $\dfrac{v_n}{v_e} = \dfrac{m_e}{m_n} = \dfrac{1}{1835}$

or $v_e = 1835\, v_n$

and $\sqrt{\dfrac{2 m_n E_n}{2 m_e E_e}} = 1$

∴ $\dfrac{E_n}{E_e} = \dfrac{m_e}{m_n} = \dfrac{1}{1835}$

or $\boxed{E_e = 1835\, E_n}$

Example 12.4: De Broglie wavelength of electrons in a monoenergetic beam is 7.2×10^{-11} metres. Calculate the momentum and energy of electrons in the beam in electron volts.

Data: $\lambda = 7.2 \times 10^{-11}$ m; $h = 6.6 \times 10^{-34}$ J-s

Formulae: $p = \dfrac{h}{\lambda}$, $E = \dfrac{p^2}{2m}$

Solution:

$p = \dfrac{6.6 \times 10^{-34}}{7.2 \times 10^{-11}}$

$= \boxed{0.916 \times 10^{-23} \text{ kg-m/sec}}$

$E = \dfrac{(0.916 \times 10^{-23})^2}{2 \times 9.1 \times 10^{-31}}$ J

$= 0.0461 \times 10^{-15}$ J

$= \dfrac{0.0461 \times 10^{-15}}{1.6 \times 10^{-19}}$ eV

$= 0.0289 \times 10^4$ eV $= \boxed{289 \text{ eV}}$

Example 12.5 : What is the De Broglie wavelength associated with a 5000 kg car having a constant speed of 20 m/sec. ?

Data : m = 5000 kg, h = 6.6×10^{-34} J-sec, v = 20 m/sec.

Formula : $\lambda = \dfrac{h}{mv}$

Solution :

$$\lambda = \dfrac{6.6 \times 10^{-34}}{5000 \times 20}$$

$$= \boxed{6.6 \times 10^{-39} \text{ m}}$$

As can be seen, the De Broglie wave associated with a macroscopic body is too small to be significant.

Example 12.6 : A beam of 10 kV electrons is passed through a thin metallic sheet whose interplanar spacing is 0.55 A°. Calculate the angle of deviation of the first-order diffraction maximum.

Data : V = 10 kV = 10×10^3 volts, d = 0.55 A° = 0.55×10^{-10} m, n = 1

Formulae : $\lambda = \dfrac{12.27}{\sqrt{V}}$ A° and $2d \sin\theta = n\lambda$

Solution :

$$\lambda = \dfrac{12.27}{\sqrt{V}} \text{ A°} = \dfrac{12.27}{\sqrt{10^4}} = 0.1227 \text{ A°}$$

$$2d \sin\theta = n\lambda$$

Substituting for n, λ and d,

$$\sin\theta = \dfrac{0.1227 \times 10^{-10}}{2 \times 0.55 \times 10^{-10}} = 0.111545$$

$$\theta = \sin^{-1}(0.111545) = \boxed{6.40° = 6°24'}$$

Example 12.7 : The spacing between the atoms of a certain crystal is 1.2 A°. At what angle will the first-order Bragg reflection occur for thermal neutrons ?

Kinetic energy = 0.025 eV, Mass of neutron is 1.67×10^{-27} kg

Data : d = 1.2 A°, n = 1, E = 0.025 eV = $0.025 \times 1.6 \times 10^{-19}$ J

Formulae : $\lambda = \dfrac{h}{\sqrt{2mE}}$ and $2d \sin\theta = n\lambda$

Solution :

$$\lambda = \dfrac{6.6 \times 10^{-34}}{\sqrt{2 \times 1.67 \times 10^{-27} \times 0.025 \times 1.6 \times 10^{-19}}}$$

$$= 18.057 \times 10^{-11} \text{ m} = 1.8057 \text{ A°}$$

ENGG. PHYSICS (F.Y. B. TECH. B.V.)   QUANTUM MECHANICS

$$\sin\theta = \frac{\lambda}{2d} = \frac{1.8057 \times 10^{-11}}{2 \times 1.2 \times 10^{-11}}$$

$$= 0.7524$$

$$\theta = \sin^{-1}(0.7524)$$

$$= \boxed{48.79° = 48°48'}$$

Example 12.8 : Find the K.E. of a neutron which has a wavelength of 3 A°. At what angle will such a neutron undergo first-order Bragg reflection from a calcite crystal for which the grating space is 3.036 A° ? Mass of neutron is 1.67×10^{-27} kg.

Data : $\lambda = 3$ A° $= 3 \times 10^{-10}$ m, n = 1, d = 3.036 A° = 3.036×10^{-10} m, m = 1.67×10^{-27} kg

Formulae : (i) $\lambda = \dfrac{h}{\sqrt{2mE}}$

          (ii) $2d\sin\theta = n\lambda$

Solution :

(i) $$E = \frac{h^2}{2m\lambda^2}$$

$$= \frac{(6.6 \times 10^{-34})^2}{2 \times 1.67 \times 10^{-27} \times (3 \times 10^{-10})^2}$$

$$= \boxed{1.449 \times 10^{-21} \text{ J}}$$

(ii) $$\sin\theta = \frac{\lambda}{2d} = \frac{3 \times 10^{-10}}{2 \times 3.036 \times 10^{-10}} = 0.49407$$

$$\theta = \sin^{-1}(0.49407)$$

$$= \boxed{29.6085° = 29°36'}$$

Example 12.9 : An electron initially at rest is accelerated through a p.d. of 5000 V. Compute (i) the momentum, (ii) the De Broglie wavelength and (iii) the wave number of the electron. Also calculate the Bragg angle for its first-order reflection from (111) planes of nickel which are 2.04 A° apart.

Data : V = 5000 V, n = 1, d = 2.04 A° = 2.04×10^{-11} m

Formulae : (i) $p = \sqrt{2meV}$, (ii) $\lambda = \dfrac{12.27}{\sqrt{V}}$ A°, (iii) $\bar{\upsilon} = \dfrac{1}{\lambda}$, (iv) $2d\sin\theta = n\lambda$

Solution :

(i) $$p = \sqrt{2 \times 9.1 \times 10^{-31} \times 1.6 \times 10^{-19} \times 5000}$$

$$= \boxed{3.815 \times 10^{-23} \text{ kg - m/sec}}$$

(ii) $$\lambda = \frac{12.27}{\sqrt{5000}} \text{ A°}$$

$$= 0.17352 \text{ A°} = \boxed{0.17352 \times 10^{-10} \text{ m}}$$

(iii) Wave number, $\bar{\upsilon} = \dfrac{1}{\lambda} = \boxed{5.76 \times 10^{10} \text{ m}}$

(iv) $2d \sin \theta = n\lambda$

$$\sin \theta = \dfrac{\lambda}{2d} = \dfrac{0.17352 \times 10^{-10}}{2 \times 2.04 \times 10^{-10}}$$

$$= 0.0425$$

$$\theta = \sin^{-1}(0.0425)$$

$$= \boxed{2.43° = 2°26'}$$

Example 12.10 : Electrons from a heated filament accelerated by a p.d. of 10 kV are passed through a thin film of a metal for which the atomic spacing is 0.55 A. What is the angle of deviation of the first-order maximum ?

Solution :

We have the relation

$$\lambda = \dfrac{h}{mv} = \dfrac{h}{\sqrt{2meV}} = \dfrac{12.27}{\sqrt{V}} \text{ A}°$$

∴ $\lambda = \dfrac{12.27}{\sqrt{10 \times 10^3}}$

$$= \boxed{0.122 \text{ A}°}$$

Now, from Bragg's law, $2d \sin \theta = n\lambda$

Here, $n = 1$ $\sin \theta = \dfrac{n\lambda}{2d} = \dfrac{1 \times 0.122}{2 \times 0.55} = 0.111$

$$\boxed{\theta = 6° 22'}$$

Hence, required angle of deviation for the first-order maximum is 6° 22'.

Example 12.11 : In an experiment, the wavelength of a photon is measured to an accuracy of one part per million. What is the uncertainty Δx in a simultaneous measurement of the position of the photon having a wavelength of 6000 A° ?

Data : $\lambda = 6000 \text{ A}° = 6000 \times 10^{-10}$ m, $h = 6.6 \times 10^{-34}$ J-sec

$$\dfrac{\Delta \lambda}{\lambda} = \dfrac{1}{10^6}$$

Formulae : $\Delta p = \dfrac{h}{\Delta \lambda}$, $\Delta x \cdot \Delta p \approx h$

Solution :

$$\Delta p = \dfrac{6.6 \times 10^{-34}}{6000 \times 10^{-16}}$$

$$= 1.1 \times 10^{-21} \text{ kg-m/sec}$$

$$\Delta x = \dfrac{h}{\Delta p} = \dfrac{6.6 \times 10^{-34}}{1.1 \times 10^{-21}} = \boxed{6 \times 10^{-13} \text{ m}}$$

Example 12.12 : In order to locate the electron in an atom within a distance of 5×10^{-12} m using electromagnetic waves, the wavelength must be of the same order. Calculate the energy and momentum of the photon. What is the corresponding uncertainty in its momentum ?

Data : $\lambda = \Delta x = 5 \times 10^{-12}$ m

Formulae : $p = \dfrac{h}{\lambda}$, $E = \dfrac{hc}{\lambda}$, $\Delta p_x = \dfrac{h}{\Delta x}$

Solution :

$$p = \dfrac{6.6 \times 10^{-34}}{5 \times 10^{-12}} = 1.32 \times 10^{-22} \text{ kg-m/sec}$$

$$E = \dfrac{6.6 \times 10^{-34} \times 3 \times 10^{8}}{5 \times 10^{-12}} = 3.96 \times 10^{-14} \text{ J}$$

$$\Delta p_x = \dfrac{6.6 \times 10^{-34}}{5 \times 10^{-12}} = \boxed{1.32 \times 10^{-22} \text{ kg-m/sec}}$$

Example 12.13 : Compute the uncertainty in the location of a 2 gram mass moving with a speed of 1.5 m/sec. and the minimum uncertainty in the location of an electron moving with a speed of 0.5×10^{8} m/sec. Given, $\Delta p = 10^{-3}$ p.

Data : $v_e = 0.5 \times 10^{8}$ m/sec, $\Delta p = 10^{-3}$ p, m = 2 grams = 2×10^{-3} kg,

v for the body = 1.5 m/sec

Formula : $\Delta x \, \Delta p = h$

Solution :

(i) For the body,

$$\Delta p = 10^{-3} p = 10^{-3} (mv)$$

$$\Delta x \cdot \Delta p = h$$

$$\Delta x = \dfrac{h}{\Delta p} = \dfrac{6.6 \times 10^{-34}}{10^{-3} \times 2 \times 1.5 \times 10^{-3}}$$

$$= \boxed{2.2 \times 10^{-28} \text{ m}}$$

(ii) For the electron,

$$\Delta x = \dfrac{6.6 \times 10^{-34}}{10^{-3} \times 9.1 \times 10^{-31} \times 0.5 \times 10^{8}}$$

$$= \boxed{1.45 \times 10^{-8} \text{ m}}$$

It can be seen that the uncertainty associated with a microscopic body is very large and therefore, it plays a significant role in measurements.

Example 12.14 : Assume that the uncertainty in the location of a particle is equal to its De Broglie wavelength. Show that the uncertainty in its velocity is equal to its velocity.

Data : $\Delta x = \lambda$

Formula : $\Delta x \cdot \Delta p = h$

Solution :

$$\Delta x \cdot m \Delta v_x = h$$

$$\Delta v_x = \frac{h}{\Delta x \cdot m} = \frac{h}{m \lambda}$$

Using
$$\lambda = \frac{h}{mv}$$

we have
$$\Delta v_x = \frac{h m v}{mh} = v$$

Example 12.15 : An electron is confined to a box of length 1 A°. Calculate the minimum uncertainty in its velocity, given mass of electron = 9.1×10^{-31} kg, h = 6.6×10^{-34} J-sec.

Data : $\Delta x = 1$ A° = 10^{-10} m, h = 6.6×10^{-34} J-sec, m = 9.1×10^{-31} kg

Formula : $\Delta x \, \Delta p_x = h$

Solution :

$$(\Delta x)_{max} (\Delta p_x)_{min} = h$$

$$(\Delta x)_{max} (\Delta v)_{min} = h$$

$$(\Delta v)_{min} = \frac{h}{m \, \Delta x}$$

$$= \frac{6.6 \times 10^{-34}}{9.1 \times 10^{-31} \times 10^{-10}}$$

$$= \boxed{0.725 \times 10^7 \text{ m/sec.}}$$

This is comparable to the speed of the electron and is therefore very large.

Example 12.16 : What accelerating potential would be required for a proton with zero velocity to acquire a velocity corresponding to De Broglie wavelength of 10^{-14} m ?

Data : h = 6.62×10^{-34} J-sec, m = 1.67×10^{-27} kg, e = 1.6×10^{-19} C

Formula : $V = \dfrac{h^2}{2 \, me\lambda^2}$

Solution :

$$V = \frac{(6.62 \times 10^{-34})^2}{2 \times 1.67 \times 10^{-27} \times 1.6 \times 10^{-19} \times (10^{-14})^2}$$

$$= 8.2 \times 10^6 \text{ volts} = \boxed{8.2 \text{ M volts}}$$

Example 12.17 : Find De Broglie wavelength of 10 keV electrons.

Data : E = 10 keV = $10 \times 10^3 \times 1.6 \times 10^{-19}$ J

Formula : $\lambda = \dfrac{h}{\sqrt{2mE}}$

Solution :

$$\lambda = \frac{6.6 \times 10^{-34}}{\sqrt{2 \times 9.1 \times 10^{-31} \times 10^4 \times 1.6 \times 10^{-19}}}$$

$$= 1.22 \times 10^{-11} \text{ m} = \boxed{0.122 \text{ A}°}$$

Example 12.18 : Calculate the minimum uncertainty in the velocity of an electron confined to a box of length 10 A°.

Data : $L = 10 \text{ A}° = 10 \times 10^{-10}$ m

Formula : $\Delta x \cdot \Delta p_x = h$

Solution :

$$(\Delta x)_{max} (\Delta p_x)_{min} = h$$

i.e. $(\Delta x)_{max} \, m (\Delta v_x)_{min} = h$

$$\Delta v_x = \frac{h}{m \cdot (\Delta x)_{max}}$$

$$= \frac{6.6 \times 10^{-34}}{9.1 \times 10^{-31} \times 10^{-9}}$$

$$= \boxed{0.725 \times 10^6 \text{ m/sec.}}$$

Example 12.19 : Electrons moving with a speed of 7.3×10^7 m/sec have a wavelength of 0.1 A°. Calculate the Planck's constant.

Data : $\lambda = 0.1 \text{ A}° = 0.1 \times 10^{-10}$ m

$v = 7.3 \times 10^7$ m/sec.

Formula : $h = \lambda \cdot m v$

Solution :

$$h = 0.1 \times 10^{-10} \times 9.1 \times 10^{-31} \times 7.3 \times 10^7$$

$$= \boxed{6.643 \times 10^{-34} \text{ J-sec.}}$$

Example 12.20 : Calculate the wavelength of an electron of energy 291 eV.

Data : $E = 291 \text{ eV} = 291 \times 1.6 \times 10^{-19}$ J

Formula : $\lambda = \dfrac{h}{\sqrt{2 m E}}$

Solution :

$$\lambda = \frac{6.6 \times 10^{-34}}{\sqrt{2 \times 9.1 \times 10^{-31} \times 291 \times 1.6 \times 10^{-19}}}$$

$$= \boxed{0.717 \text{ A}°}$$

Example 12.21 : An electron has a speed of 600 m/sec with an accuracy of 0.005 %. Calculate the uncertainty with which we can locate the position of the electron.

Data :
$$v = 600 \text{ m/sec}$$
$$\Delta v = 0.005 \text{ \% of } v$$
$$= \frac{0.005}{100} \times 600 \text{ m/sec}$$

Formula : $\Delta x \cdot \Delta p = h$

Solution :
$$\Delta x = \frac{h}{\Delta p}$$
$$= \frac{h}{m \, \Delta v} = \frac{6.6 \times 10^{-34}}{9.1 \times 10^{-31}} \times \frac{0.005}{100} \times 600$$
$$= \boxed{0.024 \text{ m}}$$

Example 12.22 : Proton and deuteron are accelerated by the same potential. Compare their De Broglie wavelengths. Assume mass of deuterium to be twice the mass of a proton.

Data : $m_d = 2 m_p$

Formula : $\lambda = \dfrac{h}{\sqrt{2 \, meV}}$

Solution :

For proton, $\lambda_p = \dfrac{h}{\sqrt{2 \, m_p \, eV}}$

For deuteron, $\lambda_d = \dfrac{h}{\sqrt{2 \, m_d eV}} = \dfrac{h}{\sqrt{4 \, m_p eV}}$

$$\frac{\lambda_p}{\lambda_d} = \frac{h/\sqrt{2 \, m_p \, eV}}{h/\sqrt{4 \, m_p \, eV}} = \sqrt{2}$$

∴ $\boxed{\lambda_p : \lambda_d = \sqrt{2} : 1}$

Example 12.23 : Find the kinetic energy of a neutron in eV, whose De-Broglie wavelength is 1 A° ($M_n = 1.67 \times 10^{-27}$ kg).

Solution :

Given :
$$\lambda_n = 1 \text{ A°} = 1 \times 10^{-10} \text{ m}$$
$$M_n = 1.67 \times 10^{-27} \text{ kg}$$
$$h = 6.63 \times 10^{-34} \text{ J.sec}$$
$$\lambda = \frac{h}{\sqrt{2mE}}$$

∴ $E = \dfrac{h^2}{2m\lambda^2} = \dfrac{(6.63 \times 10^{-34})^2}{2 \times 1.67 \times 10^{-27} \times (1 \times 10^{-10})^2}$

∴ $E = 1.3160 \times 10^{-20}$ J

$\boxed{E = 8.225 \times 10^{-2} \text{ eV}}$

Example 12.24 : Find the De-Broglie wavelength of an electron accelerated through a potential difference of 100 volts.

Data : $V = 100$ volts

Formula : $\lambda = \dfrac{12.27}{\sqrt{V}}$ A°

Solution :

$\lambda = \dfrac{12.27}{\sqrt{100}} = \boxed{1.227 \text{ A°}}$

12.6 CONCEPT OF WAVE FUNCTION

A wave motion appears in almost all branches of physics. A wave motion is defined as a periodic disturbance travelling with finite velocity through a medium or space. The simplest form of vibration is simple harmonic motion (S.H.M.) and a particle executing S.H.M. acts as a source which radiates waves. The wave motion provides a way for energy and momentum to move from one place to another without material particles making that journey. The waves can be classified according to their broad physical properties into mainly three categories :

(a) Electromagnetic waves which need not require any medium to propagate.

(b) Matter waves which give the probability amplitude of finding a particle at a given position and time.

(c) **Mechanical Waves :** The mechanical waves are simplest one to understand because they are produced by some sort of mechanical vibrations which we can see.

When a mechanical wave passes through a medium, the medium particles perform an S.H.M. given by equation

$y = A \cos \omega t$ ... (1)

where A is the amplitude of the oscillation and $\omega = 2\pi\upsilon$, where υ is the frequency.

This equation is applicable to all individual particles affected by the wave. Suppose the wave is progressing forward with velocity v. If P is the origin of the wave, then a particle at Q at a distance x from P will receive the wave x/v sec later than P did.

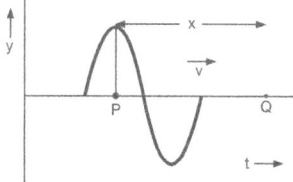

Fig. 12.7 : Progressive wave moving with velocity v

Hence, its displacement at time t and distance x from the origin will be

$$y = A \cos \omega \left(t - \frac{x}{v}\right) \quad \ldots (2)$$

The wave equation of such a wave is

$$\frac{d^2y}{dt^2} = v^2 \frac{d^2y}{dx^2} \quad \ldots (3)$$

The solution of equation (3) is given by

$$y = A e^{-i\omega(t - x/v)} \quad \ldots (4)$$

In a string we can represent the wave disturbance by the transverse displacement of y. Similarly, for light waves the field vectors E and B vary in space and time, for sound waves, pressure P varies in space and time. In the same way, for matter waves, the wave function ψ varies in space and time. So ψ in wave mechanics is analogous to electric field E in electromagnetic waves or to pressure P in the sound waves. However, ψ itself unlike E and P has no direct physical significance, but gives a measure of the probability of finding a particle at a particular position. Hence, it is called **probability amplitude**.

12.7 PHYSICAL SIGNIFICANCE OF THE WAVE FUNCTION ψ

Schroedinger interpreted ψ in terms of charge density. If A is the amplitude of an electromagnetic wave, then the energy per unit volume, i.e. energy density is equal to A^2. Also, the photon energy $h\upsilon$ is constant. So the number of photons per unit volume, i.e. the photon density is equal to $\frac{A^2}{h\upsilon}$, and it is proportional to the amplitude square.

Similarly, if ψ is the amplitude of matter waves at any point in space, the particle density at that point may be taken as proportional to $|\psi|^2$. So $|\psi|^2$ is a measure of particle density and on multiplying this by the charge of the particle, we shall get the charge density. Thus, $|\psi|^2$ is a measure of **'charge density'**.

According to Max Born, the value of $|\psi|^2$ at a point at a given time is related to the probability of finding the body described by its wave function ψ at that point at that instant. A large value of $|\psi|^2$ means a strong possibility of the presence of the body, while a small value of $|\psi|^2$ means a slight possibility of its presence. As long as $|\psi|^2$ is not actually zero somewhere, there is a definite chance, however small, of detecting the body there.

Although the wave function ψ of a particle is spread out in space, this does not mean that the particle itself is also thus spread out. When an experiment is performed to detect a particle, an electron for instance, a whole electron is either found at a certain place and time, or it is not. There is nothing like 20 % of an electron. However, it is certainly possible that there is 20 % chance that the electron be found at that place and time, and it's likelihood that is specified by $|\psi|^2$ or ψψ*, ψ* being the complex conjugate of ψ.

$|\psi|^2$ or $\psi\psi^*$ is taken as the probability density, i.e. the probability of finding the particle in unit volume. So the probability of the particle being present in a volume element dx · dy · dz is $|\psi|^2$ dx dy dz. Then, the wave function ψ is called the **'probability density amplitude'**.

Since the particle is certainly to be found somewhere in space, we must have,

$$\iiint |\psi|^2 \, dx \, dy \, dz = 1 \qquad \ldots (1)$$

the triple integral extending over all possible values of x, y, z.

A function ψ satisfying this relation is called a **'normalised wave function'** and equation (1) is known as the **'normalisation condition'**. Thus, ψ has to be a normalisable function.

Besides being normalisable, ψ must also satisfy the following conditions:

(1) ψ must be a single valued function, because ψ is related to the probability of finding the particle at a given place and time, and the probability can have only one value at a given point and time.

(2) ψ must be finite, because the particle exists somewhere in space, and so integral over all space must be finite.

(3) ψ and its derivatives $\frac{\partial \psi}{\partial x}, \frac{\partial \psi}{\partial y}, \frac{\partial \psi}{\partial z}$ must be continuous everywhere in the region where ψ is defined.

12.8 SCHROEDINGER'S WAVE EQUATION

Schroedinger started with De Broglie's idea of matter waves and developed it into a mathematical theory known as **'wave mechanics'**. Schroedinger's wave equation is the mathematical representation of matter waves associated with a moving particle. There are two types of Schroedinger's wave equations:

(1) Schroedinger's time independent wave equation
(2) Schroedinger's time dependent wave equation.

12.8.1 Schroedinger's Time Independent Wave Equation

According to De Broglie's theory, a particle of mass m moving with a velocity v has a wave system of some kind associated with it, and its wavelength is given by $\lambda = \frac{h}{mv}$. The waves are produced only when something oscillates. Though we do not know the quantity that vibrates to produce the matter waves, but we can indicate that quantity by ψ. The periodic changes in ψ produce the wave system associated with the particle, just as the periodic changes in the displacement y of a string produce a wave system along the string. In quantum mechanics, ψ corresponds to the displacement y of wave motion in a string. However, ψ, unlike y, is not itself a measurable quantity and it may be complex.

Consider a system of stationary waves associated with a particle. Let (x, y, z) be the coordinates of the particle and let ψ denote the wave displacement of matter waves at time t.

By analogy with the wave equation

$$\frac{d^2 y}{dt^2} = v^2 \frac{d^2 y}{dx^2}$$ of a two-dimensional wave (in xy plane), the wave equation for a three-dimensional wave with wave velocity u can be written as

$$\frac{\partial^2 \psi}{\partial t^2} = u^2 \left(\frac{\partial^2 \psi}{\partial x^2} + \frac{\partial^2 \psi}{\partial y^2} + \frac{\partial^2 \psi}{\partial z^2} \right)$$

$$\frac{\partial^2 \psi}{\partial t^2} = u^2 \nabla^2 \psi \qquad \ldots (1)$$

where $\nabla^2 = \frac{\partial^2}{\partial x^2} + \frac{\partial^2}{\partial y^2} + \frac{\partial^2}{\partial z^2}$ is the **'Laplacian operator'**.

The solution of equation (1) is

$$\psi(x, y, z, t) = \psi_0(x, y, z) e^{-i\omega t} \qquad \ldots (2)$$

where $\psi_0(x, y, z)$ represents the amplitude of the wave at the point considered.

The position vector of a point whose Cartesian coordinates are (x, y, z) is given by

$$\vec{r} = x\hat{i} + y\hat{j} + z\hat{k}$$

$\hat{i}, \hat{j}, \hat{k}$ being unit vectors along the axes. So equation (2) can be written as

$$\psi(\vec{r}, t) = \psi_0(\vec{r}) e^{-i\omega t} \qquad \ldots (3)$$

Differentiating equation (3) twice with respect to time t, we get

$$\frac{\partial \psi}{\partial t} = -i\omega \psi_0(r) e^{-i\omega t}$$

and

$$\frac{\partial^2 \psi}{\partial t^2} = (-i\omega)^2 \psi_0(\vec{r}) e^{-i\omega t} = -\omega^2 \psi \qquad \ldots (4)$$

From equations (1) and (4), we get

$$u^2 \nabla^2 \psi = -\omega^2 \psi$$

$$\therefore \quad \nabla^2 \psi + \frac{\omega^2}{u^2} \psi = 0 \qquad \ldots (5)$$

But $\omega = 2\pi \nu$, and $u = \nu \lambda$

∴ Equation (5) becomes

$$\nabla^2 \psi + \frac{4\pi^2}{\lambda^2} \psi = 0 \qquad \ldots (6)$$

The De Broglie wavelength of the waves associated with the particle is given by

$$\lambda = \frac{h}{mv} = \frac{h}{p} \qquad \ldots (7)$$

Substituting equation (7) in (6), we get

$$\nabla^2 \psi + \frac{4\pi^2 p^2}{h^2} \psi = 0 \qquad \ldots (8)$$

The total energy E of the particle is the sum of it's K.E. $= \frac{1}{2}mv^2$ and potential energy V.

$$\therefore \quad E = \frac{1}{2}mv^2 + V$$

$$E = \frac{p^2}{2m} + V$$

This gives
$$p^2 = 2m(E-V) \quad \ldots (9)$$

Substituting equation (9) in (8), we get

$$\nabla^2 \psi + \frac{8\pi^2 m(E-V)}{h^2} \psi = 0 \quad \ldots (10)$$

Equation (10) is called **'Schroedinger's time independent wave equation'**.

Taking $H = \frac{h}{2\pi}$, equation (10) becomes

$$\nabla^2 \psi + \frac{2m(E-V)}{H^2} \psi = 0 \quad \ldots (11)$$

12.8.2 Schroedinger's Time Dependent Wave Equation

Schroedinger's time independent wave equation is

$$\nabla^2 \psi + \frac{8\pi^2 m}{h^2}(E-V)\psi = 0 \quad \ldots (1)$$

The time dependent wave equation is obtained by eliminating E from the time independent equation.

Consider a system of stationary waves associated with a particle. Let (x, y, z) be the coordinates of the particle and let ψ denote the wave displacement of the matter waves at time t. If u be the wave velocity, then the equation for a three-dimensional wave motion can be written as,

$$\frac{\partial^2 \psi}{\partial t^2} = u^2 \left(\frac{\partial^2 \psi}{\partial x^2} + \frac{\partial^2 \psi}{\partial y^2} + \frac{\partial^2 \psi}{\partial z^2} \right) = u^2 \nabla^2 \psi \quad \ldots (2)$$

where $\nabla^2 = \frac{\partial^2}{\partial x^2} + \frac{\partial^2}{\partial y^2} + \frac{\partial^2}{\partial z^2}$ is the **'Laplacian operator'**

The solution of equation (2) is

$$\psi(x, y, z, t) = \psi_0(x, y, z) e^{-i\omega t} = \psi_0(\vec{r}) e^{-i\omega t} \quad \ldots (3)$$

where $\psi_0(x, y, z)$ is the amplitude of the wave at the point considered.

Differentiating equation (3) with respect to time t, we get

$$\frac{\partial \psi}{\partial t} = (-i\omega) \psi_0(\vec{r}) e^{-i\omega t} = -i\omega \psi \quad \ldots (4)$$

Now, $\omega = 2\pi\upsilon$ and $E = h\upsilon$ or $\upsilon = \dfrac{E}{h}$

$$\therefore \quad \omega = \dfrac{2\pi E}{h}$$

Putting this value of ω in equation (4), we get

$$\dfrac{\partial \psi}{\partial t} = -i\,\dfrac{2\pi E}{h}\,\psi \qquad \ldots (5)$$

Multiplying both sides of equation (5) by i,

$$i\dfrac{\partial \psi}{\partial t} = i^2 \dfrac{2\pi}{h} E\psi$$

$$\therefore \quad E\psi = i\dfrac{h}{2\pi}\dfrac{\partial \psi}{\partial t} = iH\dfrac{\partial \psi}{\partial t} \qquad \ldots (6)$$

From equations (1) and (6), we get

$$\nabla^2 \psi + \dfrac{8\pi^2 m}{h^2}\left(\dfrac{ih}{2\pi}\dfrac{\partial \psi}{\partial t} - V\psi\right) = 0$$

Multiplying both sides of this equation by $\dfrac{-h^2}{8\pi^2 m}$, we get

$$-\dfrac{h^2}{8\pi^2 m}\nabla^2 \psi - \dfrac{ih}{2\pi}\dfrac{\partial \psi}{\partial t} + V\psi = 0$$

$$\left(-\dfrac{h^2}{8\pi^2 m}\nabla^2 + V\right)\psi = \dfrac{ih}{2\pi}\dfrac{\partial \psi}{\partial t} \qquad \ldots (7)$$

or $\quad \left(\dfrac{-h^2}{2m}\nabla^2 + V\right)\psi = iH\dfrac{\partial \psi}{\partial t} \qquad \ldots (8)$

Equation (8) is called **'Schroedinger's time dependent wave equation'**.

Taking $\quad H = \left(-\dfrac{h^2}{8\pi^2 m}\nabla^2 + V\right) = \left(\dfrac{-h^2}{2m}\nabla^2 + V\right)$ as **'Hamiltonian operator'**

and $\quad E = \dfrac{ih}{2\pi}\dfrac{\partial}{\partial t} = iH\dfrac{\partial}{\partial t}$ as **'Eigen operator'**,

equation (8) becomes

$$H\psi = E\psi \qquad \ldots (9)$$

12.9 APPLICATIONS OF SCHROEDINGER'S TIME INDEPENDENT WAVE EQUATION

In quantum mechanics, the wave function of a system gives the description of that system. We apply Schroedinger's wave equation to a system, and then solve it to find the wave function of the system. We shall study how Schroedinger's time independent wave equation can be applied to a system and then solved to find the energy and wave function of the system under given conditions. We also aim at learning characteristic properties of solutions of this equation and comparing the predictions of quantum mechanics with those of Newtonian mechanics. As simple applications of Schroedinger's time independent wave equation, here we shall discuss the problems of :

(1) Particle in a rigid box
(2) Particle in a non-rigid box
(3) Tunneling effect.

12.9.1 Particle in a Rigid Box

Consider a particle confined to a rigid box and restricted to travelling along x-axis between $x = 0$ and $x = L$ (See Fig. 12.7). Such a box has infinitely hard walls, and a particle does not lose energy when it collides with such walls. So the total energy E of the particle remains constant. The case under discussion is also called **'infinite potential well'**.

As shown in Fig. 12.8, the potential energy V of the particle is infinite on both sides of the box, while V is constant (say $V = 0$ for convenience) inside the box. This means that $V(x) = 0$ in the region $0 < x < L$; and $V(x) = \infty$ for $x \leq 0$ and $x \geq L$.

The particle cannot have an infinite amount of energy. So it cannot exist outside the box and hence particle wave function ψ is zero for $x \leq 0$ and $x \geq L$. We now find the wave function ψ of the particle within the box, i.e. in the region $0 < x < L$. We use Schroedinger's time independent wave equation and solve it for this purpose.

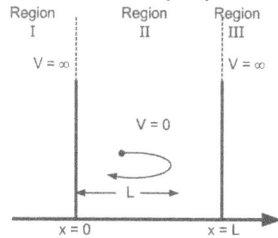

Fig. 12.8 : Infinite potential well

Schroedinger's time independent wave equation is

$$\nabla^2 \psi + \frac{8\pi^2 m}{h^2}(E - V)\psi = 0 \qquad \ldots (1)$$

Now, the motion of the particle is along x-axis. So $\nabla^2 \psi$ can be replaced by the total derivative $\frac{d^2\psi}{dx^2}$. Also $V(x) = 0$ inside the box. So for this problem, Schroedinger's equation (1) becomes

$$\frac{d^2\psi}{dx^2} + \frac{8\pi^2 m E}{h^2}\psi = 0$$

i.e. $$\frac{d^2\psi}{dx^2} + k^2\psi = 0 \qquad \ldots (2)$$

where
$$k^2 = \frac{8\pi^2 m E}{h^2} \quad \ldots (3)$$

Equation (2) is a total differential equation of second order with imaginary roots, and its general solution will involve two arbitrary constants. So the solution of equation (2) can be taken as

$$\psi(x) = A e^{ikx} + B e^{-ikx} \quad \ldots (4)$$

We now apply boundary conditions, namely $\psi(0) = 0$ and $\psi(L) = 0$. So from equation (4), we get

From first boundary condition, $\psi(0) = 0$.
$$\psi(0) = A + B = 0 \quad \text{i.e.} \quad B = -A$$

and from second boundary condition, $\psi(L) = 0$.
$$\psi(L) = A e^{ikL} + B e^{-ikL} = 0$$

Taking $B = -A$, we get
$$A e^{ikL} - A e^{-ikL} = 0$$

Multiplying and dividing by $2i$.

$$\therefore \quad 2i \cdot A \frac{(e^{ikL} - e^{-ikL})}{2i} = 0$$

or $\quad 2i A \sin kL = 0 \quad \ldots (5)$

As $A \neq 0$, we infer from equation (5) that
$$\sin kL = 0$$
i.e. $\quad kL = n\pi,$ where $n = 1, 2, 3, \ldots\ldots$

$$\therefore \quad k = \frac{n\pi}{L} \quad \ldots (6)$$

From equations (3) and (6), we have
$$k^2 = \frac{8\pi^2 m E}{h^2} = \frac{n^2 \pi^2}{L^2}$$

or $\quad E_n = \dfrac{n^2 \cdot h^2}{8 m L^2} \quad \ldots (7)$

Equation (7) gives the energy values of the particle and it is evident that the energy of the particle can have only certain specific values as specified by equation (7). These energy values are called **'Eigen values'**. Thus, the energy of a particle confined to a rigid box is quantized. It cannot have an arbitrary energy; the fact of its confinement leads to restrictions on its wave function that permit it to have only those energies as specified by equation (7).

The integer n corresponding to the energy level E_n is called its **'quantum number'**. $n = 0$ is not possible because the particle cannot have zero energy; and if it did, the particle wave function ψ would have to be zero everywhere in the box, and this means that the particle cannot be present there.

The exclusion of E = 0 as a possible value for the energy of a trapped particle, like the limitation of E to a discrete set of definite values, is a quantum mechanical result. Classically, all energies, including zero, are presumed possible.

We shall compute the permitted energy levels of an electron in a rigid box of width 1 A°.

Putting $m = 9.1 \times 10^{-31}$ kg, $h = 6.63 \times 10^{-34}$ J-s and $L = 10^{-10}$ m in equation (7), we get

$$E_n = 6 \times 10^{-18} n^2 \text{ joules}$$

$$= \frac{6 \times 10^{-18}}{1.6 \times 10^{-19}} n^2 \text{ eV}$$

$$\cong 38 n^2 \text{ eV}$$

The energy levels of such electron trapped in a potential well of width 1 A° is shown in Fig. 12.9.

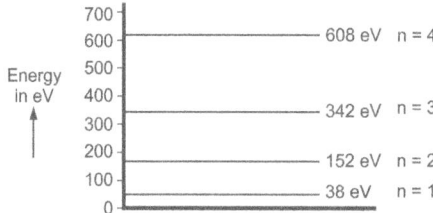

Fig. 12.9 : Energy levels of electron in a rigid box of width 1 A°

Wave Function of a Particle in a Rigid Box

The wave function $\psi(x)$ of a particle inside a rigid box of width L is given by

$$\psi(x) = 2iA \sin kx \qquad \ldots (1)$$

where

$$k = \sqrt{\frac{8\pi^2 m E}{h^2}}$$

$$= \frac{n\pi}{L} \qquad \ldots (2)$$

From equations (1) and (2),

$$\psi(x) = 2iA \sin \frac{n\pi}{L} x \qquad \ldots (3)$$

Equation (3) gives Eigen functions corresponding to energy Eigen values

$$E_n = \frac{n^2 h^2}{8mL^2} \qquad \ldots (4)$$

The complex conjugate of $\psi(x)$ is

$$\psi(x) = -2iA \sin \frac{n\pi}{L} x$$

To evaluate the constant A, we use the normalization condition.

i.e.
$$\int_0^L \psi \psi^* \, dx = 1$$

$$\int_0^L 4A^2 \sin^2 \frac{n\pi}{L} x \, dx = 1$$

This gives $2A^2 L = 1$ or $A = \frac{1}{\sqrt{2L}}$

Putting this value of A in equation (3), we get the normalized wave function of the particle as

$$\psi_n = \frac{2i}{\sqrt{2L}} \sin \frac{n\pi}{L} x = i \sqrt{\frac{2}{L}} \cdot \sin \cdot \frac{n\pi}{L} x \qquad \ldots (5)$$

The normalized wave functions ψ_1, ψ_2 and ψ_3 together with the corresponding probability densities $|\psi_1|^2$, $|\psi_2|^2$ and $|\psi_3|^2$ are shown in Fig. 12.10 (a) and (b) respectively.

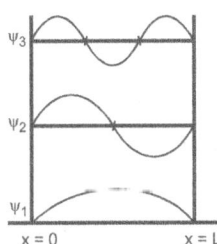
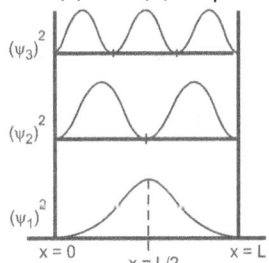

Fig. 12.10 (a) : Wave function   **Fig. 12.10 (b) : Probability densities**

While ψ_n may be negative as well as positive, $|\psi_n|^2$ is always positive. It is seen from Fig. 12.10 (b) that

(1) In every case $|\psi_n|^2 = 0$ at $x = 0$ and $x = L$, the boundaries of the box.

(2) The probability of the particle being present at a particular point in the box may be different for different quantum numbers. e.g. For $n = 1$, the probability is maximum at $x = \frac{L}{2}$. For $n = 2$ there is zero probability of the particle being present at $x = \frac{L}{2}$ and there are two maxima at $x = \frac{L}{4}$ and $x = \frac{3L}{4}$. Classical physics predicts the same probability for the particle to be present anywhere in the box.

The wave function shown in Fig. 12.10 (a) resembles the possible vibrations of a string fixed at both ends. This is so because the waves in a stretched string and the waves representing a particle obey wave equation of the same form, and when similar restrictions are placed upon each kind of wave, the solutions are identical.

Comparison of Quantum Mechanical and Classical Mechanical Predictions

Quantum Mechanical	Classical Mechanical
1. The energy of the particle confined is quantized i.e. can have only discrete energy levels.	1. The energy of the particle has continuous values i.e. can have all possible values from 0 to ∞.
2. Energy E = 0 is not possible as the result of Heisenberg's uncertainty principle.	2. Can have energy E = 0.
3. Probability of finding the particle is different at different position.	3. Probability of finding the particle is same energy where.
4. Probability of finding the particle depends on the principle number and hence on energy state.	4. Probability of finding the particle is independent of energy level.
5. Probability is zero at the walls of the potential well.	5. Probability is maximum at the walls of the potential well i.e. at the boundaries.

12.9.2 Particle in a Non-Rigid Box

Consider a particle trapped in a non-rigid box and restricted to travelling along x-axis between x = 0 and x = L (See Fig. 12.11). The walls of the box are non-rigid. The potential outside the box is finite, say V_0. The potential V_0 is greater than the energy E of the particle inside the box. The potential energy of the particle inside the box is considered to be zero, i.e. V = 0. The case under discussion is also called **'finite potential well'**.

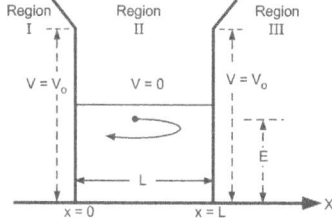

Fig. 12.11 : Finite potential well

As shown in Fig. 12.11, the potential outside the box is finite, say V_0, and inside the box V = 0. This means that $V(x) = 0$ in the region $0 < x < L$ and $V(x) = V_0$ for $x \leq 0$ and $x \geq L$.

Now, it is possible for the particle to have energy E that exceeds V_0. So the particle can exist outside the box and wave function ψ of the particle will not be zero at the boundaries of the box. We use Schroedinger's time independent wave equation to find wave function of the particle inside and on the two sides of the box.

The Schroedinger's time independent wave equation is

$$\nabla^2 \psi + \frac{8\pi^2 m}{h^2} (E - V) \psi = 0 \qquad \ldots (1)$$

Now, the motion of the particle is only along x-axis. So $\nabla^2 \psi$ can be replaced by $\frac{d^2\psi}{dx^2}$. Also $V(x) = V_0$ outside the box. So the Schroedinger's equation (1) becomes

$$\frac{d^2\psi}{dx^2} + \frac{8\pi^2 m}{h^2} (E - V_0) \psi = 0$$

i.e.
$$\frac{d^2\psi}{dx^2} - k'^2 \psi = 0 \qquad \ldots (2)$$

where
$$k'^2 = \frac{8\pi^2 m}{h^2} (V_0 - E) \qquad \ldots (3)$$

Let the wave functions be denoted by ψ_I, ψ_{II} and ψ_{III} respectively in regions I, II and III.

Equation (2) is a total differential equation of second order with real roots, and its general solution will involve two arbitrary constants. So the solutions of equation (2) can be written as :

For region I, i.e. for $x < 0$,
$$\psi_I(x) = A e^{k'x} + B e^{-k'x} \qquad \ldots (4)$$

and for region III, i.e. for $x > L$,
$$\psi_{III}(x) = C e^{k'x} + D e^{-k'x} \qquad \ldots (5)$$

If the wave function of the particle is not to be infinite as we go away from the boundaries of the box, the negative exponential term in equation (4) and the positive exponential term in equation (5) should be absent. i.e. $B = 0$ and $C = 0$.

∴
$$\psi_I(x) = A e^{k'x} \qquad \ldots (6)$$
and
$$\psi_{III}(x) = D e^{-k'x} \qquad \ldots (7)$$

Equations (6) and (7) give wave functions of the particle on the two sides of the non-rigid box.

Now, to find the wave function inside the box, we take $V(x) = 0$ inside the box. So the equation (1) becomes,

$$\frac{d^2\psi}{dx^2} + \frac{8\pi^2 mE}{h^2} \psi = 0$$

i.e.
$$\frac{d^2\psi}{dx^2} + k^2 \psi = 0 \qquad \ldots (8)$$

where
$$k^2 = \frac{8\pi^2 mE}{h^2} \qquad \ldots (9)$$

Equation (8) is a total differential equation of second order with imaginary roots. So its solution can be taken as

$$\psi_{II}(x) = P e^{ikx} + Q e^{-ikx} \qquad \ldots (10)$$

Equation (10) gives the wave function inside the box.

The wave function of the particle will be known completely, both outside and inside the box, if we can evaluate the four constants A, D, P and Q of equations (6), (7) and (10).

For this we need four independent equations among these constants, and they can be obtained by using the property of the wave function that ψ and $\dfrac{\partial \psi}{\partial x}$ must be continuous everywhere in the region where ψ is defined.

So, $\psi_I(0) = \psi_{II}(0)$

i.e. $\quad A = P + Q \quad$ ... (11)

and $\psi_{II}(L) = \psi_{III}(L)$

i.e. $\quad P e^{ikL} + Q e^{-ikL} = D e^{-k'L} \quad$ ... (12)

Similarly, $\left.\dfrac{\partial \psi_I}{\partial x}\right|_{x=0} = \left.\dfrac{\partial \psi_{II}}{\partial x}\right|_{x=0}$

i.e. $\quad A k' = i P k - i Q k \quad$ ... (13)

and $\left.\dfrac{\partial \psi_{II}}{\partial x}\right|_{x=L} = \left.\dfrac{\partial \psi_{III}}{\partial x}\right|_{x=L}$

i.e. $\quad P i k e^{ikL} - Q i k e^{-ikL} = -D k' e^{-k'L} \quad$ ... (14)

The constants A, D, P and Q can be evaluated by solving equations (11), (12), (13) and (14). Thus, the wave function of the particle in a non-rigid box is known completely.

The first few wave functions of a particle in a non-rigid box and the corresponding probability densities are shown in Fig. 12.12 (a) and (b).

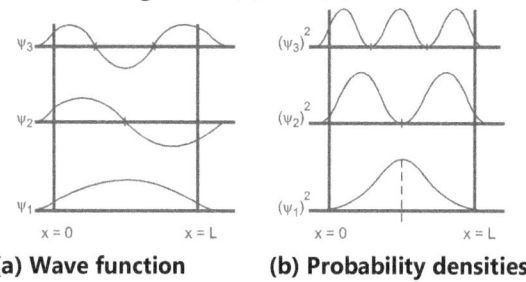

(a) Wave function (b) Probability densities

Fig. 12.12

It can be seen from Fig. 12.12 (a) that the wave functions ψ_n are not equal to zero outside the box. This means that even though the particle energy E is smaller than the value of potential outside the box, there is still a definite probability that the particle be found outside the box. In other words, even though the particle does not have sufficient energy to break through the walls of the box, it may nevertheless somehow penetrate them and leak out.

The wave functions of a particle in a box, with rigid walls are zero at the walls. [See Fig. 12.12 (a)]. But when the confining box has non-rigid walls, the wave functions of the particle are not equal to zero at the walls. This means that the particle wave functions are somewhat longer in the case of a non-rigid box than the wave functions in the case of rigid box. i.e. wavelengths of the particle are larger when it is in a non-rigid box than the wavelengths when it is in a rigid box. A larger wavelength means a smaller frequency and hence smaller energy. Hence energy levels of a particle in a non-rigid box are lower than the corresponding energy levels of a particle in a rigid box. This is shown in Fig. 12.13 where full lines show energy levels of a particle in a rigid box and dotted lines show energy levels of a particle in a non-rigid box.

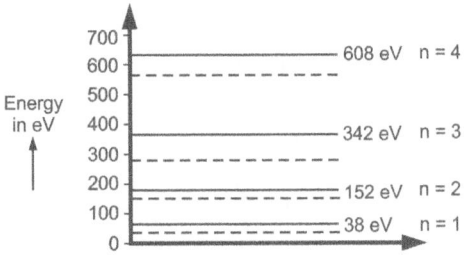

Fig. 12.13 : Energy levels

It is seen that the energy of the particle in a non-rigid box is quantized if $E < V_0$.

When the potential energy outside the box is finite, say V_0, it will be possible for a particle to have energy E that exceeds V_0. Such a particle is not trapped inside the box, for it always has sufficient energy to penetrate the walls of the box. Energy of the particle is not quantized but it may have any value above V_0. However, the K.E. of the particle outside the box is $(E - V_0)$ and it is always less than its K.E. inside the box. This is because whole energy E of the particle inside the box is K.E. as $V = 0$ there. Less energy means longer wavelength. o wave function ψ has a longer wavelength outside the box than inside.

Example 12.25 : Compute the permitted energy levels of an electron in an infinite potential well of width 1 A°.

Data : $m = 9.1 \times 10^{-31}$ kg, $L = 1$ A° $= 10^{-10}$ m

Formula : $E_n = \dfrac{n^2 h^2}{8 mL^2}$

Solution :

$$E_n = \dfrac{n^2 (6.6 \times 10^{-34})^2}{8 \times 9.1 \times 10^{-31} \times (10^{-10})^2}$$

$$\approx 6 \times 10^{-18} \, n^2 \, J$$

$$E_n \approx 38 \, n^2 \, eV$$

For $\quad n = 1, \quad \boxed{E_1 = 38 \text{ eV}}$

$\quad n = 2, \quad \boxed{E_2 = 152 \text{ eV}}$

$\quad n = 3, \quad \boxed{E_3 = 342 \text{ eV}}$ etc.

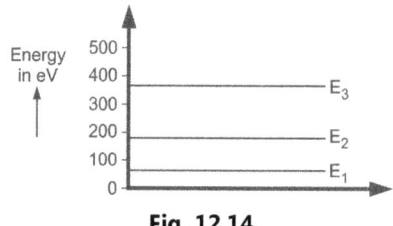

Fig. 12.14

Example 12.26 : An infinite square well has a width of 1 A°. What is the fractional change in the lowest two permissible energies of one electron in this well if the width is increased to 2 A° ?

Data : $L = 1 \, A° = 10^{-10}$ m, $L' = 2 \times 10^{-10}$ m

Formula : $$E_n = \frac{n^2 h^2}{8 \, mL^2}$$

Solution :

From previous numerical,

For $L = 1$, $E_n \approx 38 \, n^2$ eV

i.e. $E_1 = 38$ eV and $E_2 = 152$ eV

For $L = 2$ the energies reduce by a factor of 4

$\therefore \quad E_1' = 9.5$ eV and $E_2' = 38$ eV

Fractional change, $\Delta E_1 = E_1 - E_1'$

$\Delta E_2 = E_2 - E_2'$

$\Delta E_1 = 38 - 9.5 = \boxed{28.5 \text{ eV}}$

$\Delta E_2 = 152 - 38 = \boxed{114 \text{ eV}}$

Example 12.27 : Lowest energy level of an electron trapped in a potential well is 38 eV. Find the width of the well.

Data : $E = 38$ eV, $n = 1$.

Formula : $$E = \frac{n^2 h^2}{8 \, mL^2}$$

Solution :

$$L^2 = \frac{n^2 h^2}{8 \, mE}$$

$$L = \sqrt{\frac{(6.6 \times 10^{-34})^2}{8 \times 9.1 \times 10^{-31} \times 38 \times 1.6 \times 10^{-19}}}$$

$= \boxed{10^{-10} \text{ m} = 1 \, A°}$

Example 12.28 : An electron is trapped in a rigid box of width 1 A°. Find its lowest energy level and momentum. Hence find energy of 5th level.

Data : $L = 1 \text{ A}° = 10^{-10}$ m

Formula : $E_n = \dfrac{n^2 h^2}{8 mL^2} \approx 38 n^2$

Solution :

$$E_1 = 38 \text{ eV}$$

$$E_1 = \dfrac{p_1^2}{2m}$$

∴ $p_1^2 = 2 m E_1$

$= 2 \times 9.1 \times 10^{-31} \times 38 \times 1.6 \times 10^{-19}$

$= 1106.56 \times 10^{-50}$

$\boxed{p_1 = 33.26 \times 10^{-25} \text{ kg - m/sec}}$

$E_5 \approx 25 \times 38 \text{ eV} \approx \boxed{950 \text{ eV}}$

Example 12.29 : An electron is accelerated through a potential difference of 10 kV. Calculate the De-Broglie wavelength and momentum of the electron.

Data : $V = 10{,}000$ volts

Formulae : (I) $\lambda = \dfrac{12.27}{\sqrt{V}}$ A°, (ii) $p = \dfrac{h}{\lambda}$

Solution :

(i) $\lambda = \dfrac{12.27}{\sqrt{10000}}$

$\boxed{\lambda = 0.1227 \text{ A}°}$

(ii) $p = \dfrac{6.6 \times 10^{-34}}{0.1227 \times 10^{-10}}$

$\boxed{p = 5.378 \times 10^{-23} \text{ kg-m/sec}}$

Example 12.30 : Proton and alpha particles are accelerated through same potential difference. Compute the ratio of their De-Broglie wavelengths.

Data : $M_\alpha = 4 M_p$, $e_\alpha = 2 e_p$

Formula : $\lambda = \dfrac{L}{\sqrt{2meV}}$

Solution :

For proton, $\lambda_p = \dfrac{h}{\sqrt{2 m_p e_p V}}$

For alpha particle, $\lambda_\alpha = \dfrac{h}{\sqrt{2m_\alpha e_\alpha V}}$

But, $m_\alpha = 4m_p$ and $e_\alpha = 2e_p$

$\therefore \lambda_\alpha = \dfrac{h}{\sqrt{16 m_p e_p V}}$

$\therefore \dfrac{\lambda_\alpha}{\lambda_p} = \dfrac{h}{\sqrt{16 m_p e_p V}} \cdot \dfrac{\sqrt{2 m_p e_p V}}{h} = \boxed{\dfrac{1}{\sqrt{8}}}$

Example 12.31 : Find the De-Broglie wavelength of an electron accelerated through a potential difference of 100 volts.

Data : $V = 100$ volts

Formula : $\lambda = \dfrac{12.27}{\sqrt{V}}$ A°

Solution :

$$\lambda = \dfrac{12.27}{\sqrt{100}}$$

$$\boxed{\lambda = 1.227\ \text{A°}}$$

Example 12.32 : What potential difference must be applied to an electron microscope to obtain electrons of wavelength 0.3 A° ?

Data : $\lambda = 0.3$ A°

Formula : $\lambda = \dfrac{12.27}{\sqrt{V}}$ A°

Solution :

$$0.3 = \dfrac{12.27}{\sqrt{V}}$$

$$\sqrt{V} = 40.9$$

$\therefore \quad \boxed{V = 1672.8\ \text{volts}}$

Example 12.33 : Calculate the velocity and De-Broglie wavelength of an α-particle of energy 1 keV.

Data : $E = 1$ keV, $m_\alpha = 4 m_p$

Formula : $\lambda = \dfrac{h}{\sqrt{2mE}}$

Solution :

$$\lambda = \dfrac{6.6 \times 10^{-34}}{\sqrt{2 \times 4 \times 1.67 \times 10^{-27} \times 1 \times 10^3 \times 1.6 \times 10^{-19}}}$$

$$\lambda = 4.514 \times 10^{-13}\ \text{m}$$

$$\boxed{\lambda = 0.00451\ \text{A°}}$$

Example 12.34 : Which has a shorter wavelength of 1 eV photon or 1 eV electron? Calculate the value and explain.

Data :
$$E_p = 1 \text{ eV}$$
$$E_e = 1 \text{ eV}$$

Formula :
$$\lambda = \frac{h}{\sqrt{2mE}}$$

Solution :

$$\lambda_p = \frac{h}{\sqrt{2m_p E_p}}$$

$$\lambda_p = \frac{6.6 \times 10^{-34}}{\sqrt{2 \times 1.67 \times 10^{-27} \times 1 \times 1.6 \times 10^{-19}}}$$

$$\lambda_p = 2.855 \times 10^{-11} \text{ m} = \boxed{0.2855 \text{ A}°}$$

$$\lambda_e = \frac{h}{\sqrt{2m_e E_e}}$$

$$\lambda_e = \frac{6.6 \times 10^{-34}}{\sqrt{2 \times 9.1 \times 10^{-31} \times 1 \times 1.6 \times 10^{-19}}}$$

$$\lambda_e = 1.223 \times 10^{-9} \text{ m} = \boxed{12.23 \text{ A}°}$$

$$\lambda_e > \lambda_p$$

Because lighter the particle, greater will be the wavelength of the matter waves $\left(\lambda \propto \frac{1}{m}\right)$.

Example 12.35 : An electron has kinetic energy equal to its rest mass energy. Calculate De-Broglie's wavelength associated with it.

Data :
$$E = m$$

Formula :
$$\lambda = \frac{h}{\sqrt{2mE}}$$

Solution :

$$\lambda = \frac{h}{\sqrt{2m^2}}$$

$$\lambda = \frac{6.6 \times 10^{-34}}{9.1 \times 10^{-31}\sqrt{2}}$$

$$\boxed{\lambda = 5.129 \times 10^{-4} \text{ m}}$$

Example 12.36 : Find the De Broglie's wavelength associated with monoenergetic electron beam having momentum 10^{-23} kg m/s.

Data :
$$p = 10^{-23} \text{ kg m/s}$$

Formula : $\lambda = \dfrac{h}{p}$

Solution :

$$\lambda = \dfrac{h}{p}$$

$$\lambda = \dfrac{6.63 \times 10^{-34}}{10^{-23}}$$

$$\lambda = 6.63 \times 10^{-11} \text{ m}$$

or

$$\boxed{\lambda = 0.663 \text{ A}°}$$

Example 12.37 : Find the energy of neutron in unit of electron volt whose De-Broglie wavelength is 1 A°. (**Given :** $M_n = 1.674 \times 10^{-27}$ kg).

Data : $M_n = 1.674 \times 10^{-27}$, $\lambda = 1$ A°

Formula : $\lambda = \dfrac{h}{\sqrt{2mE}}$

Solution :

$$E = \dfrac{h^2}{2m\lambda^2}$$

$$E = \dfrac{(6.63 \times 10^{-34})^2}{2 \times 1.67 \times 10^{-27} \times (1 \times 10^{-10})^2}$$

$$E = 1.316 \times 10^{-20} \text{ J}$$

$$\boxed{E = 8.225 \times 10^{-2} \text{ eV}}$$

Example 12.38 : Calculate the De-Broglie wavelength of 10 keV protons in eV.

Data : $E = 10$ keV, $m = 1.67 \times 10^{-27}$ kg

Formula : $\lambda = \dfrac{h}{\sqrt{2mE}}$

Solution :

$$\lambda = \dfrac{6.63 \times 10^{-34}}{\sqrt{2 \times 1.67 \times 10^{-27} \times 10 \times 10^3 \times 1.6 \times 10^{-19}}}$$

$$\lambda = 2.868 \times 10^{-13} \text{ m}$$

$$\boxed{\lambda = 2.868 \times 10^{-3} \text{ A}°}$$

Example 12.39 : At what kinetic energy an electron will have a wavelength of 5000 A° ?

Data : $\lambda = 5000$ A°

Formula : $\lambda = \dfrac{h}{\sqrt{2mE}}$

Solution :

$$\lambda^2 = \frac{h^2}{2mE}$$

$$\therefore \quad E = \frac{(6.63 \times 10^{-34})^2}{2\,(9.1 \times 10^{-31})\,(5000 \times 10^{-10})^2}$$

$$E = 9.66 \times 10^{-25} \text{ J}$$

$$\boxed{E = 6.038 \times 10^{-6} \text{ eV}}$$

Example 12.40 : Calculate the wavelength of a photon and an electron both having an energy 1.0 eV. (**Given :** Planck's constant $h = 6.63 \times 10^{-34}$ J-s, Mass of electron $= 9.1 \times 10^{-31}$ kg).

Data : $E = 1.0$ eV

Formulae : (i) For electron, $\lambda = \dfrac{h}{\sqrt{2mE}}$ (ii) For photon, $E = h\nu$ i.e. $\lambda = \dfrac{hc}{E}$

Solution :

(i) For electron,

$$\lambda = \frac{6.63 \times 10^{-34}}{\sqrt{2 \times 9.1 \times 10^{-31} \times 1 \times 1.6 \times 10^{-19}}}$$

$$\lambda = 1.228 \times 10^{-9} \text{ m} = \boxed{12.28 \text{ A}^\circ}$$

(ii) For photon,

$$\lambda = \frac{6.63 \times 10^{-34} \times 3 \times 10^8}{1 \times 1.6 \times 10^{-19}}$$

$$\lambda = 1.243 \times 10^{-6} \text{ m} = \boxed{12430 \text{ A}^\circ}$$

Example 12.41 : Assuming atomic nucleus to be a rigid box (infinite potential well), calculate the ground state energy of an electron if it existed inside the nucleus.
(**Given :** Planck's constant $= 6.63 \times 10^{-34}$ J-s, Mass of the electron $= 9.1 \times 10^{-31}$ kg and size of the nucleus $\sim 10^{-15}$ m. Using this result, argue that electron cannot exist inside the nucleus. Given maximum binding energy per nucleon $= 8.8$ MeV).

Data : $d = 10^{-15}$ m, $m = 9.1 \times 10^{-31}$ kg, $\dfrac{\text{B.E.}}{N} = 8.8$ MeV

Formulae : (i) $E_n = \dfrac{n^2 h^2}{8mL^2}$ (ii) $\Delta x \Delta p = h$

Solution :

(i)

$$E_n = \frac{(1)^2 (6.63 \times 10^{-34})^2}{8 \times 9.1 \times 10^{-31} \times (10^{-15})^2}$$

$$E_n = 6.038 \times 10^{-10} \text{ J}$$

$$\boxed{E_n = 3.774 \times 10^9 \text{ eV}}$$

(ii) $\Delta x \Delta p = h$

$$\Delta p = \frac{6.63 \times 10^{-34}}{10^{-15}}$$

$$\boxed{\Delta p = 6.63 \times 10^{-19} \text{ kg m/s}}$$

If this is the uncertainty in the momentum of electron in the nucleus, the momentum itself must be at least comparable to Δp i.e. $p \sim \Delta p$.

$$\therefore \quad E = \frac{p^2}{2m} = \frac{(6.63 \times 10^{-19})^2}{2 \times 9.1 \times 10^{-31}}$$

$$E = 2.415 \times 10^{-7} \text{ J}$$

$$\boxed{E = 1.510 \times 10^{12} \text{ eV}}$$

This shows that if the electron exist in the nucleus, the energy must be at least 1.51×10^{12} eV, which is much more than B.E. per nucleon. Therefore, it cannot exist in the nucleus.

Example 12.42 : An electron is trapped in a rigid box of width 2 A°. Find its lowest energy level and momentum. Hence, find energy of the 3rd energy level.

Data : $\quad L = 2 \text{ A}°.$

Formulae : $\quad E_n = \dfrac{n^2 h^2}{8mL^2}, \quad P_n = \sqrt{2mE_n}$

Solution :

For lowest energy level, $n = 1$

$$E_1 = \frac{1^2 \times (6.6 \times 10^{-34})^2}{8 \times 9.1 \times 10^{-31} \times (2 \times 10^{-10})^2}$$

$$E_1 = 1.50 \times 10^{-18} \text{ J}$$

or $\quad E_1 = 9.37 \text{ eV}$

$\therefore \quad P_1 = \sqrt{2 \times 9.1 \times 10^{-31} \times 1.51 \times 10^{-18}}$

$$P_1 = 1.66 \times 10^{-24} \text{ kg-m/sec}$$

For third energy level, $n = 3$.

$$\therefore \quad E_3 = \frac{3^2 \times (6.6 \times 10^{-34})^2}{8 \times 9.1 \times 10^{-31} \times (2 \times 10^{-10})}$$

$$\boxed{E_3 = 13.5 \times 10^{-18} \text{ J}}$$

or $\quad \boxed{E_3 = 84.33 \text{ eV}}$

Example 12.43 : Compare the lowest three energy states for an electron confined in an infinite potential well of width 10 A°.

Data : $\quad L = 10 \text{ A}°$

Formula : $\quad E_n = \dfrac{n^2 h^2}{8mL^2}$

Solution :

$$E_n = \frac{n^2 h^2}{8mL^2}$$

$$E_n = \frac{n^2 (6.63 \times 10^{-34})^2}{8 \times 9.1 \times 10^{-31} \times (10 \times 10^{-10})^2}$$

$$E_n = 0.603 \times 10^{-19} n^2 \text{ J}$$

or

$$E_n = 0.38 n^2 \text{ eV}$$

For first energy level, $n = 1$

∴ $\boxed{E_1 = 0.38 \text{ eV}}$

For second energy level, $n = 2$

∴ $\boxed{E_2 = 1.52 \text{ eV}}$

For third energy level, $n = 3$

∴ $\boxed{E_3 = 3.42 \text{ eV}}$

Example 12.44 : Compute energy difference between the ground state and first excited state for an electron in a one-dimensional rigid box of length 10^{-8} cm.

Data : $L = 10^{-8}$ cm

Formula : $E_n = \dfrac{n^2 h^2}{8mL^2}$

Solution :

$$E_1 = \frac{(1)^2 h^2}{8mL^2}$$

and

$$E_2 = \frac{(2)^2 h^2}{8mL^2}$$

∴ $E_2 - E_1 = \dfrac{4h^2}{8mL^2} - \dfrac{h^2}{8mL^2} = \dfrac{3 \times (6.63 \times 10^{-34})^2}{8 \times (9.1 \times 10^{-31})(10^{-10})^2}$

$= 1.8114 \times 10^{-17}$ J

$\boxed{E_2 - E_1 = 113.21 \text{ eV}}$

SUMMARY

- De Broglie's hypothesis states that a material particle of mass 'm' moving with a velocity v has a wave associated with it. This wave is called as a De Broglie wave and its wavelength is given by, $\lambda = h/mv$.

- De Broglie wavelength in terms of kinetic energy of a particle is $\lambda = \dfrac{h}{\sqrt{2mE}}$.
- For a charged particle accelerated through a potential difference of V, the De Broglie wavelength, $\lambda = \dfrac{h}{\sqrt{2mqV}}$.

  For an electron, the De Broglie wavelength is $\lambda = \dfrac{12.27}{\sqrt{V}}$ A°.

- Schroedinger's wave equation is the mathematical representation of matter waves associated with a moving particle. They are of two types :

  (i) Schroedinger's time independent wave equation :
  $$\nabla^2 \psi + \dfrac{8\pi^2 m}{h^2}(E - V)\psi = 0$$

  (ii) Schroedinger's time dependent wave equation :
  $$\left(\dfrac{-h^2}{8\pi^2 m}\nabla^2 + V\right)\psi = \dfrac{ih}{2\pi}\dfrac{\partial \psi}{\partial t}$$

  i.e. $H\psi = E\psi$

- The variable quantity characterizing De Broglie waves is denoted by ψ and it is called the wave function of the particle. This wave function contains all the information about the particle.
- The quantity $|\psi(x, y, z, t)|^2$, called the probability density or probability distribution function, determines the probability in unit volume of finding a particle at a given position at a given time.
- The probability of a particle being present in a volume element dx·dy·dz is $|\psi|^2 \cdot dx\, dy\, dz$.

  The probability of finding the particle in all space is $\iiint\limits_{\text{all space}} |\psi|^2\, dx\, dy\, dz = 1$.

  This is the normalization condition. A wave function ψ satisfying this relation is called a normalized wave function.

- The wave function should satisfy the following conditions :

  (i) It should be a normalized function.

  (ii) It should be a well behaved function i.e., single valued, finite and continuous.

- For a particle in a rigid box, the wave function is given by

  $$\psi_n(x, t) = i \cdot \sqrt{\dfrac{2}{L}} \cdot \sin\left(\dfrac{n\pi}{L}\right) x$$

The energy level of the particle is given by

$E_n = \dfrac{n^2 h^2}{8mL^2}$ and is quantized. $n = 1, 2, 3$.

- For a non-rigid box, the particle wave functions are longer than the wave functions in the case of rigid box.
- Particles trapped in a box, despite having insufficient energy ($E < V_o$) to penetrate the walls some how leak out. This is a tunneling effect which is a behaviour unique to Quantum Mechanics.

IMPORTANT FORMULAE

- $\lambda = \dfrac{h}{mv} = \dfrac{h}{p}$

- $E = h\upsilon$, $\quad E = \dfrac{p^2}{2m}$

- $E = mc^2$

- $\lambda = \dfrac{h}{\sqrt{2mE}}$

- $\lambda = \dfrac{h}{\sqrt{2meV}}$ and $\lambda \simeq \dfrac{12.27}{\sqrt{V}} \, \text{A}°$

- $\nabla^2 \psi + \dfrac{8\pi^2 m}{h^2} (E - V) \psi = 0$

- $\left(-\dfrac{h^2}{8\pi^2 m} \nabla^2 + V\right) \psi = \dfrac{ih}{2\pi} \dfrac{\partial \psi}{\partial t}$; $H\psi = E\psi$

- $E_n = \dfrac{n^2 h^2}{8mL^2}$; where $n = 1, 2, ...$

- Normalization condition $\displaystyle\int\int\int_{-\infty}^{+\infty} \psi^* \psi \, dx\, dy\, dz = 1$.

EXERCISE

1. Explain briefly the wave nature of matter and obtain an expression for the De-Broglie wavelength.
2. Starting from the De-Broglie concept, obtain Heisenberg's uncertainty principle. Give an illustration of the principle.

3. Show that De-Broglie wavelength of a charged particle is inversely proportional to the square root of the accelerating potential.
4. Write a short note on duality of matter and radiation.
5. Write a note on properties of matter waves. How are they different from electromagnetic and mechanical waves?
6. What are group and phase velocities? Explain them.
7. Discuss the properties of matter waves.
8. What are matter waves? Show that the wavelength λ associated with an electron of mass m and kinetic energy E is given by $\lambda = \dfrac{h}{\sqrt{2\,mE}}$.
9. Write a short note on Heisenberg's uncertainty principle.
10. State Heisenberg's uncertainty principle and explain it using the concept of De-Broglie wave groups.
11. Derive Schroedinger's time dependent and time independent wave equation.
12. Derive an expression for the energy levels and wave function of a particle enclosed in an infinite potential well.
13. Explain Harmonic oscillator classically and quantum mechanically. Compare between the two.
14. Explain the physical significance of ψ, ψ^2.
15. Explain particle in a non-rigid box. How is this situation different from a rigid box?
16. Write a note on a particle in a potential well with infinite sides.
17. Write a short note on Eigen values of particle in a rigid box.
18. Starting with the wave function for a particle moving in a one-dimensional potential well, show that the probability of existence within the well changes with quantum number.
19. Using Schroedinger's wave equation, find energy and wave function of a particle in a rigid box.
20. Explain De-Broglie's concept of matter waves. Show that the wavelength associated with electrons accelerated by a potential difference of V volts is given by $\dfrac{h}{\sqrt{2\,meV}}$.
21. Explaining De-Broglie's hypothesis of matter waves, describe an experiment in support of it.
22. State De-Broglie's hypothesis of matter waves. Show that the De-Broglie wavelength of a charged particle is inversely proportional to the square root of the accelerating potential.

23. Explain wave nature of matter. Show that the De-Broglie wavelength of a charged particle is inversely proportional to the square root of the accelerating potential. Comment on its significance.
24. State De-Broglie hypothesis.
25. Derive an expression for the De-Broglie wavelength in terms of energy.
26. Explain in short De-Broglie's hypothesis of matter waves.
27. Explain De-Broglie's hypothesis of matter waves and obtain the equation of De-Broglie wavelength of matter waves in terms of energy by analogy with radiation. Also obtain equation of De-Broglie wavelength of an electron.

UNSOLVED PROBLEMS

1. Calculate the De-Broglie wavelength of a 10 keV neutron.
   Given : Mass of the neutron = 1.67×10^{-27} kg. **(Ans.** λ = 0.285 A°)
2. The De-Broglie wavelength of electrons in a monoenergetic beam is 7.2×10^{-11} m. Calculate the momentum and energy of electrons in the beam in electron volts.
   (Ans. 0.92×10^{-23} kg-m/sec., E = 288 eV)
3. An electron is bound by a potential box of infinite height having a width 2.5 A°. Calculate the minimum uncertainty in its velocity. **(Ans.** 0.725×10^7 m/sec.)
4. Calculate the wavelength associated with a particle of mass 1 g and moving with a velocity of 2×10^5 cm/sec. Describe the possibility of performing a successful diffraction experiment with a beam of such particles.
   (Ans. 3.312×10^{-34} m, experiment not successful)
5. A bullet of mass 25 gm is moving with a speed of 400 m/sec. The speed is measured accurately upto 0.02 %. Calculate the certainty with which the position of the bullet can be located. Given h = 6.6×10^{-34} J.s. **(Ans.** 5.25×10^{-32} m)
6. Assume that a particle cannot be confined to a spherical volume of diameter less than the De-Broglie wavelength of the particle. Estimate the minimum K.E. a proton confined to a nucleus of diameter 10^{-14} m may have. What K.E. would an electron have to possess if it were confined to this nucleus ? **(Ans.** 8.2 MeV, 124 MeV)
7. What potential difference must be applied to an electron microscope to produce electrons of wavelength 0.4 A° ? **(Ans.** 937.9 volts)

8. The average time that an atom retains excess excitation energy before emitting it as electromagnetic radiation is 10^{-8} sec. Calculate the limit of accuracy with which the excitation energy of the emitted radiation can be determined. **(Ans.** 6.63×10^{-26} J)

9. Find the lowest K.E. permissible for an electron in (i) A cubical box of side 1 cm. (ii) Same box of side 3 A°. **(Ans.** 1.13×10^{-14} eV, 12.6 eV)

10. An electron is bounded by a potential that is approximated by an infinite square well of width 2×10^{-8} cm. Calculate the lowest two permissible energies of the electron.

(Ans. 19 eV, 38 eV)

✠ ✠ ✠

SOLVED UNIVERSITY QUESTION PAPER
DECEMBER 2014

Constants :

$$e = 1.6 \times 10^{-19} \text{ C}$$
$$m_e = 9.1 \times 10^{-31} \text{ kg}$$
$$h = 6.63 \times 10^{-34} \text{ J-s}$$
$$m_p = 1.66 \times 10^{-27} \text{ kg}$$
$$N_a = 6.025 \times 10^{23} \text{ atoms/gm-mole}$$

Q.1 (a) Why chemical method can not be used for separating isotopes ? Hence explain the mechanism of Bainbridge mass spectrograph for separating isotopes. **(6 M)**

(b) In a certain cyclotron, the maximum radius that the path of a deuteron may have before it is defected out of magnetic field is 20cm. Calculate the energy of deuteron in MeV. **(4 M)**

Data : R = 20 cm

Formula : $E = \dfrac{R^2 Q^2 B^2}{2M}$

Solution : As value of B is not given problem can not be solved.

OR

Q.2 (a) What are thermonuclear reaction ? Explain p-p cycle. **(6 M)**

(b) A beam of electrons moving with an uniform speed of 4×10^7 m/s is projected normal to the magnetic field of strength $B = 1 \times 10^{-3}$ Wb/m². What is the path of the beam in magnetic field ? **(4 M)**

Data :
$V = 4 \times 10^7$ m/s
$B = 1 \times 10^{-3}$ Wb/m²

Formula : $R = \dfrac{mV}{Be}$

Solution : $R = \dfrac{9.1 \times 10^{-31} \times 4 \times 10^7}{1 \times 10^{-3} \times 1 - 6 \times 10^{-19}}$

$R = 0.227$ M

The electron will follow circular path of radius 0.2275 m

Q.3 (a) State and explain the following terms related to superconductivity. **(6 M)**
  (a) Critical temperature (b) Critical magnetic field
  (c) Critical current density

 (b) Draw the band structure of p-n junction diode under forward and reverse biasing.
  (4 M)

OR

Q.4 (a) What is Hall effect ? Derive the formula for Hall coefficient and Hall voltage ?**(6 M)**
 (b) State and explain any two commercial applications of superconductors. **(4 M)**

Q.5 (a) What are nanoparticles ? Give any one method for producing nanoparticles **(6 M)**
 (b) State and explain the second law of thermodynamics. **(4 M)**

OR

Q.6 (a) What are the different steps involved in a Carnot cycle ? **(6 M)**
 (b) How the following properties make the nanoparticle different from bulk material?
  (a) Electrical (b) Magnetic **(4 M)**

Q.7 (a) Derive the formula for condition of brightness in reflected system when the light is reflected from thin film of uniform thickness. **(6 M)**
 (b) Light of wavelength 6×10^{-5} cm falls on a screen at a distance of 100 cm from a narrow slit. Find the width of the slit if the first minima lie 1 mm on either side of the central maxima. **(4 M)**

Data :
$\lambda = 6 \times 10^{-5}$ cm
$D = 100$ cm
$d = 1$ mm
$n = 1$

Formula : (i) $a \sin \theta = n\lambda$

 (ii) $\tan \theta = \dfrac{d}{D}$

Solution : Form Fig.

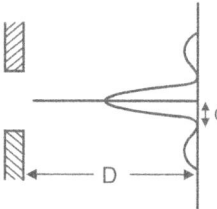

Fig.

$$\tan\theta = \frac{d}{D}$$

for large value of D and small value of d.

$$\tan\theta \simeq \theta \simeq \sin\theta$$

$$\therefore \quad a\frac{d}{D} = n\lambda$$

$$a = \frac{1 \times 6 \times 10^{-5} \times 100}{1 \times 10^{-1}}$$

$$a = 6 \times 10^{-2} \text{ cm}$$

Q.8 (a) Explain the diffraction at a grating. Derive formula for intensity distribution. **(6 M)**

(b) White Light falls normally on film of soapy water whose thickness is 5×10^{-5} cm. Which wavelength will be reflected most strongly in the visible region? **(4 M)**

Solution : Ref. Example 7.3.

Q.9 (a) What is Nicols prism? How it can be used for producing plane polarized light?

(6 M)

(b) With band diagram, explain the working of semiconductor laser. **(4 M)**

OR

Q.10 (a) What is Holography? Explain the method of hologram construction and reillumination. **(6 M)**

(b) Calculate the thickness of a half wave plate, given that **(4 M)**

$\mu_e = 1.533 \; \mu_0 = 1.544$ and $\lambda = 5000$ A°

Data :
$$\lambda = 5000 \text{ A}°$$
$$\mu_e = 1.533$$
$$\mu_0 = 1.544$$

Formula :
$$t = \frac{\lambda}{2(\mu_0 - \mu_e)}$$
$$t = \frac{5000 \times 10^{-8}}{2(1.544 - 1.533)}$$
$$t = 2.272 \times 10^{-3} \text{ cm}$$

Q.11 (a) A particle is confined in a potential well of infinite depth, derive the formula fort energy engine values. **(6 M)**

(b) A cinema hall has volume of 7500m³. It is required to have reverberation time of 1.5 sec. What should be the total absorption in the hall ? **(4 M)**

Solution : Ref. Example 11.2.

Q.12 (a) What is reverberation ? Discuss the Sabine's formula. How the reverberation affects acoustics of a building. **(6 M)**

(b) Find the kinetic energy of a neutron which has a wavelength of 3A°. **(4 M)**

Data : $\lambda = 3A°$

Formula : $\lambda = \dfrac{\lambda}{\sqrt{2mE}}$

Solution : $E = \dfrac{\lambda^2}{2m\lambda^2}$

$$E = \dfrac{(6.63 \times 10^{-34})^2}{2 \times 1.66 \times 10^{-27} \times (3 \times 10^{-10})^2}$$

$$E = 1.45 \times 10^{-21} \text{ J}$$

ENGINEERING PHYSICS
MAY 2015

Time : 3 Hours   Max. Marks : 60

1. (a) An electron is subjected to parallel electric field, derive the formula for impact velocity. **(07)**
   (b) In a thermonuclear reaction 1.00×10^{-3} kg hydrogen is converted into 0.993×10^{-3} kg helium. Calculate the energy released in Joules. **(03)**

OR

2. (a) Give principle, construction and working of betatron. **(06)**
   (b) An α-particle travels at right angles to a magnetic field with a speed of 6×10 m/s. The flux density of the field is 0.2 Wb/m^2. Calculate (i) force acting on α-particle and (ii) acceleration. **(04)**

3. (a) Using Fermi-Dirac probability function show that the position of Fermi level is at the centre of conduction band and valence band in an intrinsic semiconductor. **(06)**
   (b) What is super conductivity? Explain the term critical temperature. **(04)**

OR

4. (a) Explain the superconductivity on the basis of BCS theory. **(06)**
   (b) Calculate the conductivity of pure silicon at room temperature when the concentration of carrier is 1.6×10^{10} per cm^3. Given: μ_e = 1500 cm^2 V-s and μ_h = 500 cm^2 / V-sec at room temperature. **(04)**

5. (a) Describe the Joule's method of determination of j. **(06)**
   (b) State and explain any two properties of nanoparticles. **(04)**

OR

6. (a) What are colloids? How the chemical method can be used for synthesis of metal nanoparticles? **(06)**
   (b) State and explain first law of thermodynamics. **(04)**

7. (a) State Rayleigh's criterion of resolution. Derive the formula for resolving power of a diffraction grating. **(06)**
   (b) In Newton's ring experiment, the diameters of the 4th and 12'h dark rings are 0.4 cm and 0.7 cm respectively. Find the diameter of 20lh dark ring. **(04)**

OR

8. (a) Derive the formula for optical path difference in wedge shaped thin film. **(06)**
   (b) Give differences between Fresnel's and Fraunhofer's diffraction. **(04)**

9. (a) What is double refraction? Explain it on the basis of Huygen's theory. **(06)**
   (b) How a hologram can be constructed? Give its method. **(04)**

OR

10. (a) With principle and diagram, explain the working of Ruby laser. **(06)**

(b) Calculate the thickness of a quarter wave plate, given that μ_e = 1.533 μ_0 = 1.544 and λ = 6500 A°.

11. (a) What are factors affecting acoustics of a building? Give their remedies. **(06)**

(b) Derive formula for De-Broglie's wavelength of an electron accelerated by voltage V.

(04)

OR

12. (a) Derive formula for Schrodinger's time dependent wave equation. **(06)**

(b) Two sound sources are producing sound intensity level of 60 dB and 80 dB respectively. Calculate the resultant sound intensity level. **(04)**

✠ ✠ ✠

SOLVED UNIVERSITY QUESTION PAPER
DECEMBER 2014

Constants :

$$e = 1.6 \times 10^{-19} \text{ C}$$
$$m_e = 9.1 \times 10^{-31} \text{ kg}$$
$$h = 6.63 \times 10^{-34} \text{ J} - \text{s}$$
$$m_p = 1.66 \times 10^{-27} \text{ kg}$$
$$N_a = 6.025 \times 10^{23} \text{ atoms/gm-mole}$$

Q.1 (a) Why chemical method can not be used for separating isotopes ? Hence explain the mechanism of Bainbridge mass spectrograph for separating isotopes. **(6 M)**

(b) In a certain cyclotron, the maximum radius that the path of a deuteron may have before it is defected out of magnetic field is 20cm. Calculate the energy of deuteron in MeV. **(4 M)**

Data : $R = 20 \text{ cm}$

Formula : $E = \dfrac{R^2 Q^2 B^2}{2M}$

Solution : As value of B is not given problem can not be solved.

OR

Q.2 (a) What are thermonuclear reaction ? Explain p-p cycle. **(6 M)**

(b) A beam of electrons moving with an uniform speed of 4×10^7 m/s is projected normal to the magnetic field of strength $B = 1 \times 10^{-3}$ Wb/m². What is the path of the beam in magnetic field ? **(4 M)**

Data :
$$V = 4 \times 10^7 \text{ m/s}$$
$$B = 1 \times 10^{-3} \text{ Wb/m}^2$$

Formula : $R = \dfrac{mV}{Be}$

Solution :
$$R = \dfrac{9.1 \times 10^{-31} \times 4 \times 10^7}{1 \times 10^{-3} \times 1 - 6 \times 10^{-19}}$$

$$R = 0.227 \text{ M}$$

The electron will follow circular path of radius 0.2275 m

Q.3 (a) State and explain the following terms related to superconductivity. **(6 M)**
  (a) Critical temperature (b) Critical magnetic field
  (c) Critical current density
 (b) Draw the band structure of p-n junction diode under forward and reverse biasing.
    (4 M)

OR

Q.4 (a) What is Hall effect ? Derive the formula for Hall coefficient and Hall voltage ?**(6 M)**
 (b) State and explain any two commercial applications of superconductors. **(4 M)**

Q.5 (a) What are nanoparticles ? Give any one method for producing nanoparticles **(6 M)**
 (b) State and explain the second law of thermodynamics. **(4 M)**

OR

Q.6 (a) What are the different steps involved in a Carnot cycle ? **(6 M)**
 (b) How the following properties make the nanoparticle different from bulk material?
  (a) Electrical   (b) Magnetic **(4 M)**

Q.7 (a) Derive the formula for condition of brightness in reflected system when the light is reflected from thin film of uniform thickness. **(6 M)**
 (b) Light of wavelength 6×10^{-5} cm falls on a screen at a distance of 100 cm from a narrow slit. Find the width of the slit if the first minima lie 1 mm on either side of the central maxima. **(4 M)**

Data : $\lambda = 6 \times 10^{-5}$ cm
       $D = 100$ cm
       $d = 1$ mm
       $n = 1$

Formula : (i) $a \sin \theta = n\lambda$
    (ii) $\tan \theta = \dfrac{d}{D}$

Solution : Form Fig.

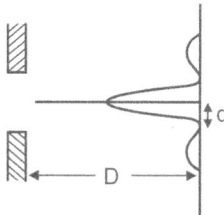

Fig.

$$\tan\theta = \frac{d}{D}$$

for large value of D and small value of d.

$$\tan\theta \simeq \theta \simeq \sin\theta$$

$$\therefore \quad a\frac{d}{D} = n\lambda$$

$$a = \frac{1 \times 6 \times 10^{-5} \times 100}{1 \times 10^{-1}}$$

$$a = 6 \times 10^{-2} \text{ cm}$$

Q.8 (a) Explain the diffraction at a grating. Derive formula for intensity distribution. **(6 M)**

(b) White Light falls normally on film of soapy water whose thickness is 5×10^{-5} cm. Which wavelength will be reflected most strongly in the visible region? **(4 M)**

Solution : Ref. Example 7.3.

Q.9 (a) What is Nicols prism? How it can be used for producing plane polarized light?

(6 M)

(b) With band diagram, explain the working of semiconductor laser. **(4 M)**

OR

Q.10 (a) What is Holography? Explain the method of hologram construction and reillumination. **(6 M)**

(b) Calculate the thickness of a half wave plate, given that **(4 M)**

$\mu_e = 1.533$ $\mu_0 = 1.544$ and $\lambda = 5000$ A°

Data :

$$\lambda = 5000 \text{ A}°$$
$$\mu_e = 1.533$$
$$\mu_0 = 1.544$$

Formula :

$$t = \frac{\lambda}{2(\mu_0 - \mu_e)}$$

$$t = \frac{5000 \times 10^{-8}}{2(1.544 - 1.533)}$$

$$t = 2.272 \times 10^{-3} \text{ cm}$$

Q.11 (a) A particle is confined in a potential well of infinite depth, derive the formula fort energy engine values. **(6 M)**

(b) A cinema hall has volume of 7500m^3. It is required to have reverberation time of 1.5 sec. What should be the total absorption in the hall ? **(4 M)**

Solution : Ref. Example 11.2.

Q.12 (a) What is reverberation ? Discuss the Sabine's formula. How the reverberation affects acoustics of a building. **(6 M)**

(b) Find the kinetic energy of a neutron which has a wavelength of 3A°. **(4 M)**

Data : $\lambda = 3A°$

Formula : $\lambda = \dfrac{\lambda}{\sqrt{2mE}}$

Solution : $E = \dfrac{\lambda^2}{2m\lambda^2}$

$E = \dfrac{(6.63 \times 10^{-34})^2}{2 \times 1.66 \times 10^{-27} \times (3 \times 10^{-10})^2}$

$E = 1.45 \times 10^{-21}$ J

SUPPLIMENT OF UNIVERSITY QUESTION PAPER (BVDU)
ENGINEERING PHYSICS
MAY 2015

Time : 3 Hours   **Max. Marks : 60**

1. (a) An electron is subjected to parallel electric field, derive the formula for impact velocity. **(07)**

   (b) In a thermonuclear reaction 1.00×10^{-3} kg hydrogen is converted into 0.993×10^{-3} kg helium. Calculate the energy released in Joules. **(03)**

OR

2. (a) Give principle, construction and working of betatron. **(06)**

   (b) An α–particle travels at right angles to a magnetic field with a speed of 6×10 m/s. The flux density of the field is 0.2 Wb/m^2. Calculate (i) force acting on α – particle and (ii) acceleration. **(04)**

3. (a) Using Fermi-Dirac probability function show that the position of Fermi level is at the centre of conduction band and valence band in an intrinsic semiconductor. **(06)**

   (b) What is super conductivity? Explain the term critical temperature. **(04)**

OR

4. (a) Explain the superconductivity on the basis of BCS theory. **(06)**

   (b) Calculate the conductivity of pure silicon at room temperature when the concentration of carrier is 1.6×10^{10} per cm^3. Given: $\mu_e = 1500$ cm^2 V-s and $\mu_h = 500$ cm^2 / V- sec at room temperature. **(04)**

5. (a) Describe the Joule's method of determination of j. **(06)**

   (b) State and explain any two properties of nanoparticles. **(04)**

OR

6. (a) What are colloids? How the chemical method can be used for synthesis of metal nanoparticles? **(06)**

   (b) State and explain first law of thermodynamics. **(04)**

7. (a) State Rayleigh's criterion of resolution. Derive the formula for resolving power of a diffraction grating. **(06)**

   (b) In Newton's ring experiment, the diameters of the 4th and 12'h dark rings are 0.4 cm and 0.7 cm respectively. Find the diameter of 201h dark ring. **(04)**

OR

8. (a) Derive the formula for optical path difference in wedge shaped thin film. **(06)**

   (b) Give differences between Fresnel's and Fraunhofer's diffraction. **(04)**

9. (a) What is double refraction? Explain it on the basis of Huygen's theory. **(06)**
   (b) How a hologram can be constructed? Give its method. **(04)**

OR

10. (a) With principle and diagram, explain the working of Ruby laser. **(06)**
    (b) Calculate the thickness of a quarter wave plate, given that $\mu_e = 1.533$ $\mu_0 = 1.544$ and $\lambda = 6500$ A°.

11. (a) What are factors affecting acoustics of a building? Give their remedies. **(06)**
    (b) Derive formula for De-Broglie's wavelength of an electron accelerated by voltage V. **(04)**

OR

12. (a) Derive formula for Schrodinger's time dependent wave equation. **(06)**
    (b) Two sound sources are producing sound intensity level of 60 dB and 80 dB respectively. Calculate the resultant sound intensity level. **(04)**

www.ingramcontent.com/pod-product-compliance
Lightning Source LLC
Chambersburg PA
CBHW080540230426
43663CB00015B/2661